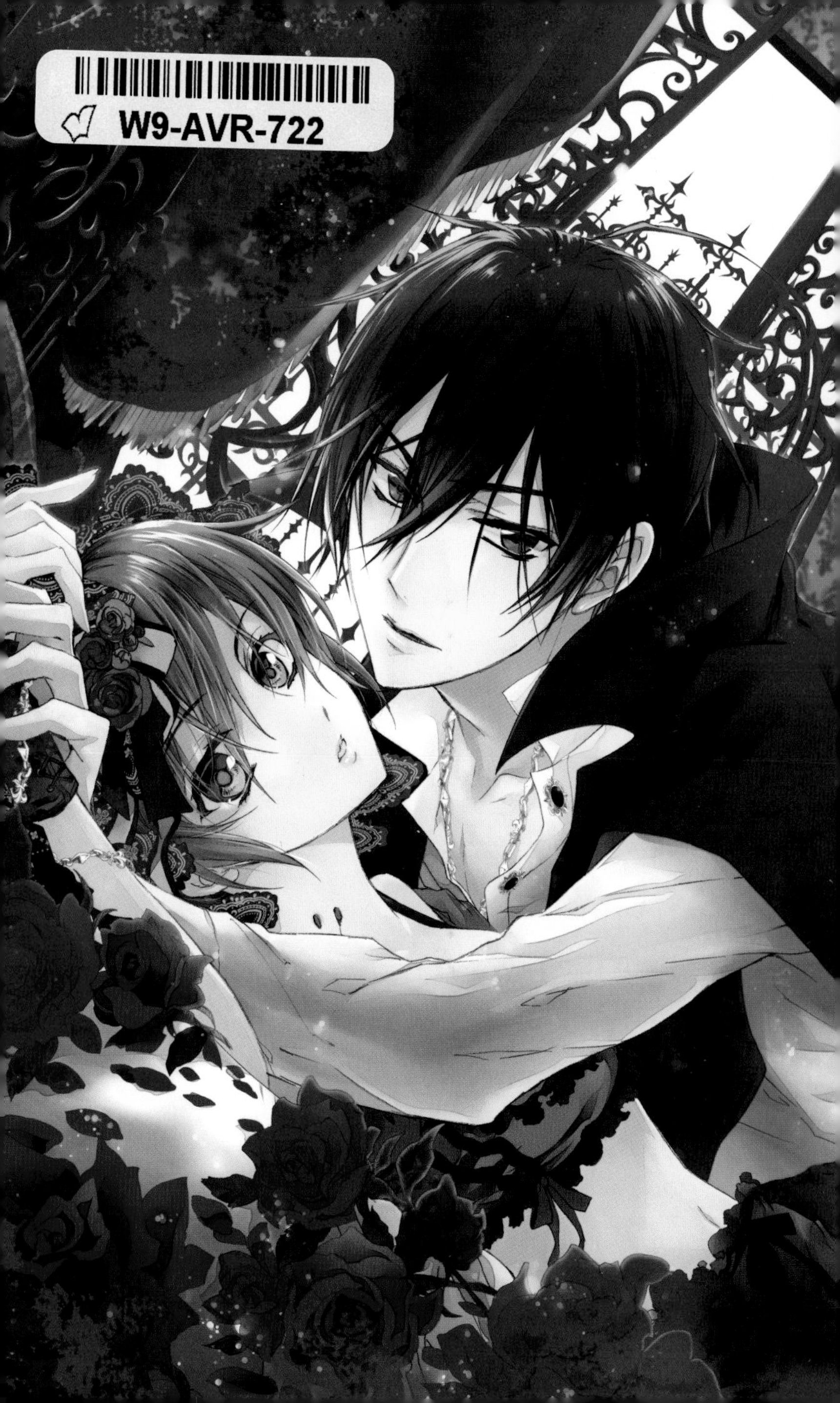

c o n t e n t s

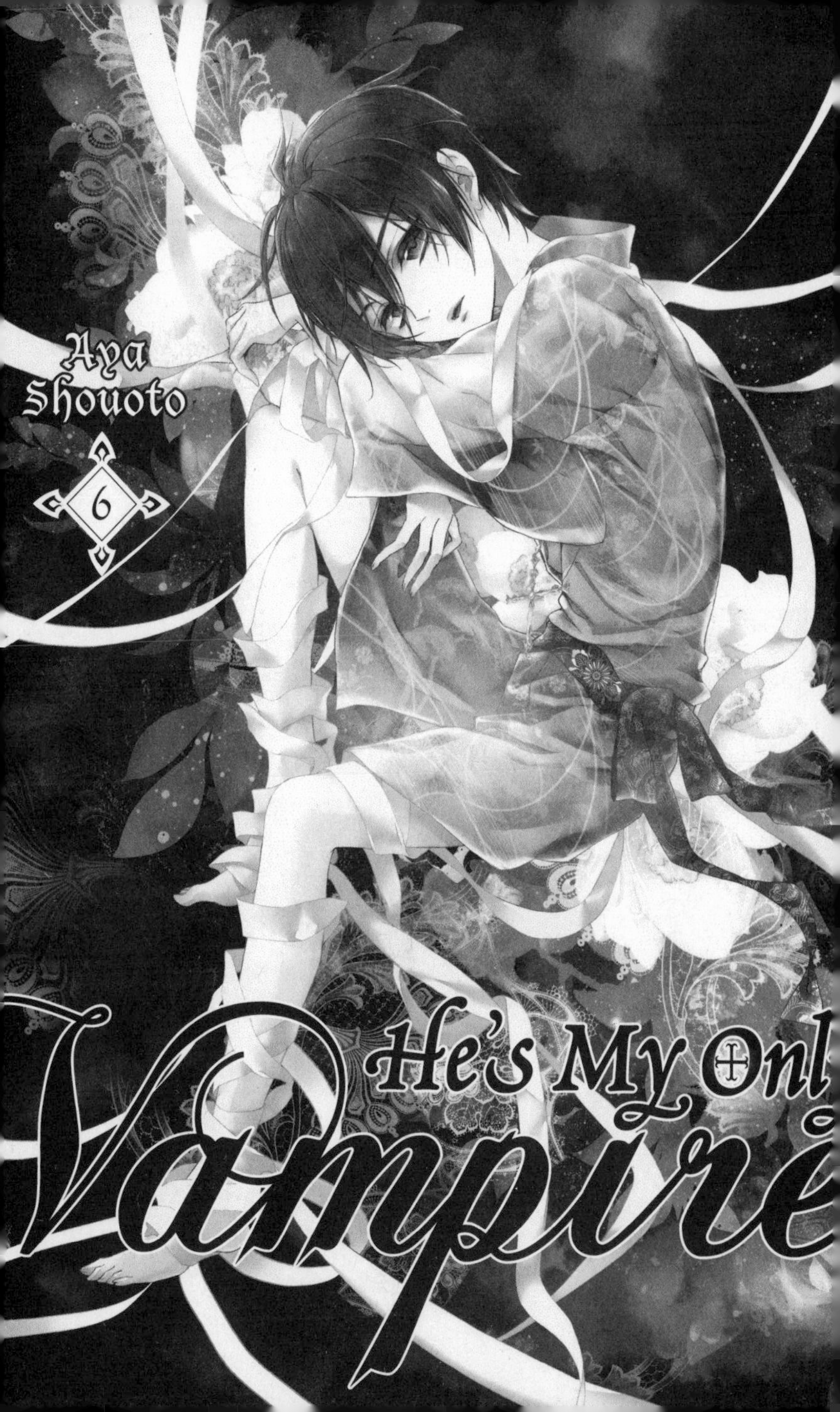
Aya Shouoto
6
He's My Only Vampire

Characters and Story

"Thrall"
One who is ageless and deathless, and shall surrender the entirety of their being to their vampire master for all of eternity...

This is the story of the vampire Aki and his thrall, Kana. Aki came to Kana's town in order to win a game to collect the seven stigmas and use their power to wake his slumbering brother, Eriya. Aki and Kana, along with their friend Jin, formed a school club called the "Curious Events Club" to gather information on the stigmas. Soon after, Kana awoke as a "true thrall," and Aki succeeded in obtaining two more stigmas.

However, the stigmas take a heavy toll on Aki's body, prompting the group to go on a hot springs vacation at a mountain resort to help him recover. But their peace is short-lived, as they suddenly find themselves surrounded by the Tsubakiins! Kana is abducted and made to regain her memories of the time she spent with Aki and Eriya seven years ago. Meanwhile, after witnessing Kana being taken from him, Aki allows his powers to run wild...

JIN SHIRANUI
(SECOND YEAR)

KANA'S CLASSMATE AND A WELL-KNOWN DELINQUENT. HE IS ACTUALLY A LYCANTHROPE. POSSESSOR OF THE "GREED" STIGMA.

DEALER SWALLOW

AKI'S SENTRY AND A JUDGE IN THE GAME OF THE SEVEN STIGMAS. HIS TRUE FORM IS THAT OF A TENGU DEMON.

ISUKA BERNSTEIN
(THIRD YEAR)
HITAKI MIYAJIMA
(THIRD YEAR)

ST. AGATHA ACADEMY'S STUDENT COUNCIL PRESIDENT AND VICE PRESIDENT. IN TRUTH, THEY ARE ANGELS. HITAKI IS IN POSSESSION OF A STIGMA.

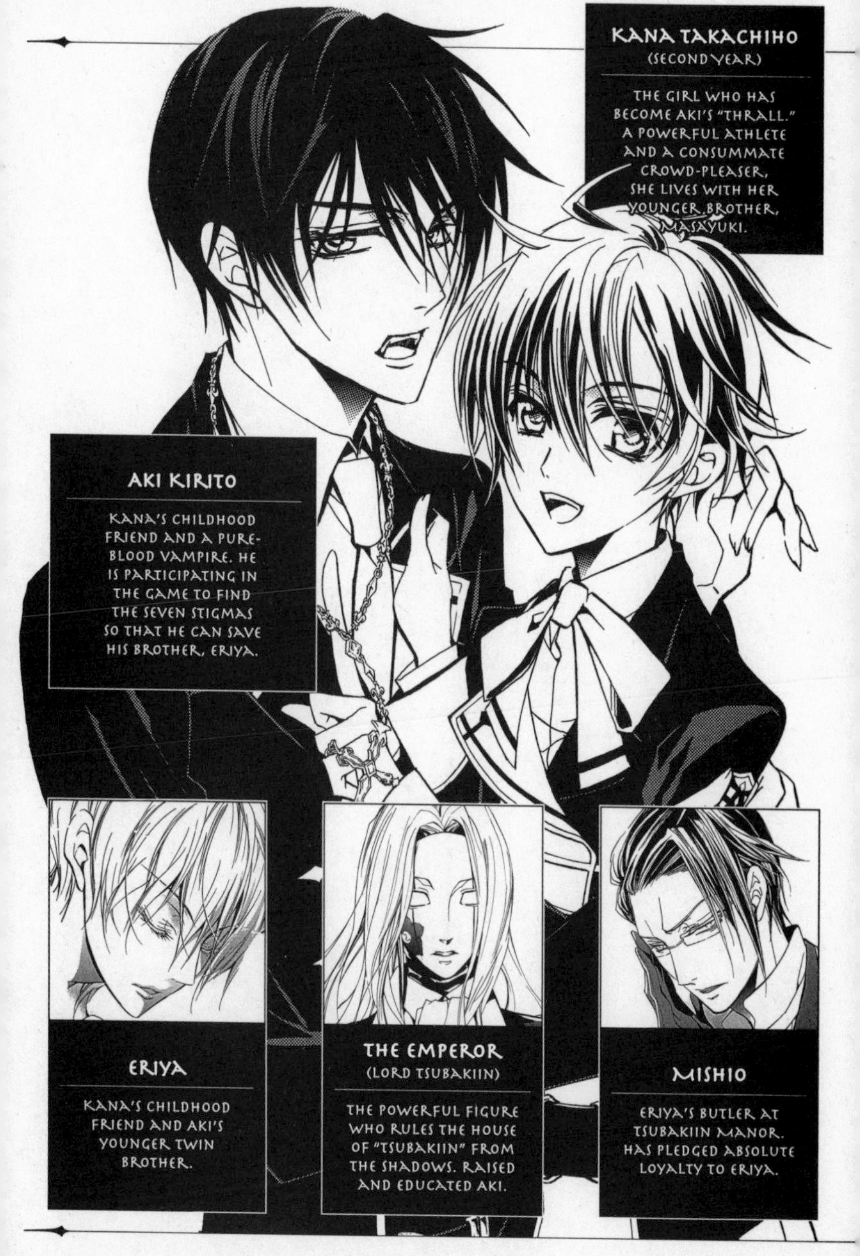
KANA TAKACHIHO
(SECOND YEAR)
THE GIRL WHO HAS BECOME AKI'S "THRALL." A POWERFUL ATHLETE AND A CONSUMMATE CROWD-PLEASER, SHE LIVES WITH HER YOUNGER BROTHER, MASAYUKI.
AKI KIRITO
KANA'S CHILDHOOD FRIEND AND A PURE-BLOOD VAMPIRE. HE IS PARTICIPATING IN THE GAME TO FIND THE SEVEN STIGMAS SO THAT HE CAN SAVE HIS BROTHER, ERIYA.
ERIYA
KANA'S CHILDHOOD FRIEND AND AKI'S YOUNGER TWIN BROTHER.
THE EMPEROR
(LORD TSUBAKIIN)
THE POWERFUL FIGURE WHO RULES THE HOUSE OF "TSUBAKIIN" FROM THE SHADOWS. RAISED AND EDUCATED AKI.
MISHIO
ERIYA'S BUTLER AT TSUBAKIIN MANOR. HAS PLEDGED ABSOLUTE LOYALTY TO ERIYA.

He's my only vampire
Aya Shouoto

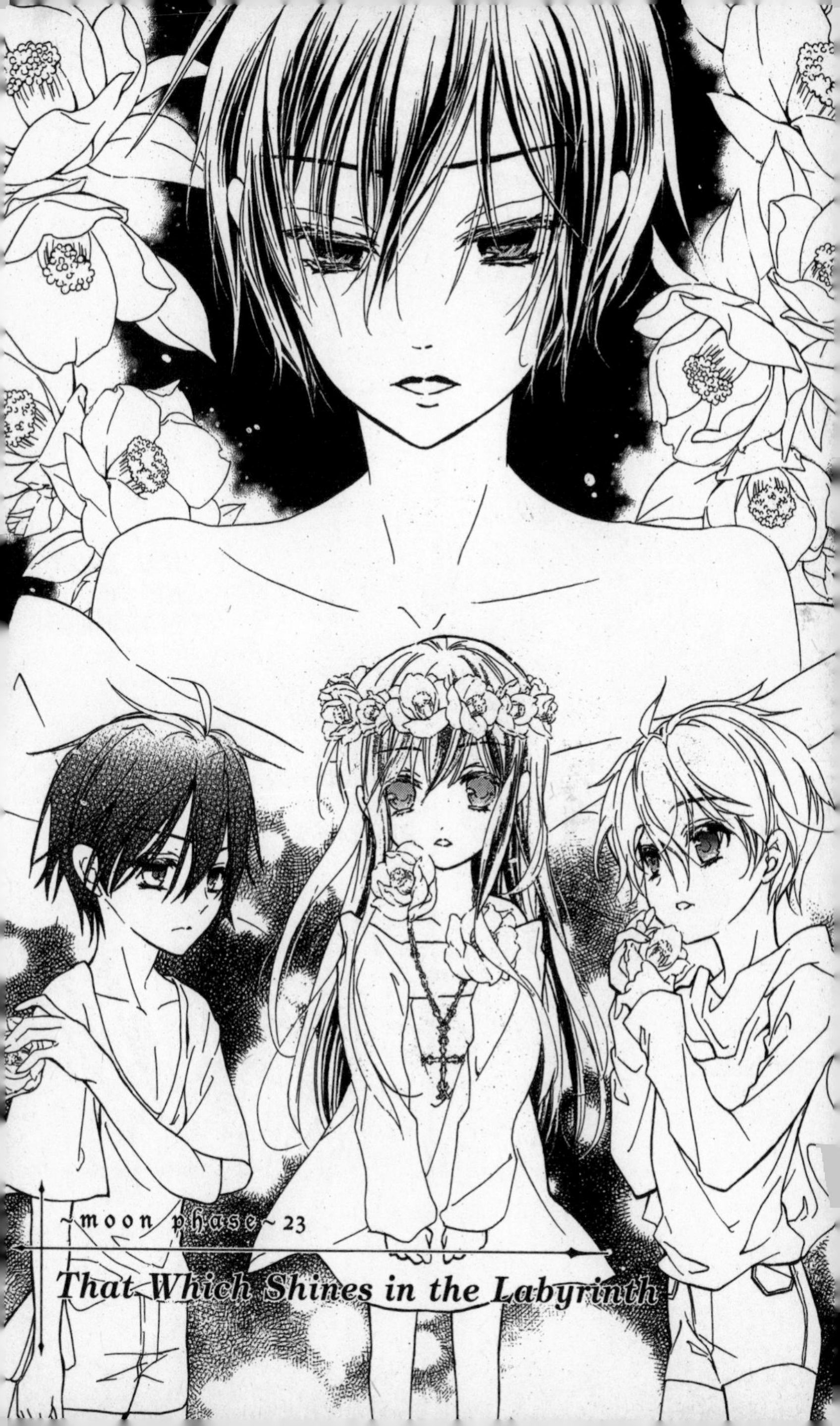
~moon phase~23
That Which Shines in the Labyrinth

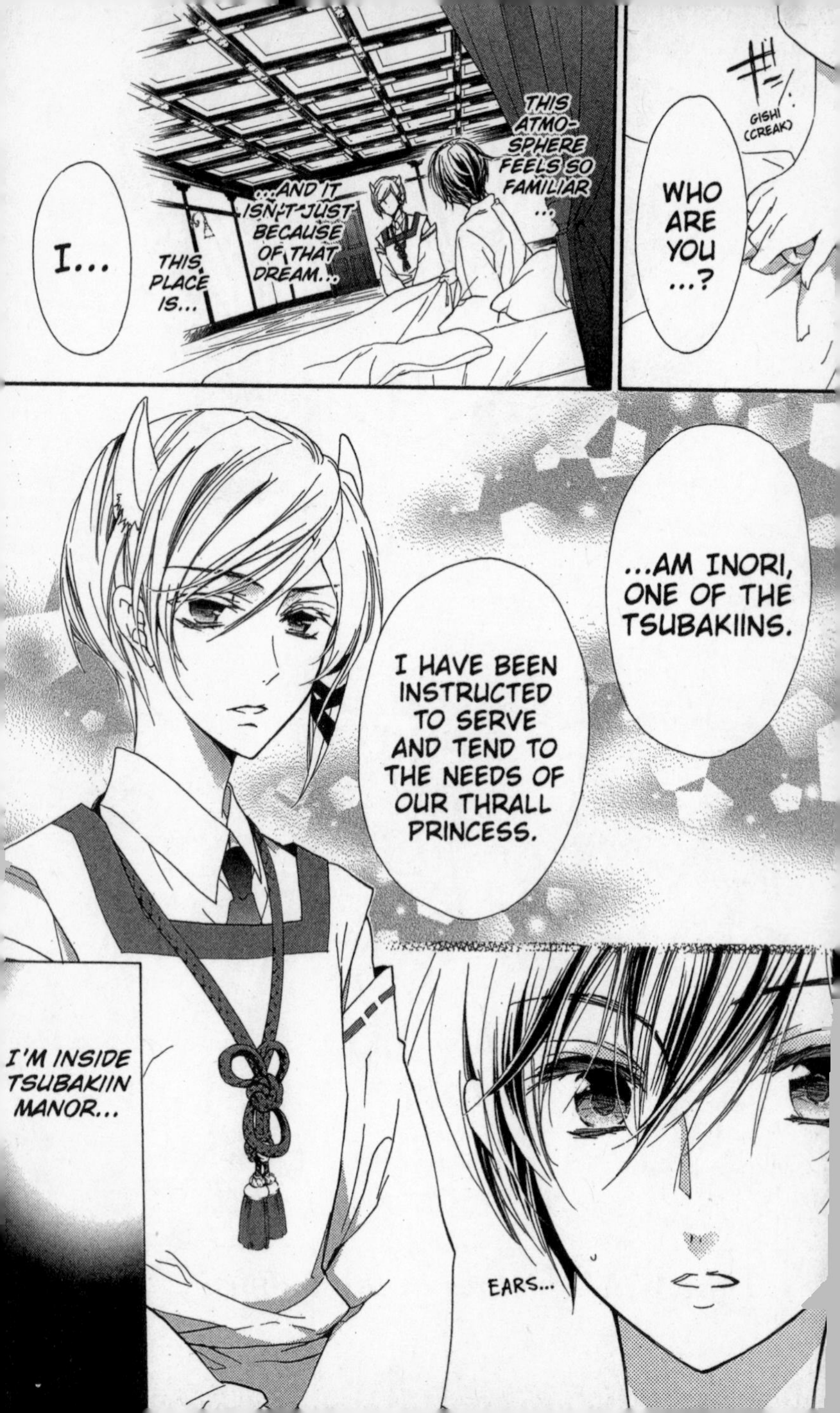
GISHI (CREAK)
WHO ARE YOU ...?
THIS ATMOSPHERE FEELS SO FAMILIAR ...
...AND IT ISN'T JUST BECAUSE OF THAT DREAM...
THIS PLACE IS...
I...
...AM INORI, ONE OF THE TSUBAKIINS.
I HAVE BEEN INSTRUCTED TO SERVE AND TEND TO THE NEEDS OF OUR THRALL PRINCESS.
EARS...
I'M INSIDE TSUBAKIIN MANOR...

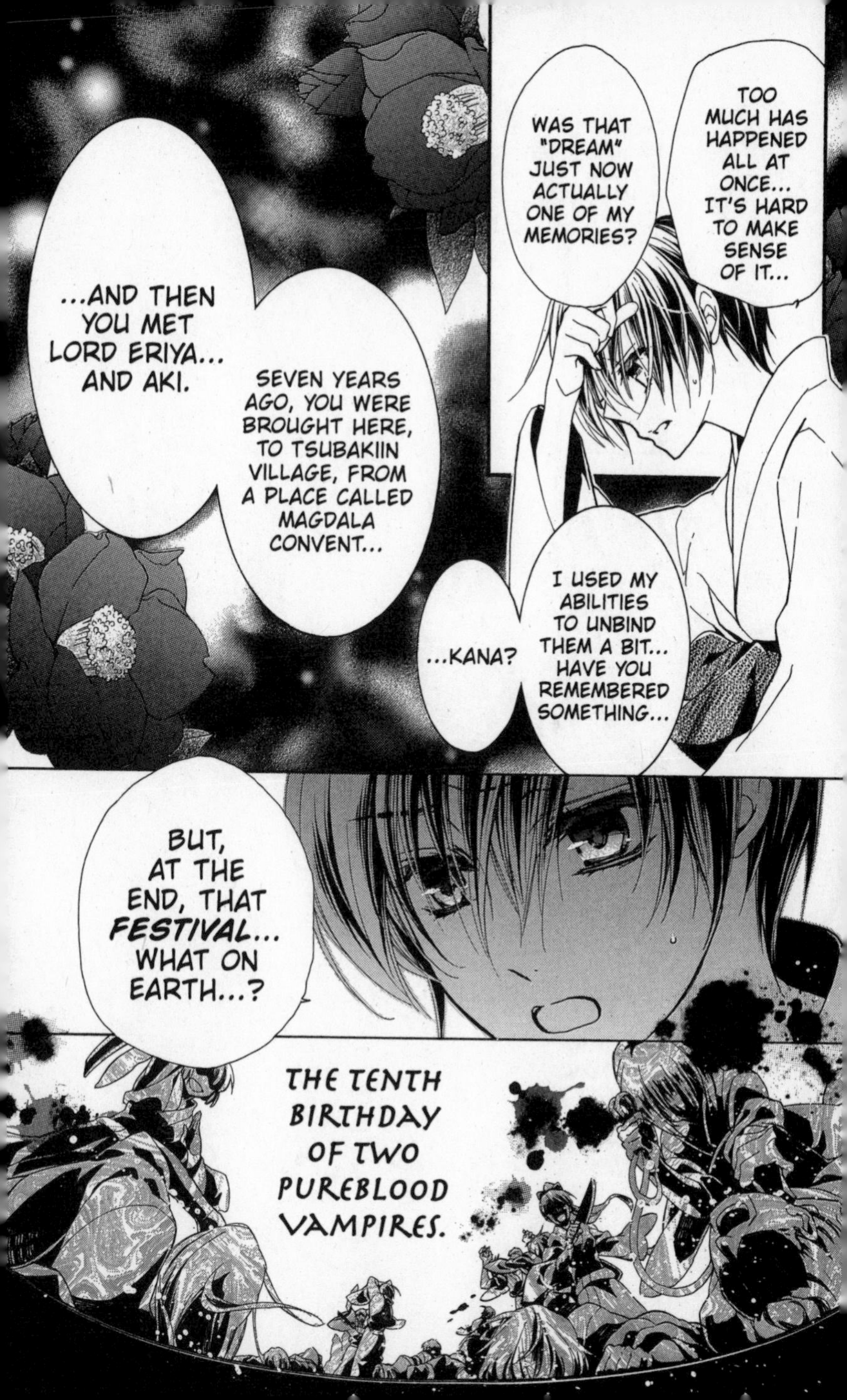
TOO MUCH HAS HAPPENED ALL AT ONCE... IT'S HARD TO MAKE SENSE OF IT...
WAS THAT "DREAM" JUST NOW ACTUALLY ONE OF MY MEMORIES?
SEVEN YEARS AGO, YOU WERE BROUGHT HERE, TO TSUBAKIIN VILLAGE, FROM A PLACE CALLED MAGDALA CONVENT...
...AND THEN YOU MET LORD ERIYA... AND AKI.
I USED MY ABILITIES TO UNBIND THEM A BIT... HAVE YOU REMEMBERED SOMETHING...
...KANA?
BUT, AT THE END, THAT *FESTIVAL*... WHAT ON EARTH...?
THE TENTH BIRTHDAY OF TWO PUREBLOOD VAMPIRES.

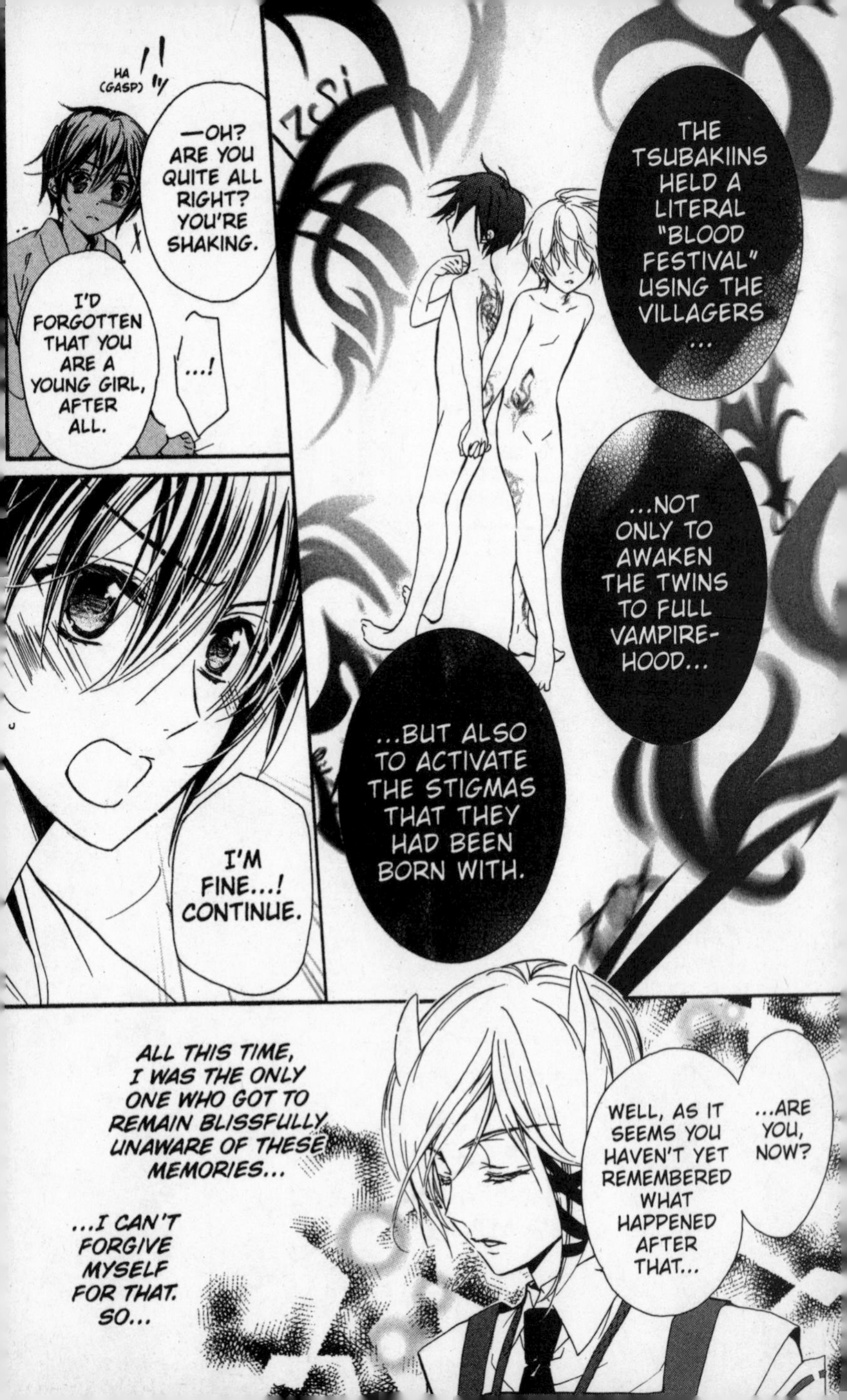
THE TSUBAKIINS HELD A LITERAL "BLOOD FESTIVAL" USING THE VILLAGERS...
...NOT ONLY TO AWAKEN THE TWINS TO FULL VAMPIRE-HOOD...
...BUT ALSO TO ACTIVATE THE STIGMAS THAT THEY HAD BEEN BORN WITH.
HA (GASP)
—OH? ARE YOU QUITE ALL RIGHT? YOU'RE SHAKING.
...!
I'D FORGOTTEN THAT YOU ARE A YOUNG GIRL, AFTER ALL.
I'M FINE...! CONTINUE.
...ARE YOU, NOW?
WELL, AS IT SEEMS YOU HAVEN'T YET REMEMBERED WHAT HAPPENED AFTER THAT...
ALL THIS TIME, I WAS THE ONLY ONE WHO GOT TO REMAIN BLISSFULLY UNAWARE OF THESE MEMORIES...
...I CAN'T FORGIVE MYSELF FOR THAT. SO...

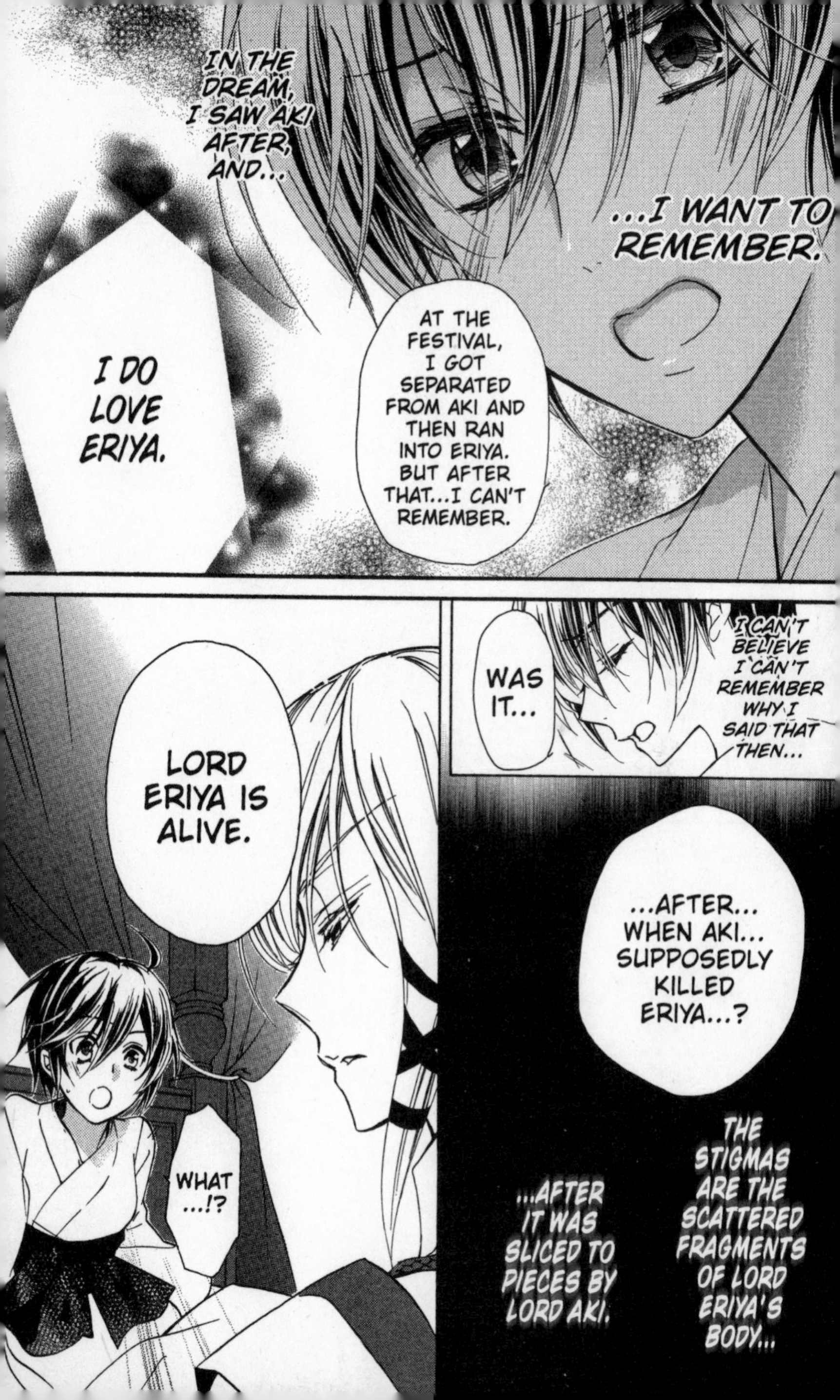
IN THE DREAM, I SAW AKI AFTER, AND...
...I WANT TO REMEMBER.
AT THE FESTIVAL, I GOT SEPARATED FROM AKI AND THEN RAN INTO ERIYA. BUT AFTER THAT...I CAN'T REMEMBER.
I DO LOVE ERIYA.
I CAN'T BELIEVE I CAN'T REMEMBER WHY I SAID THAT THEN...
WAS IT...
...AFTER... WHEN AKI... SUPPOSEDLY KILLED ERIYA...?
THE STIGMAS ARE THE SCATTERED FRAGMENTS OF LORD ERIYA'S BODY...
...AFTER IT WAS SLICED TO PIECES BY LORD AKI.
LORD ERIYA IS ALIVE.
WHAT ...!?

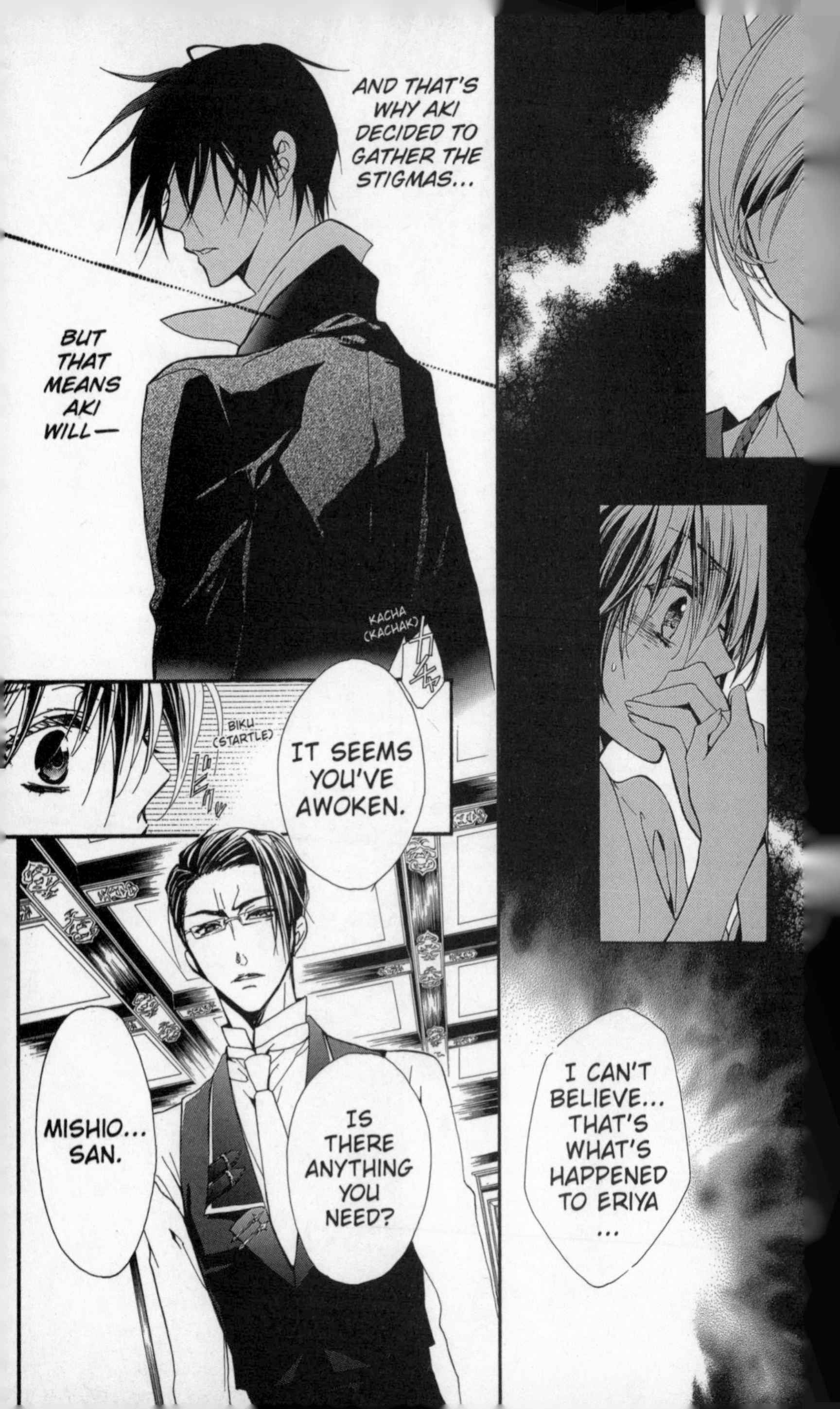
I CAN'T BELIEVE... THAT'S WHAT'S HAPPENED TO ERIYA ...
AND THAT'S WHY AKI DECIDED TO GATHER THE STIGMAS...
BUT THAT MEANS AKI WILL—
KACHA (KACHAK)
BIKU (STARTLE)
IT SEEMS YOU'VE AWOKEN.
IS THERE ANYTHING YOU NEED?
MISHIO... SAN.

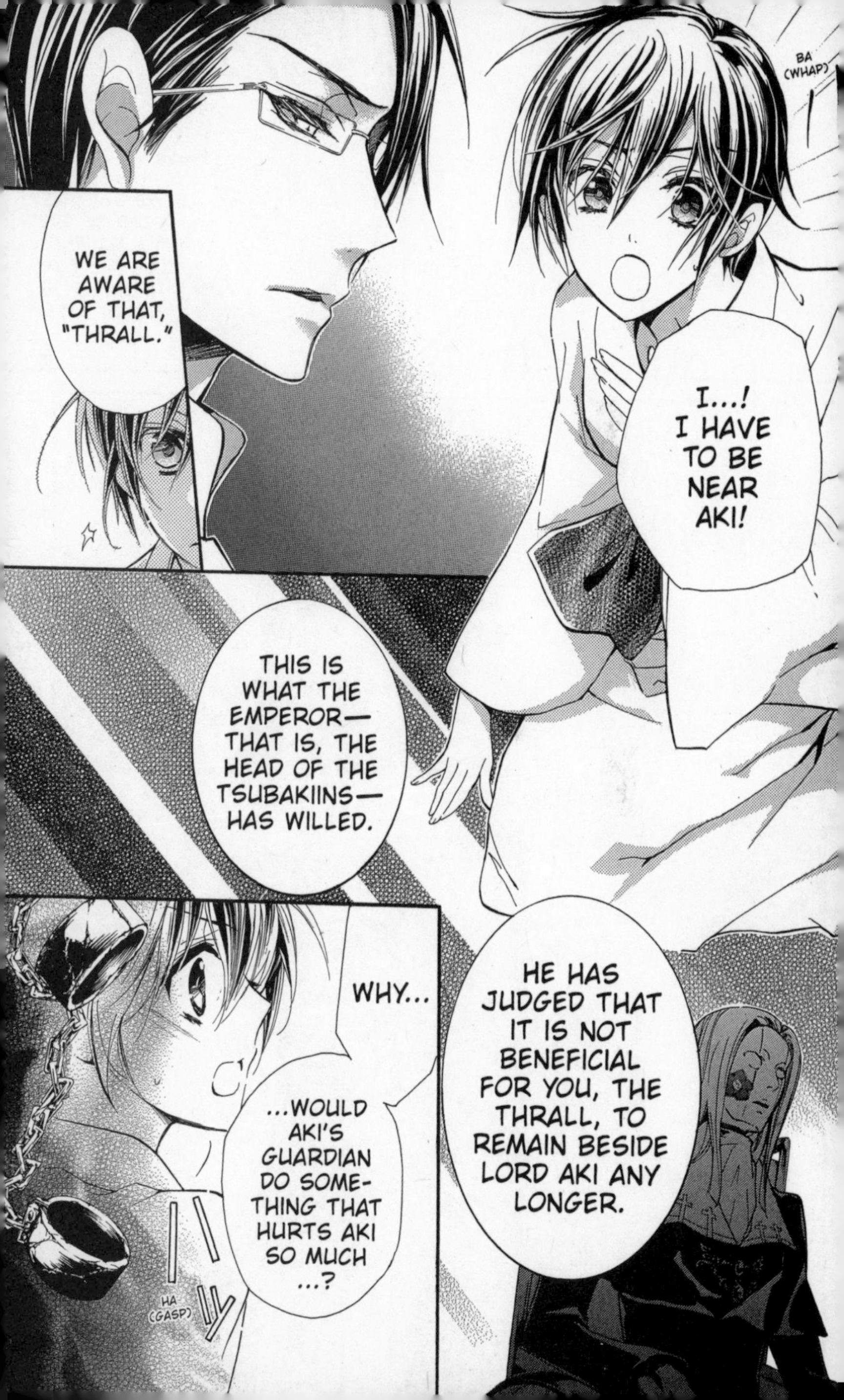
BA (WHAP)
I...! I HAVE TO BE NEAR AKI!
WE ARE AWARE OF THAT, "THRALL."
THIS IS WHAT THE EMPEROR—THAT IS, THE HEAD OF THE TSUBAKIINS—HAS WILLED.
HE HAS JUDGED THAT IT IS NOT BENEFICIAL FOR YOU, THE THRALL, TO REMAIN BESIDE LORD AKI ANY LONGER.
WHY...
...WOULD AKI'S GUARDIAN DO SOMETHING THAT HURTS AKI SO MUCH ...?
HA (GASP)

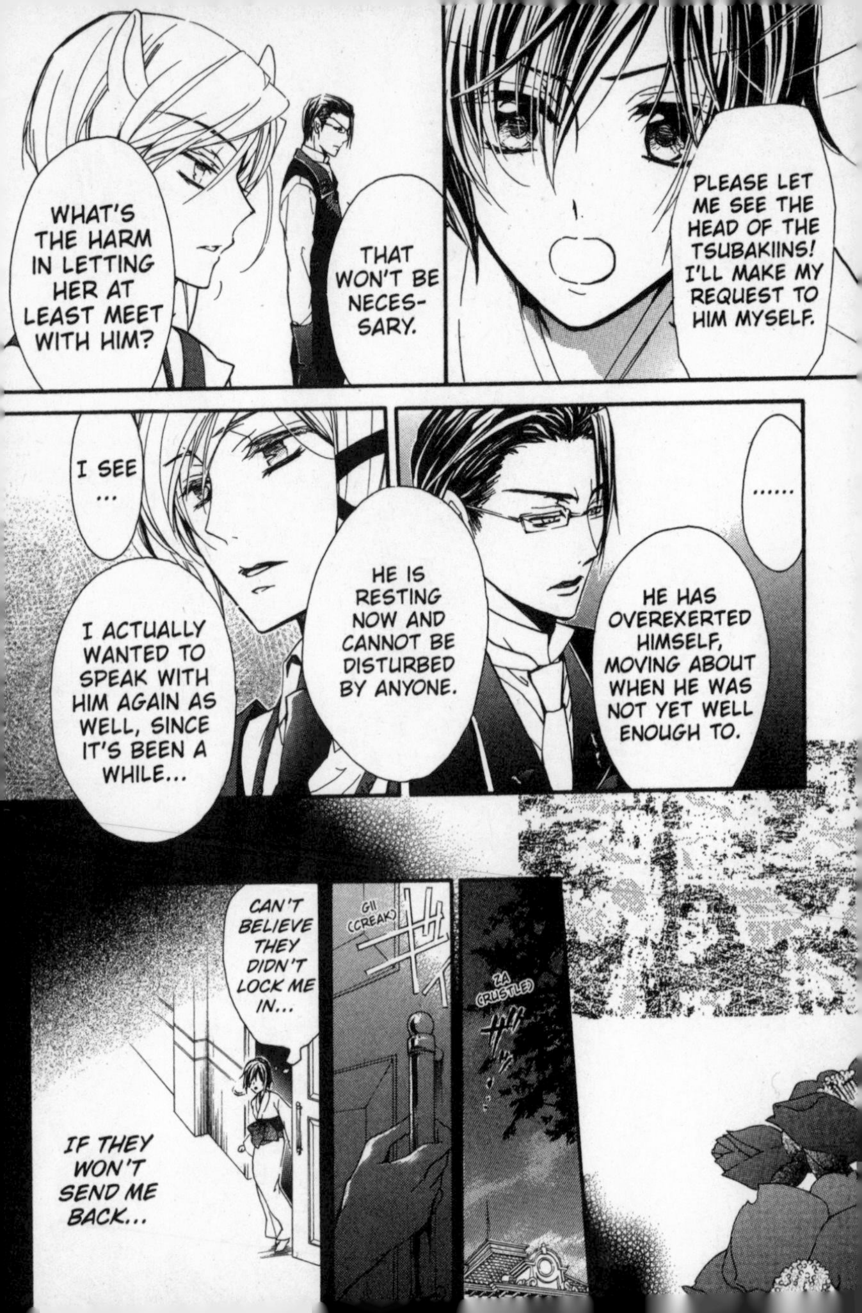
PLEASE LET ME SEE THE HEAD OF THE TSUBAKIINS! I'LL MAKE MY REQUEST TO HIM MYSELF.
THAT WON'T BE NECES-SARY.
WHAT'S THE HARM IN LETTING HER AT LEAST MEET WITH HIM?
......
HE HAS OVEREXERTED HIMSELF, MOVING ABOUT WHEN HE WAS NOT YET WELL ENOUGH TO.
HE IS RESTING NOW AND CANNOT BE DISTURBED BY ANYONE.
I SEE ...
I ACTUALLY WANTED TO SPEAK WITH HIM AGAIN AS WELL, SINCE IT'S BEEN A WHILE...
ZA (RUSTLE)
GII (CREAK)
CAN'T BELIEVE THEY DIDN'T LOCK ME IN...
IF THEY WON'T SEND ME BACK...

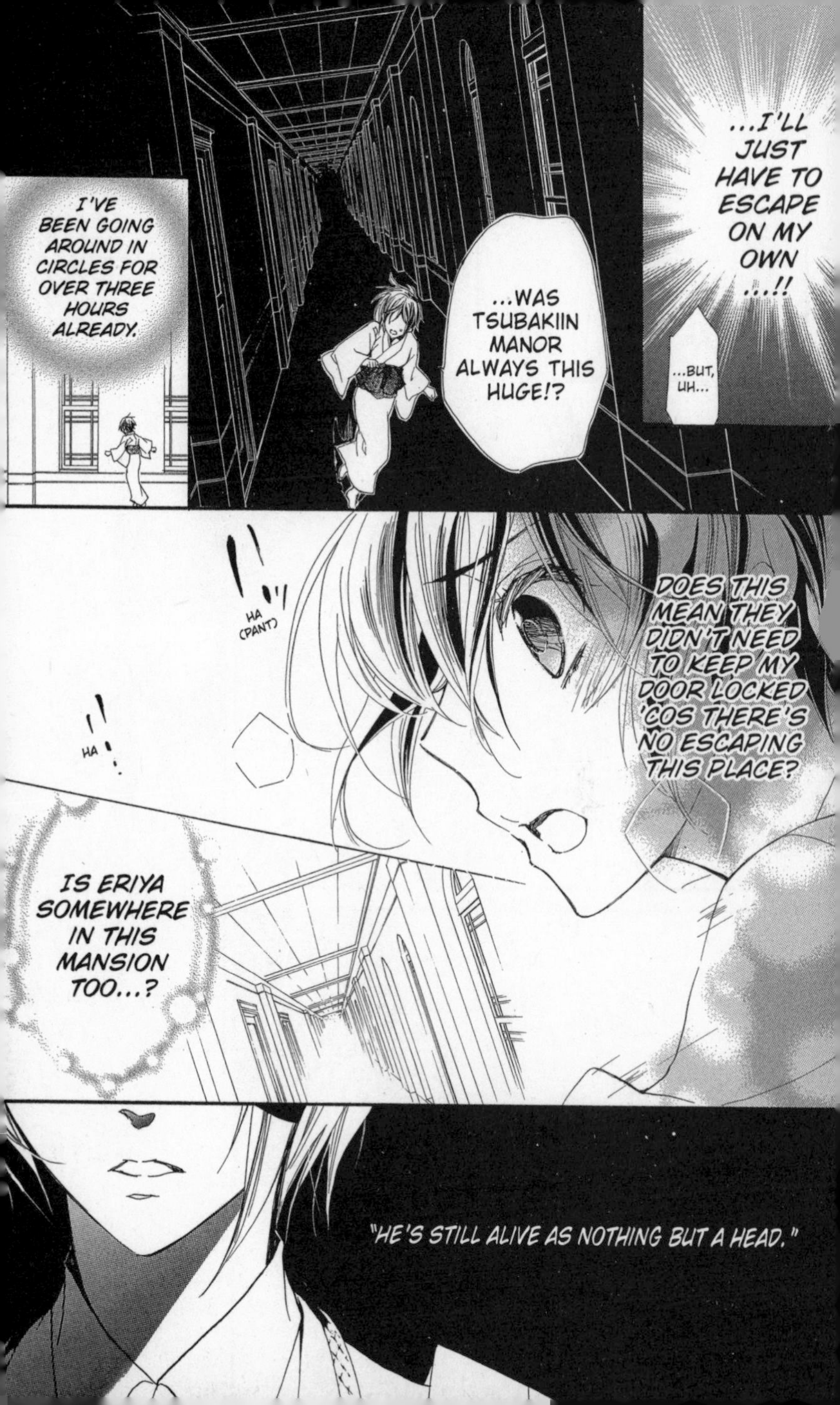
...I'LL JUST HAVE TO ESCAPE ON MY OWN ...!!
...BUT, UH...
...WAS TSUBAKIIN MANOR ALWAYS THIS HUGE!?
I'VE BEEN GOING AROUND IN CIRCLES FOR OVER THREE HOURS ALREADY.
DOES THIS MEAN THEY DIDN'T NEED TO KEEP MY DOOR LOCKED 'COS THERE'S NO ESCAPING THIS PLACE?
HA (PANT)
HA
IS ERIYA SOMEWHERE IN THIS MANSION TOO...?
"HE'S STILL ALIVE AS NOTHING BUT A HEAD."

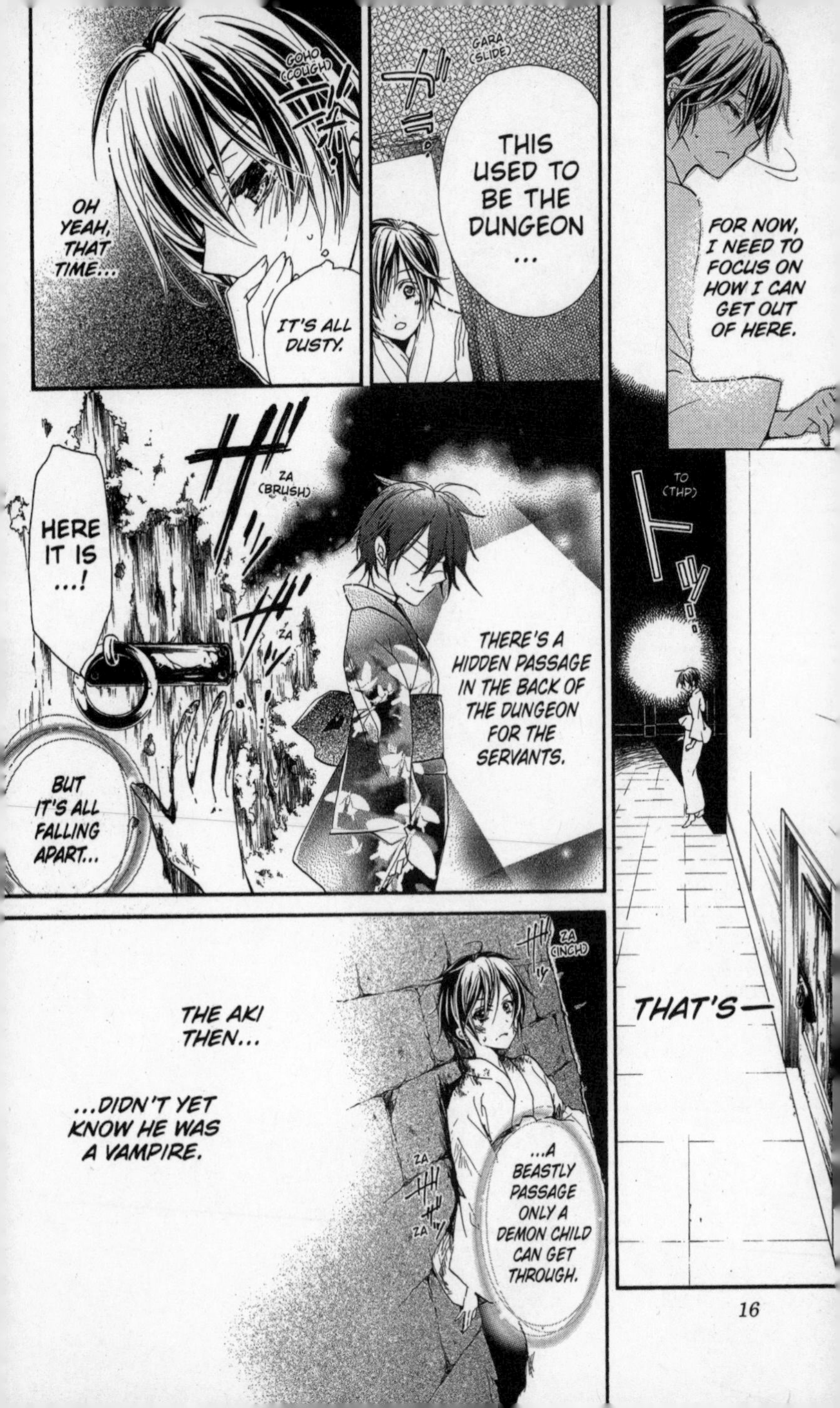
FOR NOW, I NEED TO FOCUS ON HOW I CAN GET OUT OF HERE.
GARA (SLIDE)
THIS USED TO BE THE DUNGEON ...
GOHO (COUGH)
OH YEAH, THAT TIME...
IT'S ALL DUSTY.
TO (THP)
THAT'S—
ZA (BRUSH)
ZA
THERE'S A HIDDEN PASSAGE IN THE BACK OF THE DUNGEON FOR THE SERVANTS.
HERE IT IS ...!
BUT IT'S ALL FALLING APART...
ZA (INCH)
ZA
ZA
...A BEASTLY PASSAGE ONLY A DEMON CHILD CAN GET THROUGH.
THE AKI THEN...
...DIDN'T YET KNOW HE WAS A VAMPIRE.

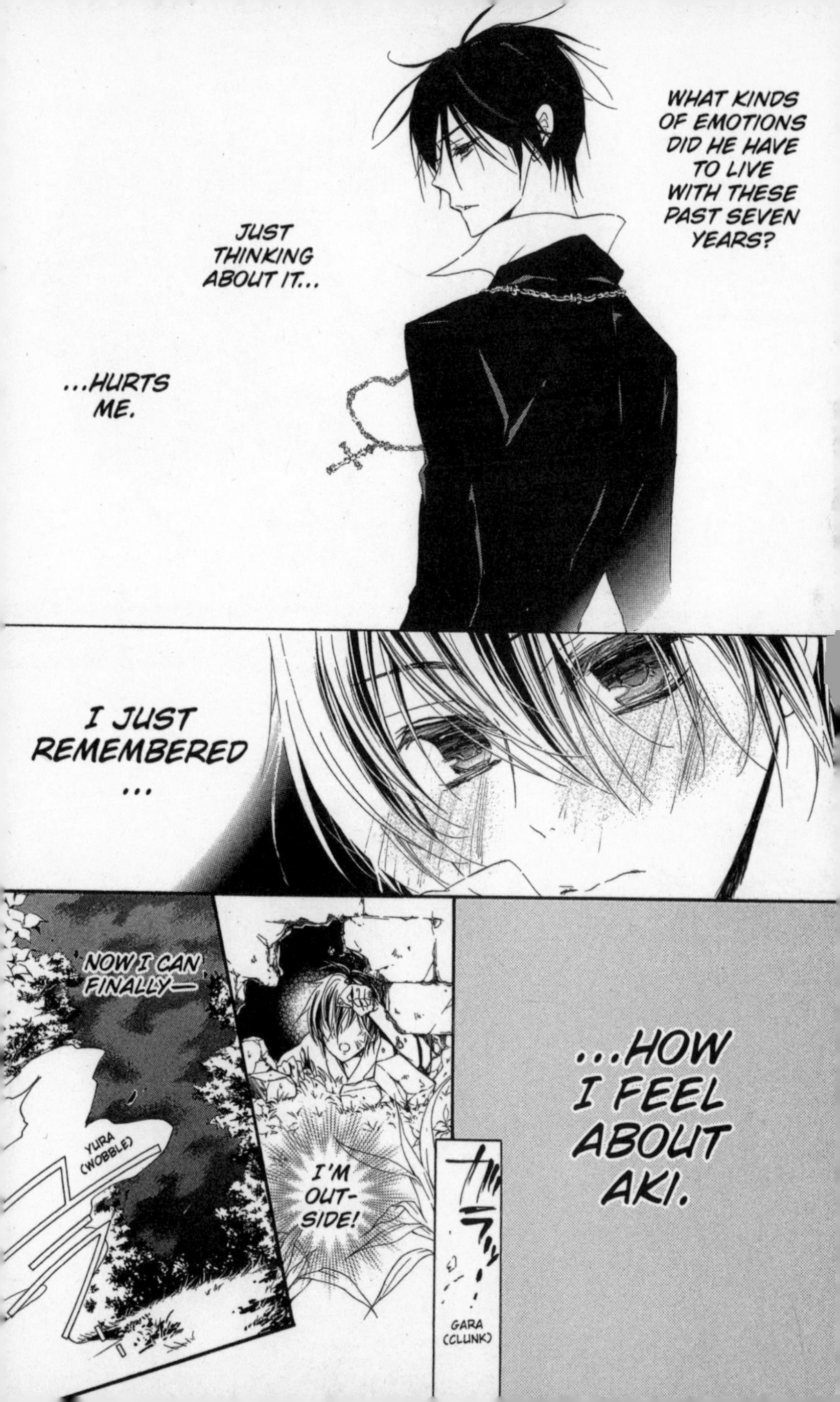
WHAT KINDS OF EMOTIONS DID HE HAVE TO LIVE WITH THESE PAST SEVEN YEARS?
JUST THINKING ABOUT IT...
...HURTS ME.
I JUST REMEMBERED...
...HOW I FEEL ABOUT AKI.
GARA (CLUNK)
I'M OUT-SIDE!
NOW I CAN FINALLY—
YURA (WOBBLE)

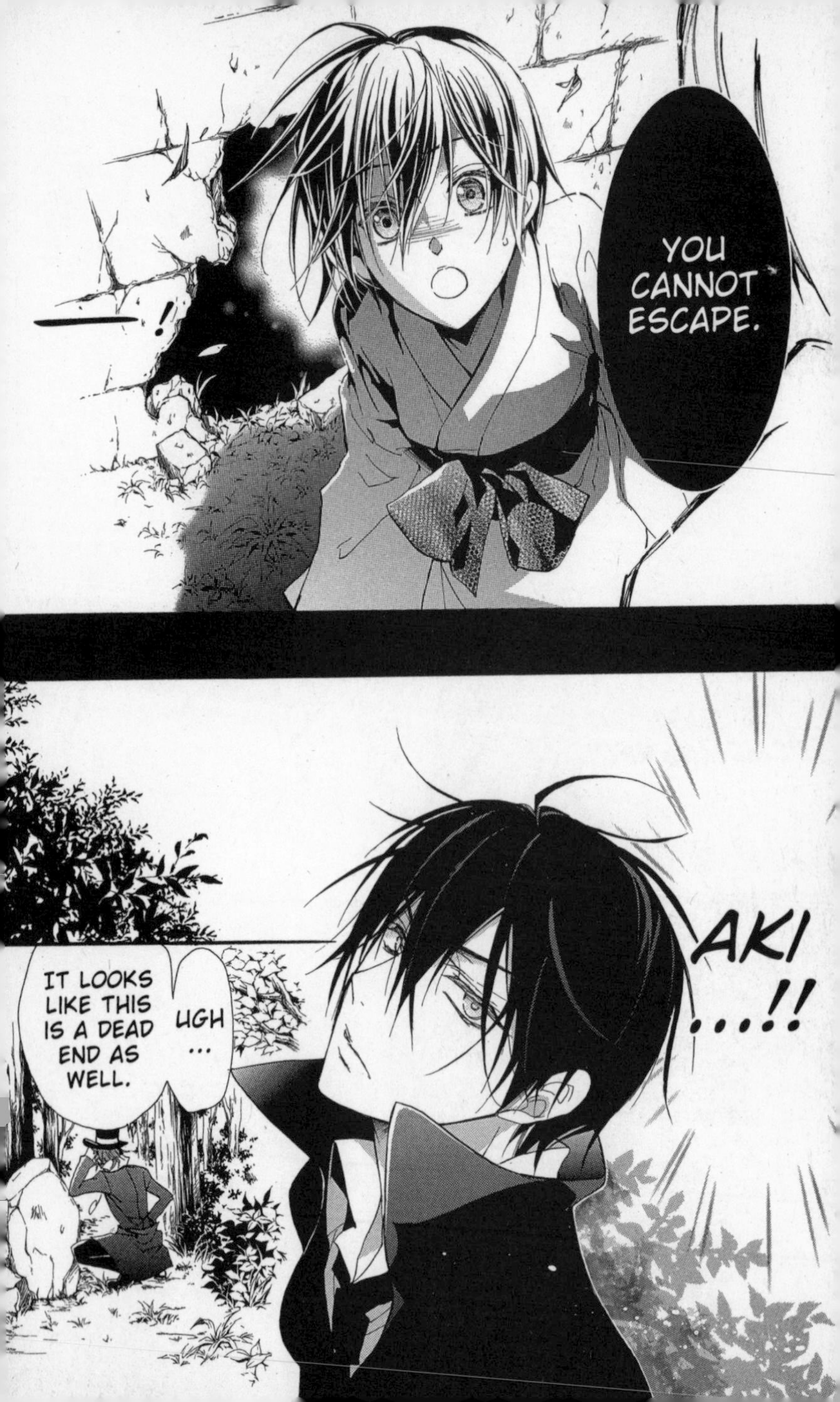
YOU CANNOT ESCAPE.
—!
AKI...!!
UGH...
IT LOOKS LIKE THIS IS A DEAD END AS WELL.

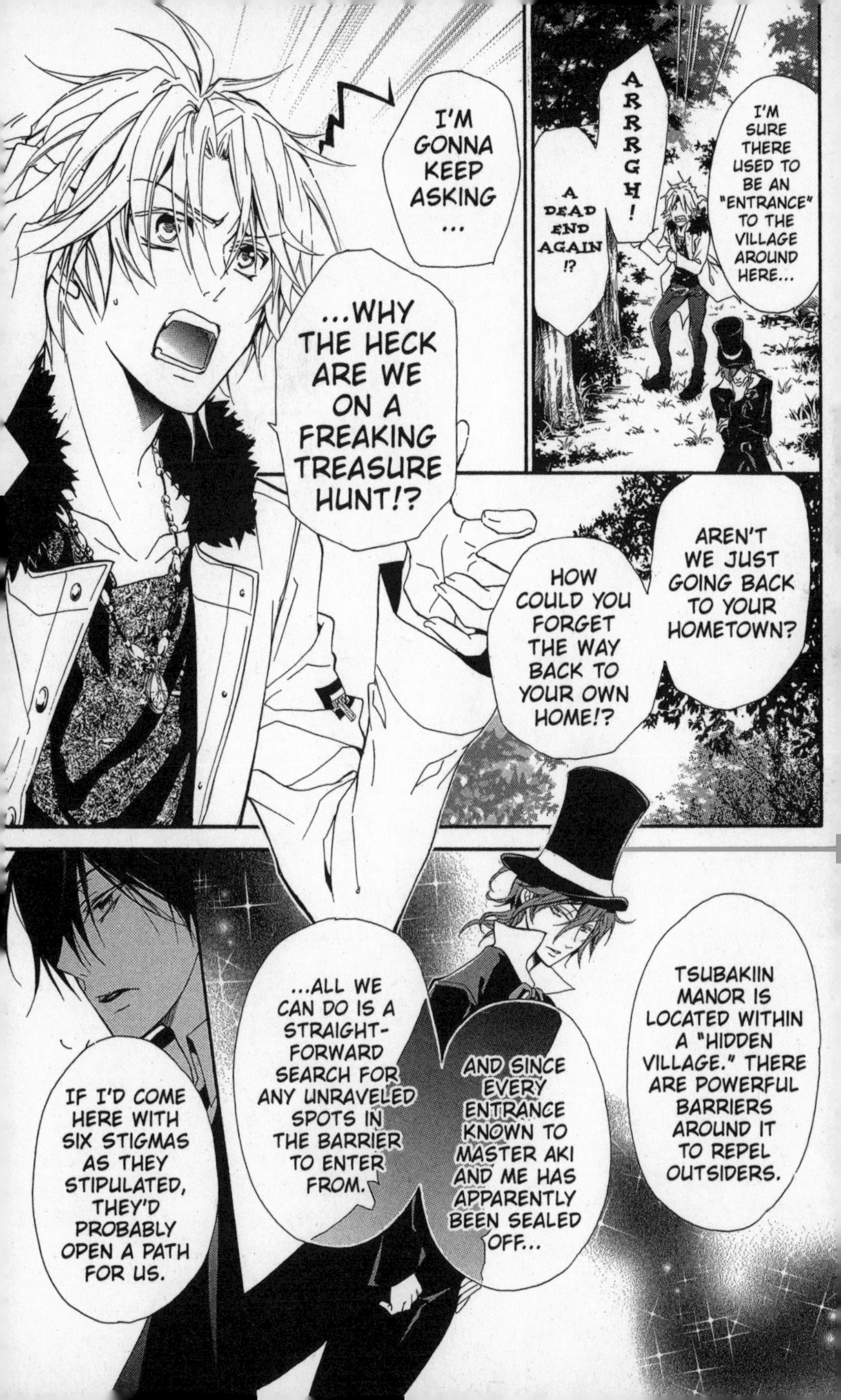
I'M SURE THERE USED TO BE AN "ENTRANCE" TO THE VILLAGE AROUND HERE...
ARRRGH!
A DEAD END AGAIN!?
I'M GONNA KEEP ASKING...
...WHY THE HECK ARE WE ON A FREAKING TREASURE HUNT!?
AREN'T WE JUST GOING BACK TO YOUR HOMETOWN?
HOW COULD YOU FORGET THE WAY BACK TO YOUR OWN HOME!?
TSUBAKIIN MANOR IS LOCATED WITHIN A "HIDDEN VILLAGE." THERE ARE POWERFUL BARRIERS AROUND IT TO REPEL OUTSIDERS.
AND SINCE EVERY ENTRANCE KNOWN TO MASTER AKI AND ME HAS APPARENTLY BEEN SEALED OFF...
...ALL WE CAN DO IS A STRAIGHT-FORWARD SEARCH FOR ANY UNRAVELED SPOTS IN THE BARRIER TO ENTER FROM.
IF I'D COME HERE WITH SIX STIGMAS AS THEY STIPULATED, THEY'D PROBABLY OPEN A PATH FOR US.

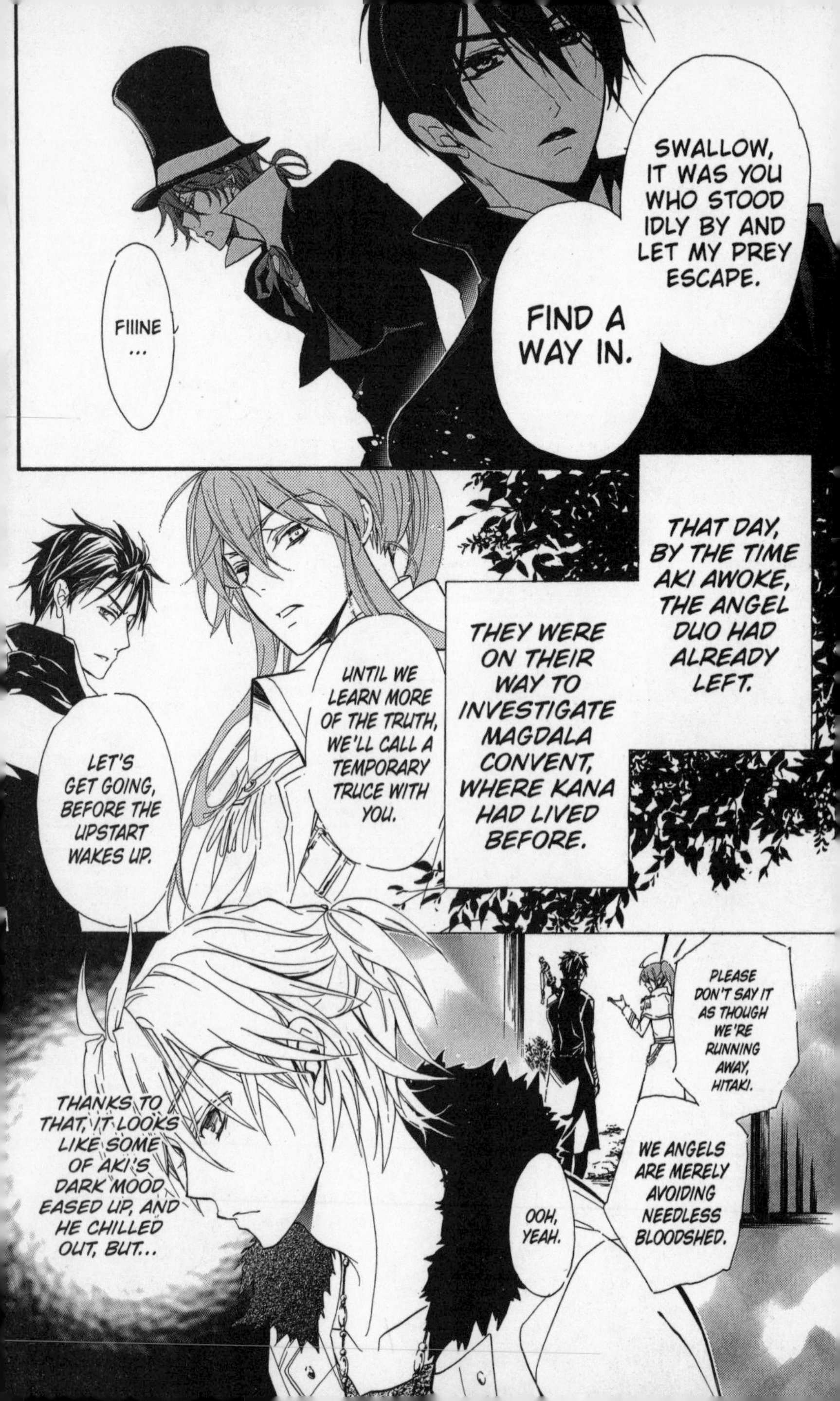
SWALLOW, IT WAS YOU WHO STOOD IDLY BY AND LET MY PREY ESCAPE.
FIND A WAY IN.
FIIINE ...
THAT DAY, BY THE TIME AKI AWOKE, THE ANGEL DUO HAD ALREADY LEFT.
THEY WERE ON THEIR WAY TO INVESTIGATE MAGDALA CONVENT, WHERE KANA HAD LIVED BEFORE.
UNTIL WE LEARN MORE OF THE TRUTH, WE'LL CALL A TEMPORARY TRUCE WITH YOU.
LET'S GET GOING, BEFORE THE UPSTART WAKES UP.
PLEASE DON'T SAY IT AS THOUGH WE'RE RUNNING AWAY, HITAKI.
WE ANGELS ARE MERELY AVOIDING NEEDLESS BLOODSHED.
OOH, YEAH.
THANKS TO THAT, IT LOOKS LIKE SOME OF AKI'S DARK MOOD EASED UP, AND HE CHILLED OUT, BUT...

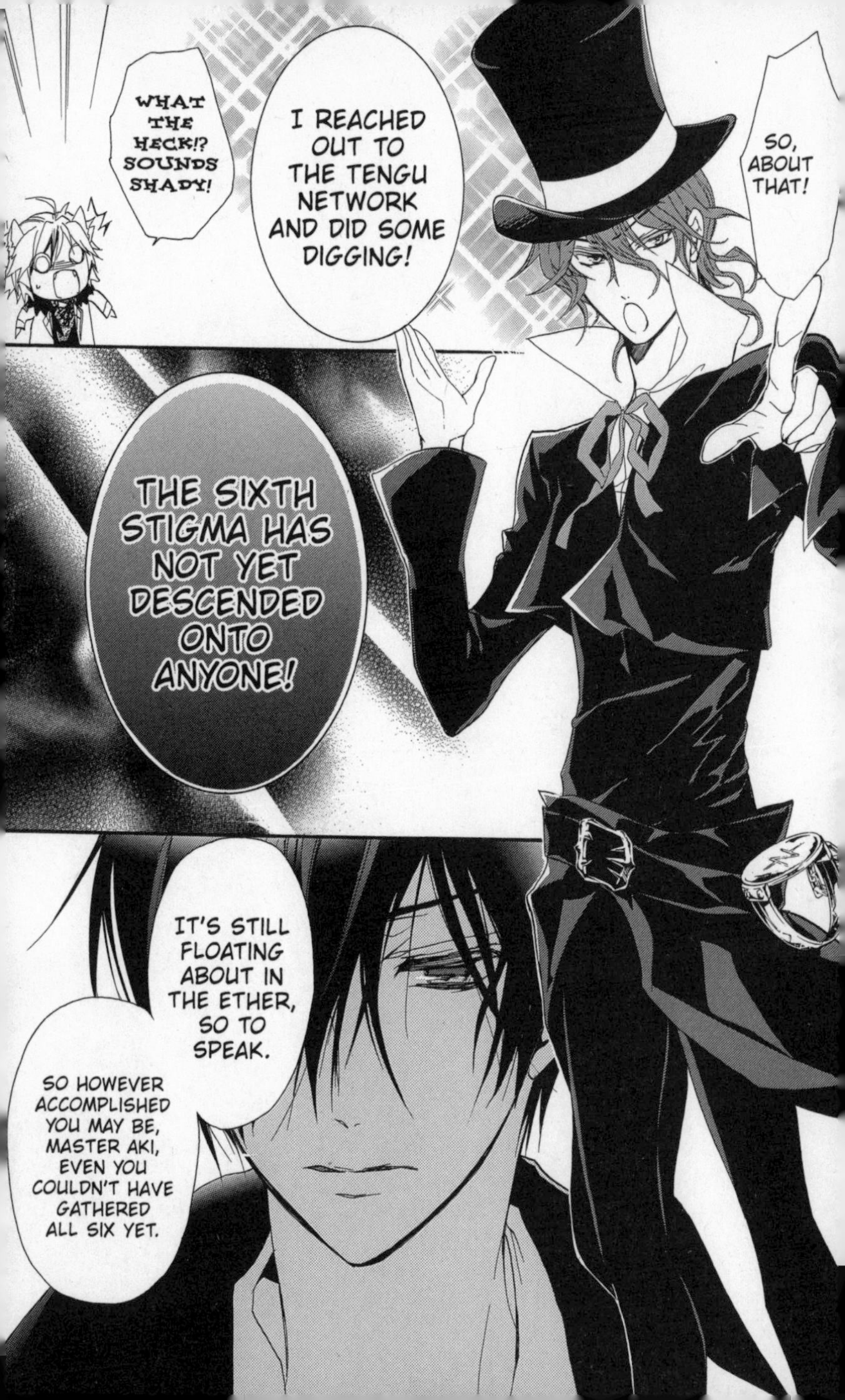
SO, ABOUT THAT!
I REACHED OUT TO THE TENGU NETWORK AND DID SOME DIGGING!
WHAT THE HECK!? SOUNDS SHADY!
THE SIXTH STIGMA HAS NOT YET DESCENDED ONTO ANYONE!
IT'S STILL FLOATING ABOUT IN THE ETHER, SO TO SPEAK.
SO HOWEVER ACCOMPLISHED YOU MAY BE, MASTER AKI, EVEN YOU COULDN'T HAVE GATHERED ALL SIX YET.

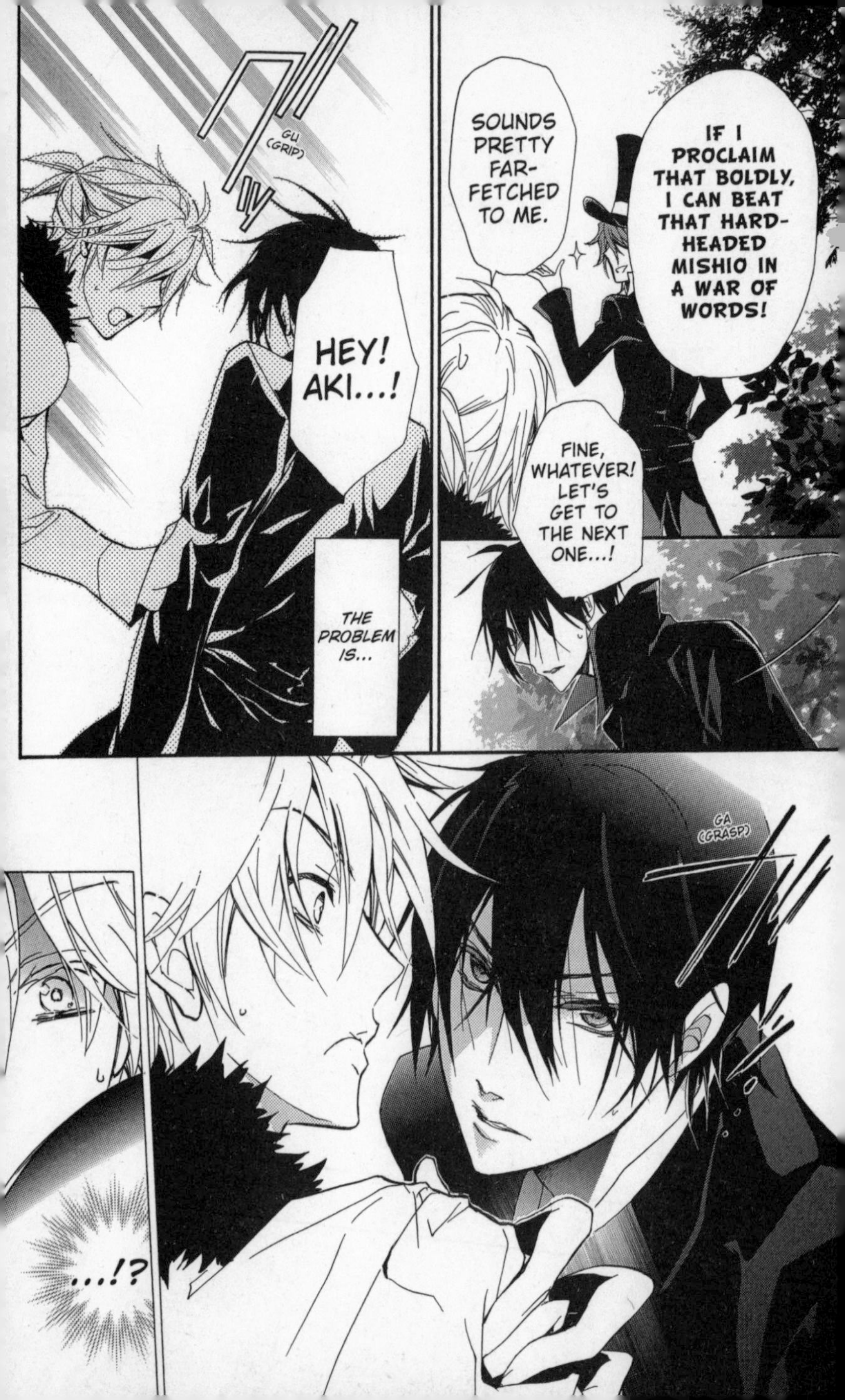
IF I PROCLAIM THAT BOLDLY, I CAN BEAT THAT HARD-HEADED MISHIO IN A WAR OF WORDS!
SOUNDS PRETTY FAR-FETCHED TO ME.
FINE, WHATEVER! LET'S GET TO THE NEXT ONE...!
GU (GRIP)
HEY! AKI...!
THE PROBLEM IS...
GA (GRASP)
...!?

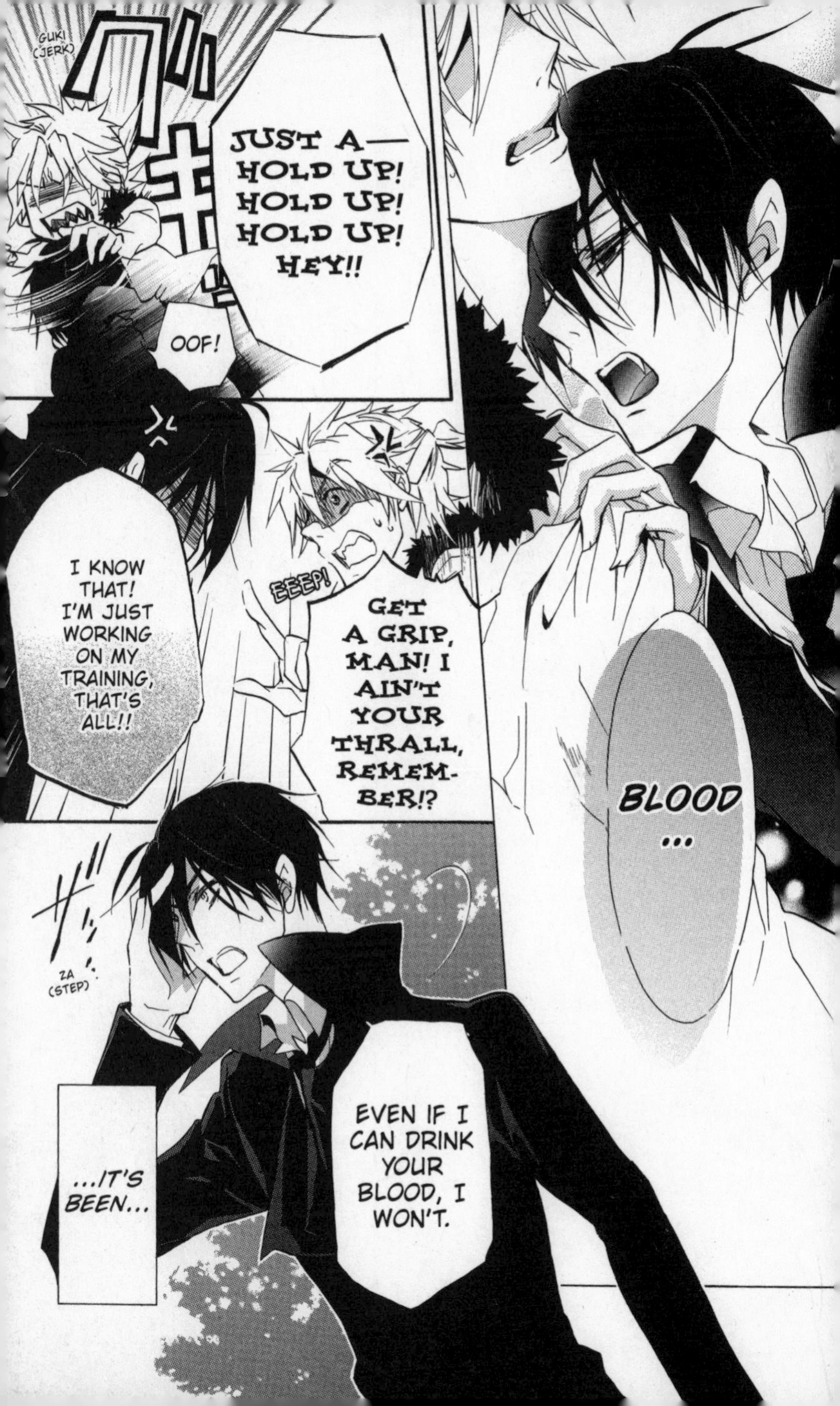
BLOOD ...
JUST A— HOLD UP! HOLD UP! HOLD UP! HEY!!
GUKI (JERK)
OOF!
GET A GRIP, MAN! I AIN'T YOUR THRALL, REMEMBER!?
EEEP!
I KNOW THAT! I'M JUST WORKING ON MY TRAINING, THAT'S ALL!!
EVEN IF I CAN DRINK YOUR BLOOD, I WON'T.
ZA (STEP)
...IT'S BEEN...

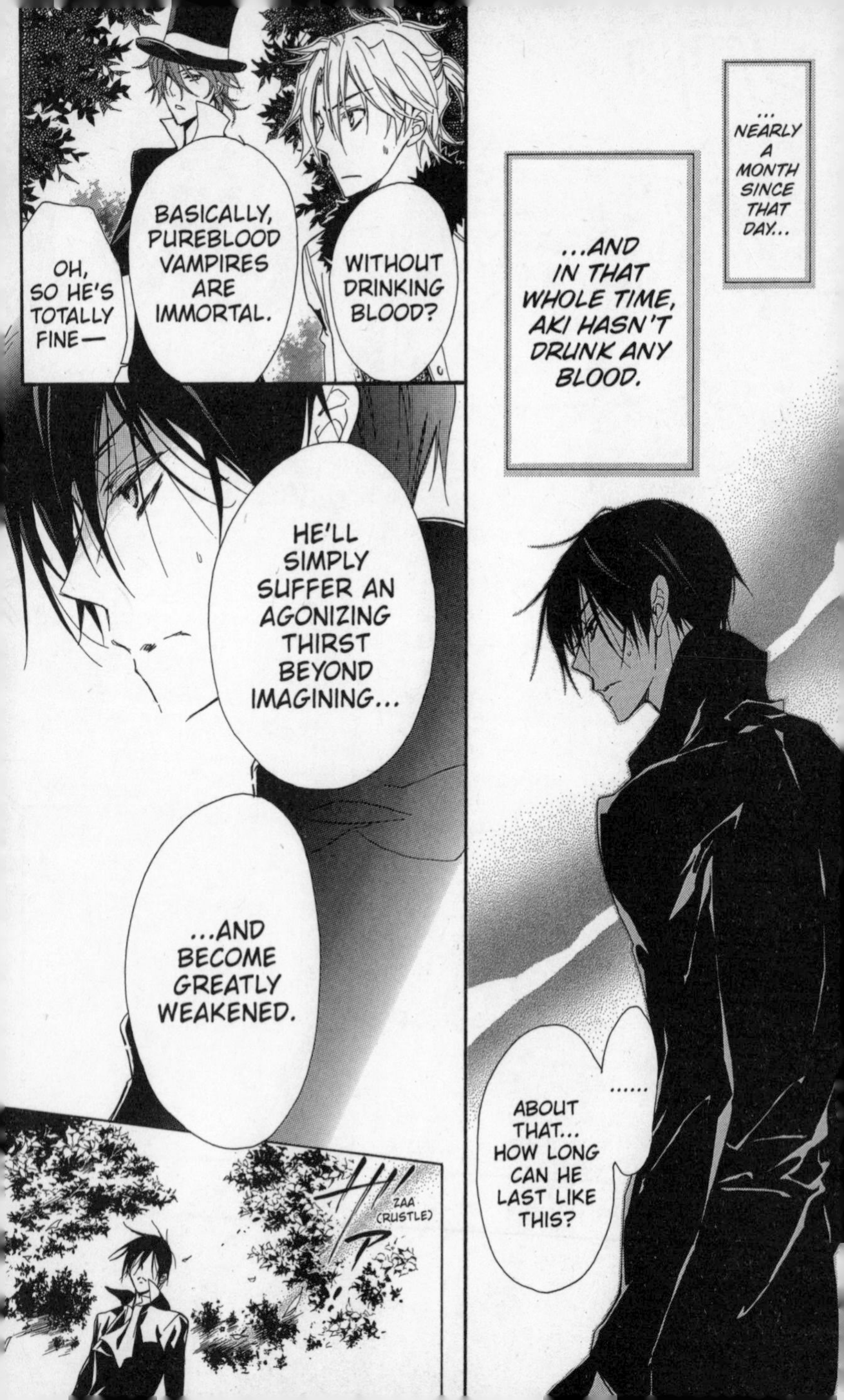
...NEARLY A MONTH SINCE THAT DAY...
...AND IN THAT WHOLE TIME, AKI HASN'T DRUNK ANY BLOOD.
......
ABOUT THAT... HOW LONG CAN HE LAST LIKE THIS?
WITHOUT DRINKING BLOOD?
BASICALLY, PUREBLOOD VAMPIRES ARE IMMORTAL.
OH, SO HE'S TOTALLY FINE—
HE'LL SIMPLY SUFFER AN AGONIZING THIRST BEYOND IMAGINING...
...AND BECOME GREATLY WEAKENED.
ZAA (RUSTLE)

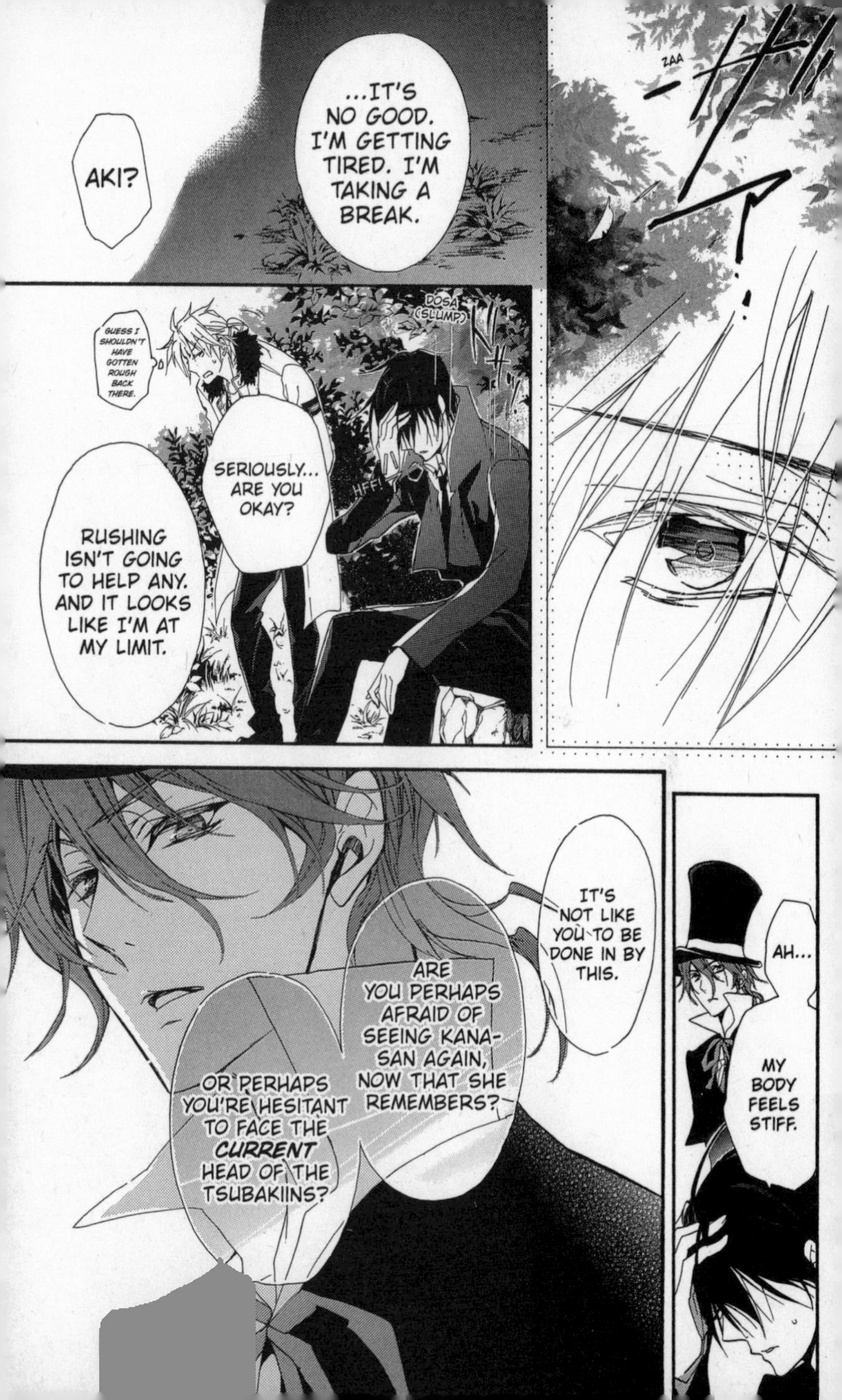
ZAA
...IT'S NO GOOD. I'M GETTING TIRED. I'M TAKING A BREAK.
AKI?
DOSA (SLUMP)
GUESS I SHOULDN'T HAVE GOTTEN ROUGH BACK THERE.
SERIOUSLY... ARE YOU OKAY?
HFF!
RUSHING ISN'T GOING TO HELP ANY. AND IT LOOKS LIKE I'M AT MY LIMIT.
AH...
MY BODY FEELS STIFF.
IT'S NOT LIKE YOU TO BE DONE IN BY THIS.
ARE YOU PERHAPS AFRAID OF SEEING KANA-SAN AGAIN, NOW THAT SHE REMEMBERS?
OR PERHAPS YOU'RE HESITANT TO FACE THE *CURRENT* HEAD OF THE TSUBAKIINS?

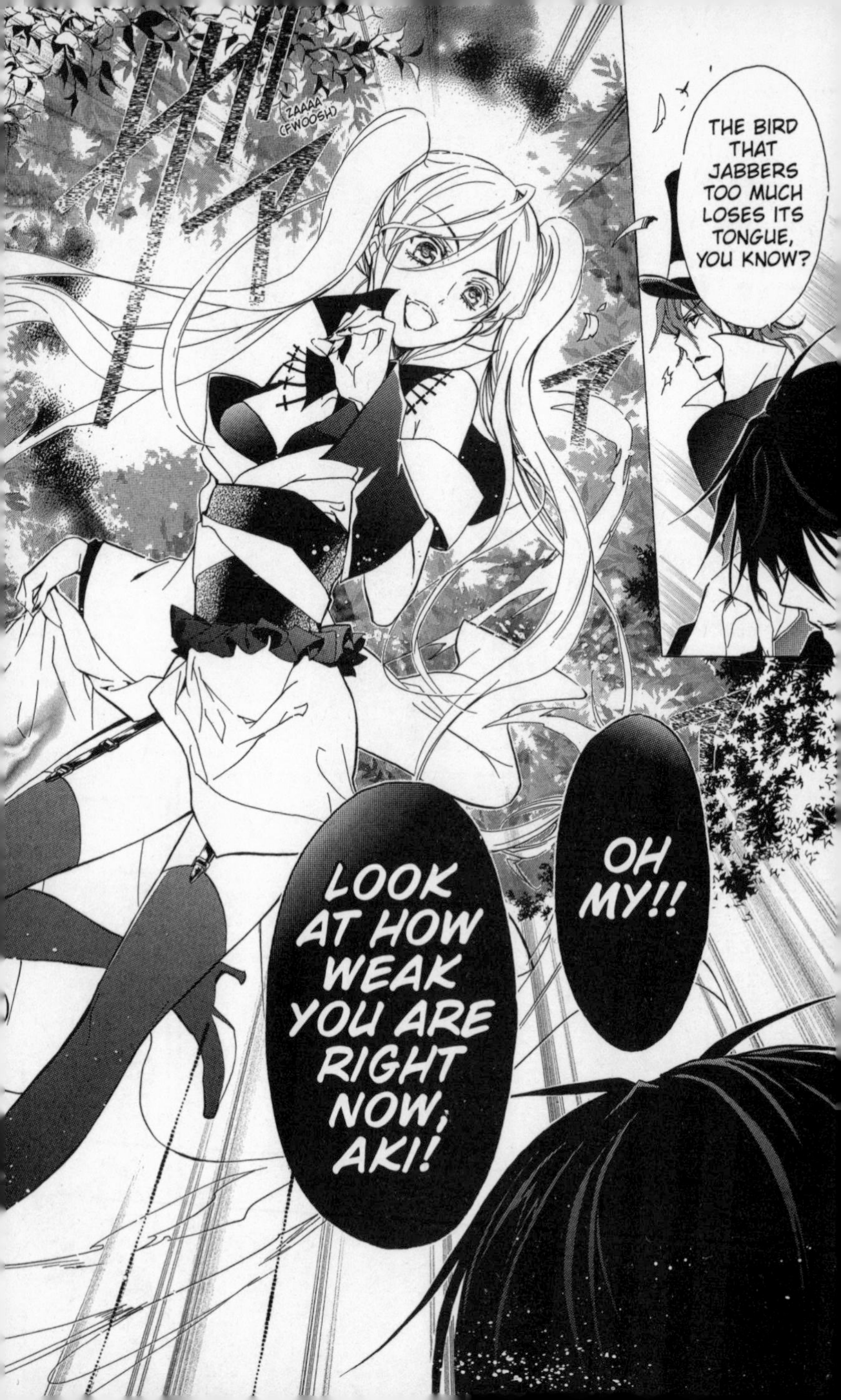
THE BIRD THAT JABBERS TOO MUCH LOSES ITS TONGUE, YOU KNOW?
ZAAAA (FWOOSH)
OH MY!!
LOOK AT HOW WEAK YOU ARE RIGHT NOW, AKI!

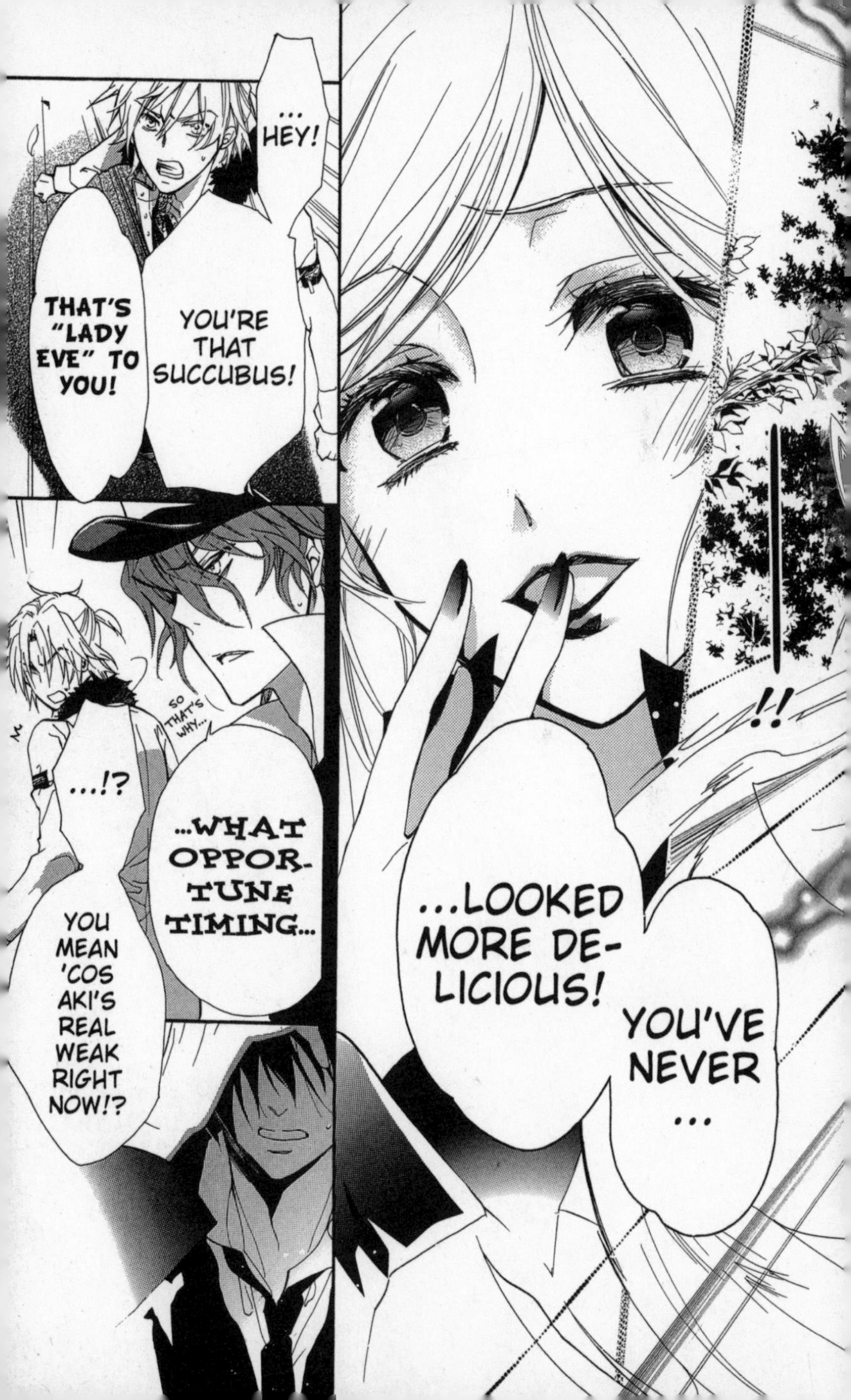
!!
YOU'VE NEVER ...
...LOOKED MORE DE-LICIOUS!
... HEY!
YOU'RE THAT SUCCUBUS!
THAT'S "LADY EVE" TO YOU!
SO THAT'S WHY...
...WHAT OPPOR-TUNE TIMING...
...!?
YOU MEAN 'COS AKI'S REAL WEAK RIGHT NOW!?

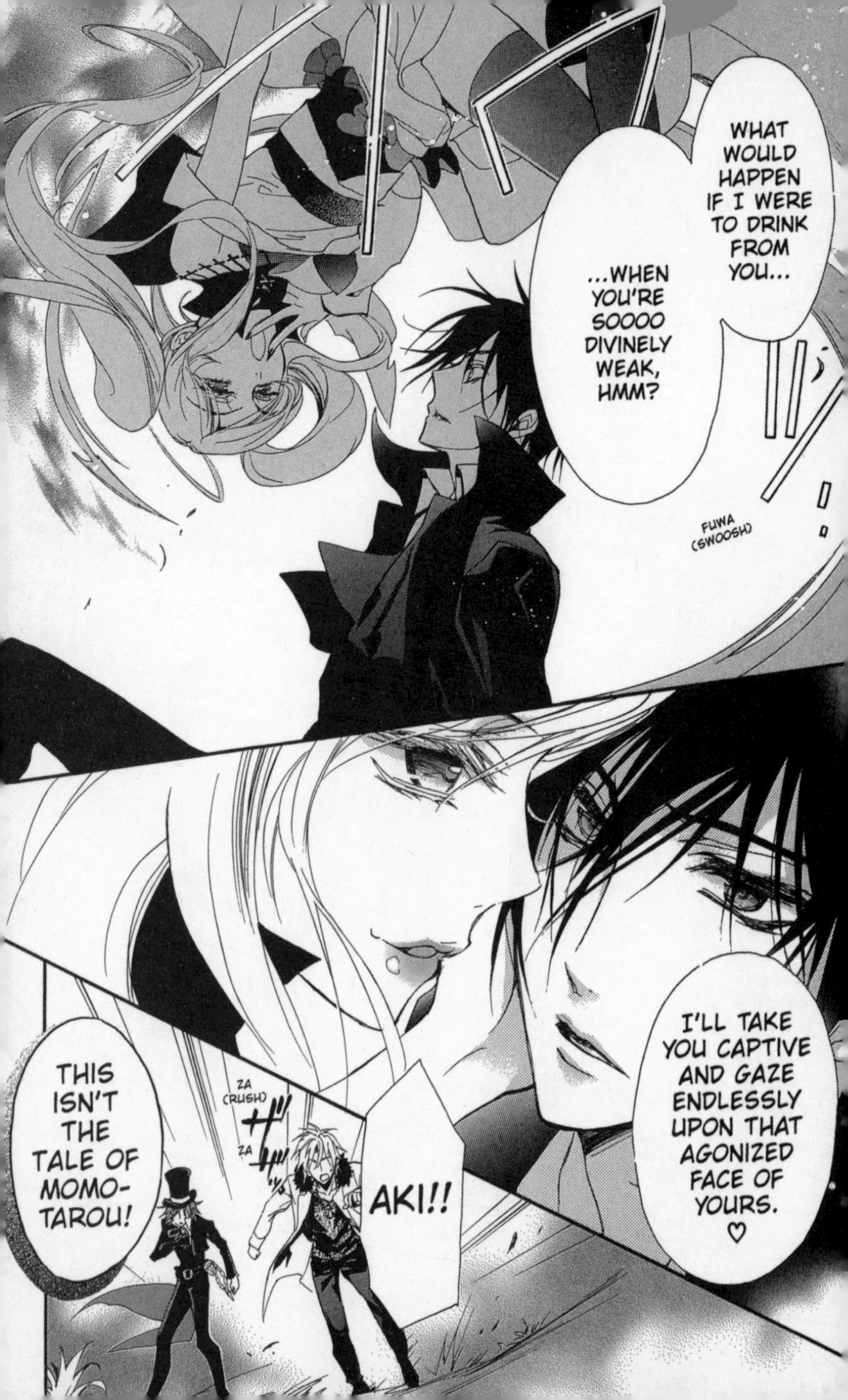
WHAT WOULD HAPPEN IF I WERE TO DRINK FROM YOU...
...WHEN YOU'RE SOOOO DIVINELY WEAK, HMM?
FUWA (SWOOSH)
I'LL TAKE YOU CAPTIVE AND GAZE ENDLESSLY UPON THAT AGONIZED FACE OF YOURS. ♡
AKI!!
ZA (RUSH) ZA
THIS ISN'T THE TALE OF MOMO-TAROU!

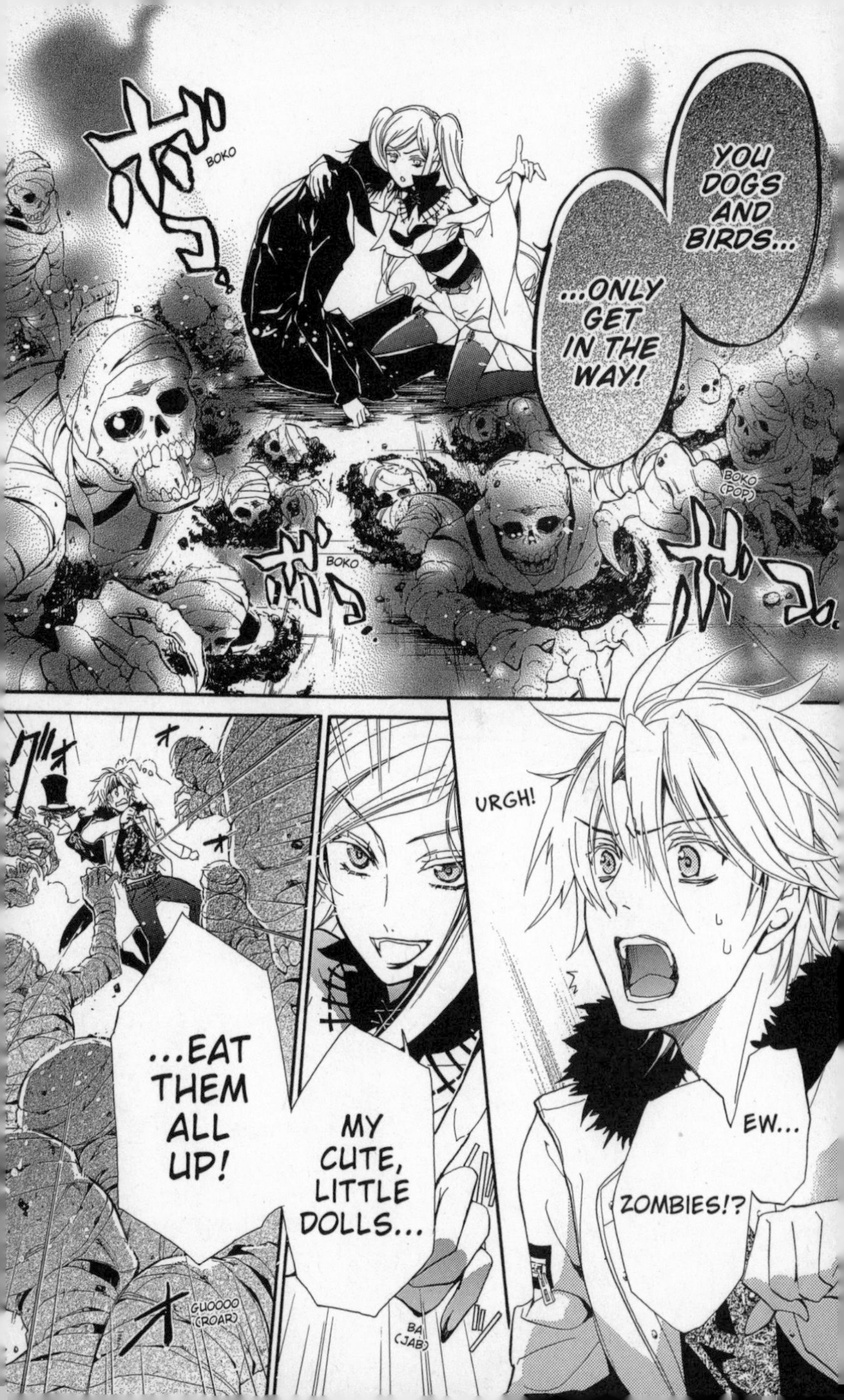
YOU DOGS AND BIRDS...
...ONLY GET IN THE WAY!
BOKO (POP)
BOKO
BOKO
URGH!
EW...
ZOMBIES!?
MY CUTE, LITTLE DOLLS...
BA (JAB)
...EAT THEM ALL UP!
GUOOOO (ROAR)

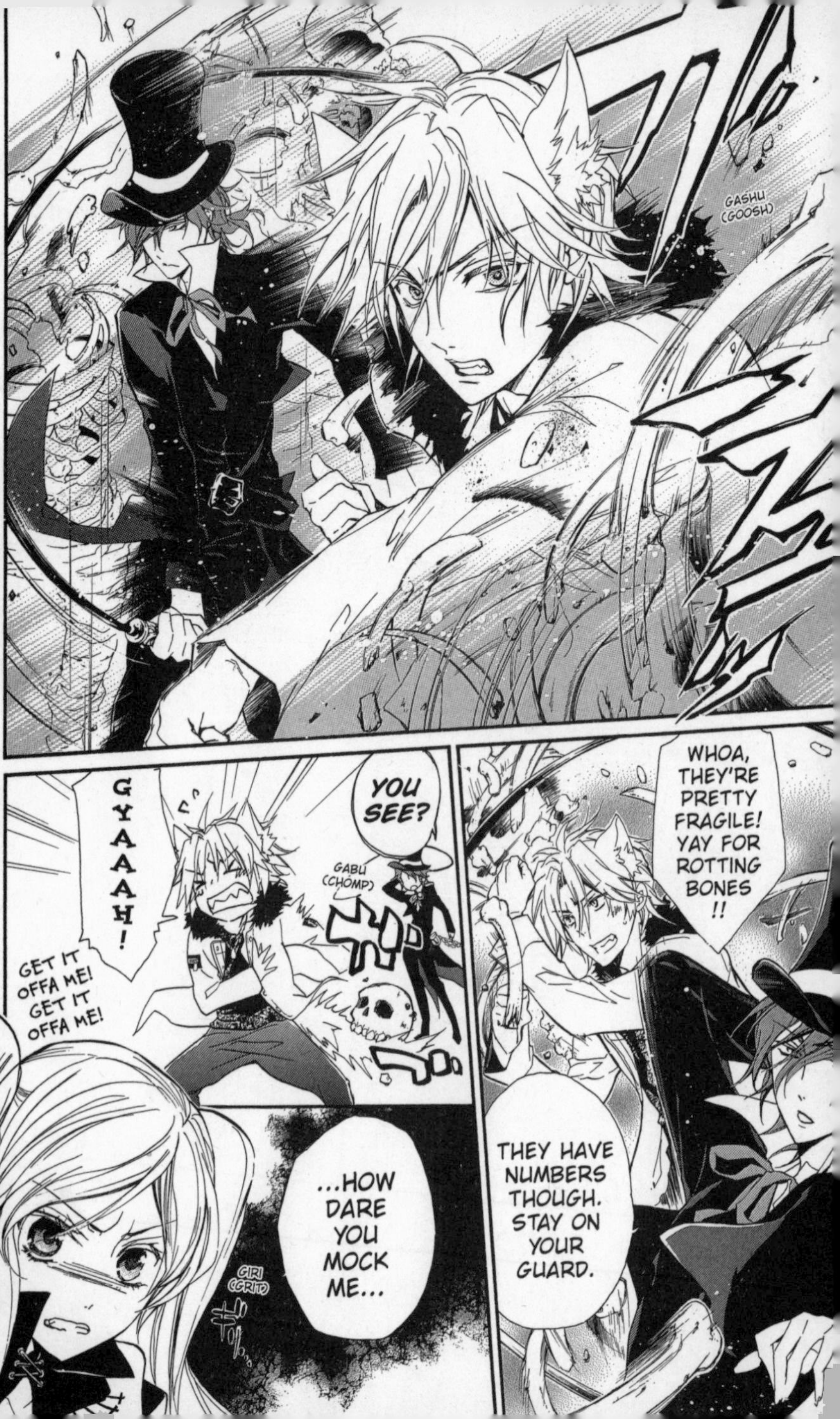
GASHU (GOOSH)
WHOA, THEY'RE PRETTY FRAGILE! YAY FOR ROTTING BONES !!
YOU SEE?
GABU (CHOMP)
GYAAAAH!
GET IT OFFA ME! GET IT OFFA ME!
THEY HAVE NUMBERS THOUGH. STAY ON YOUR GUARD.
...HOW DARE YOU MOCK ME...
GIRI (GRIT)

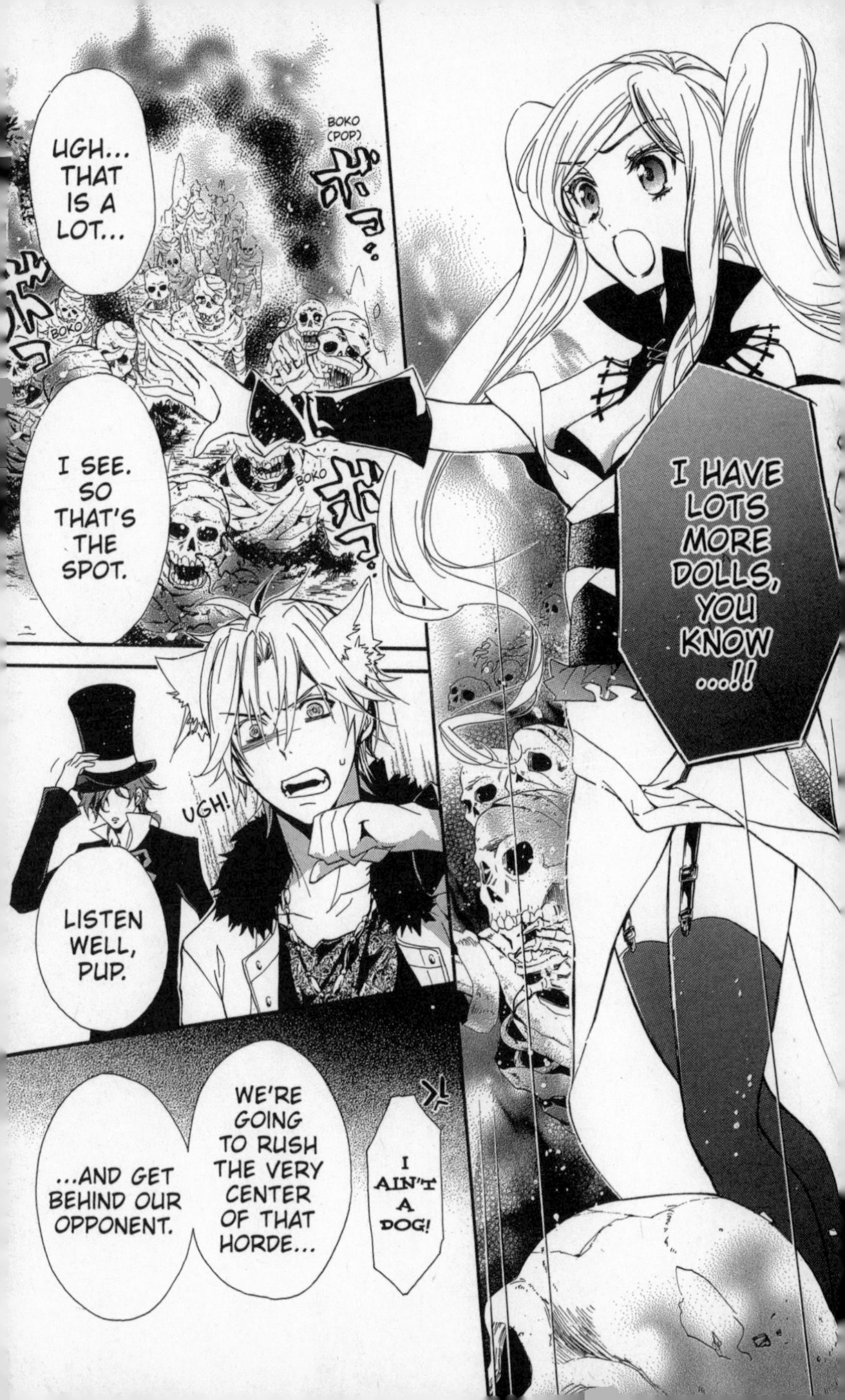
I HAVE LOTS MORE DOLLS, YOU KNOW ...!!
BOKO (POP)
UGH... THAT IS A LOT...
BOKO
BOKO
I SEE. SO THAT'S THE SPOT.
UGH!
LISTEN WELL, PUP.
I AIN'T A DOG!
WE'RE GOING TO RUSH THE VERY CENTER OF THAT HORDE...
...AND GET BEHIND OUR OPPONENT.

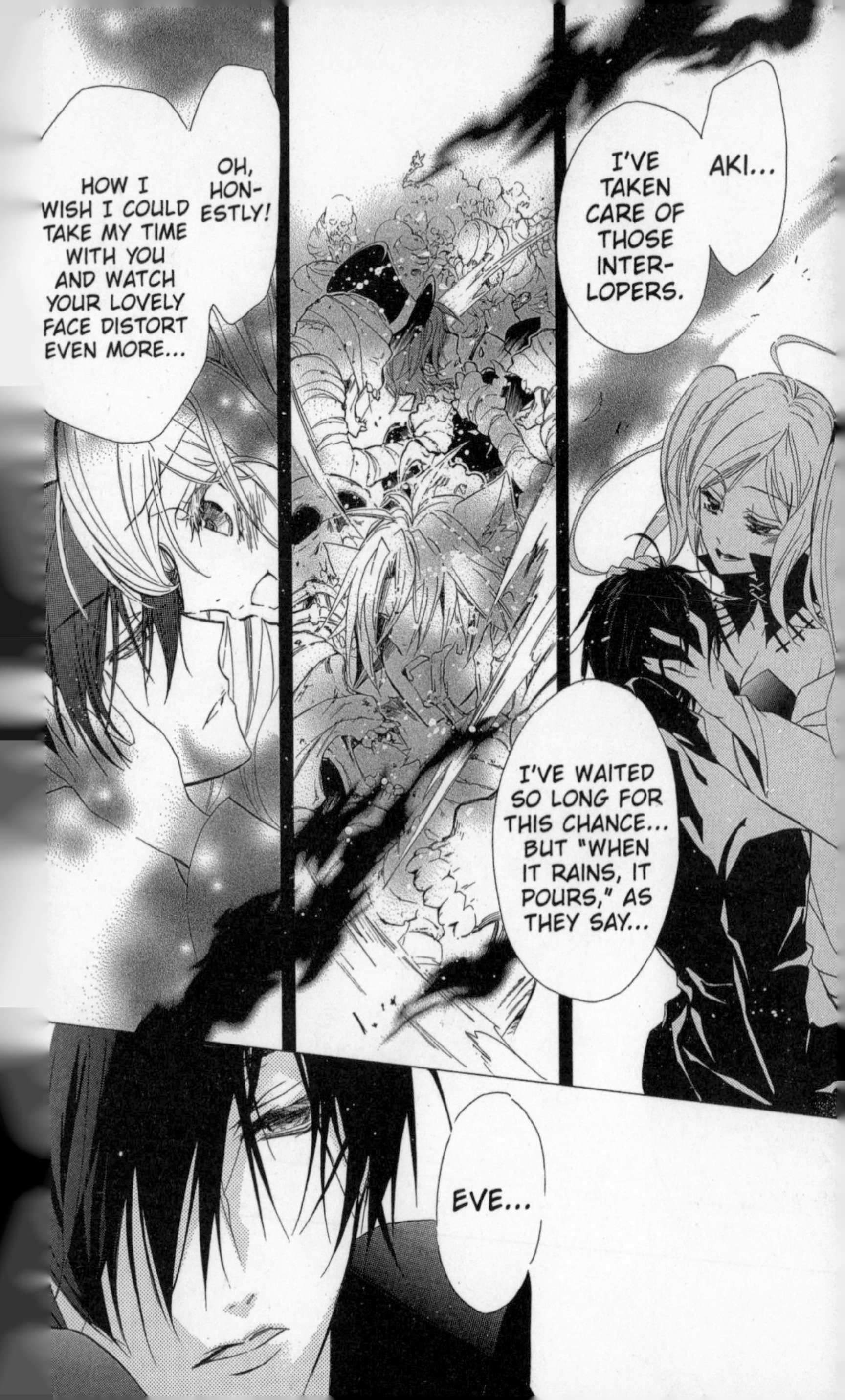
AKI...
I'VE TAKEN CARE OF THOSE INTERLOPERS.
I'VE WAITED SO LONG FOR THIS CHANCE... BUT "WHEN IT RAINS, IT POURS," AS THEY SAY...
OH, HONESTLY!
HOW I WISH I COULD TAKE MY TIME WITH YOU AND WATCH YOUR LOVELY FACE DISTORT EVEN MORE...
EVE...

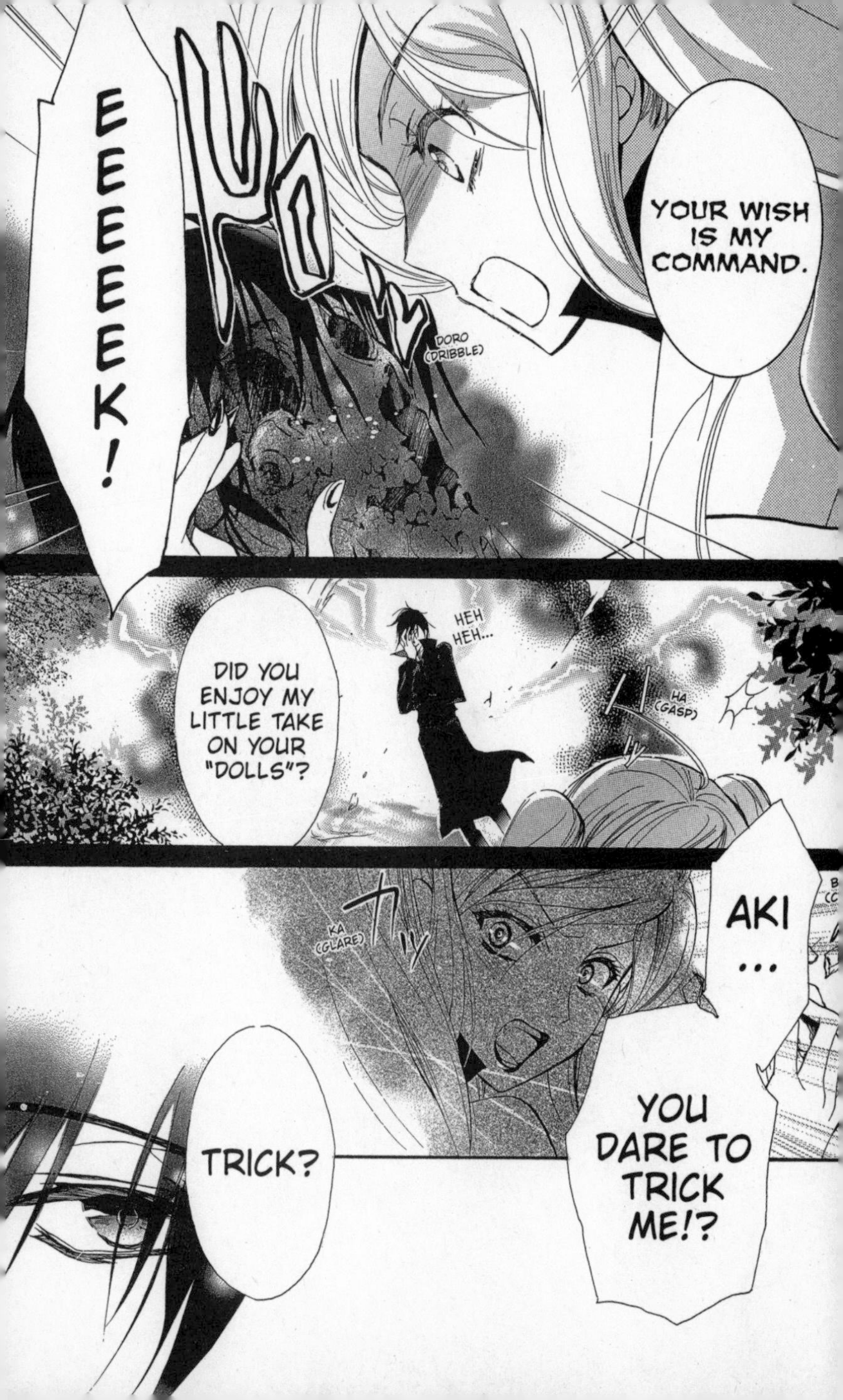
YOUR WISH IS MY COMMAND.
DORO (DRIBBLE)
EEEEEK!
HA (GASP)
HEH HEH...
DID YOU ENJOY MY LITTLE TAKE ON YOUR "DOLLS"?
AKI ...
KA (GLARE)
YOU DARE TO TRICK ME!?
TRICK?

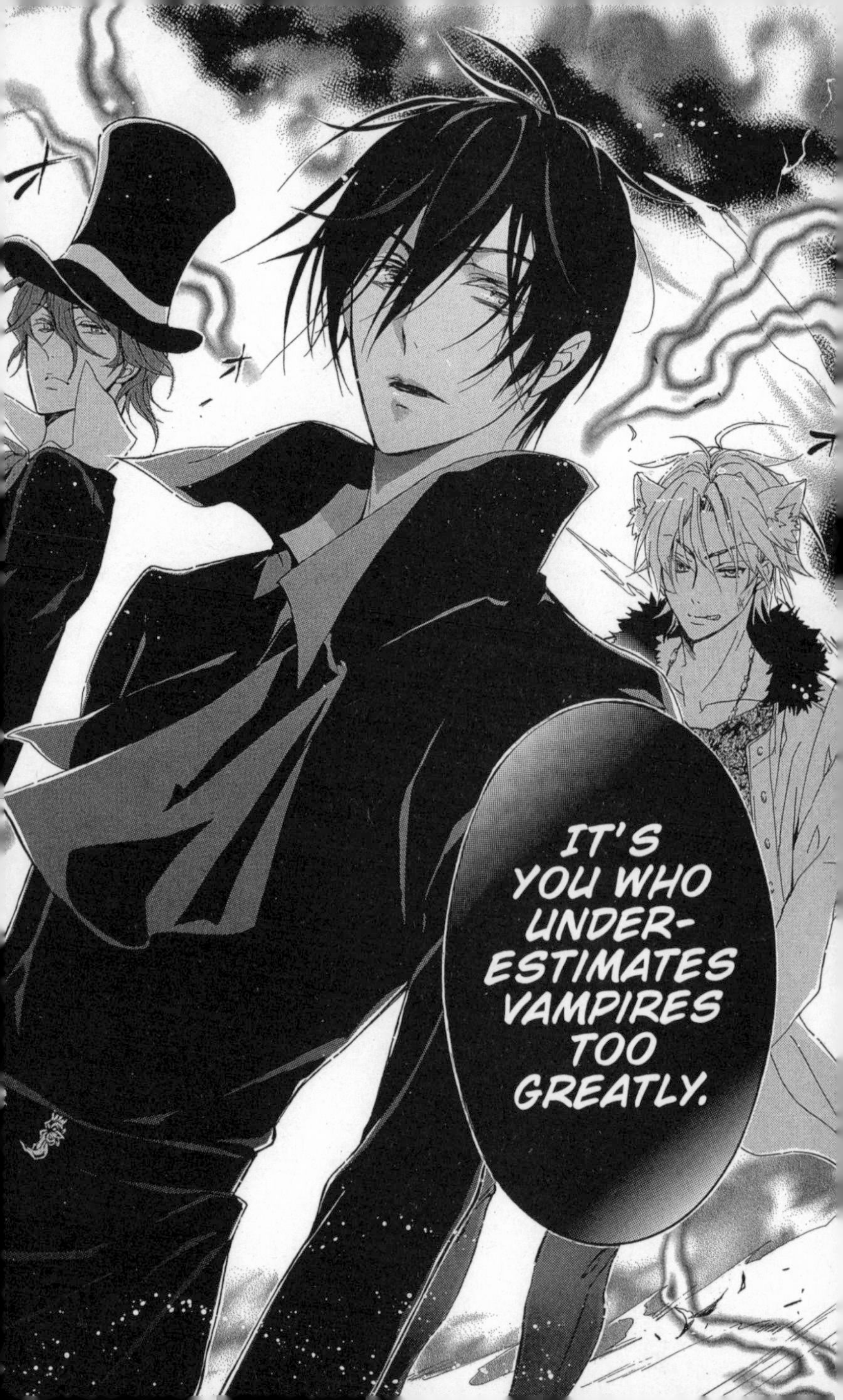
IT'S YOU WHO UNDER-ESTIMATES VAMPIRES TOO GREATLY.

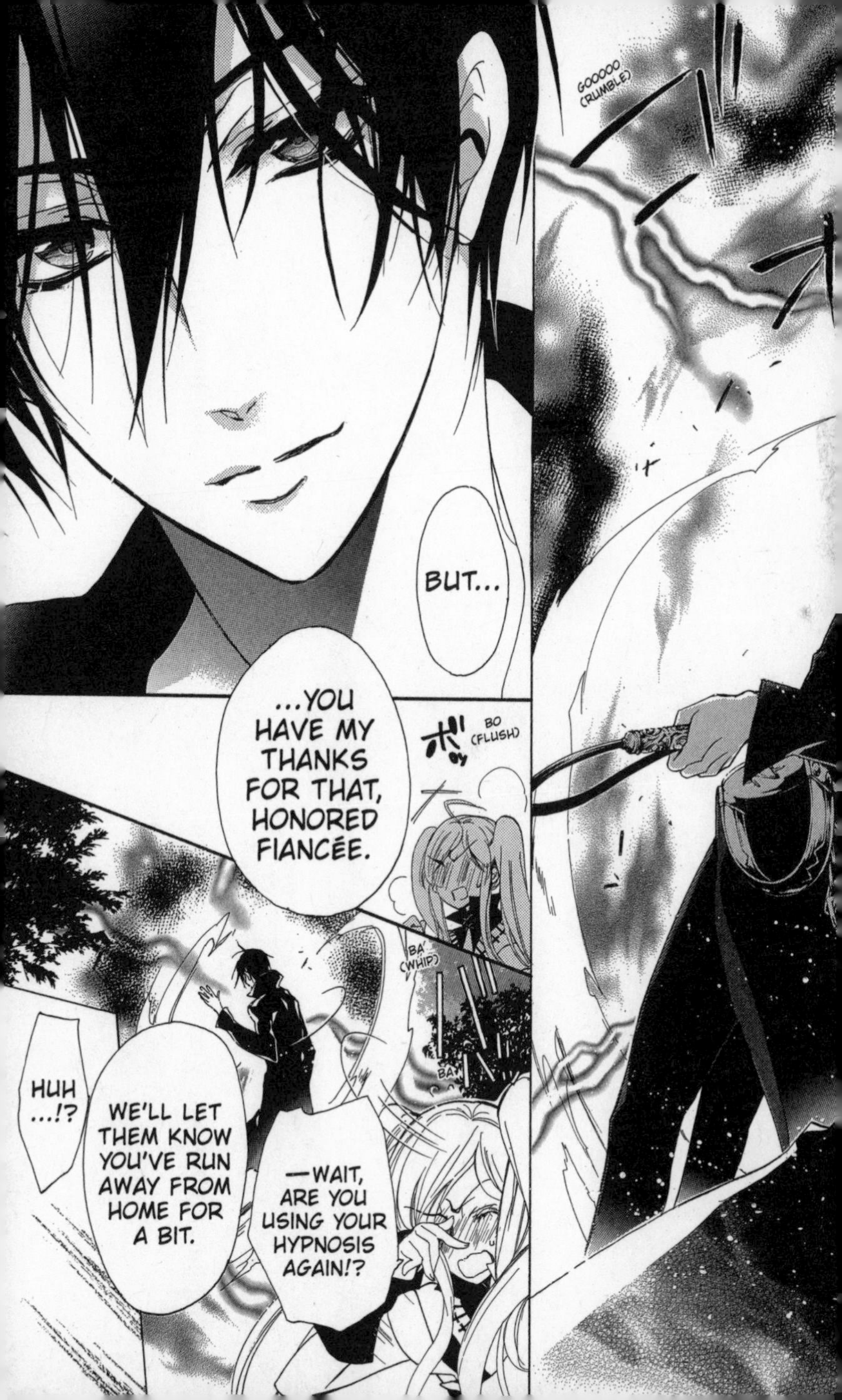
GOOOOO (RUMBLE)
BUT...
...YOU HAVE MY THANKS FOR THAT, HONORED FIANCÉE.
BO (FLUSH)
BA (WHIP)
BA
—WAIT, ARE YOU USING YOUR HYPNOSIS AGAIN!?
WE'LL LET THEM KNOW YOU'VE RUN AWAY FROM HOME FOR A BIT.
HUH ...!?

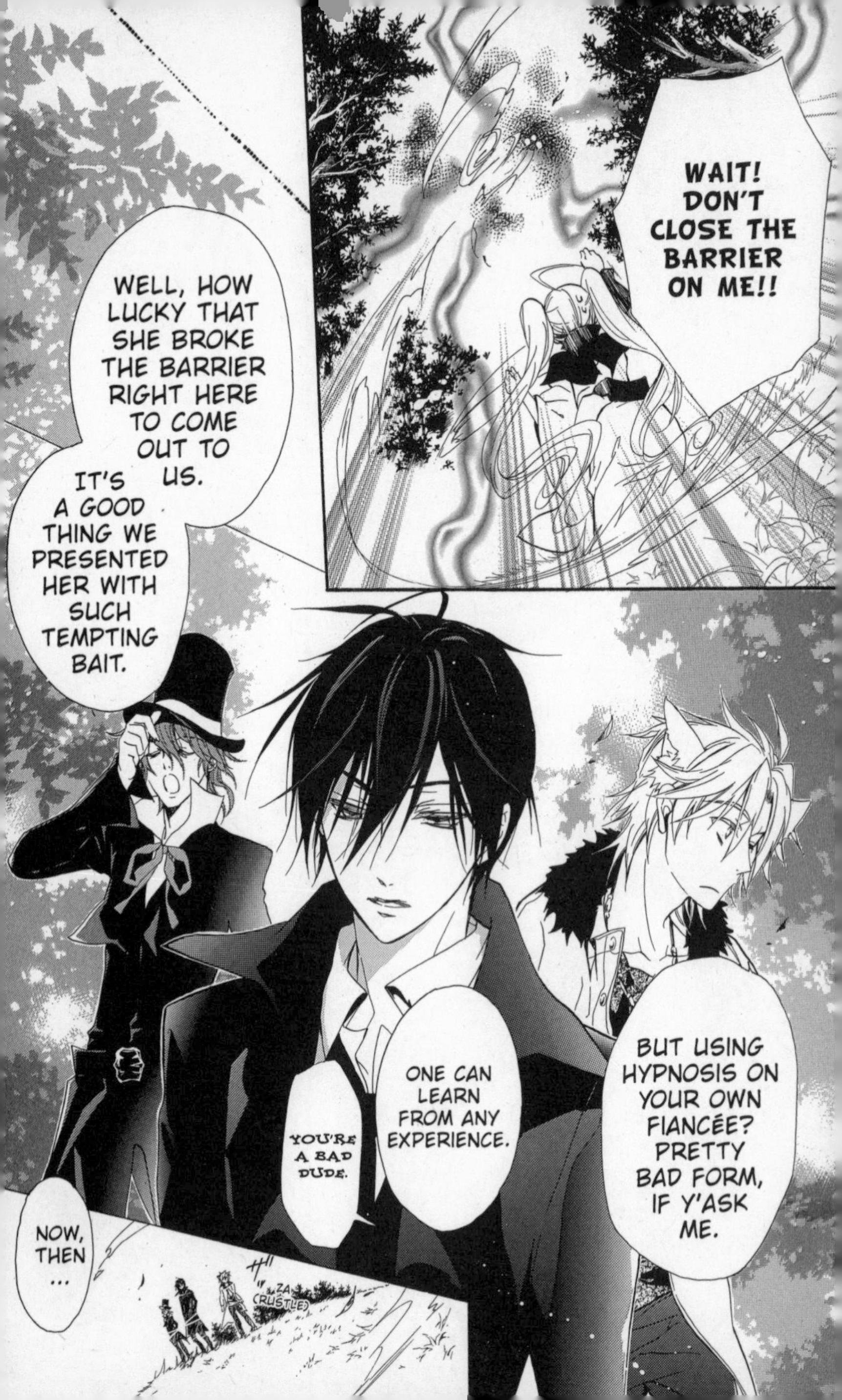
WAIT! DON'T CLOSE THE BARRIER ON ME!!
WELL, HOW LUCKY THAT SHE BROKE THE BARRIER RIGHT HERE TO COME OUT TO US.
IT'S A GOOD THING WE PRESENTED HER WITH SUCH TEMPTING BAIT.
BUT USING HYPNOSIS ON YOUR OWN FIANCÉE? PRETTY BAD FORM, IF Y'ASK ME.
ONE CAN LEARN FROM ANY EXPERIENCE.
YOU'RE A BAD DUDE.
NOW, THEN...
ZA (RUSTLE)

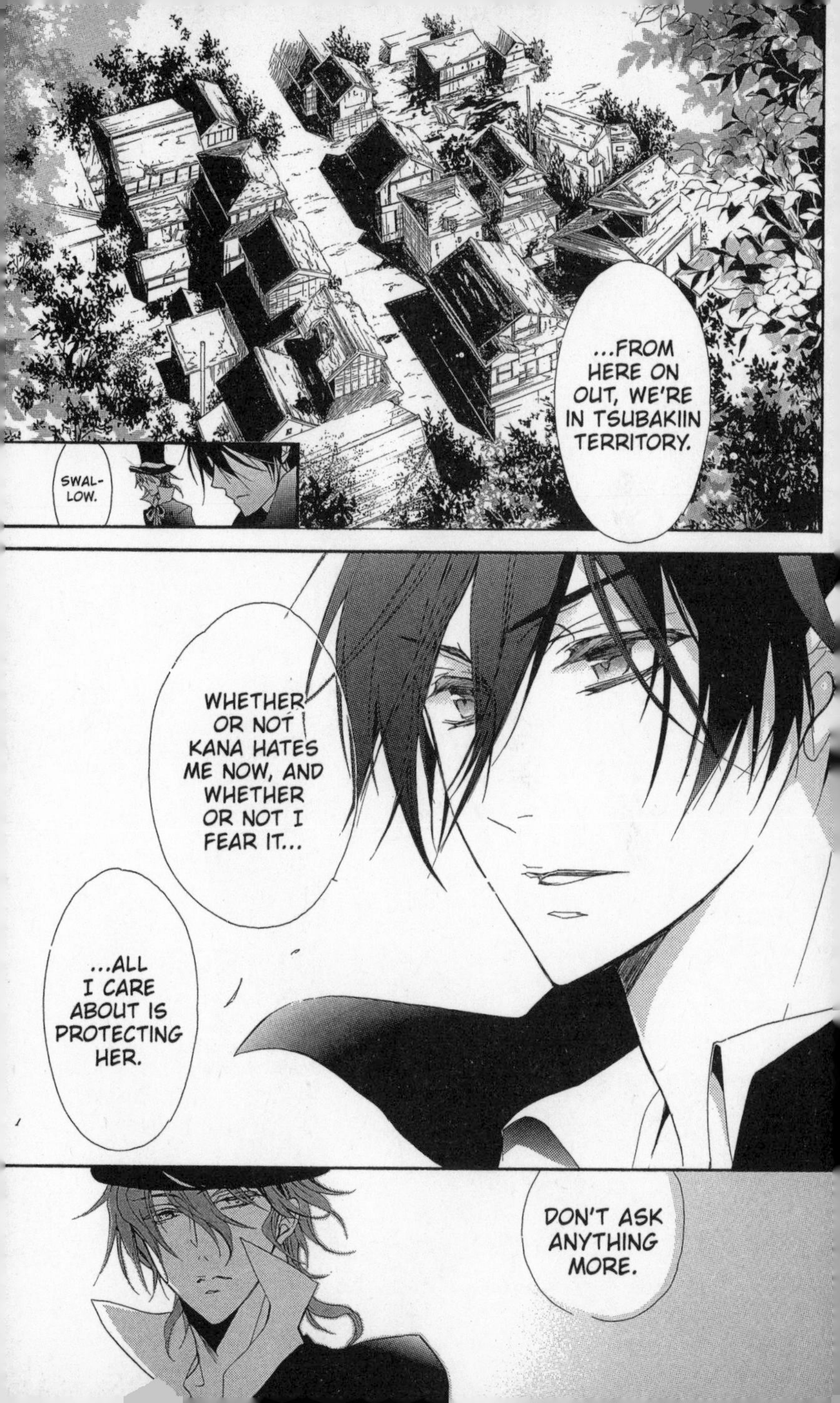
...FROM HERE ON OUT, WE'RE IN TSUBAKIIN TERRITORY.
SWAL-LOW.
WHETHER OR NOT KANA HATES ME NOW, AND WHETHER OR NOT I FEAR IT...
...ALL I CARE ABOUT IS PROTECTING HER.
DON'T ASK ANYTHING MORE.

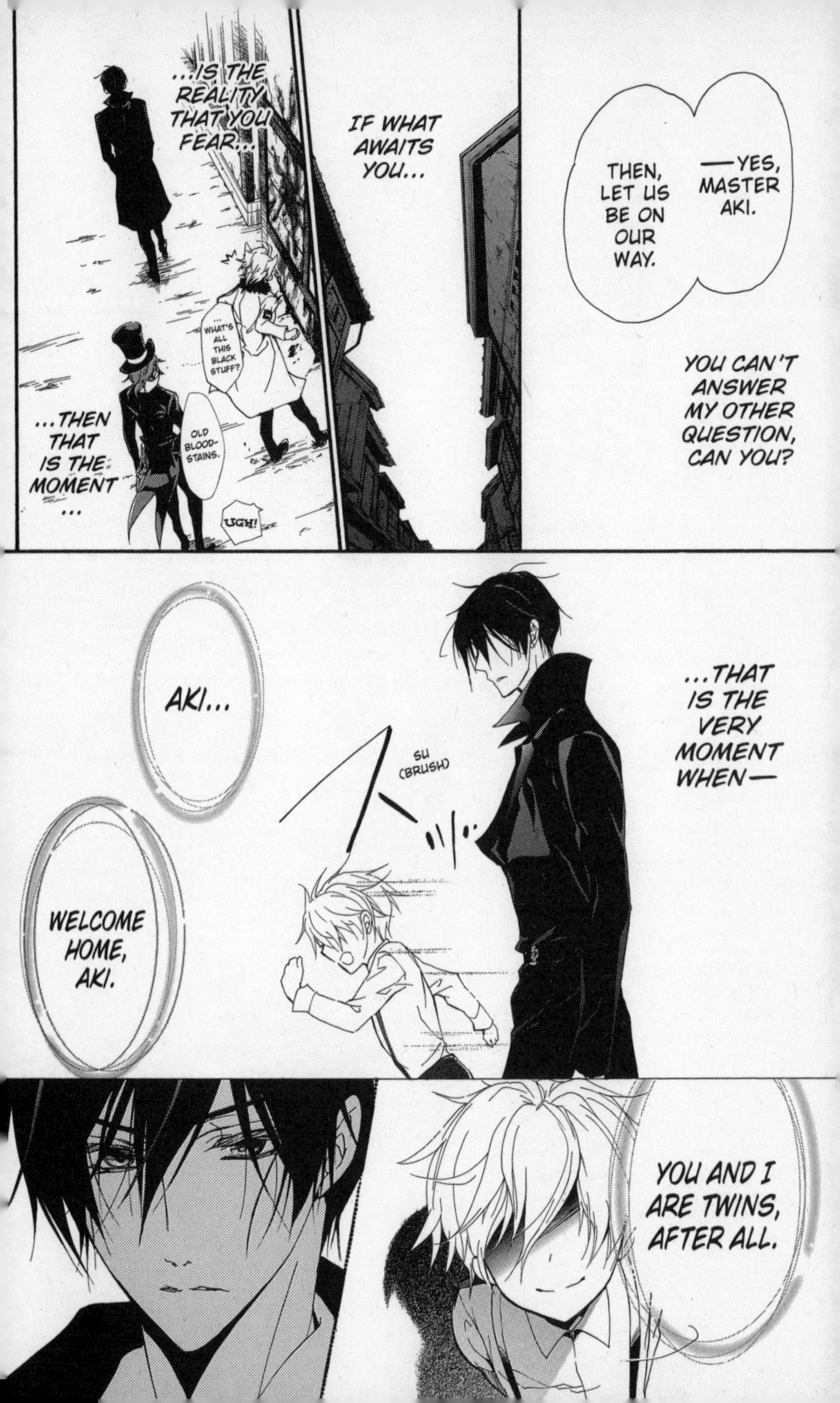
—YES, MASTER AKI.
THEN, LET US BE ON OUR WAY.
YOU CAN'T ANSWER MY OTHER QUESTION, CAN YOU?
IF WHAT AWAITS YOU...
...IS THE REALITY THAT YOU FEAR...
...WHAT'S ALL THIS BLACK STUFF?
OLD BLOOD-STAINS.
UGH!
...THEN THAT IS THE MOMENT...
...THAT IS THE VERY MOMENT WHEN—
SU (BRUSH)
AKI...
WELCOME HOME, AKI.
YOU AND I ARE TWINS, AFTER ALL.

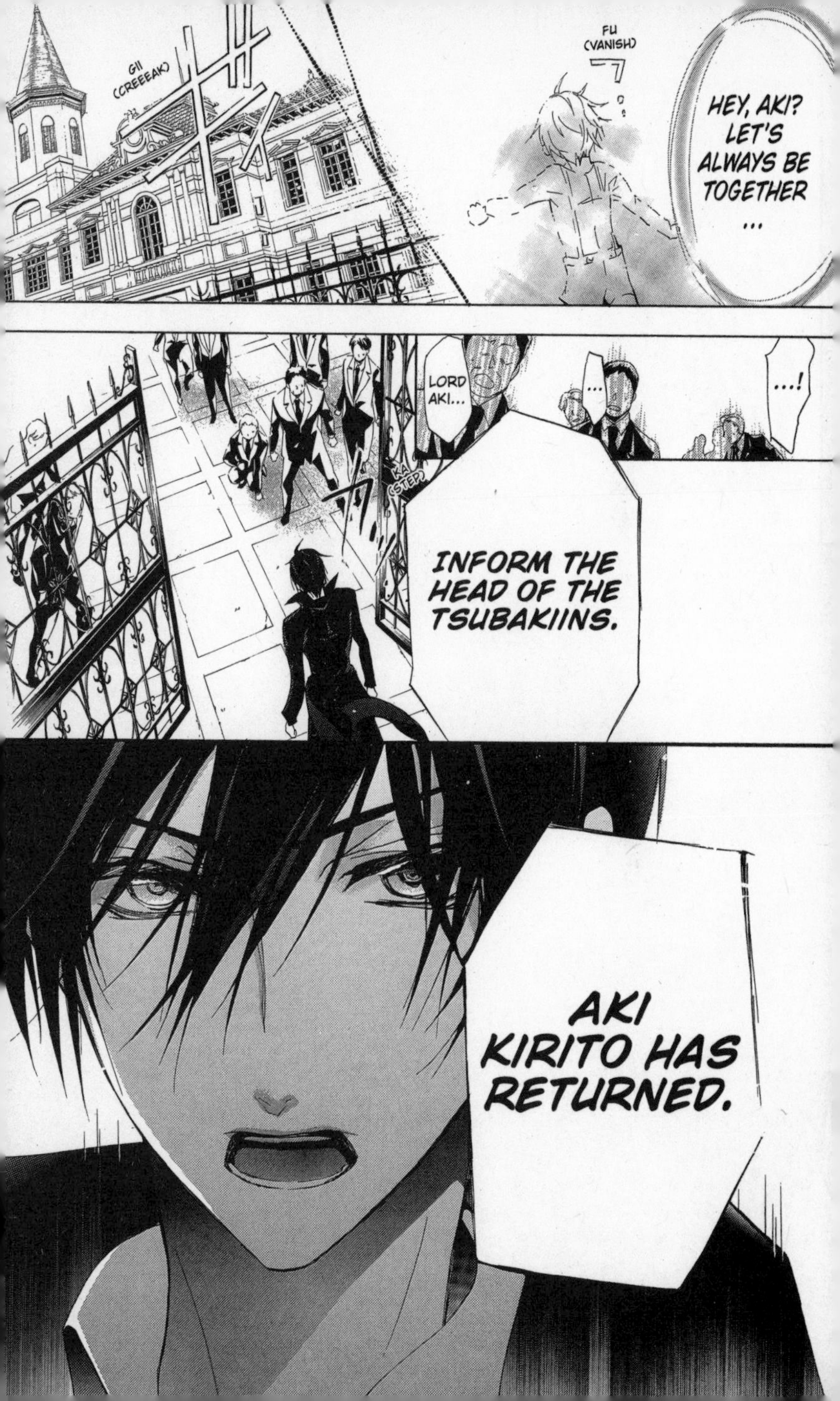
HEY, AKI? LET'S ALWAYS BE TOGETHER ...
FU (VANISH)
GII (CREEEAK)
...!
...
LORD AKI...
KA (STEP)
INFORM THE HEAD OF THE TSUBAKIINS.
AKI KIRITO HAS RETURNED.

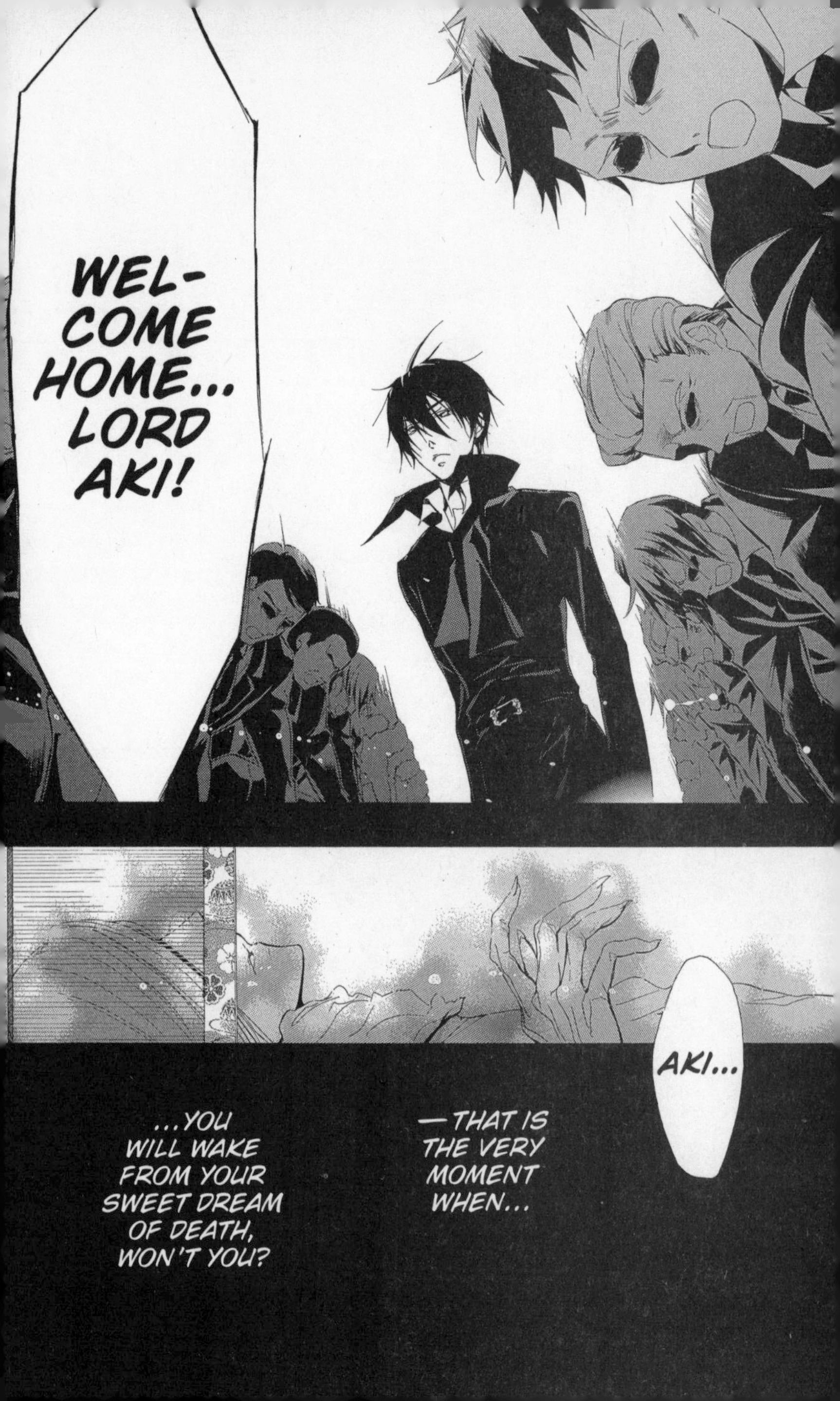
WEL-COME HOME... LORD AKI!
AKI...
—THAT IS THE VERY MOMENT WHEN...
...YOU WILL WAKE FROM YOUR SWEET DREAM OF DEATH, WON'T YOU?

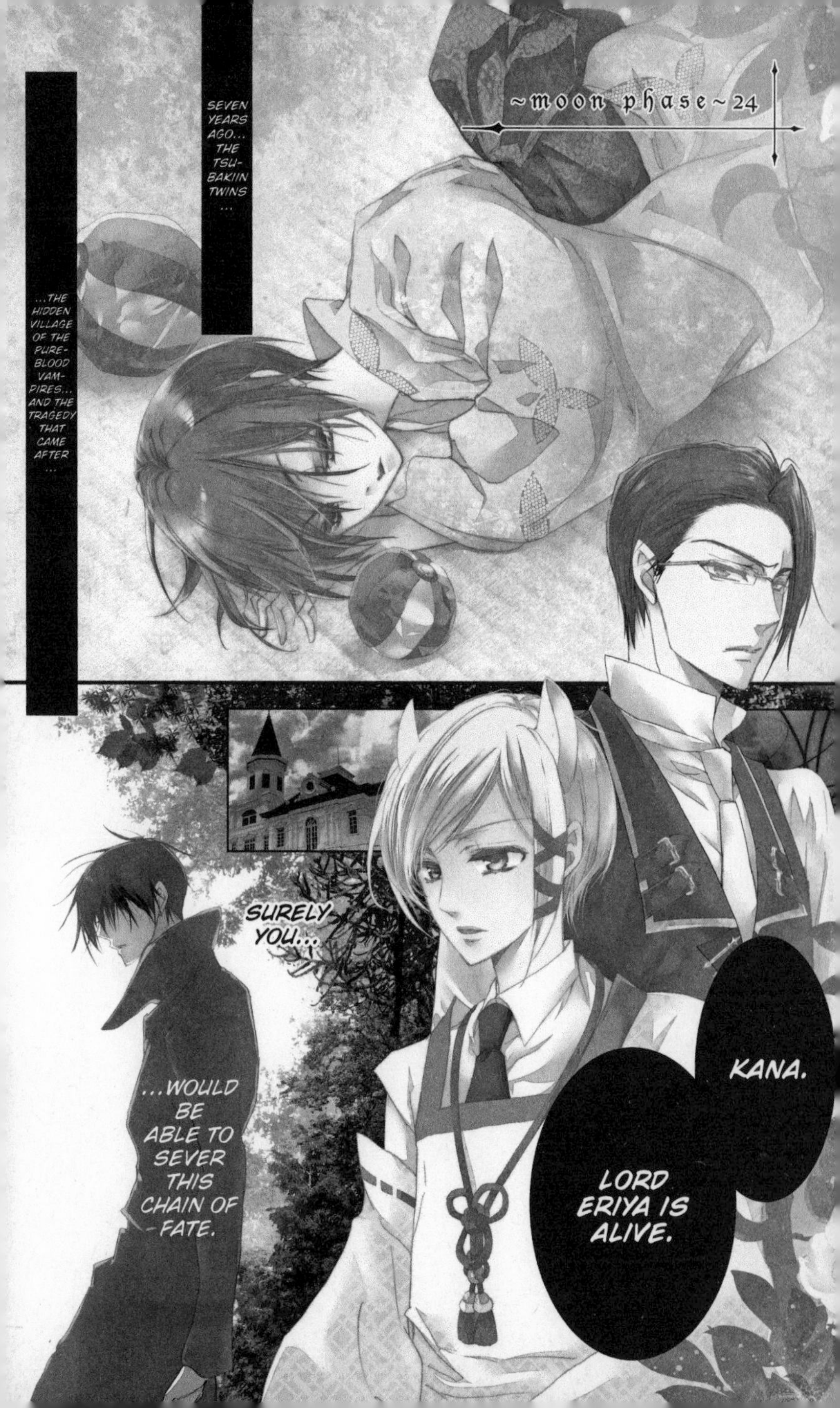
~moon phase~24
SEVEN YEARS AGO... THE TSU-BAKIIN TWINS...
...THE HIDDEN VILLAGE OF THE PURE-BLOOD VAM-PIRES... AND THE TRAGEDY THAT CAME AFTER...
KANA.
LORD ERIYA IS ALIVE.
SURELY YOU...
...WOULD BE ABLE TO SEVER THIS CHAIN OF FATE.

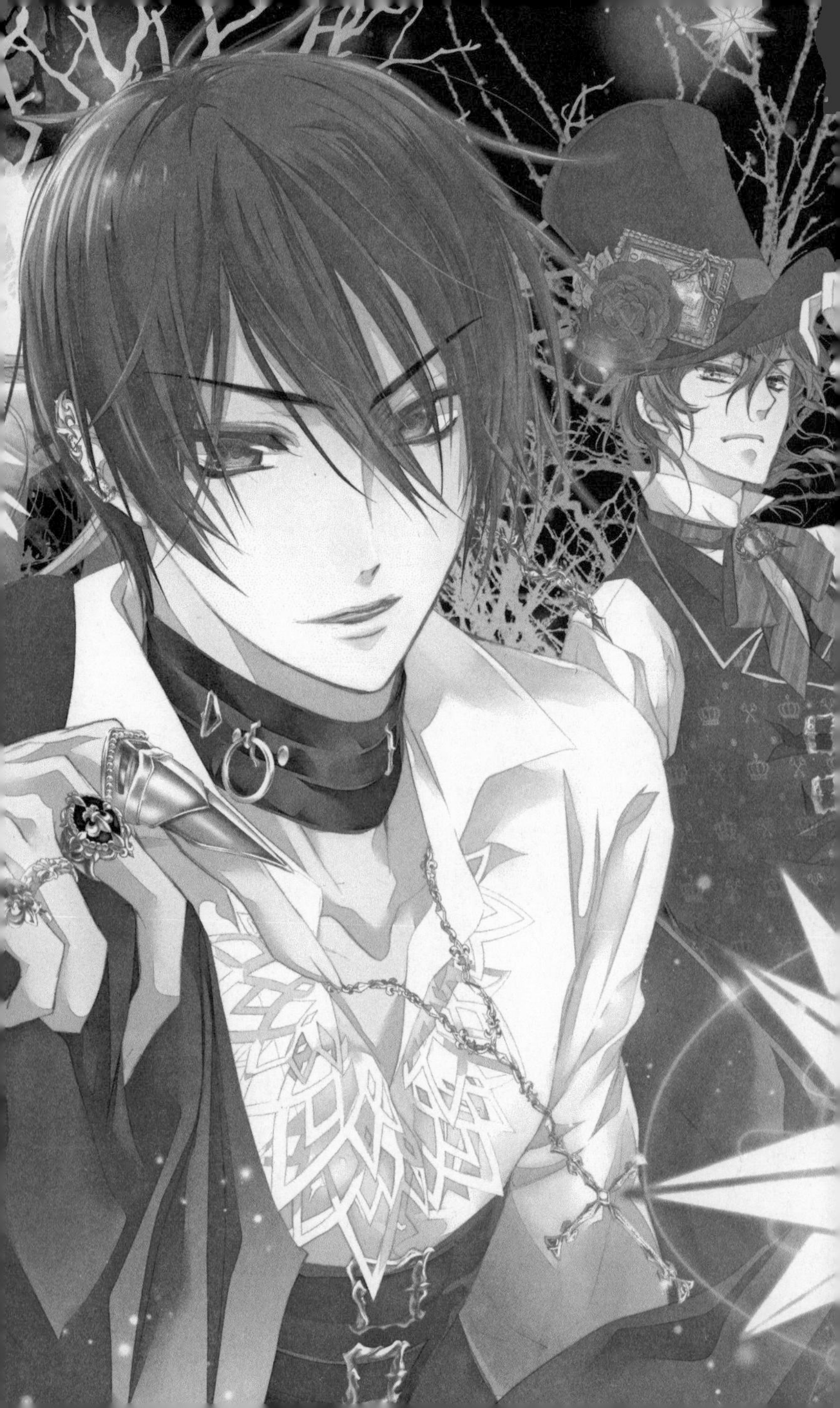

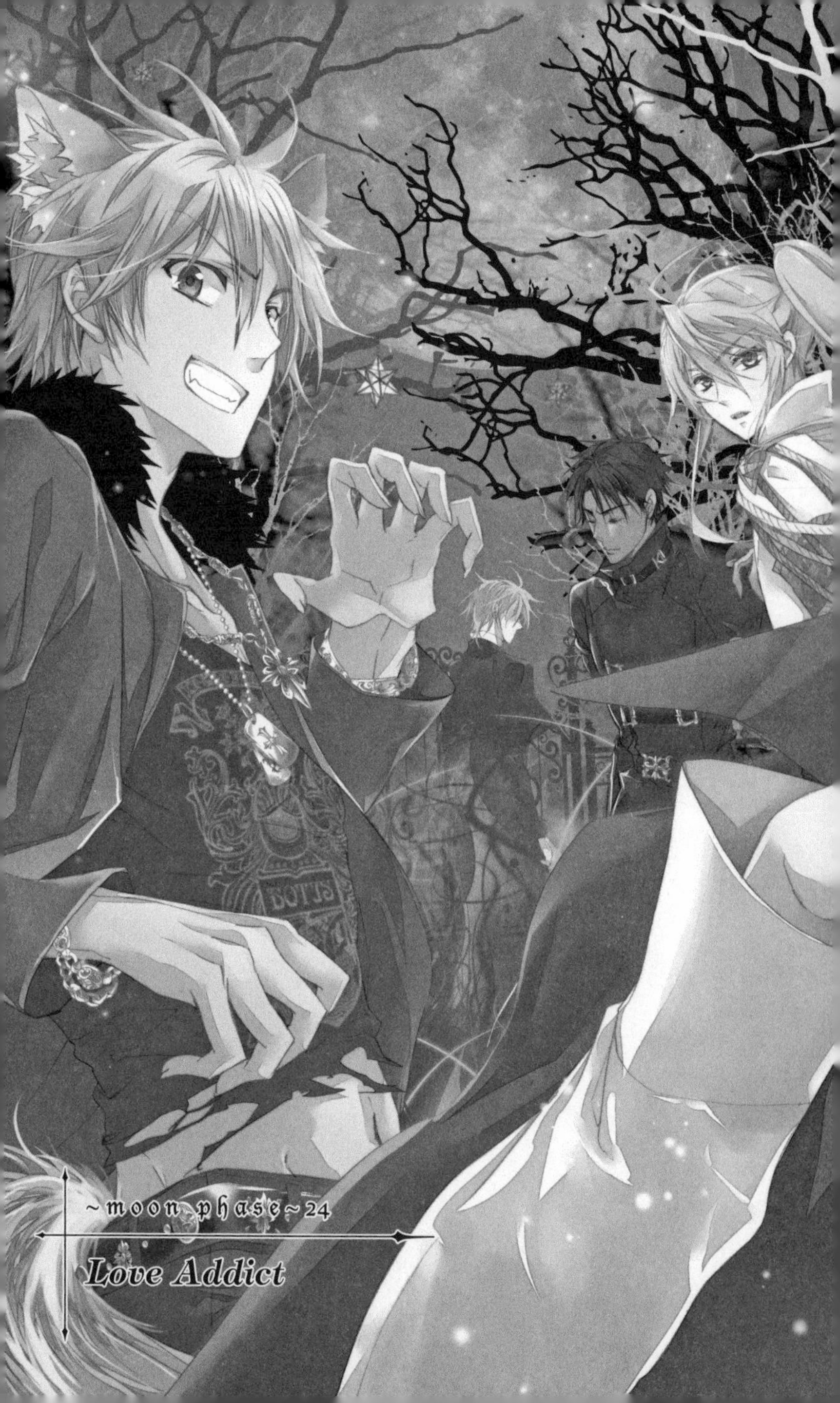
~moon phase~24
Love Addict

He's my only vampire
Aya Shouoto

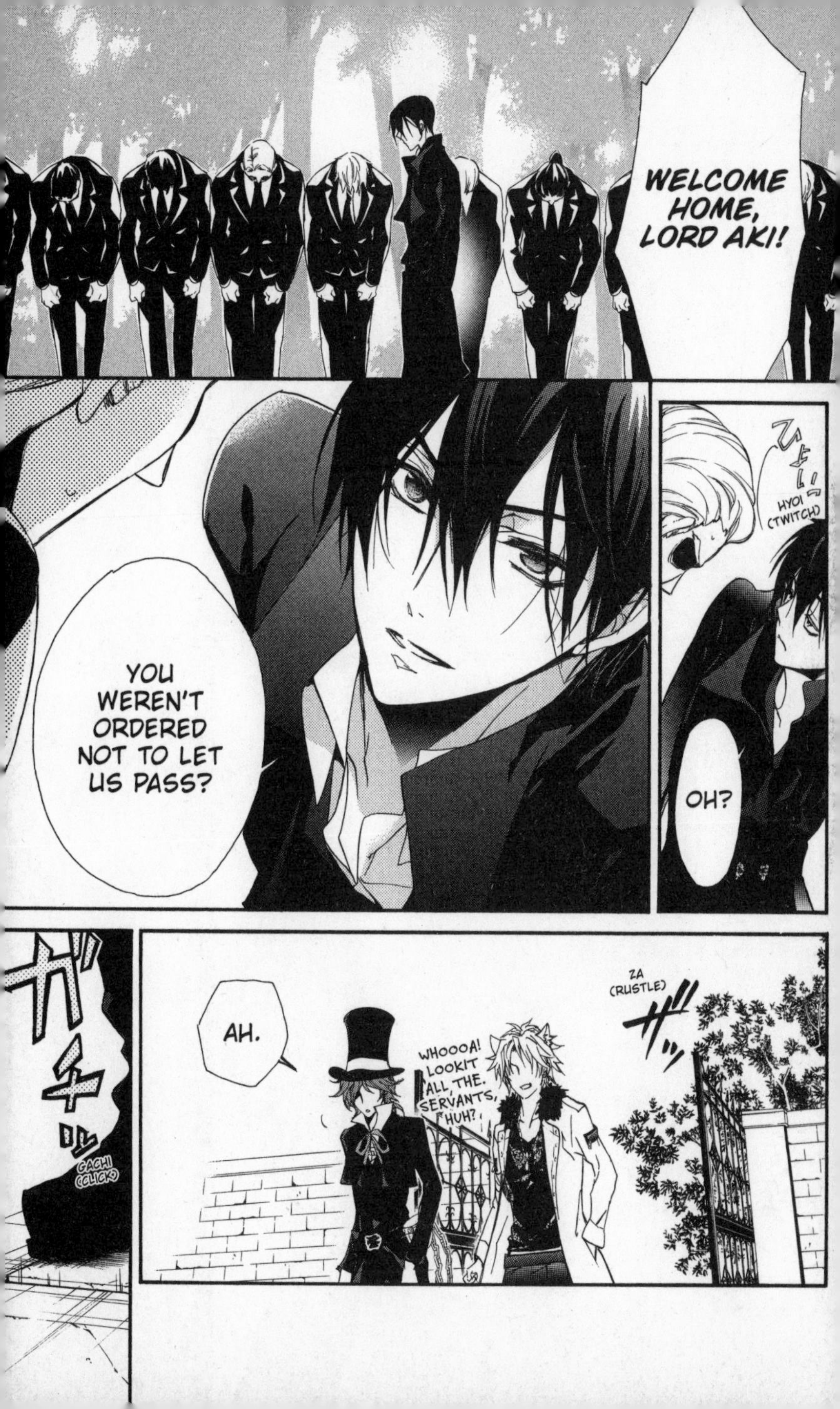
WELCOME HOME, LORD AKI!
ひょい
HYOI (TWITCH)
OH?
YOU WEREN'T ORDERED NOT TO LET US PASS?
ザッ
ZA (RUSTLE)
WHOOOA! LOOKIT ALL THE SERVANTS, HUH?
AH.
ガチッ
GACHI (CLICK)

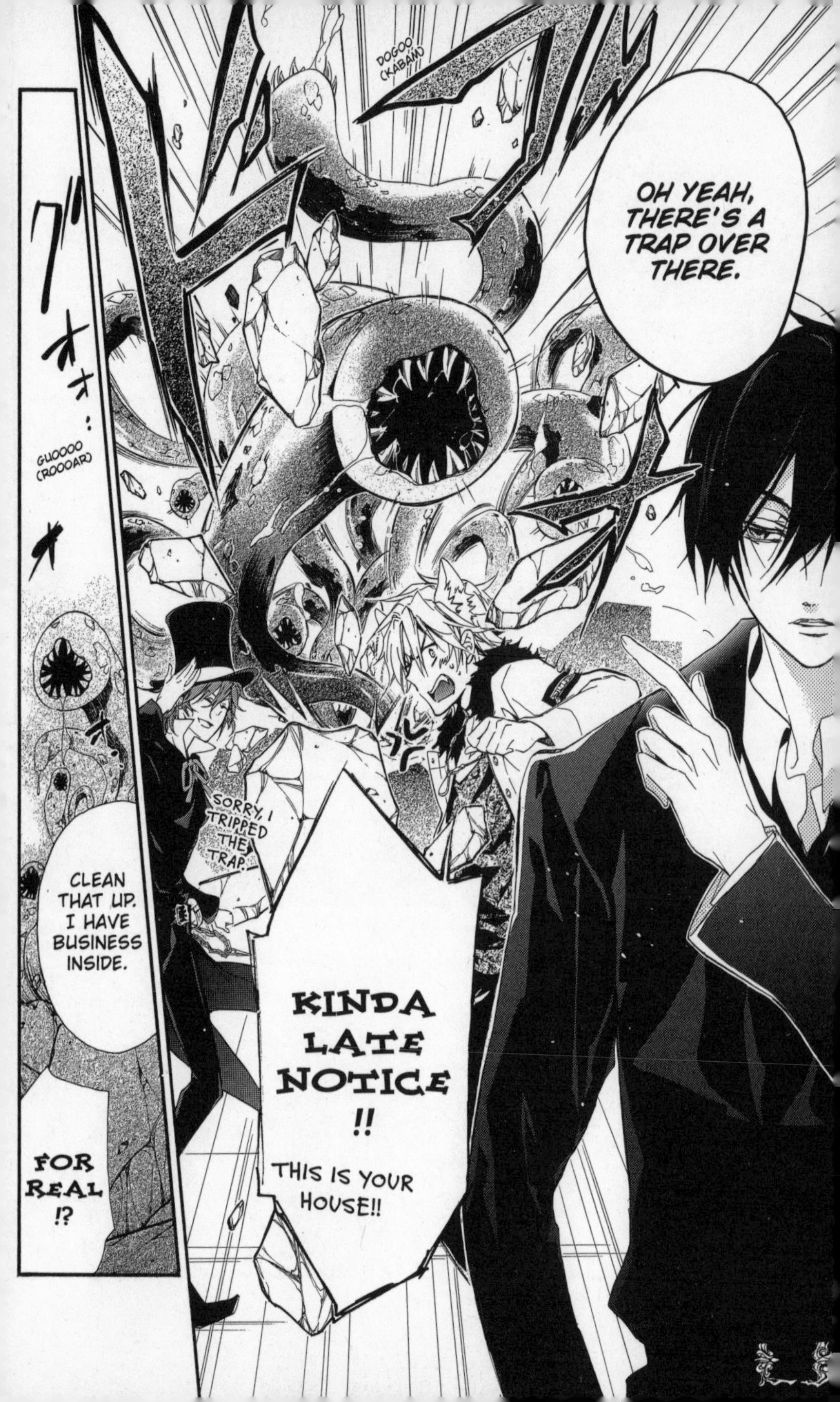
OH YEAH, THERE'S A TRAP OVER THERE.
DOGOO (KABAM)
KINDA LATE NOTICE!!
THIS IS YOUR HOUSE!!
SORRY, I TRIPPED THE TRAP.
GUOOOO (ROOOAR)
CLEAN THAT UP. I HAVE BUSINESS INSIDE.
FOR REAL!?

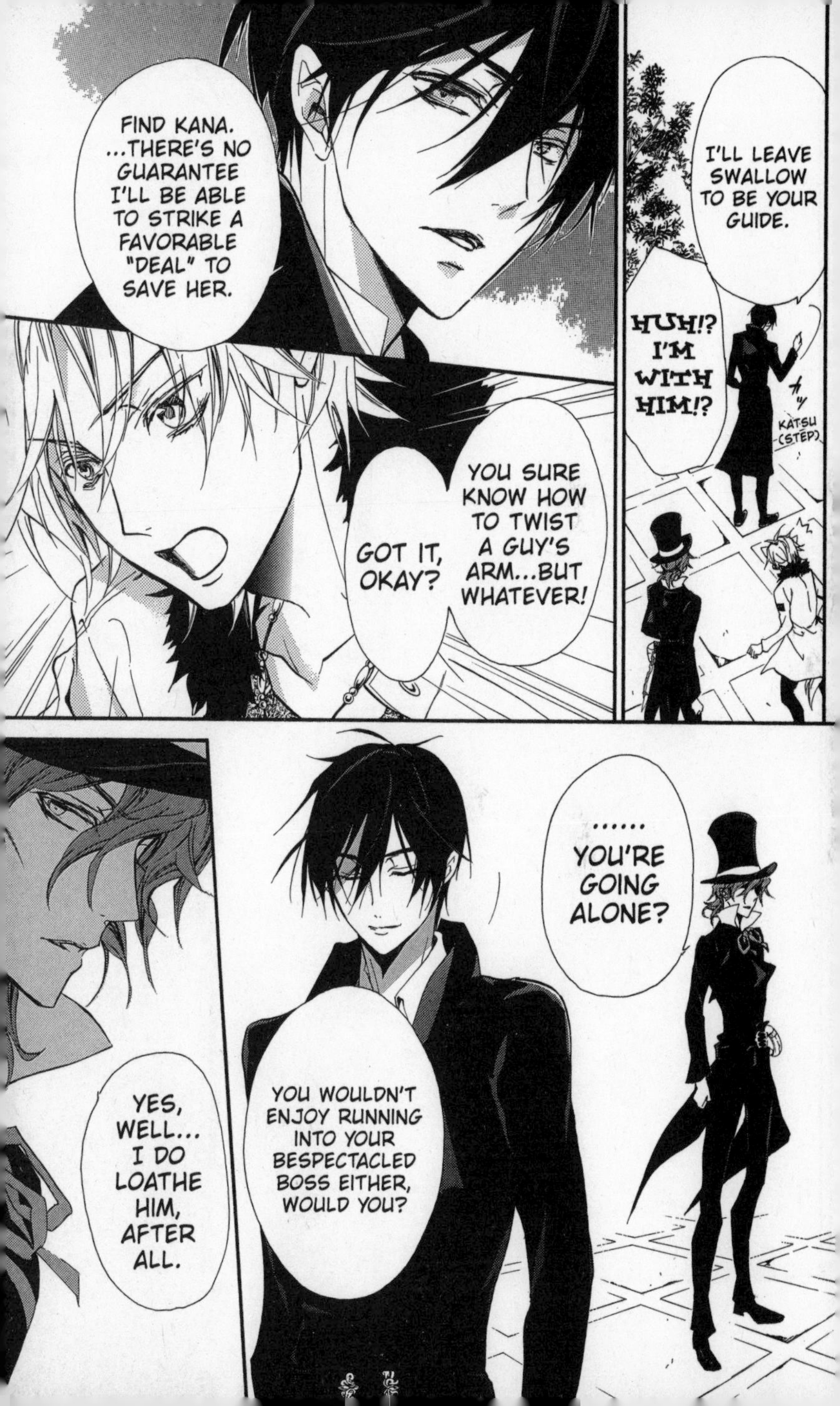
I'LL LEAVE SWALLOW TO BE YOUR GUIDE.
HUH!? I'M WITH HIM!?
カッ
KATSU (STEP)
FIND KANA. ...THERE'S NO GUARANTEE I'LL BE ABLE TO STRIKE A FAVORABLE "DEAL" TO SAVE HER.
YOU SURE KNOW HOW TO TWIST A GUY'S ARM...BUT WHATEVER!
GOT IT, OKAY?
...... YOU'RE GOING ALONE?
YOU WOULDN'T ENJOY RUNNING INTO YOUR BESPECTACLED BOSS EITHER, WOULD YOU?
YES, WELL... I DO LOATHE HIM, AFTER ALL.

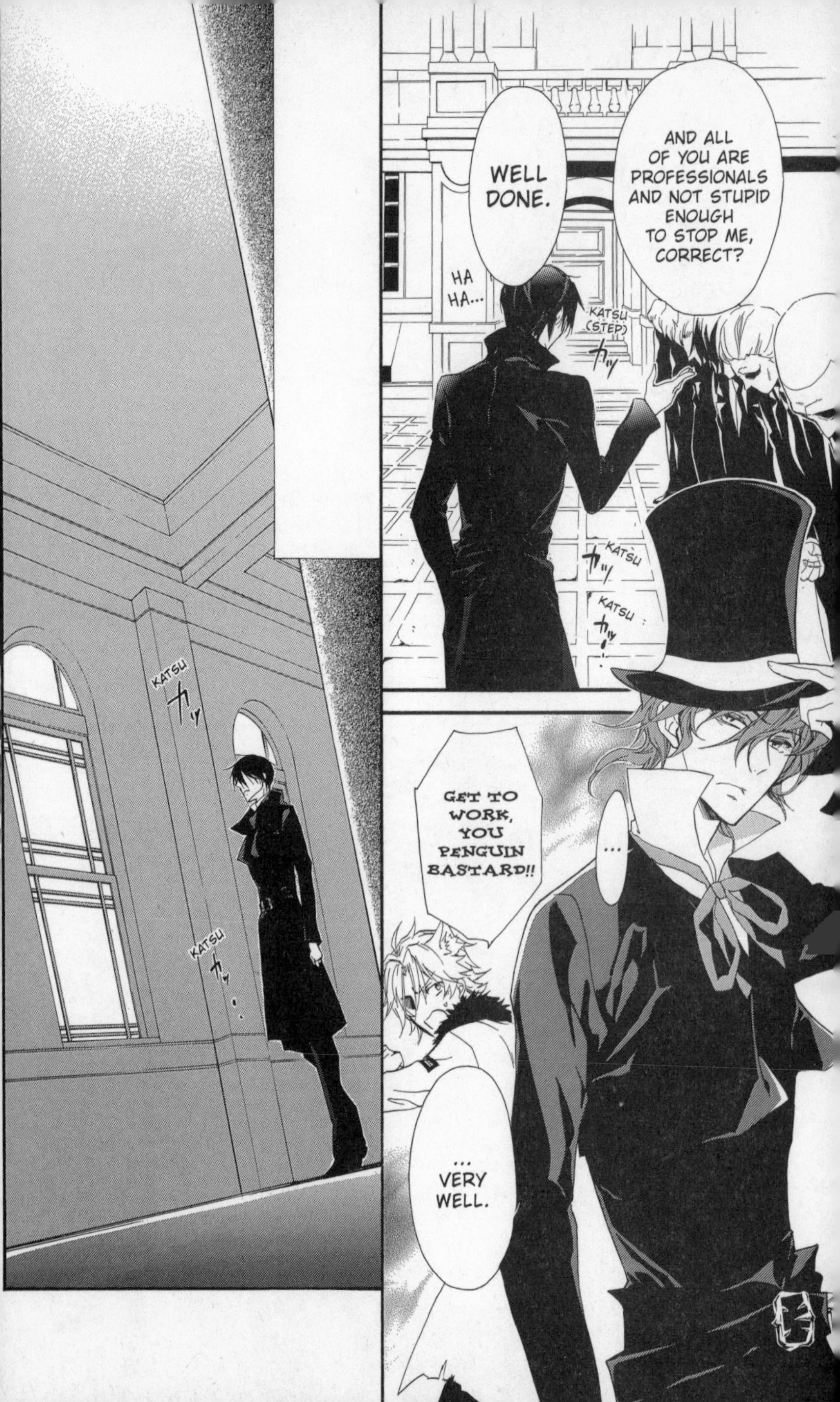
AND ALL OF YOU ARE PROFESSIONALS AND NOT STUPID ENOUGH TO STOP ME, CORRECT?
WELL DONE.
HA HA...
KATSU (STEP)
カッ
KATSU
カッ
KATSU
カッ
...
GET TO WORK, YOU PENGUIN BASTARD!!
... VERY WELL.
KATSU
カッ
KATSU
カッ

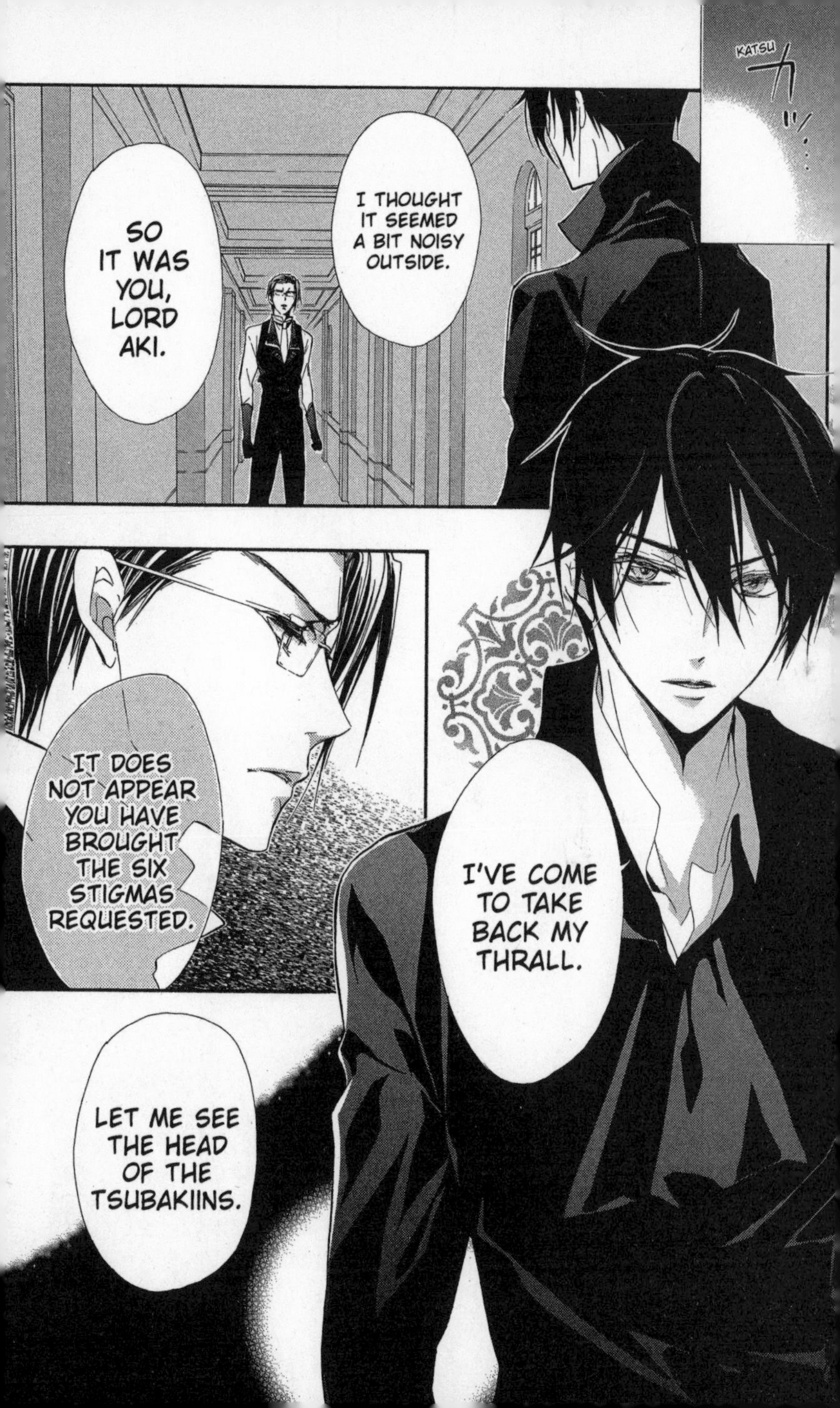
KATSU
I THOUGHT IT SEEMED A BIT NOISY OUTSIDE.
SO IT WAS YOU, LORD AKI.
I'VE COME TO TAKE BACK MY THRALL.
IT DOES NOT APPEAR YOU HAVE BROUGHT THE SIX STIGMAS REQUESTED.
LET ME SEE THE HEAD OF THE TSUBAKIINS.

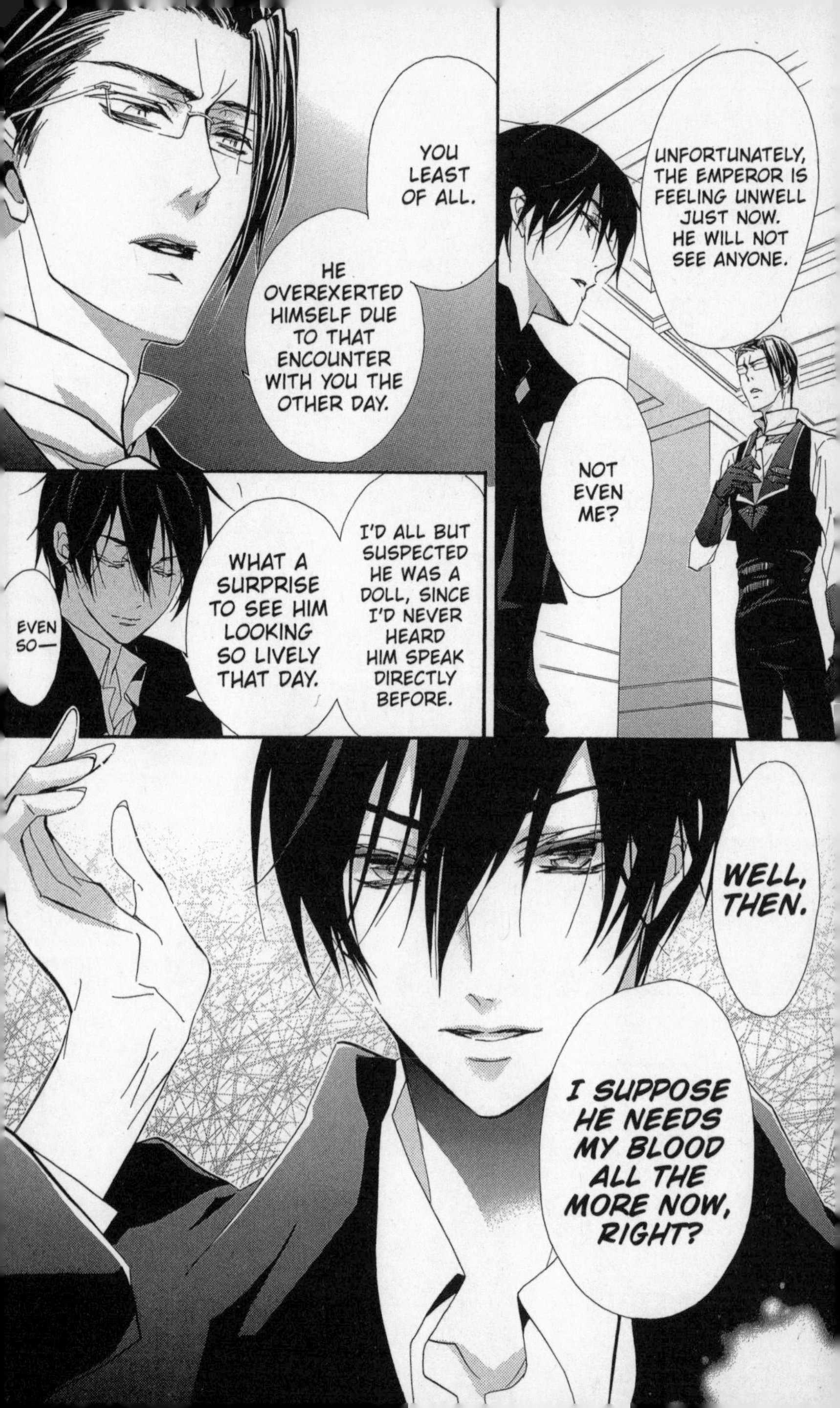
UNFORTUNATELY, THE EMPEROR IS FEELING UNWELL JUST NOW. HE WILL NOT SEE ANYONE.
NOT EVEN ME?
YOU LEAST OF ALL.
HE OVEREXERTED HIMSELF DUE TO THAT ENCOUNTER WITH YOU THE OTHER DAY.
I'D ALL BUT SUSPECTED HE WAS A DOLL, SINCE I'D NEVER HEARD HIM SPEAK DIRECTLY BEFORE.
WHAT A SURPRISE TO SEE HIM LOOKING SO LIVELY THAT DAY.
EVEN SO—
WELL, THEN.
I SUPPOSE HE NEEDS MY BLOOD ALL THE MORE NOW, RIGHT?

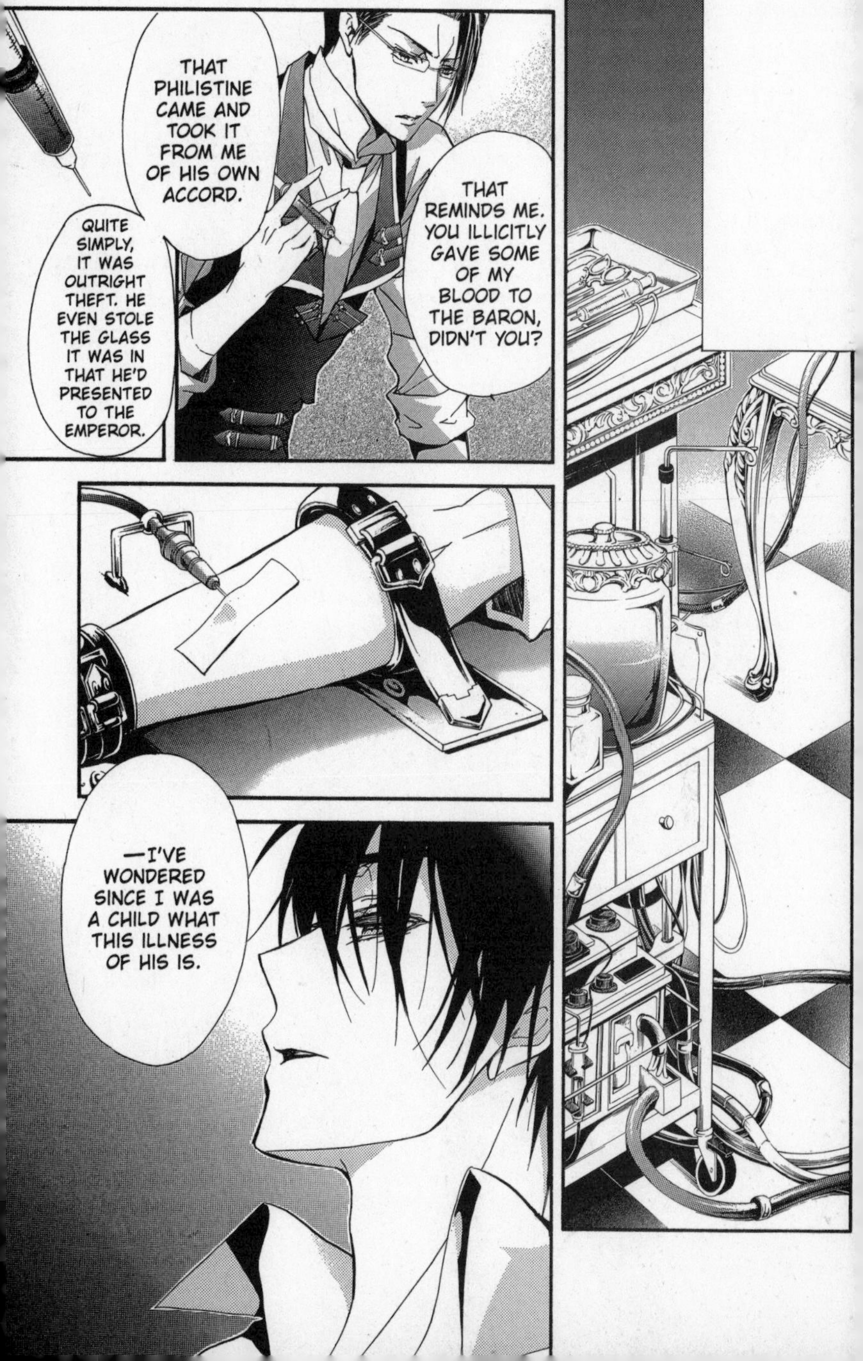
THAT REMINDS ME. YOU ILLICITLY GAVE SOME OF MY BLOOD TO THE BARON, DIDN'T YOU?
THAT PHILISTINE CAME AND TOOK IT FROM ME OF HIS OWN ACCORD.
QUITE SIMPLY, IT WAS OUTRIGHT THEFT. HE EVEN STOLE THE GLASS IT WAS IN THAT HE'D PRESENTED TO THE EMPEROR.
—I'VE WONDERED SINCE I WAS A CHILD WHAT THIS ILLNESS OF HIS IS.

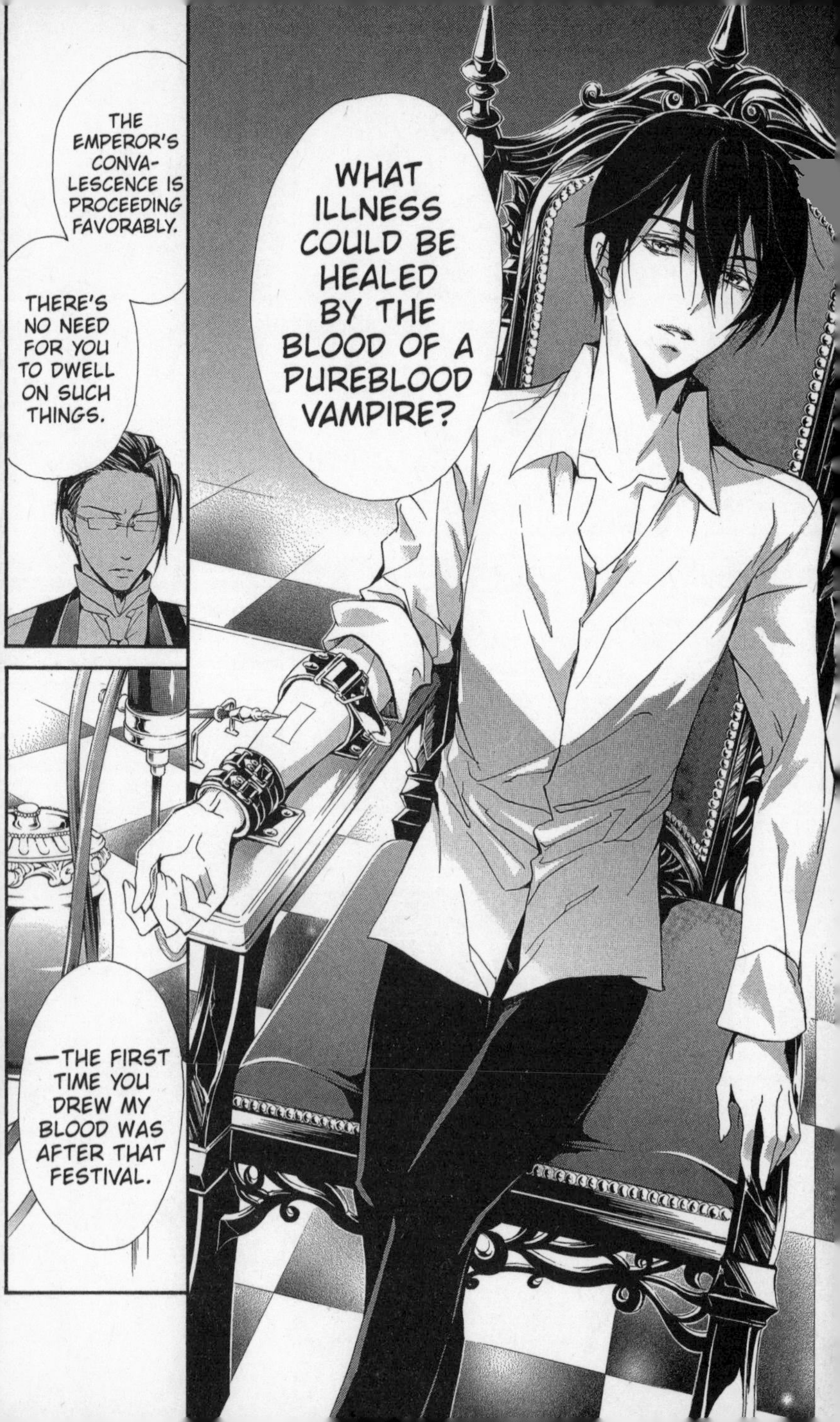
WHAT ILLNESS COULD BE HEALED BY THE BLOOD OF A PUREBLOOD VAMPIRE?
THE EMPEROR'S CONVA-LESCENCE IS PROCEEDING FAVORABLY.
THERE'S NO NEED FOR YOU TO DWELL ON SUCH THINGS.
—THE FIRST TIME YOU DREW MY BLOOD WAS AFTER THAT FESTIVAL.

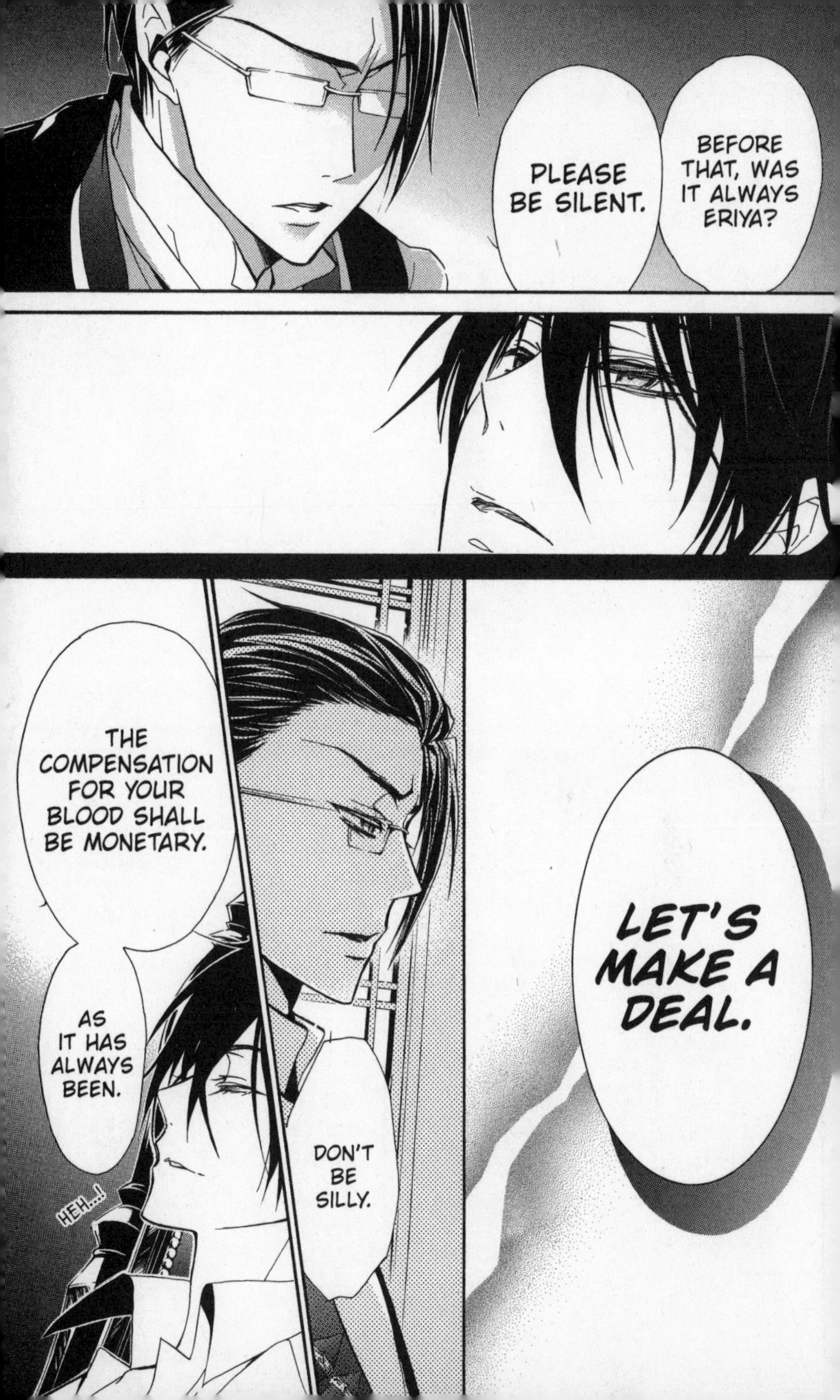
BEFORE THAT, WAS IT ALWAYS ERIYA?
PLEASE BE SILENT.
LET'S MAKE A DEAL.
THE COMPENSATION FOR YOUR BLOOD SHALL BE MONETARY.
AS IT HAS ALWAYS BEEN.
DON'T BE SILLY.
HEH...!

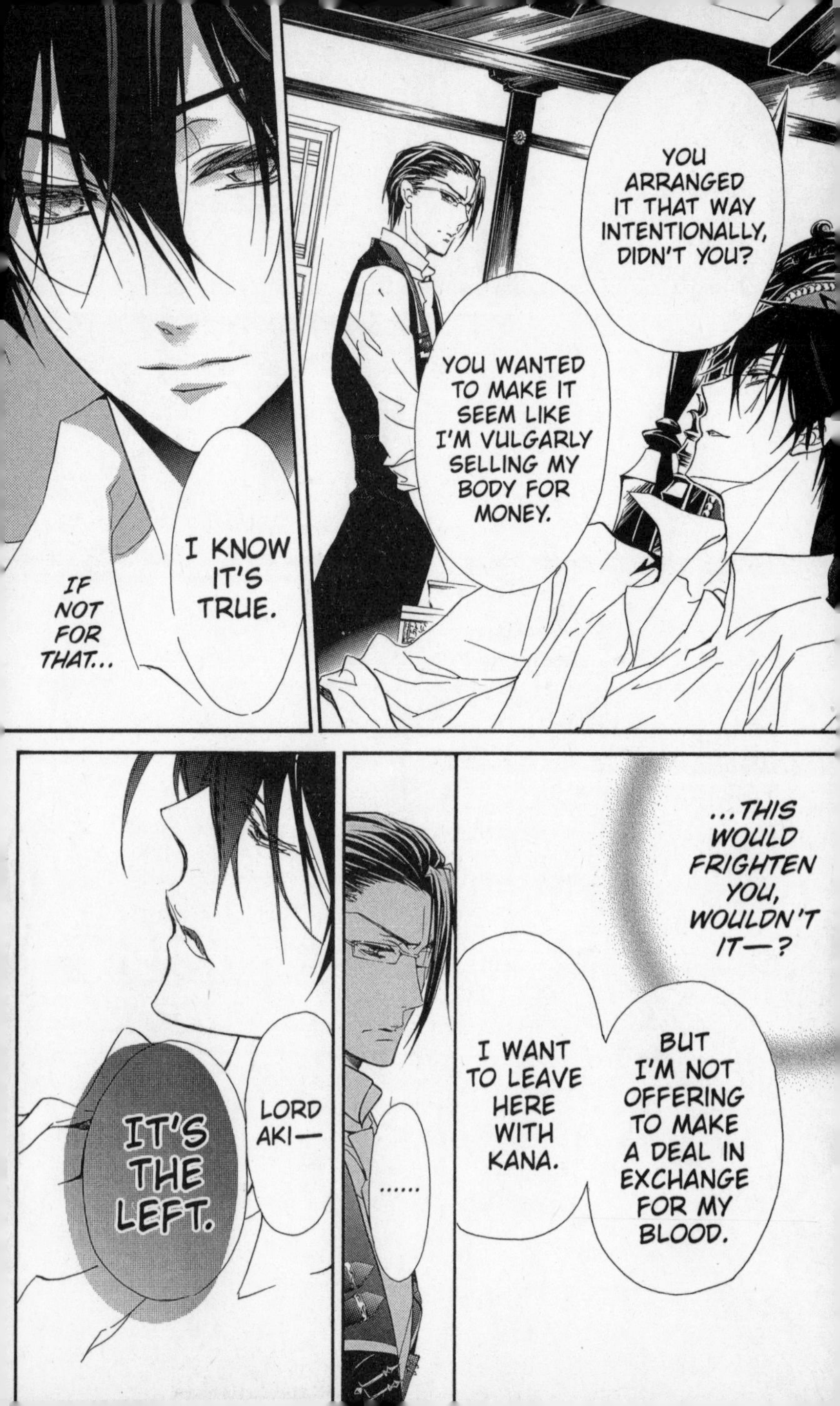
YOU ARRANGED IT THAT WAY INTENTIONALLY, DIDN'T YOU?
YOU WANTED TO MAKE IT SEEM LIKE I'M VULGARLY SELLING MY BODY FOR MONEY.
I KNOW IT'S TRUE.
IF NOT FOR THAT...
...THIS WOULD FRIGHTEN YOU, WOULDN'T IT—?
BUT I'M NOT OFFERING TO MAKE A DEAL IN EXCHANGE FOR MY BLOOD.
I WANT TO LEAVE HERE WITH KANA.
......
LORD AKI—
IT'S THE LEFT.

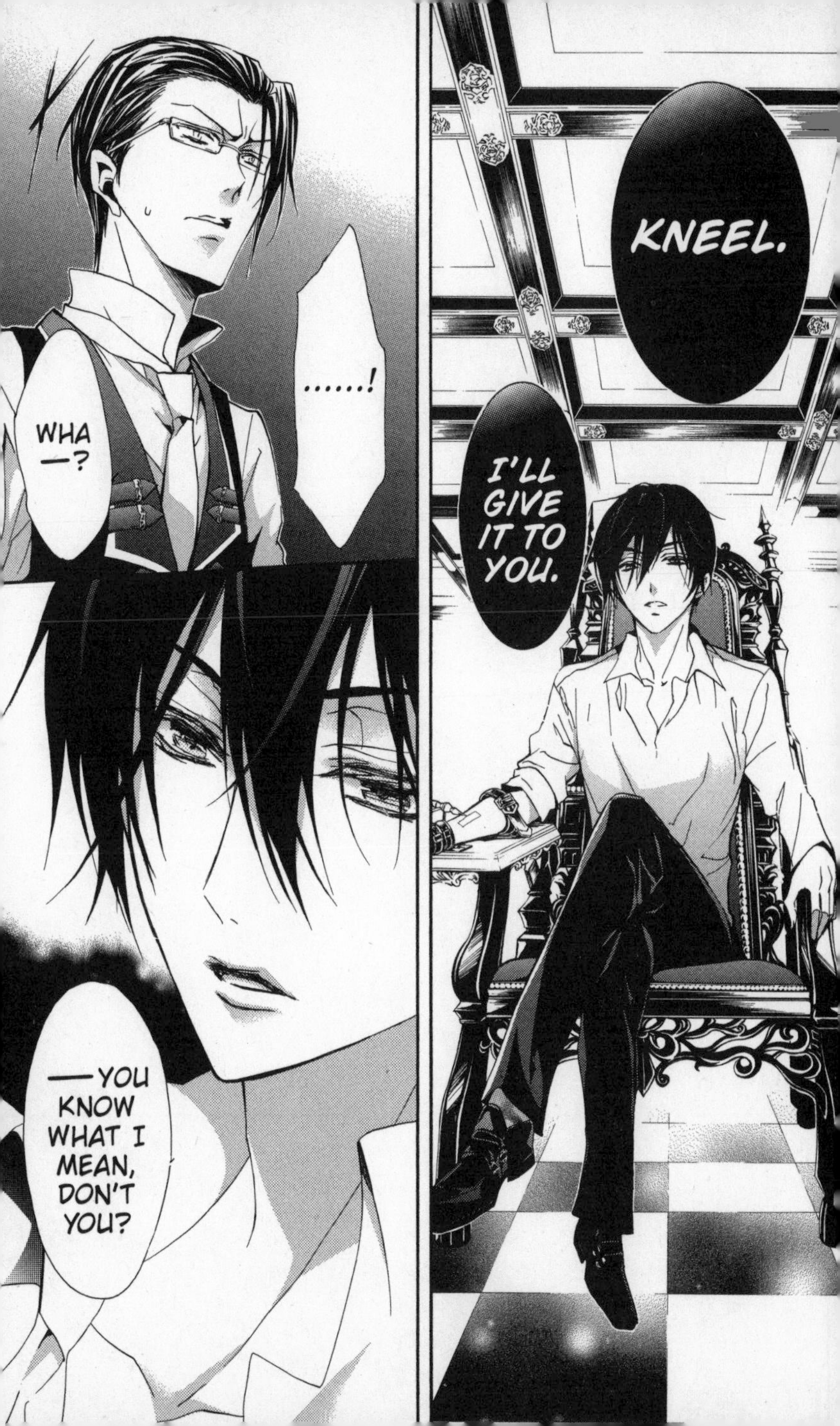
KNEEL.
I'LL GIVE IT TO YOU.
......!
WHA—?
—YOU KNOW WHAT I MEAN, DON'T YOU?

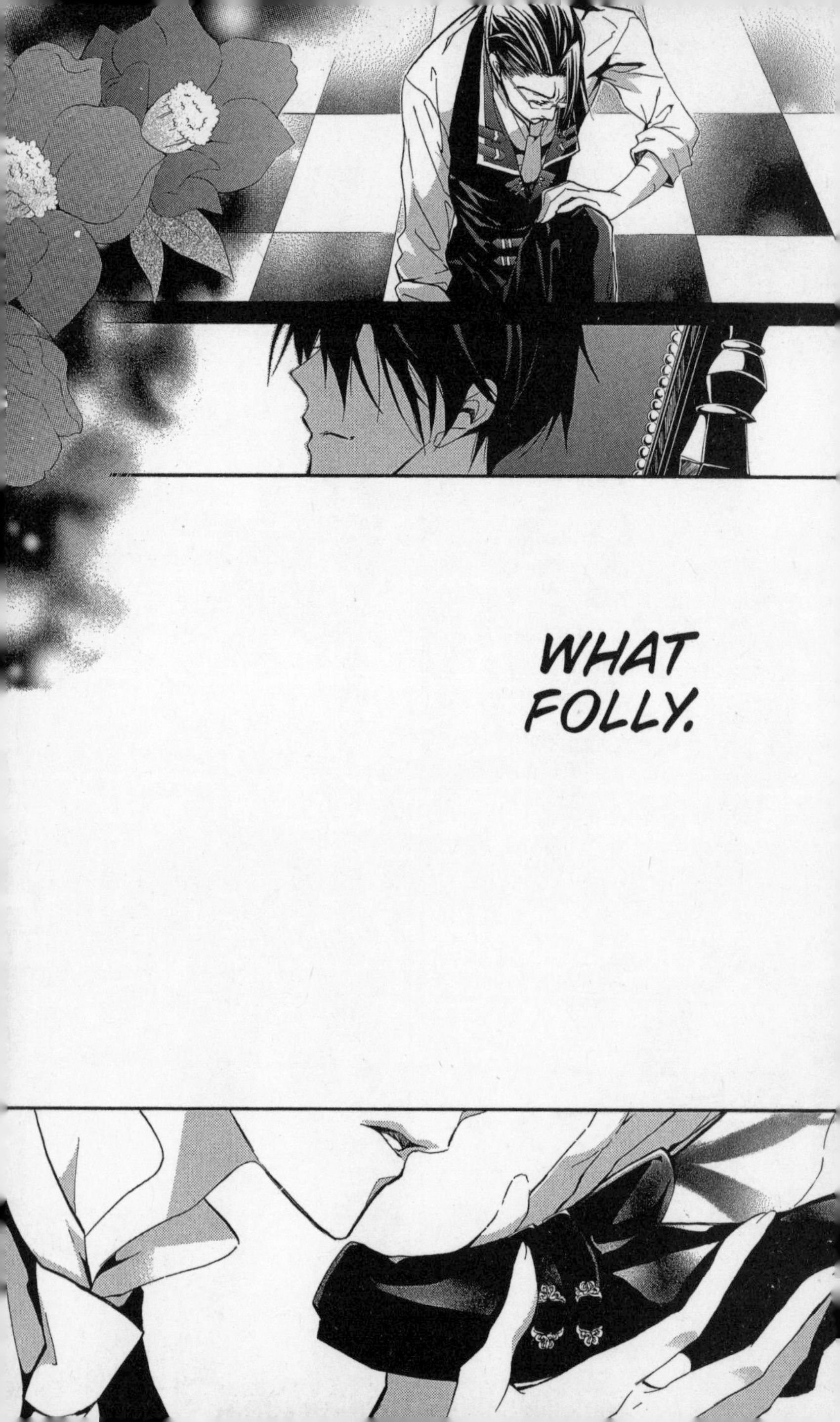
WHAT FOLLY.

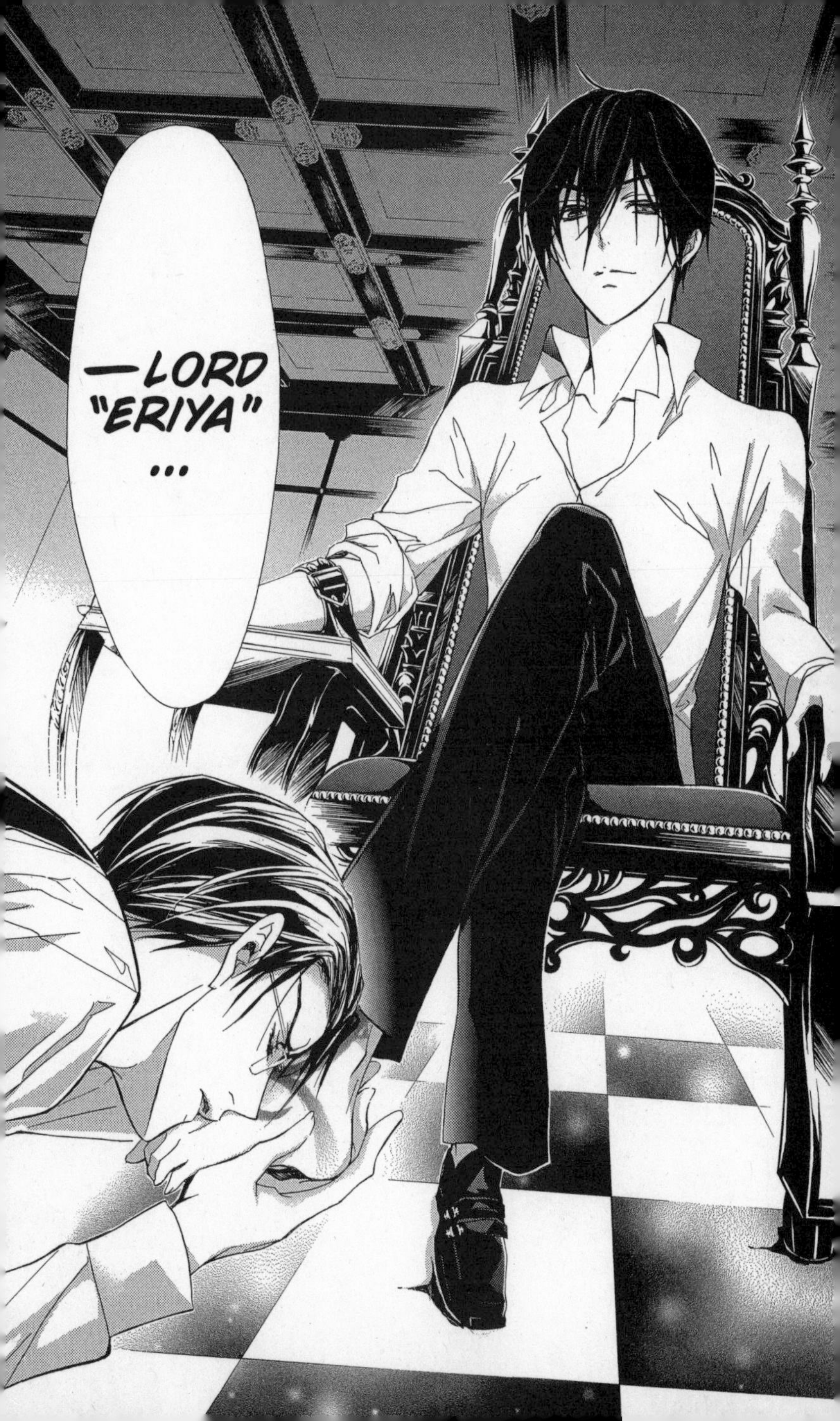
—LORD "ERIYA" ...

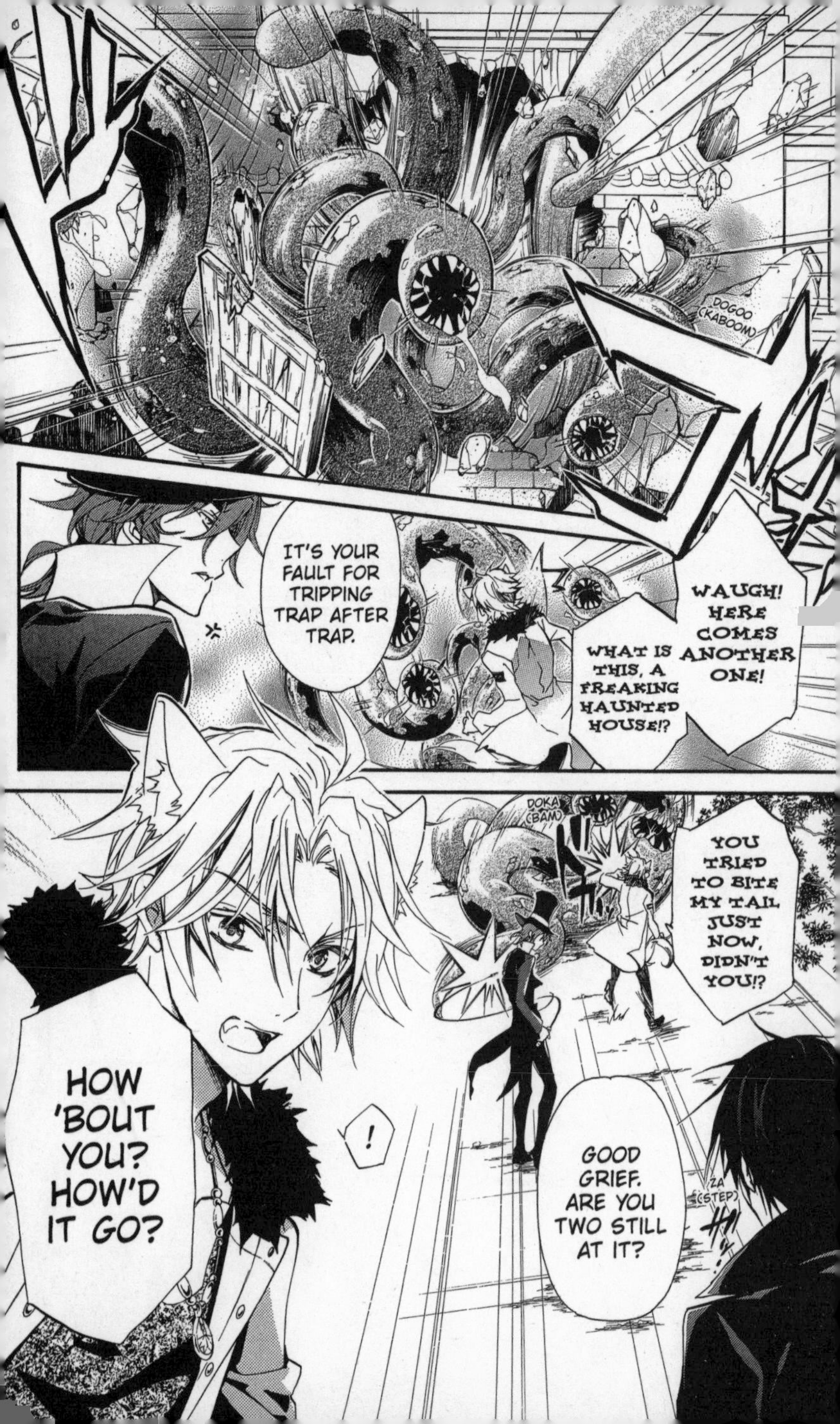
DOGOO (KABOOM)
WAUGH! HERE COMES ANOTHER ONE!
WHAT IS THIS, A FREAKING HAUNTED HOUSE!?
IT'S YOUR FAULT FOR TRIPPING TRAP AFTER TRAP.
DOKA (BAM)
YOU TRIED TO BITE MY TAIL JUST NOW, DIDN'T YOU!?
ZA (STEP)
GOOD GRIEF. ARE YOU TWO STILL AT IT?
!
HOW 'BOUT YOU? HOW'D IT GO?

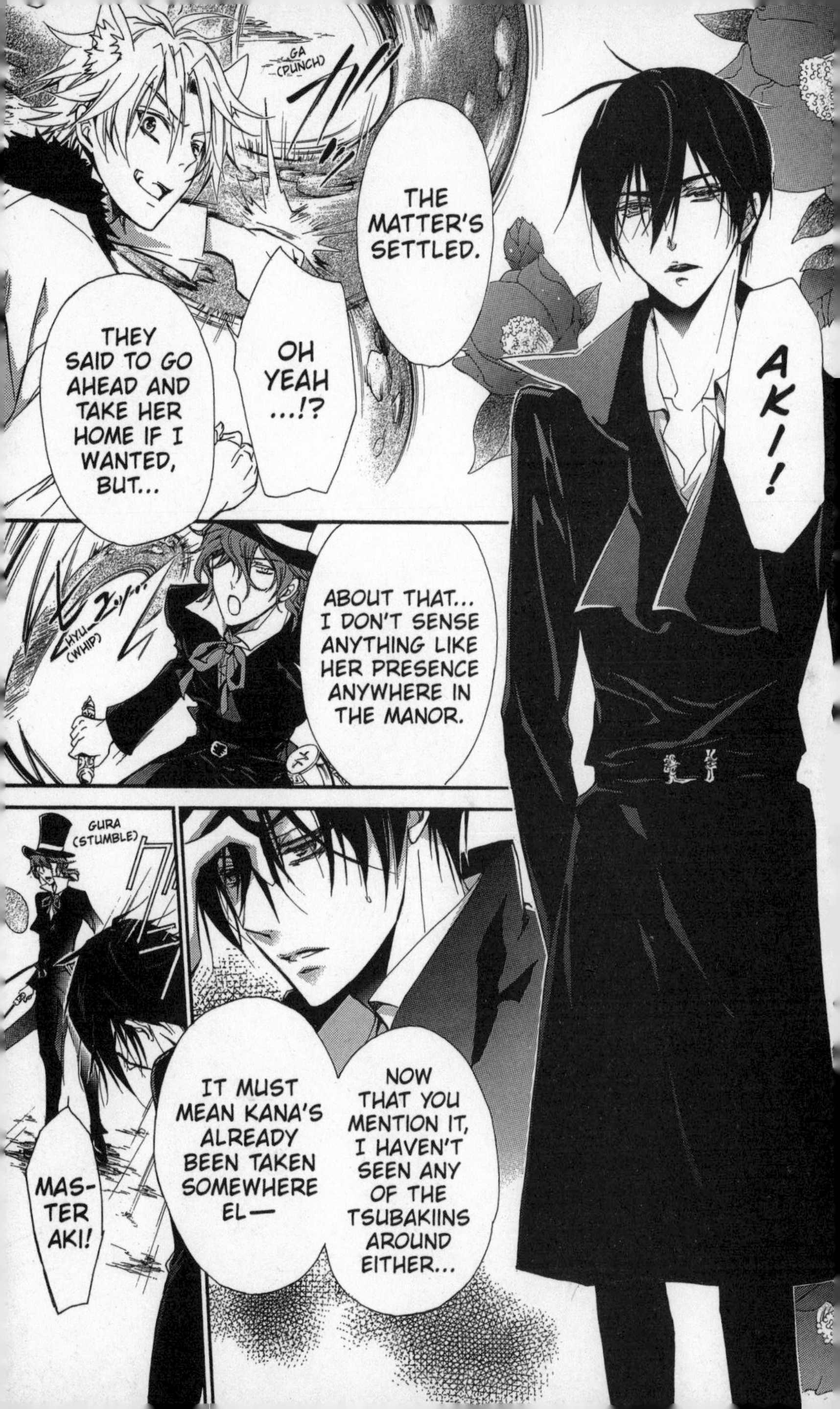
AKI!
THE MATTER'S SETTLED.
GA (PUNCH)
OH YEAH ...!?
THEY SAID TO GO AHEAD AND TAKE HER HOME IF I WANTED, BUT...
ABOUT THAT... I DON'T SENSE ANYTHING LIKE HER PRESENCE ANYWHERE IN THE MANOR.
HYU (WHIP)
NOW THAT YOU MENTION IT, I HAVEN'T SEEN ANY OF THE TSUBAKIINS AROUND EITHER...
IT MUST MEAN KANA'S ALREADY BEEN TAKEN SOMEWHERE EL—
GURA (STUMBLE)
MAS-TER AKI!

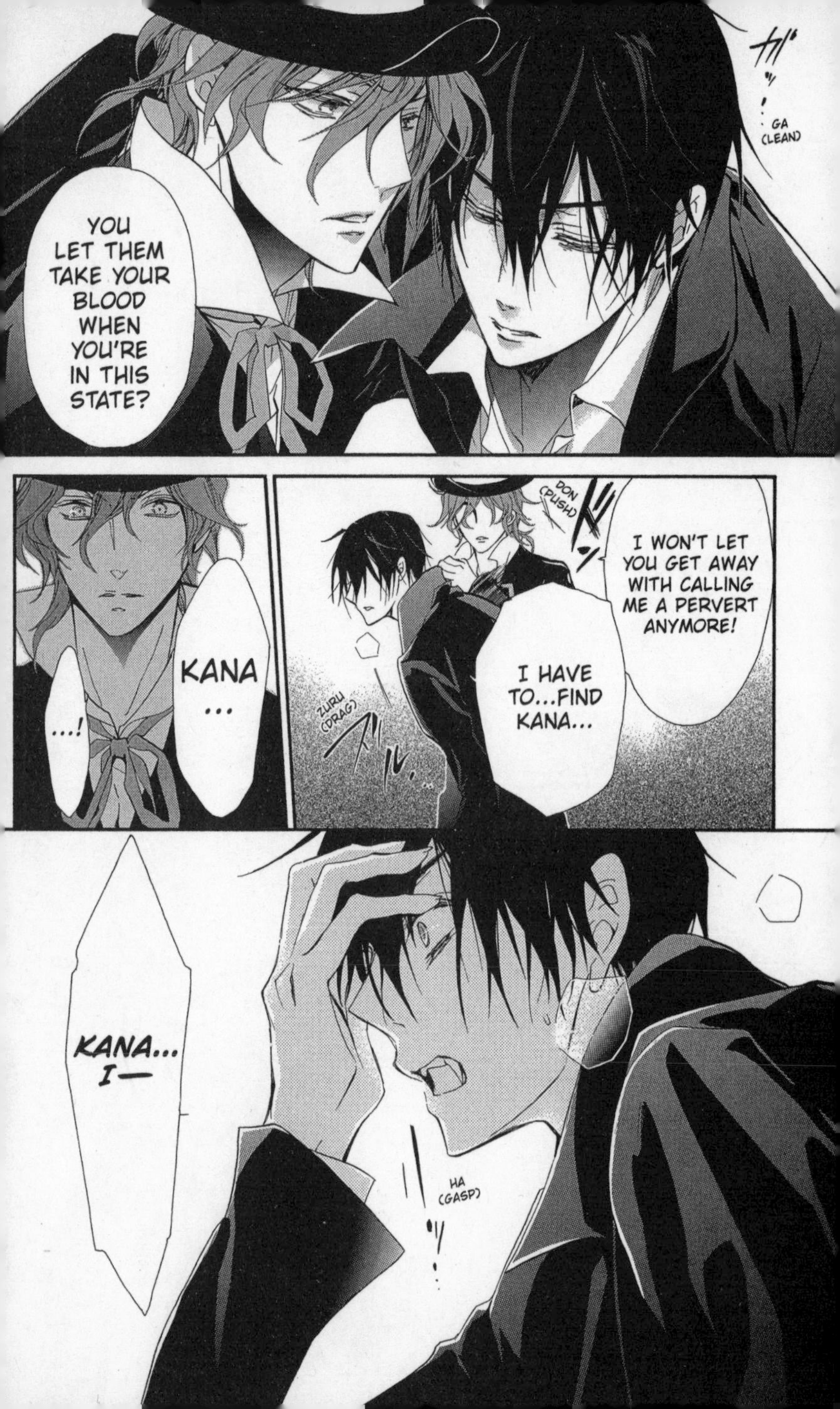
GA (LEAN)
YOU LET THEM TAKE YOUR BLOOD WHEN YOU'RE IN THIS STATE?
DON (PUSH)
I WON'T LET YOU GET AWAY WITH CALLING ME A PERVERT ANYMORE!
I HAVE TO...FIND KANA...
ZURU (DRAG)
KANA ...
...!
KANA... I—
HA (GASP)

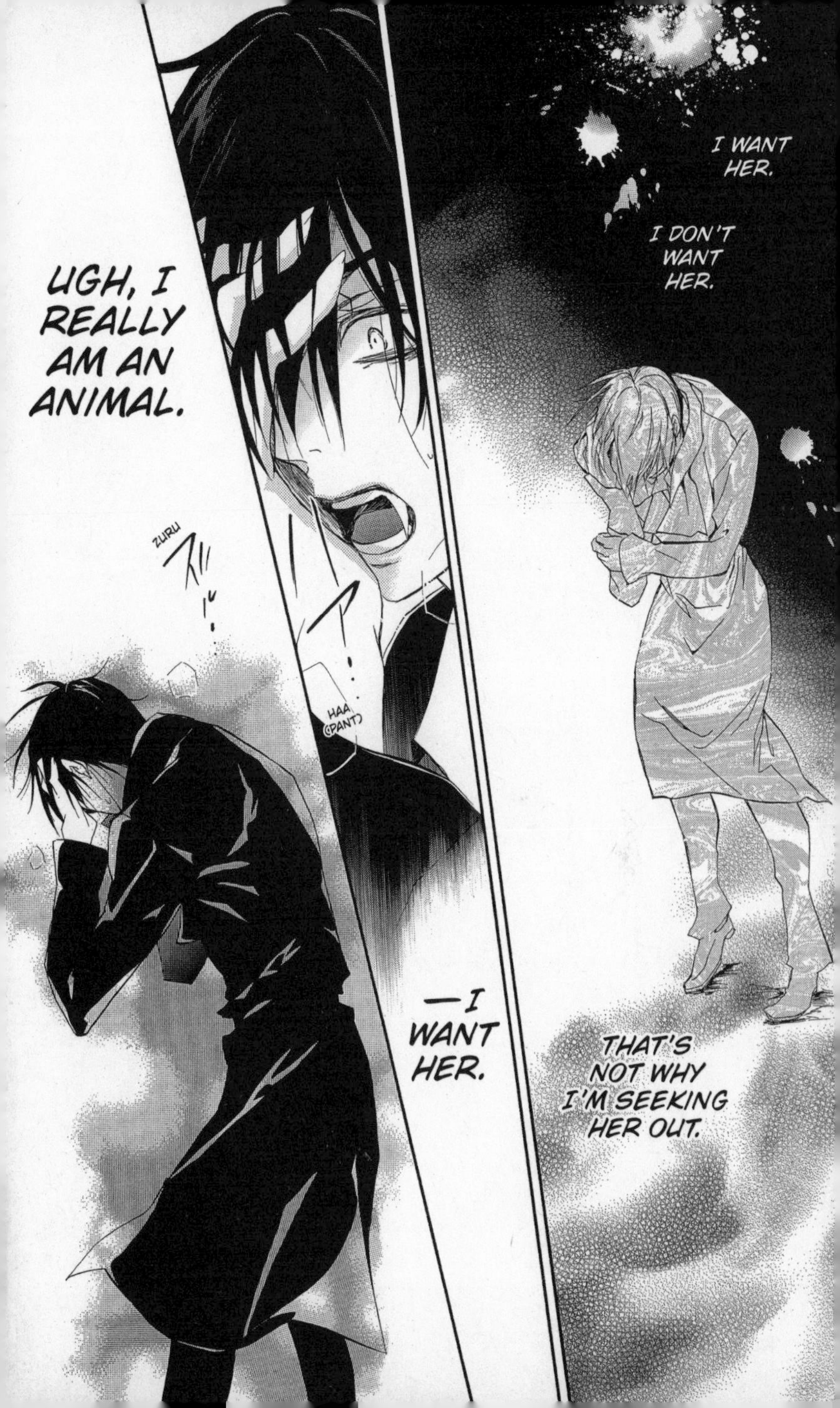
I WANT HER.
I DON'T WANT HER.
THAT'S NOT WHY I'M SEEKING HER OUT.
HAA (PANT)
—I WANT HER.
UGH, I REALLY AM AN ANIMAL.
ZURU

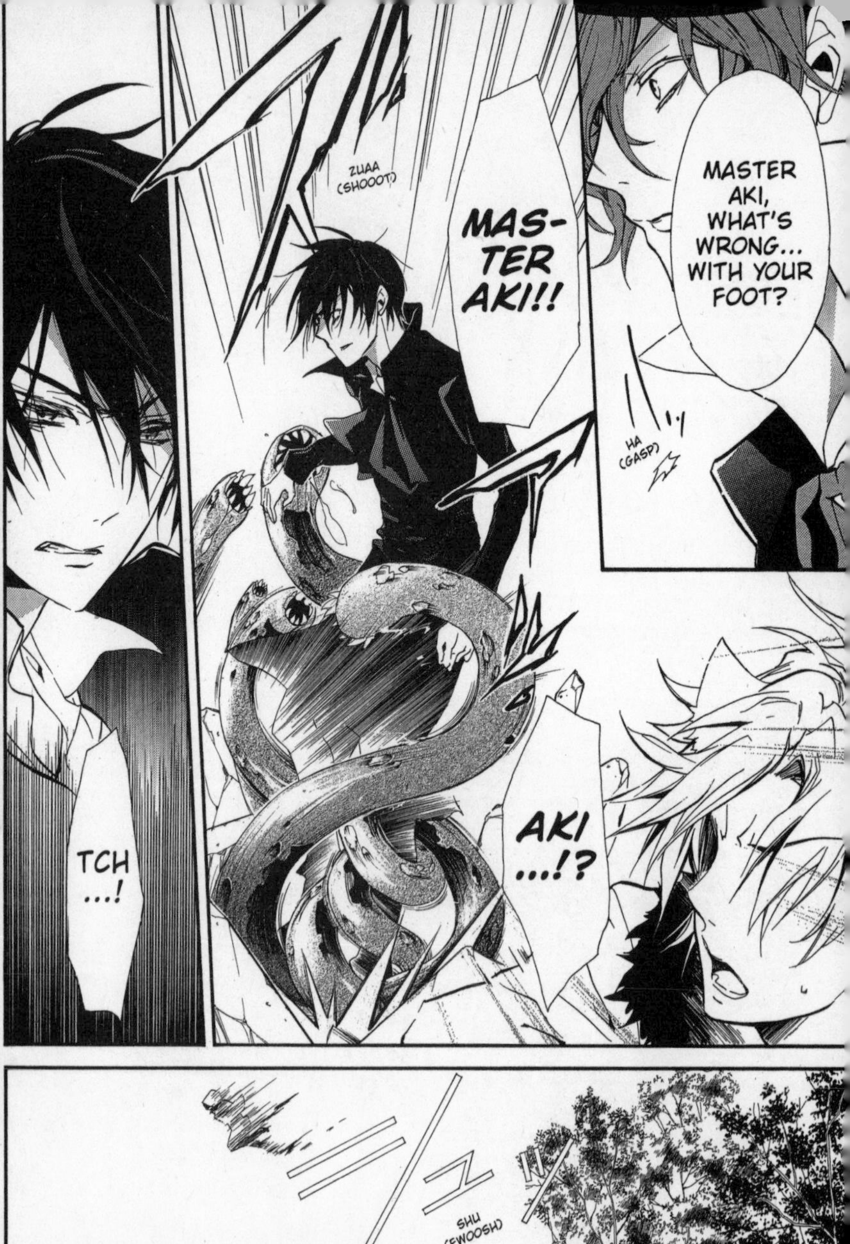
MASTER AKI, WHAT'S WRONG... WITH YOUR FOOT?
HA (GASP)
ZUAA (SHOOOT)
MAS-TER AKI!!
AKI...!?
TCH...!
SHU (FWOOSH)

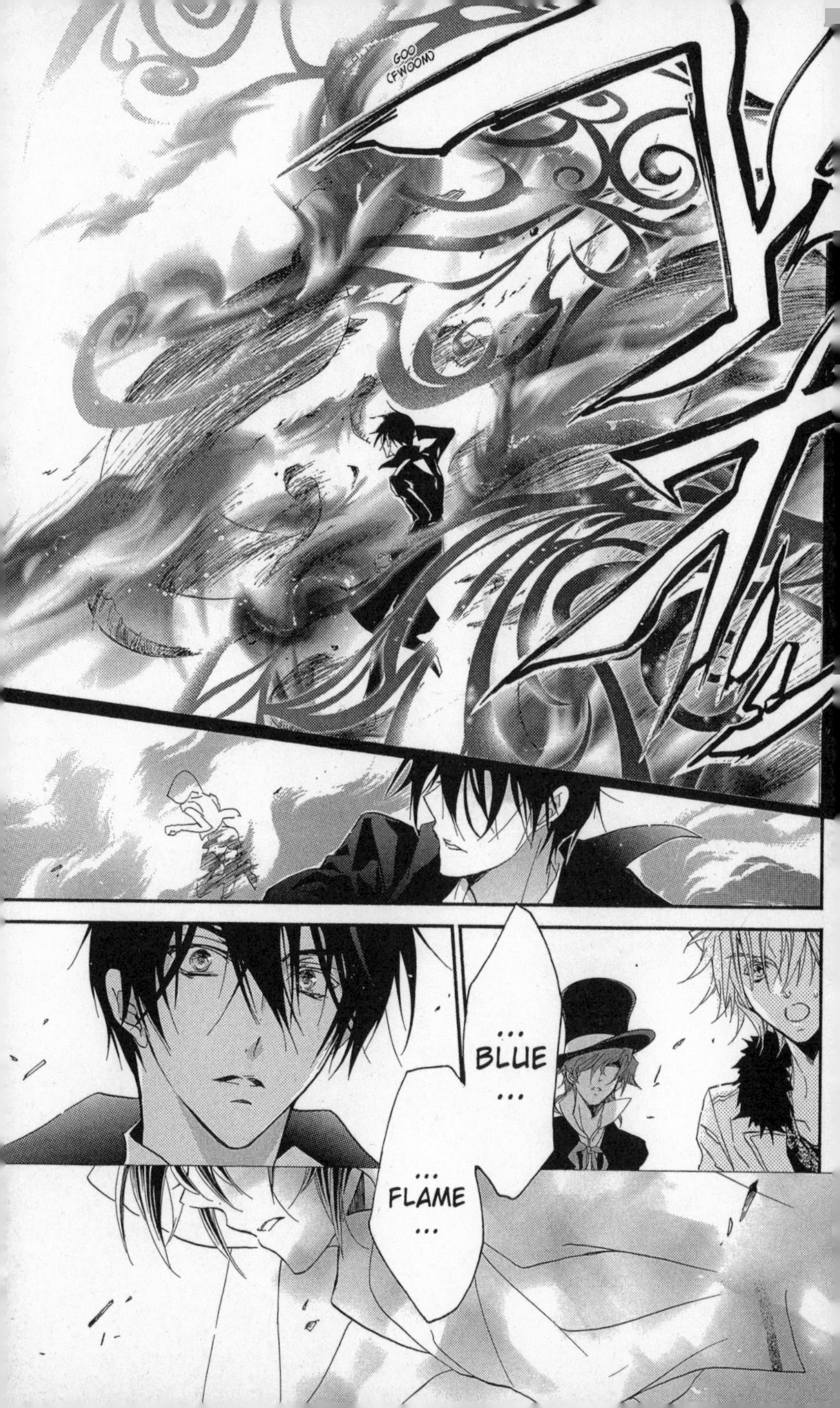
GOO (FWOOM)
... BLUE ...
... FLAME ...

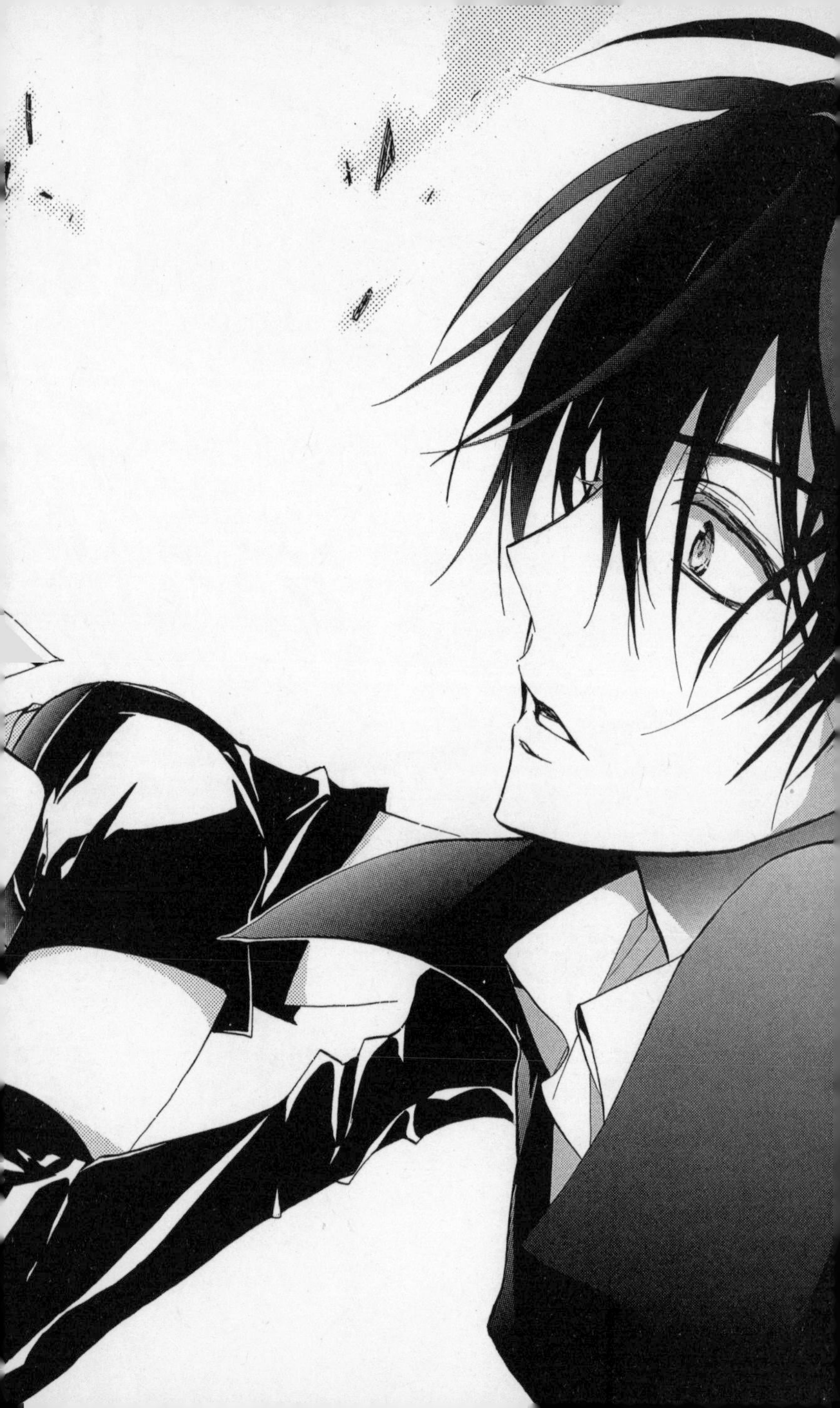

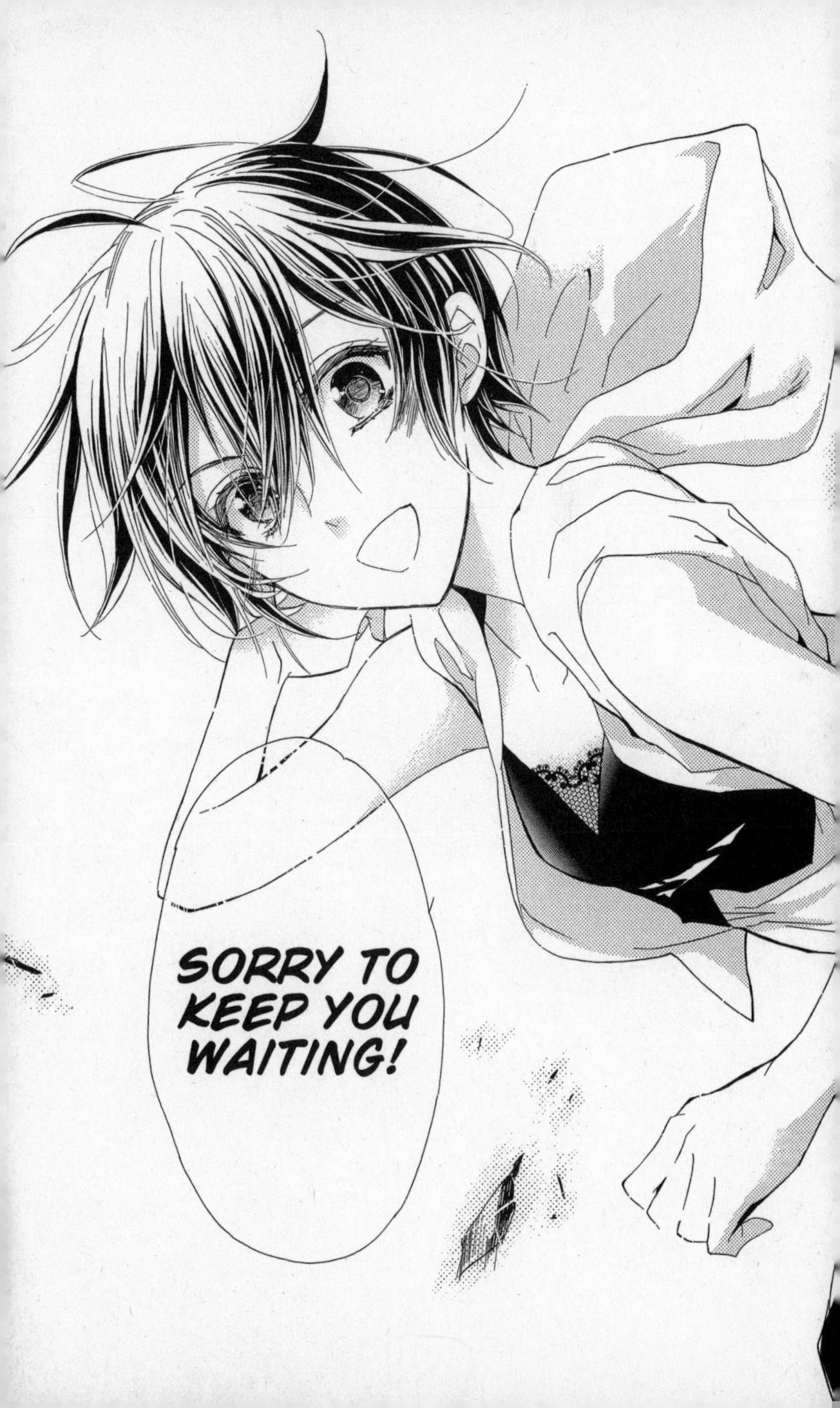
SORRY TO KEEP YOU WAITING!

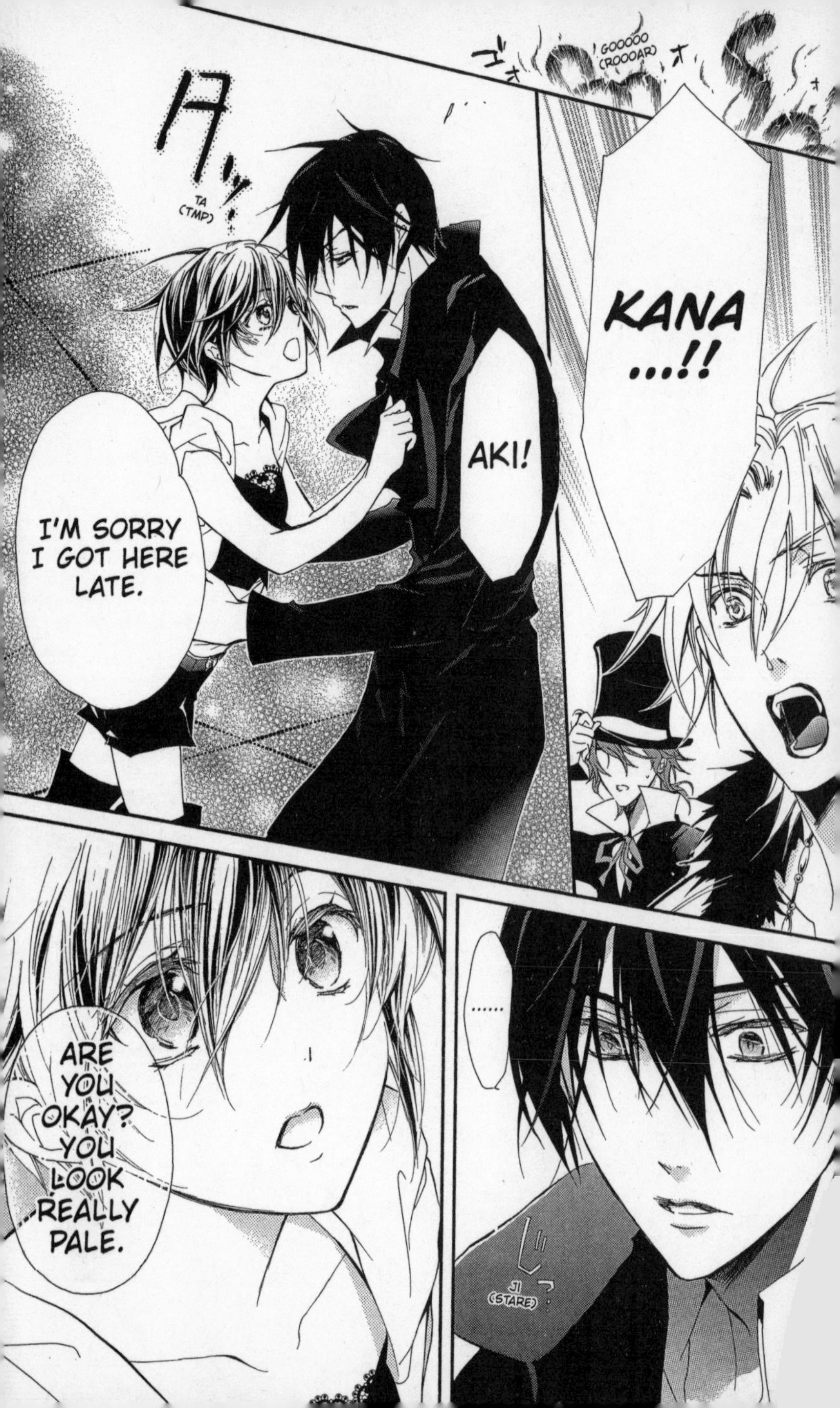

GOOOOO (ROOOAR)
KANA ...!!
TA (TMP)
AKI!
I'M SORRY I GOT HERE LATE.
......
JI (STARE)
ARE YOU OKAY? YOU LOOK REALLY PALE.

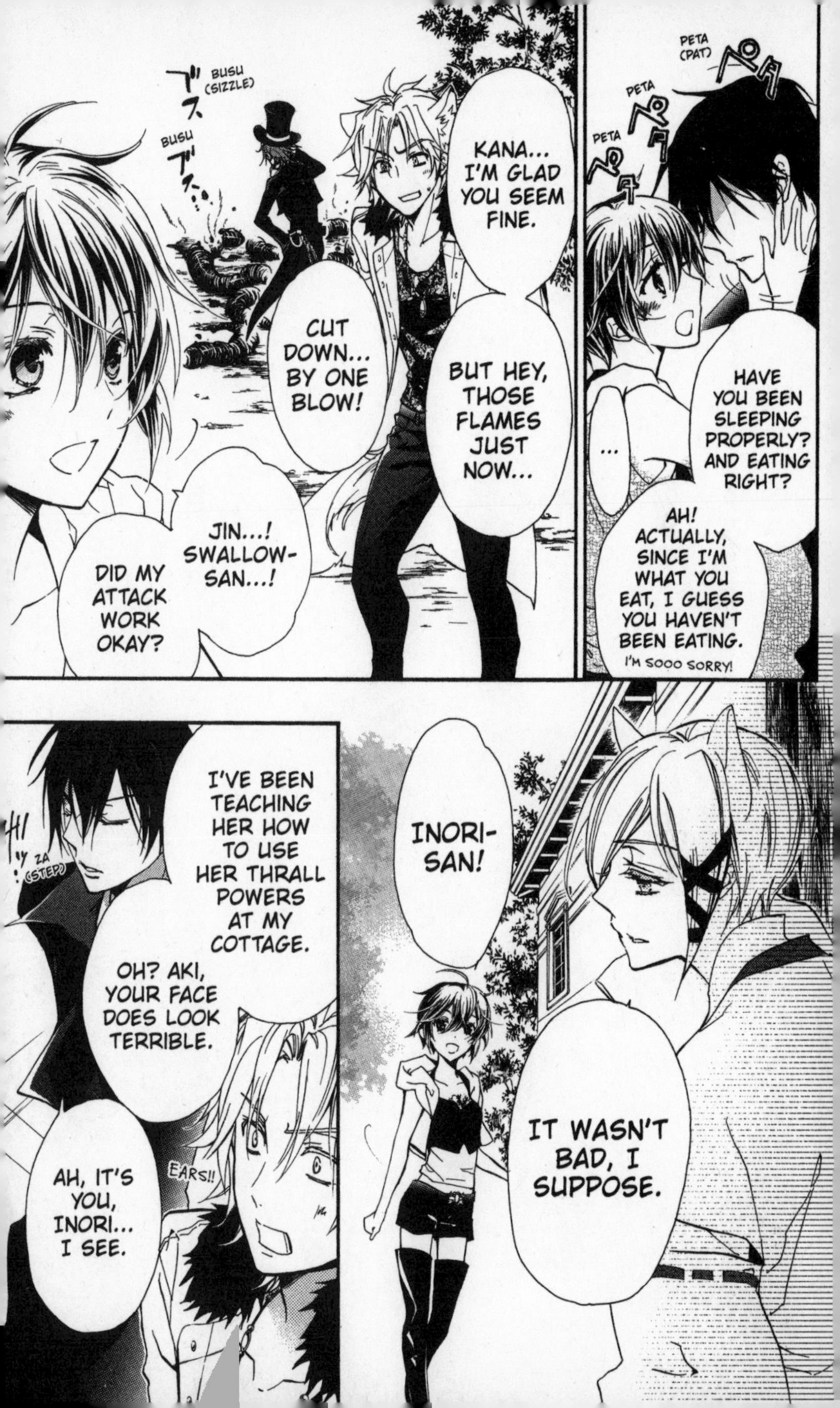
PETA (PAT)
PETA
PETA
HAVE YOU BEEN SLEEPING PROPERLY? AND EATING RIGHT?
...
AH! ACTUALLY, SINCE I'M WHAT YOU EAT, I GUESS YOU HAVEN'T BEEN EATING.
I'M SOOO SORRY!
KANA... I'M GLAD YOU SEEM FINE.
BUT HEY, THOSE FLAMES JUST NOW...
CUT DOWN... BY ONE BLOW!
BUSU (SIZZLE)
BUSU
JIN...! SWALLOW-SAN...!
DID MY ATTACK WORK OKAY?
INORI-SAN!
IT WASN'T BAD, I SUPPOSE.
ZA (STEP)
I'VE BEEN TEACHING HER HOW TO USE HER THRALL POWERS AT MY COTTAGE.
OH? AKI, YOUR FACE DOES LOOK TERRIBLE.
EARS!!
AH, IT'S YOU, INORI... I SEE.

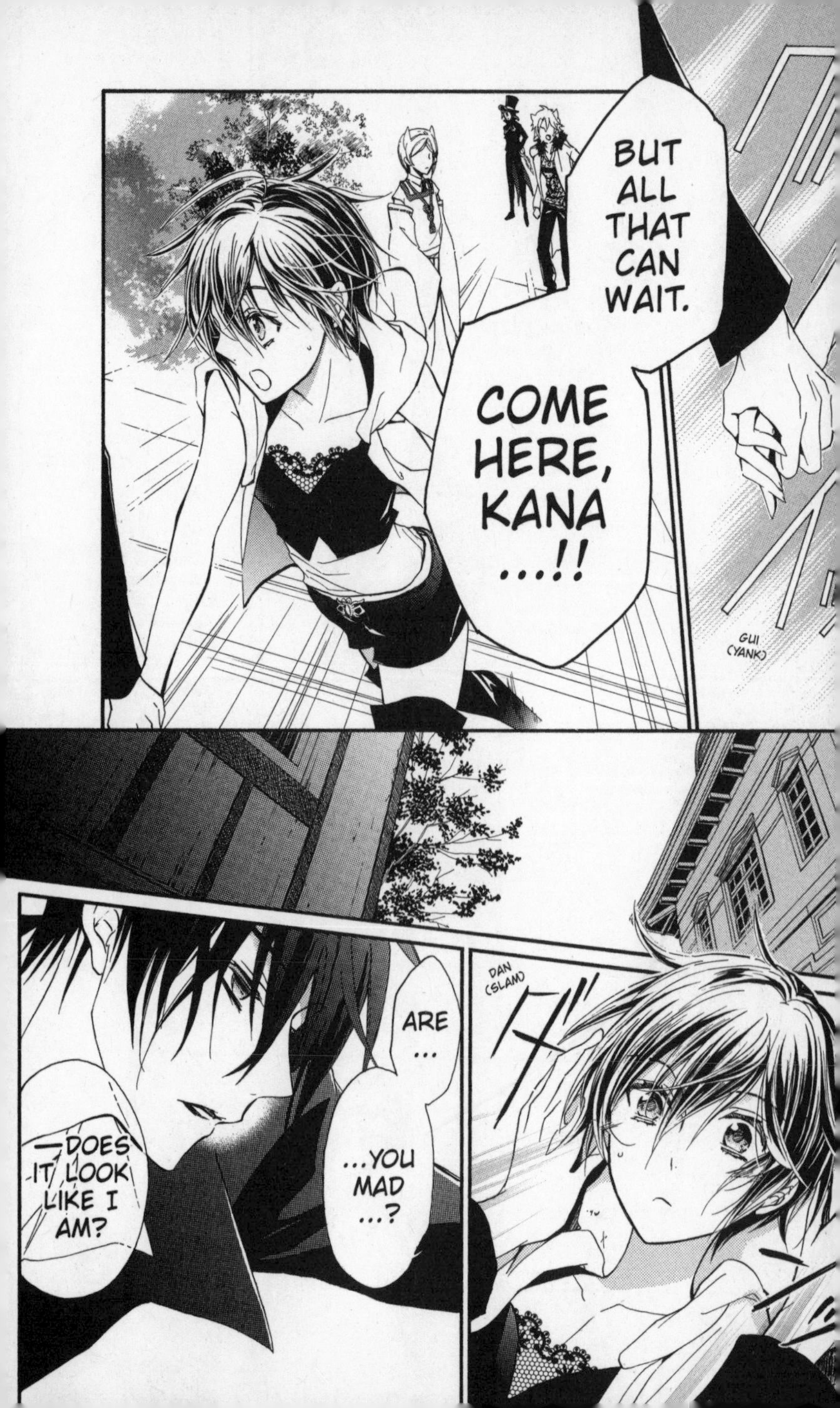
BUT ALL THAT CAN WAIT.
COME HERE, KANA ...!!
GUI (YANK)
DAN (SLAM)
ARE ...
...YOU MAD ...?
—DOES IT LOOK LIKE I AM?

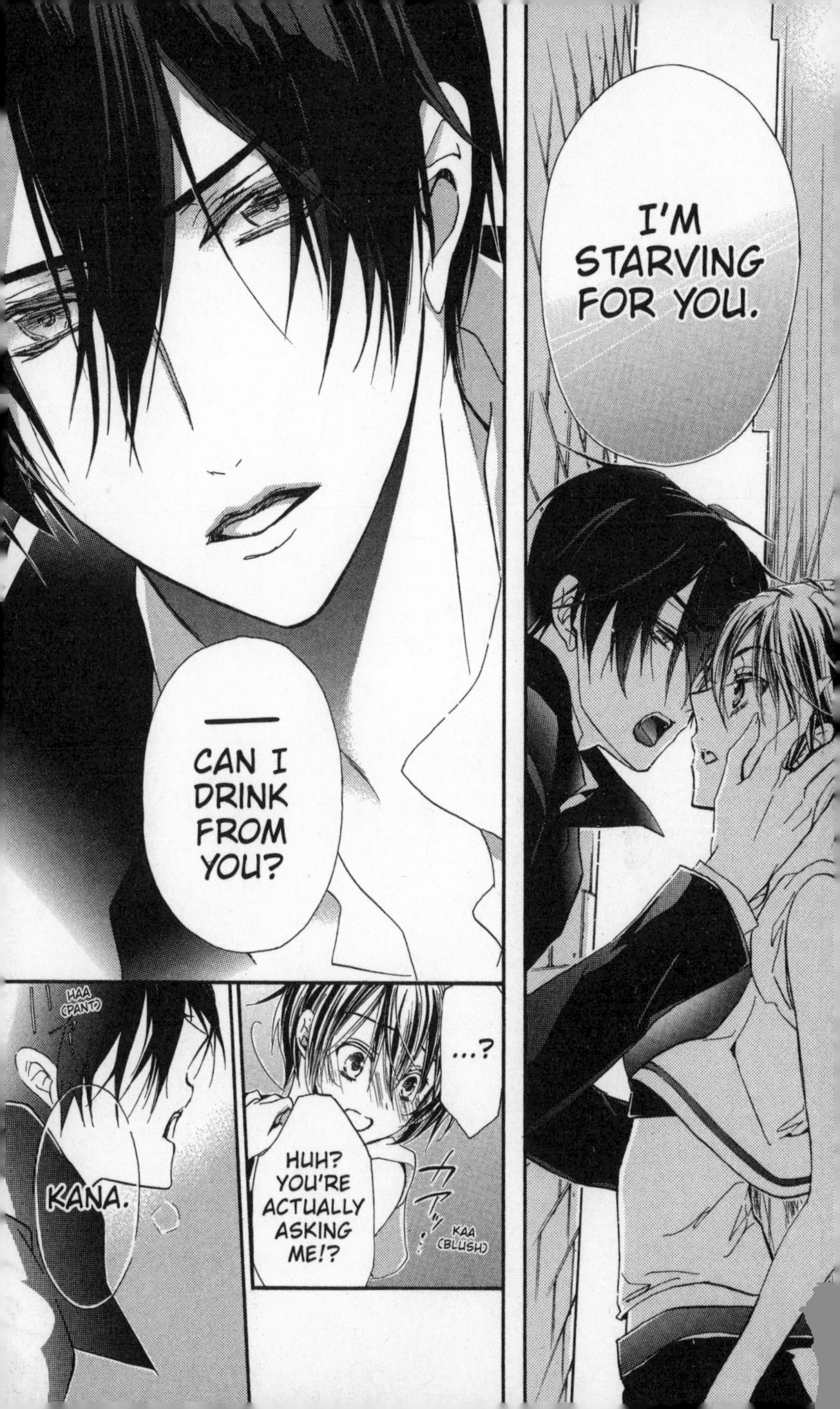

I'M STARVING FOR YOU.
— CAN I DRINK FROM YOU?
...?
HUH? YOU'RE ACTUALLY ASKING ME!?
KAA (BLUSH)
HAA (PANT)
KANA.

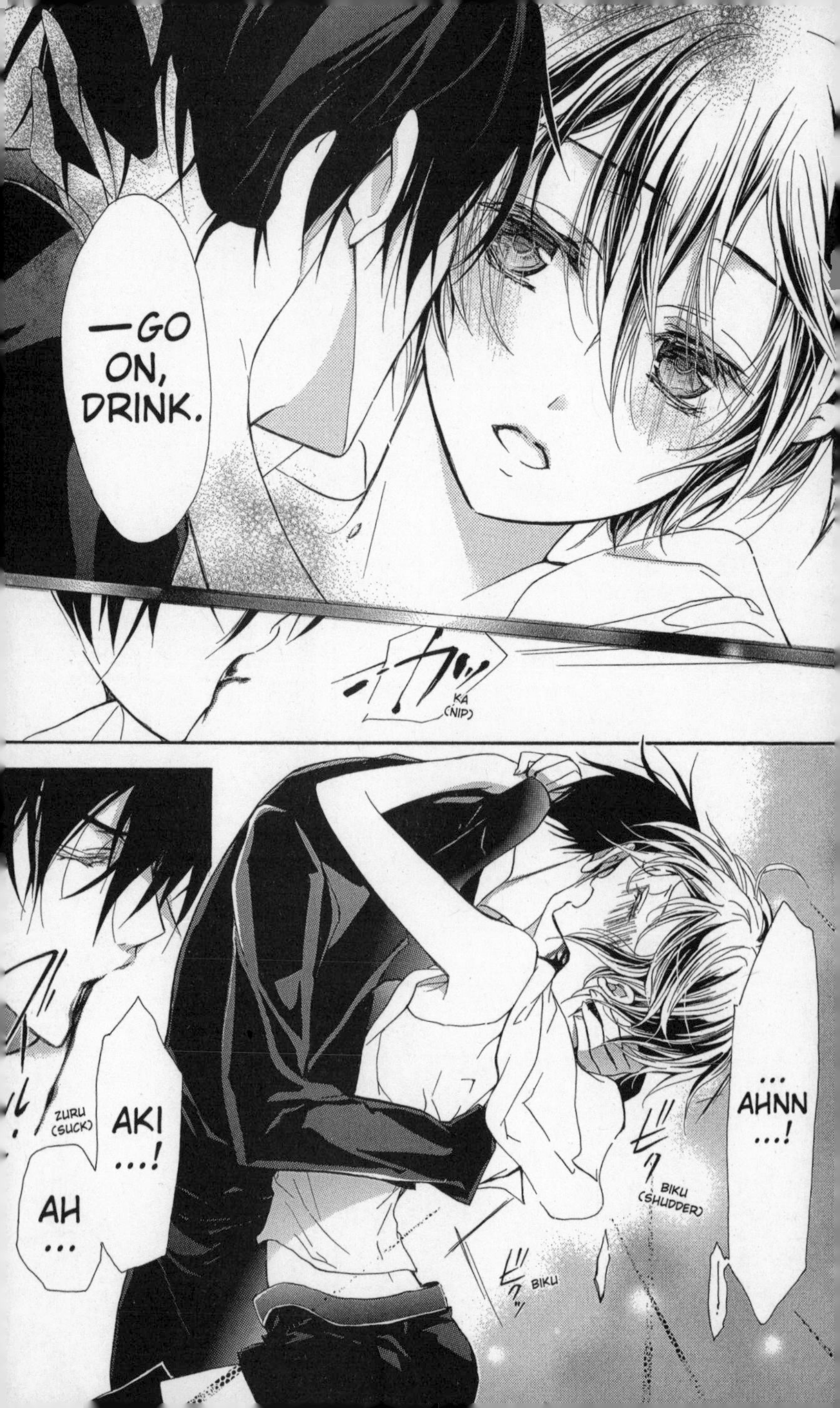
—GO ON, DRINK.
KA (NIP)
...AHNN ...!
BIKU (SHUDDER)
BIKU
ZURU (SUCK)
AKI ...!
AH ...

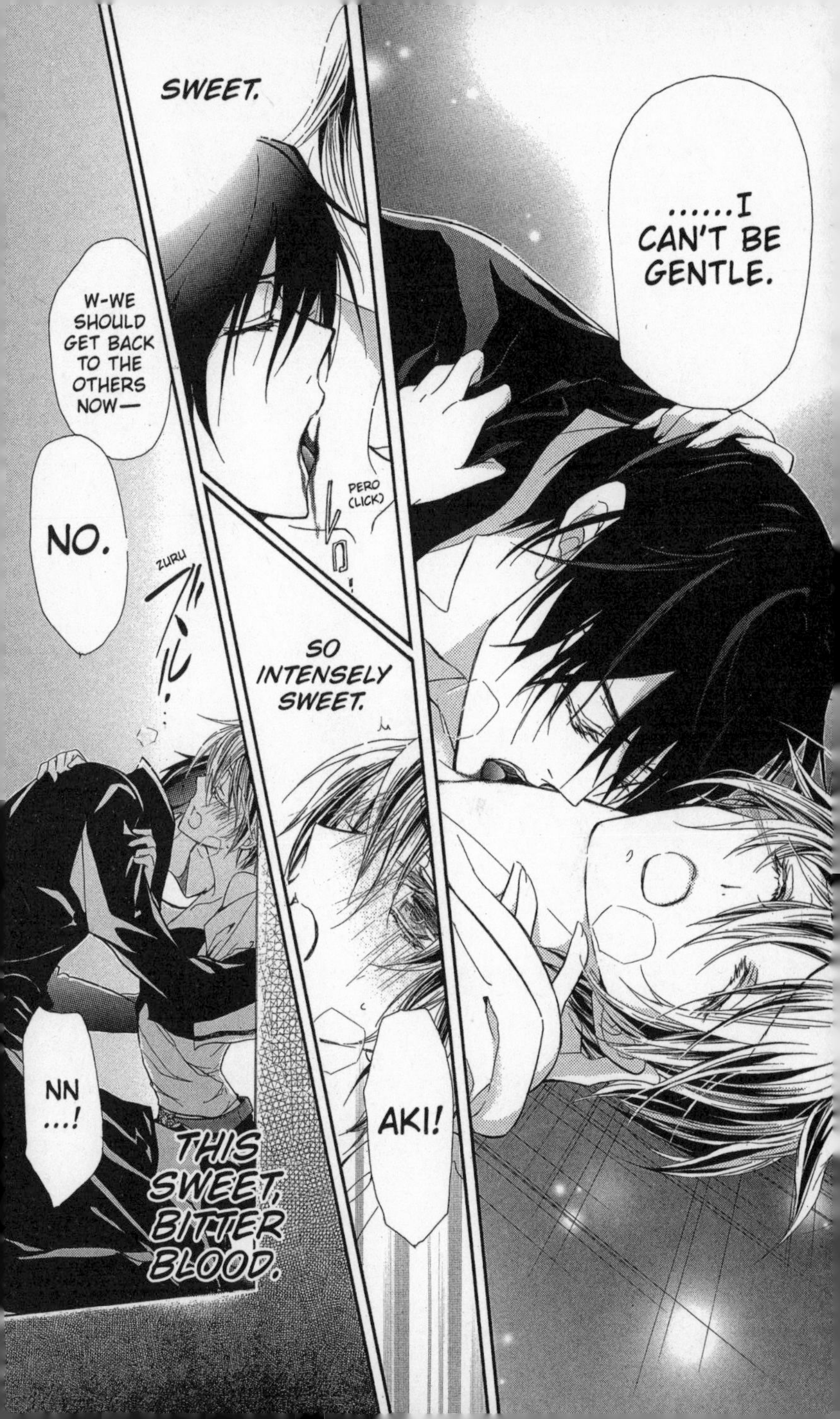
......I CAN'T BE GENTLE.
AKI!
SWEET.
PERO (LICK)
SO INTENSELY SWEET.
W-WE SHOULD GET BACK TO THE OTHERS NOW—
NO.
ZURU
NN ...!
THIS SWEET, BITTER BLOOD.

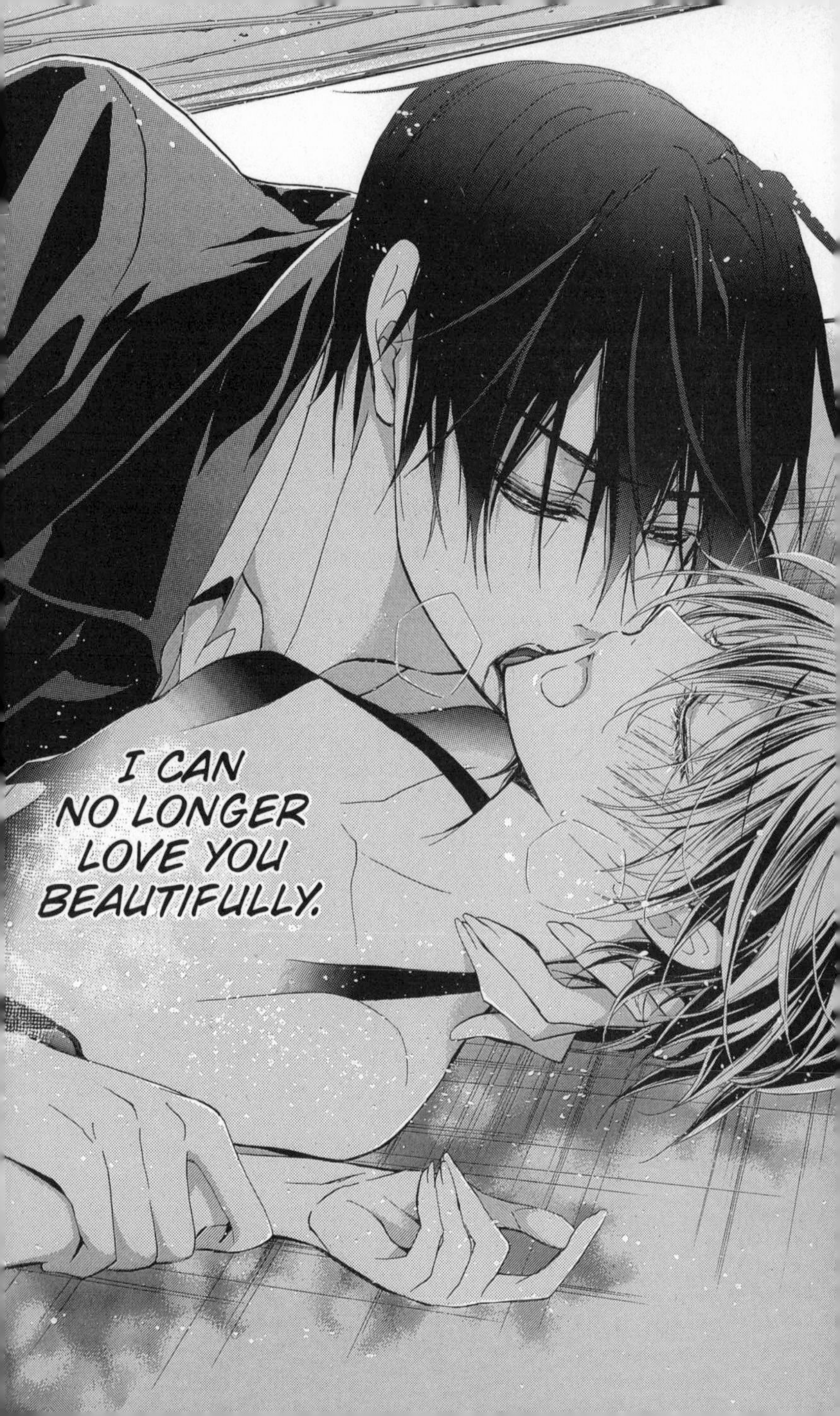
I CAN NO LONGER LOVE YOU BEAUTIFULLY.

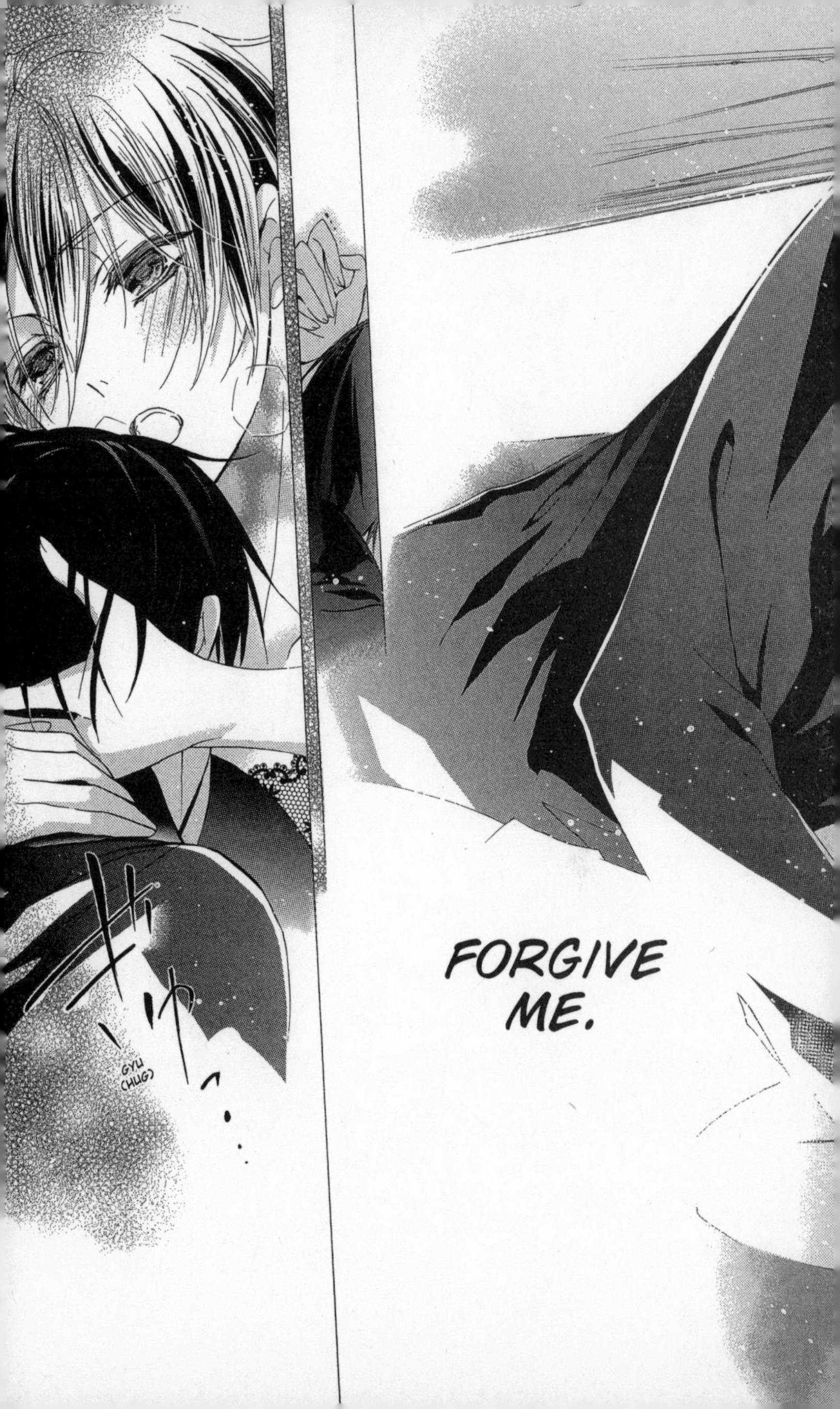
FORGIVE ME.
GYU (HUG)

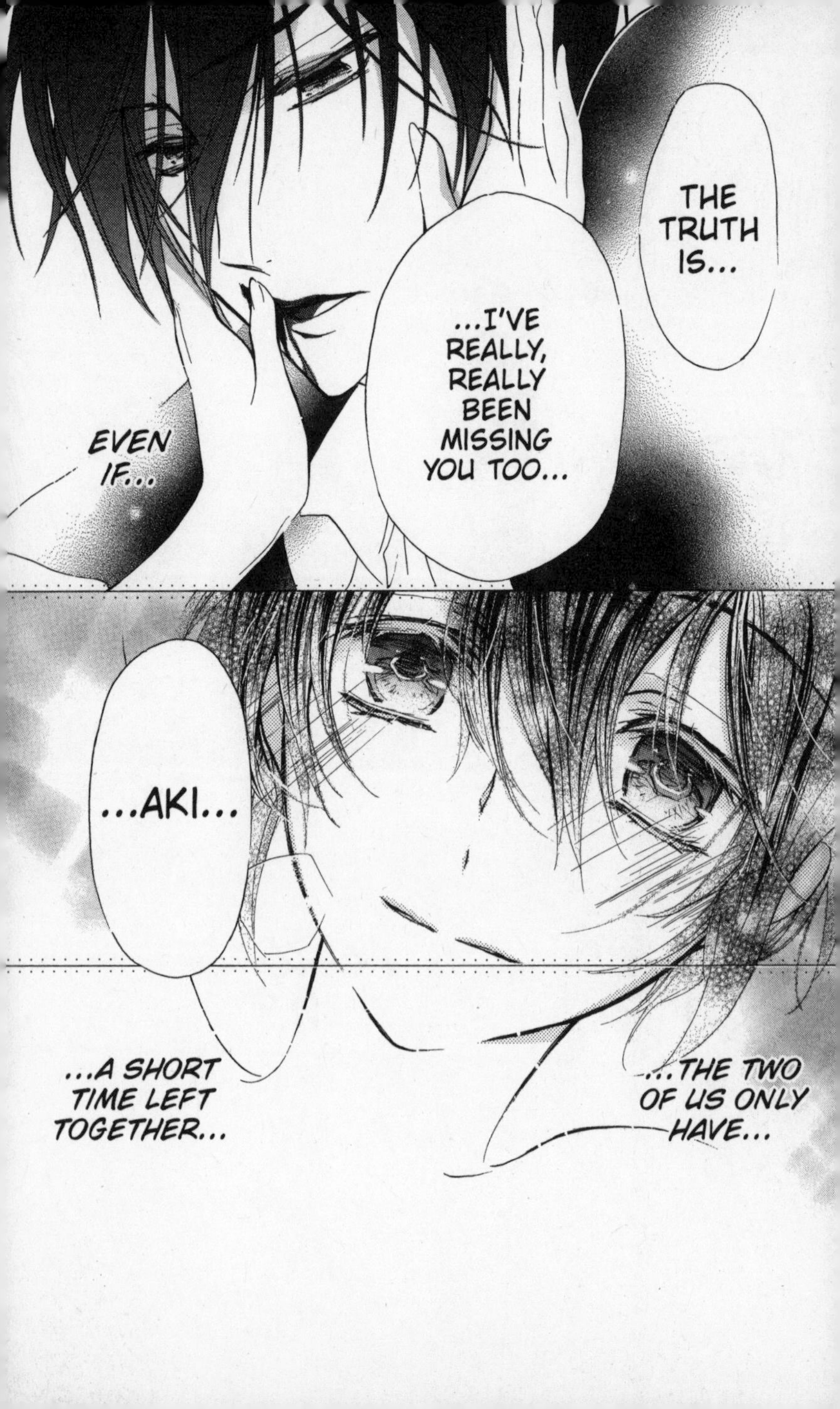
THE TRUTH IS...
...I'VE REALLY, REALLY BEEN MISSING YOU TOO...
EVEN IF...
...AKI...
...THE TWO OF US ONLY HAVE...
...A SHORT TIME LEFT TOGETHER...

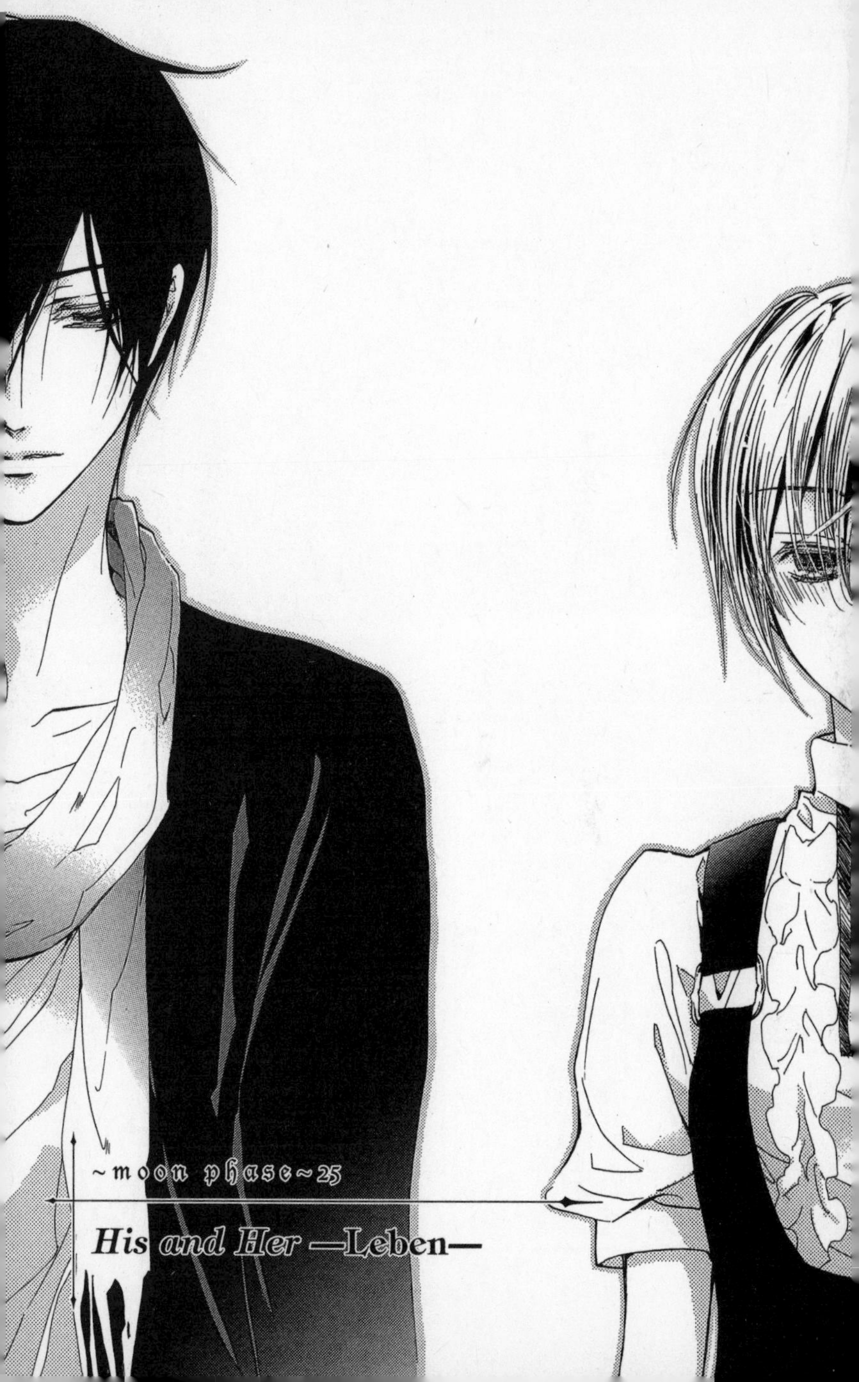
~moon phase~25
His and Her —Leben—

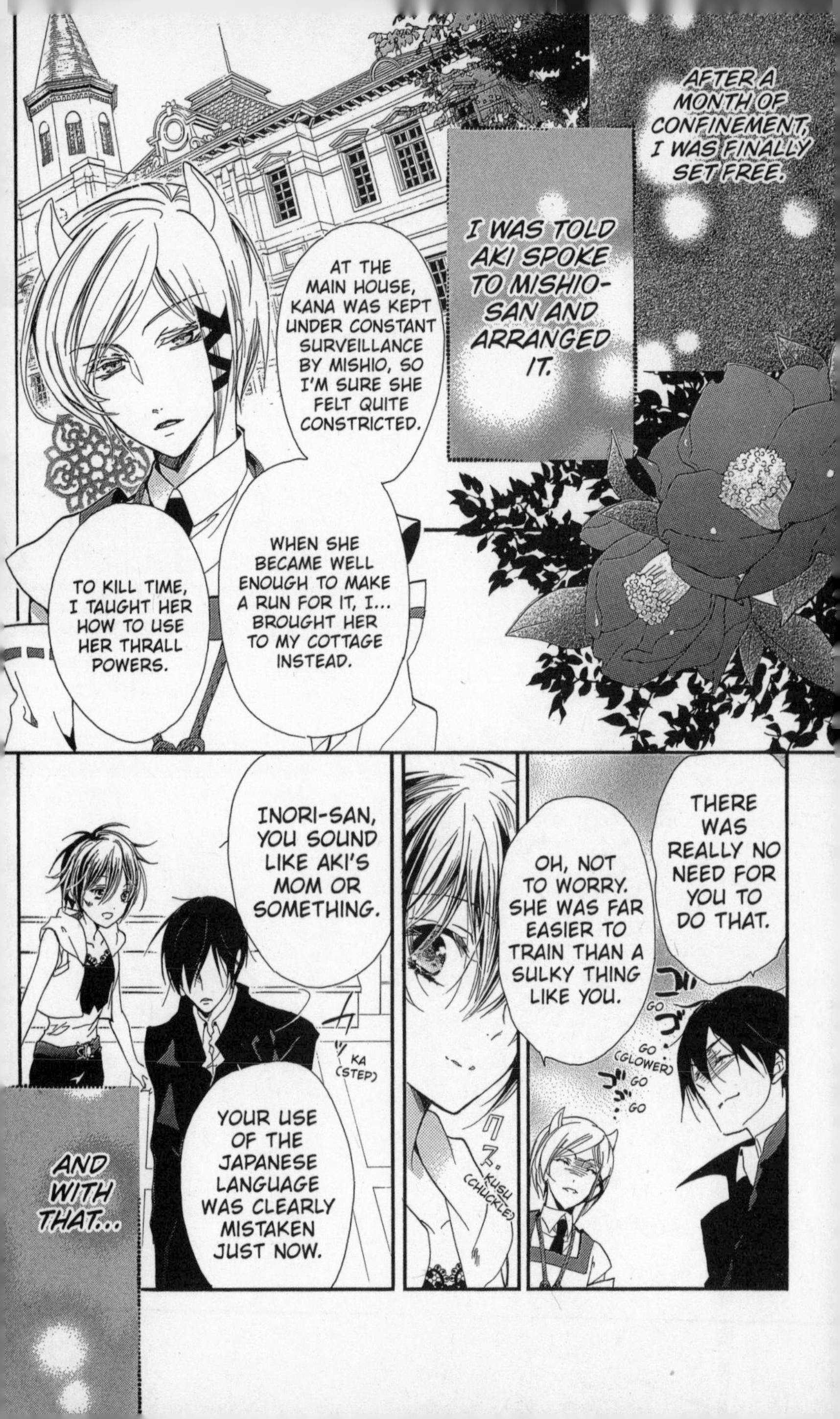
AFTER A MONTH OF CONFINEMENT, I WAS FINALLY SET FREE.
I WAS TOLD AKI SPOKE TO MISHIO-SAN AND ARRANGED IT.
AT THE MAIN HOUSE, KANA WAS KEPT UNDER CONSTANT SURVEILLANCE BY MISHIO, SO I'M SURE SHE FELT QUITE CONSTRICTED.
WHEN SHE BECAME WELL ENOUGH TO MAKE A RUN FOR IT, I... BROUGHT HER TO MY COTTAGE INSTEAD.
TO KILL TIME, I TAUGHT HER HOW TO USE HER THRALL POWERS.
THERE WAS REALLY NO NEED FOR YOU TO DO THAT.
OH, NOT TO WORRY. SHE WAS FAR EASIER TO TRAIN THAN A SULKY THING LIKE YOU.
GO GO (GLOWER) GO GO
KUSU (CHUCKLE)
INORI-SAN, YOU SOUND LIKE AKI'S MOM OR SOMETHING.
KA (STEP)
YOUR USE OF THE JAPANESE LANGUAGE WAS CLEARLY MISTAKEN JUST NOW.
AND WITH THAT...

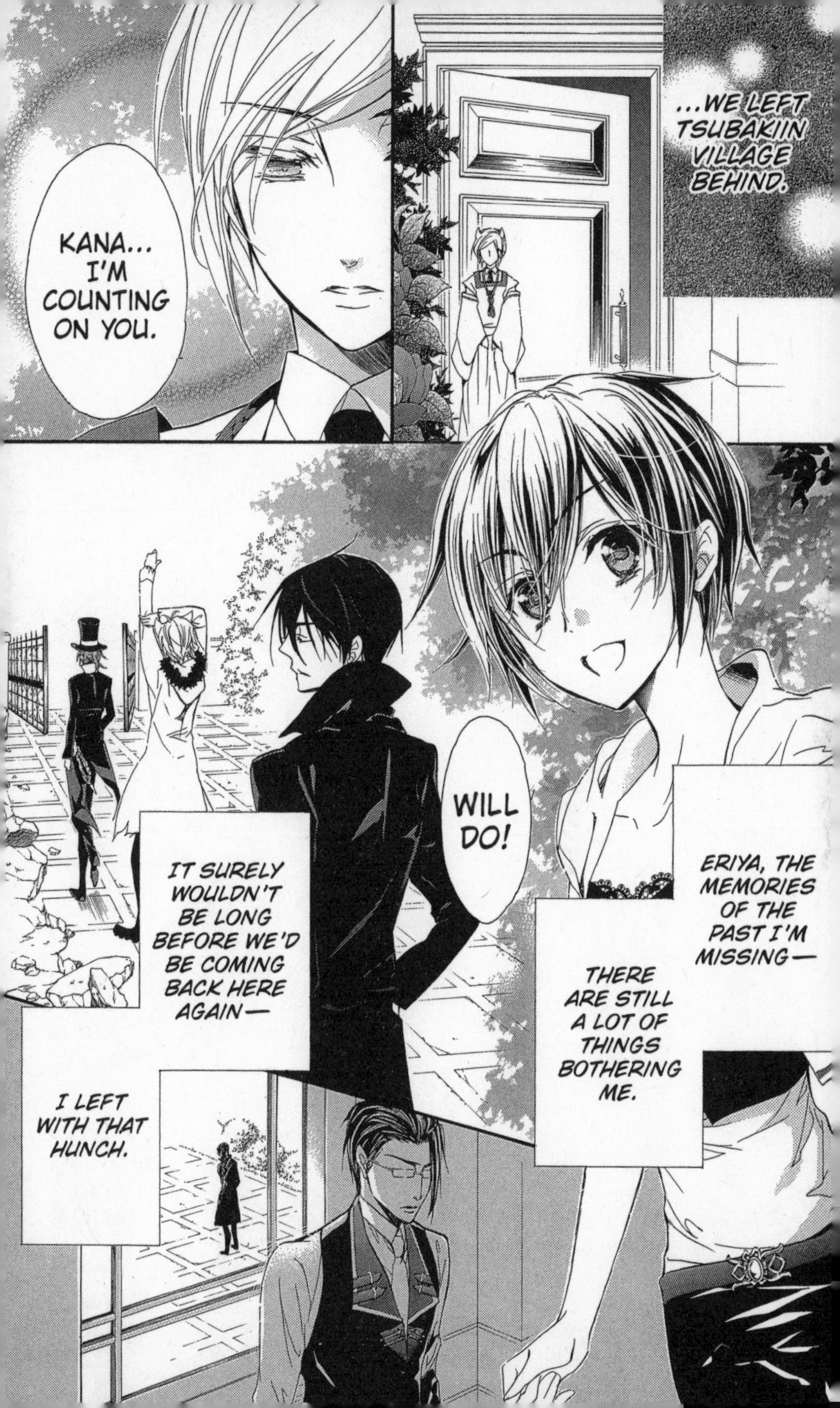
...WE LEFT TSUBAKIIN VILLAGE BEHIND.
KANA... I'M COUNTING ON YOU.
WILL DO!
ERIYA, THE MEMORIES OF THE PAST I'M MISSING—
THERE ARE STILL A LOT OF THINGS BOTHERING ME.
IT SURELY WOULDN'T BE LONG BEFORE WE'D BE COMING BACK HERE AGAIN—
I LEFT WITH THAT HUNCH.

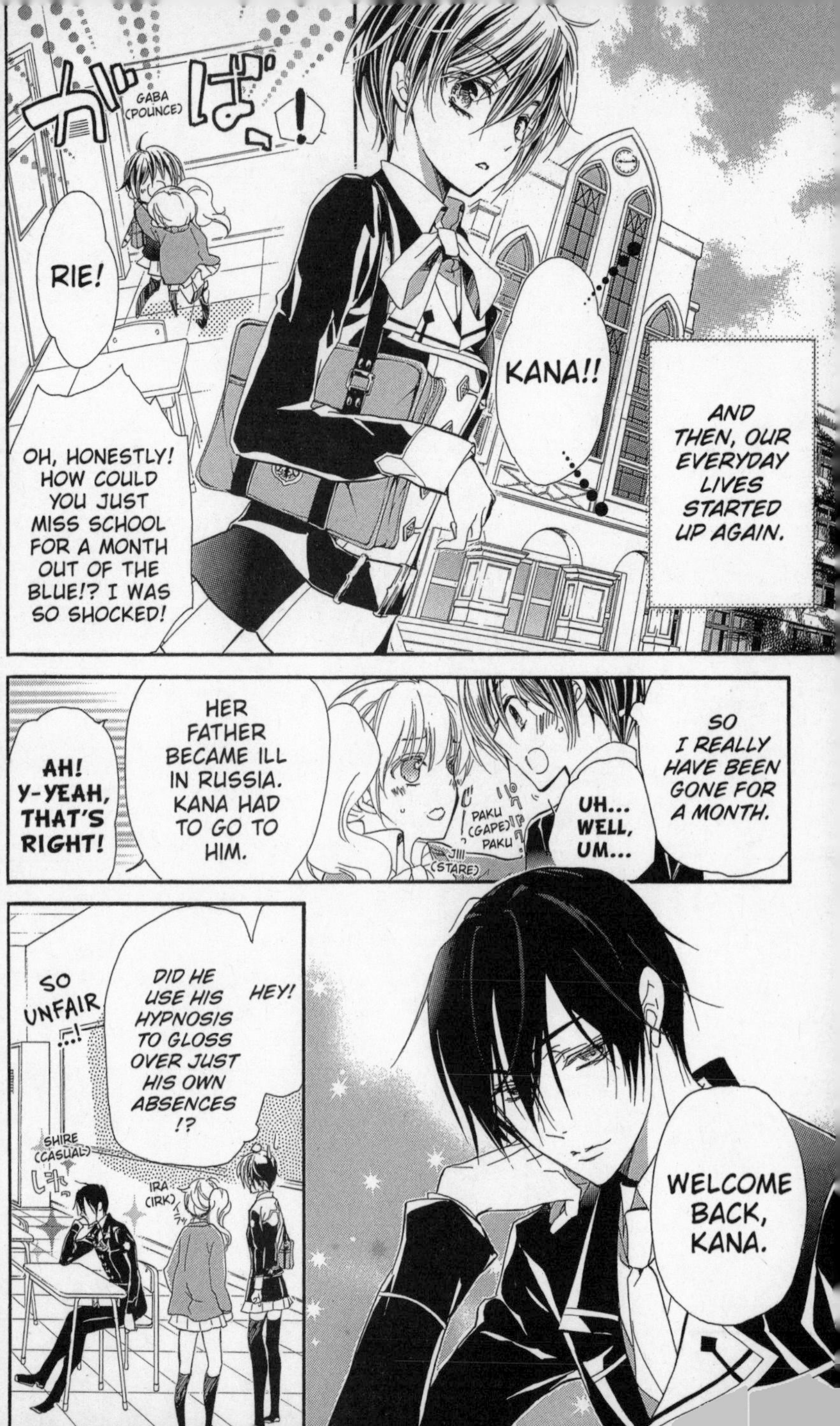
AND THEN, OUR EVERYDAY LIVES STARTED UP AGAIN.
KANA!!
GABA (POUNCE)
RIE!
OH, HONESTLY! HOW COULD YOU JUST MISS SCHOOL FOR A MONTH OUT OF THE BLUE!? I WAS SO SHOCKED!
SO I REALLY HAVE BEEN GONE FOR A MONTH.
UH... WELL, UM...
PAKU (GAPE) PAKU
JIII (STARE)
HER FATHER BECAME ILL IN RUSSIA. KANA HAD TO GO TO HIM.
AH! Y-YEAH, THAT'S RIGHT!
WELCOME BACK, KANA.
HEY!
DID HE USE HIS HYPNOSIS TO GLOSS OVER JUST HIS OWN ABSENCES !?
SO UNFAIR...!
SHIRE (CASUAL)
IRA (IRK)

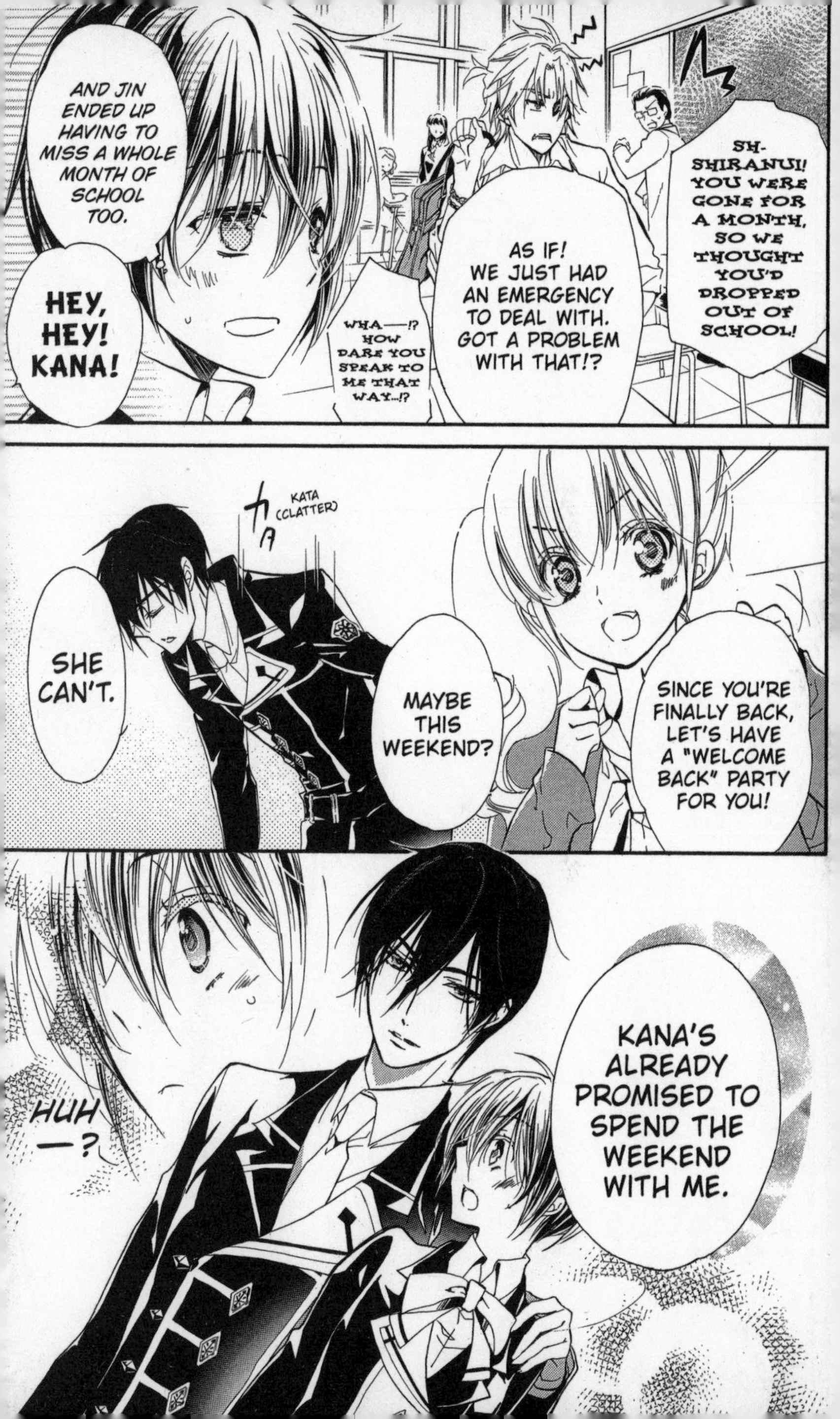
SH-SHIRANUI! YOU WERE GONE FOR A MONTH, SO WE THOUGHT YOU'D DROPPED OUT OF SCHOOL!
AS IF! WE JUST HAD AN EMERGENCY TO DEAL WITH. GOT A PROBLEM WITH THAT!?
WHA—!? HOW DARE YOU SPEAK TO ME THAT WAY...!?
AND JIN ENDED UP HAVING TO MISS A WHOLE MONTH OF SCHOOL TOO.
HEY, HEY! KANA!
SINCE YOU'RE FINALLY BACK, LET'S HAVE A "WELCOME BACK" PARTY FOR YOU!
MAYBE THIS WEEKEND?
KATA (CLATTER)
SHE CAN'T.
KANA'S ALREADY PROMISED TO SPEND THE WEEKEND WITH ME.
HUH—?

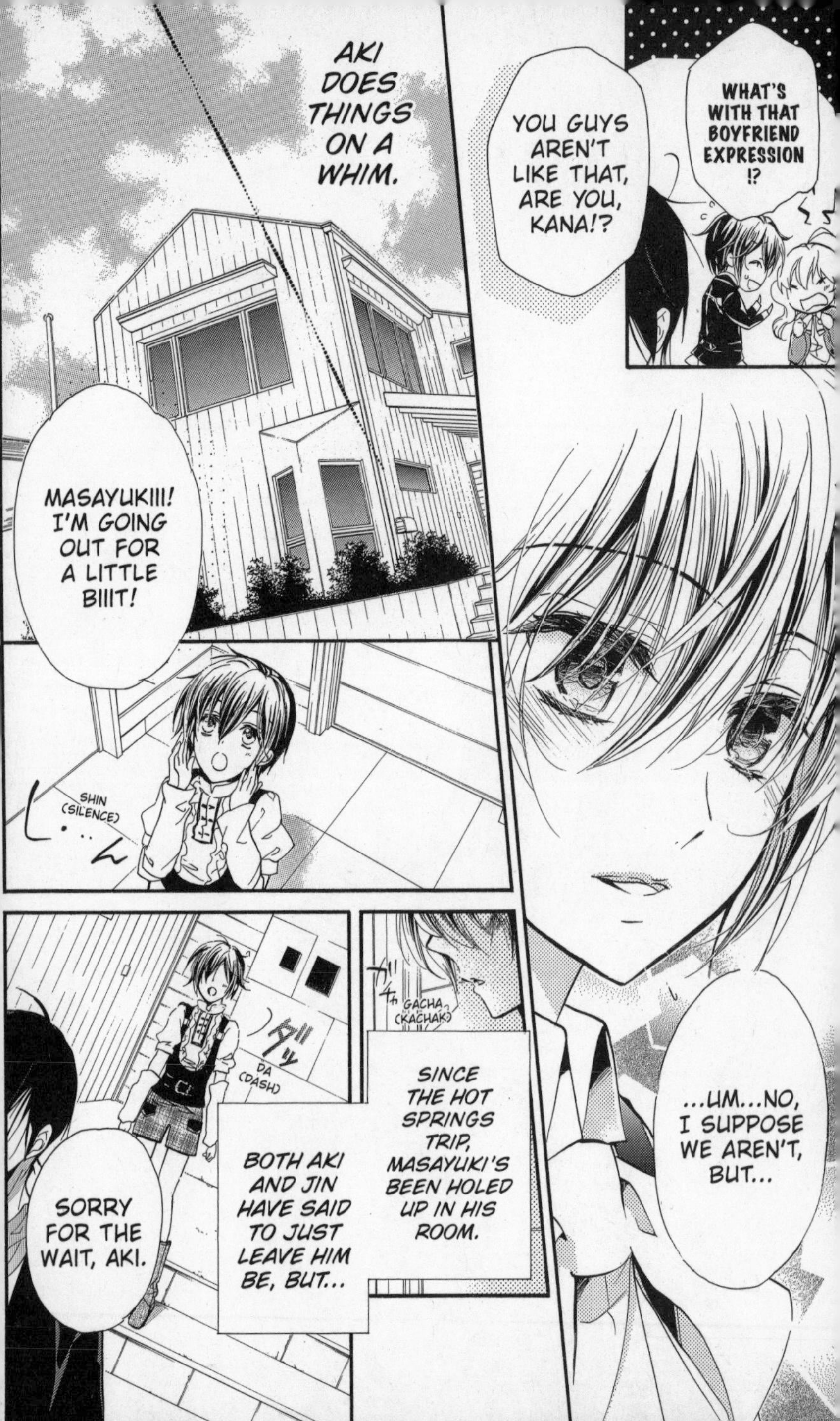
WHAT'S WITH THAT BOYFRIEND EXPRESSION!?
YOU GUYS AREN'T LIKE THAT, ARE YOU, KANA!?
...UM...NO, I SUPPOSE WE AREN'T, BUT...
AKI DOES THINGS ON A WHIM.
MASAYUKIII! I'M GOING OUT FOR A LITTLE BIIIT!
SHIN (SILENCE)
GACHA (KACHAK)
SINCE THE HOT SPRINGS TRIP, MASAYUKI'S BEEN HOLED UP IN HIS ROOM.
BOTH AKI AND JIN HAVE SAID TO JUST LEAVE HIM BE, BUT...
DA (DASH)
SORRY FOR THE WAIT, AKI.

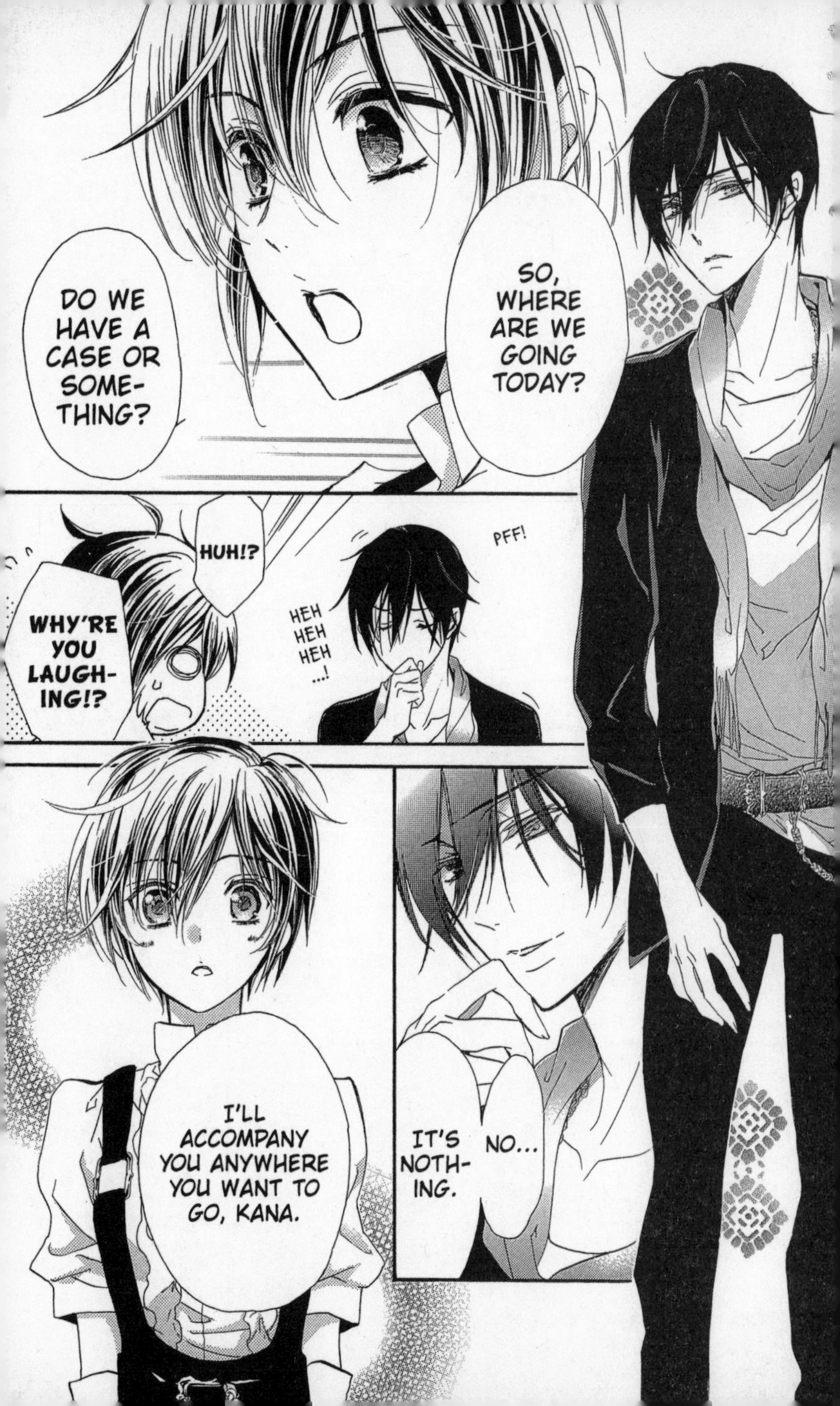
SO, WHERE ARE WE GOING TODAY?
DO WE HAVE A CASE OR SOME-THING?
PFF!
HEH HEH HEH ...!
HUH!?
WHY'RE YOU LAUGH-ING!?
NO...
IT'S NOTH-ING.
I'LL ACCOMPANY YOU ANYWHERE YOU WANT TO GO, KANA.

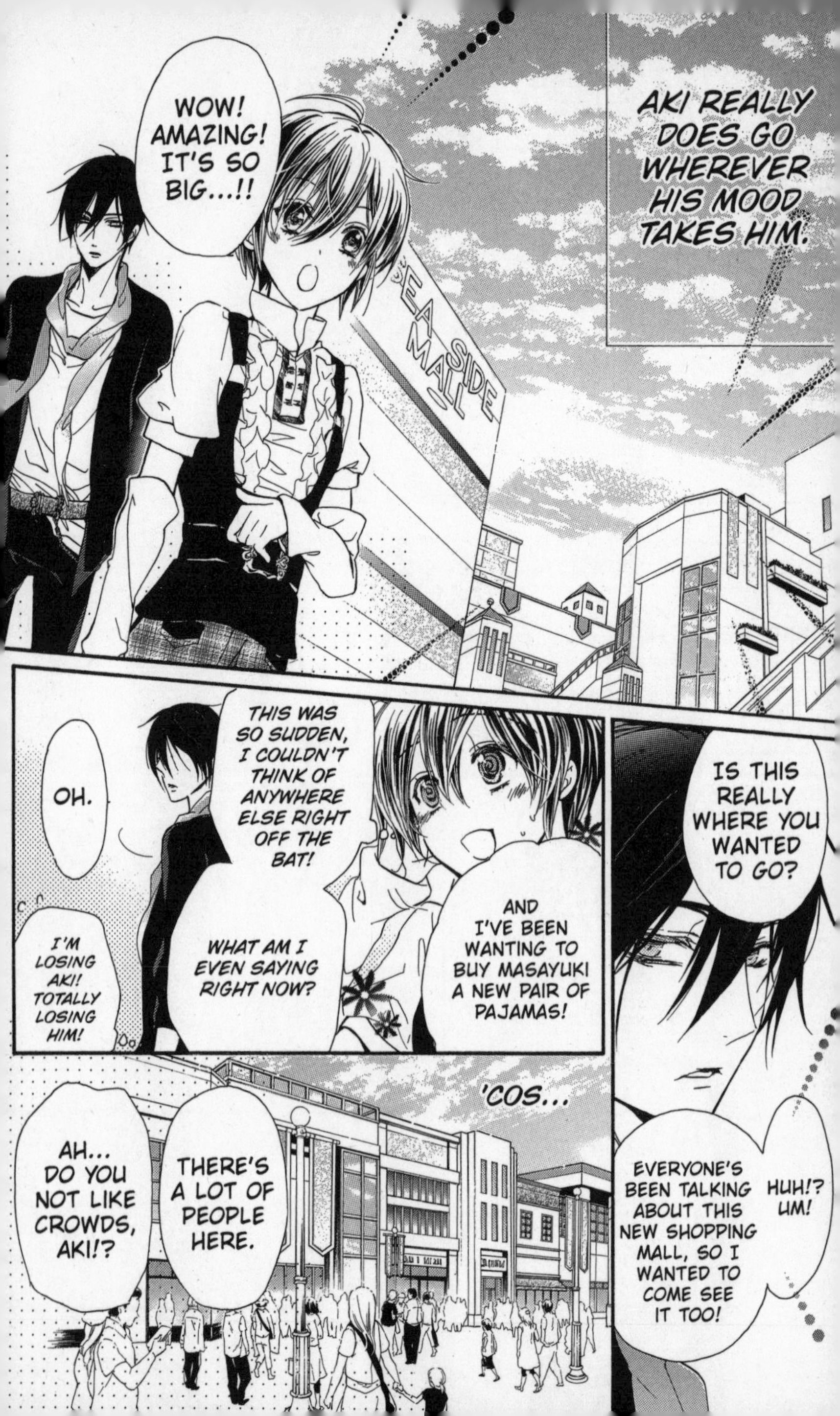
AKI REALLY DOES GO WHEREVER HIS MOOD TAKES HIM.
SEA SIDE MALL
WOW! AMAZING! IT'S SO BIG...!!
IS THIS REALLY WHERE YOU WANTED TO GO?
HUH!? UM!
EVERYONE'S BEEN TALKING ABOUT THIS NEW SHOPPING MALL, SO I WANTED TO COME SEE IT TOO!
THIS WAS SO SUDDEN, I COULDN'T THINK OF ANYWHERE ELSE RIGHT OFF THE BAT!
OH.
AND I'VE BEEN WANTING TO BUY MASAYUKI A NEW PAIR OF PAJAMAS!
WHAT AM I EVEN SAYING RIGHT NOW?
I'M LOSING AKI! TOTALLY LOSING HIM!
'COS...
THERE'S A LOT OF PEOPLE HERE.
AH... DO YOU NOT LIKE CROWDS, AKI!?

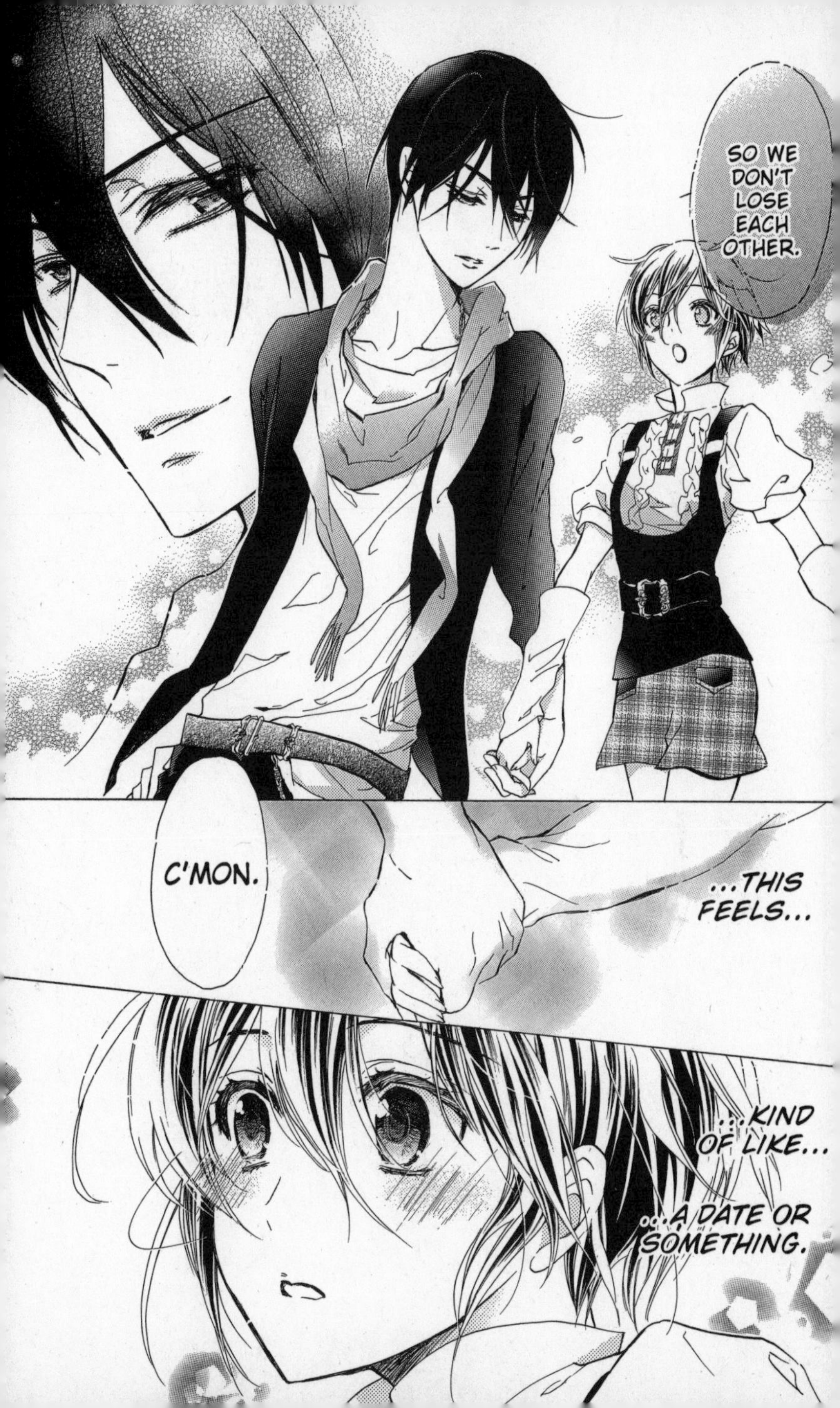
SO WE DON'T LOSE EACH OTHER.
C'MON.
...THIS FEELS...
...KIND OF LIKE...
...A DATE OR SOMETHING.

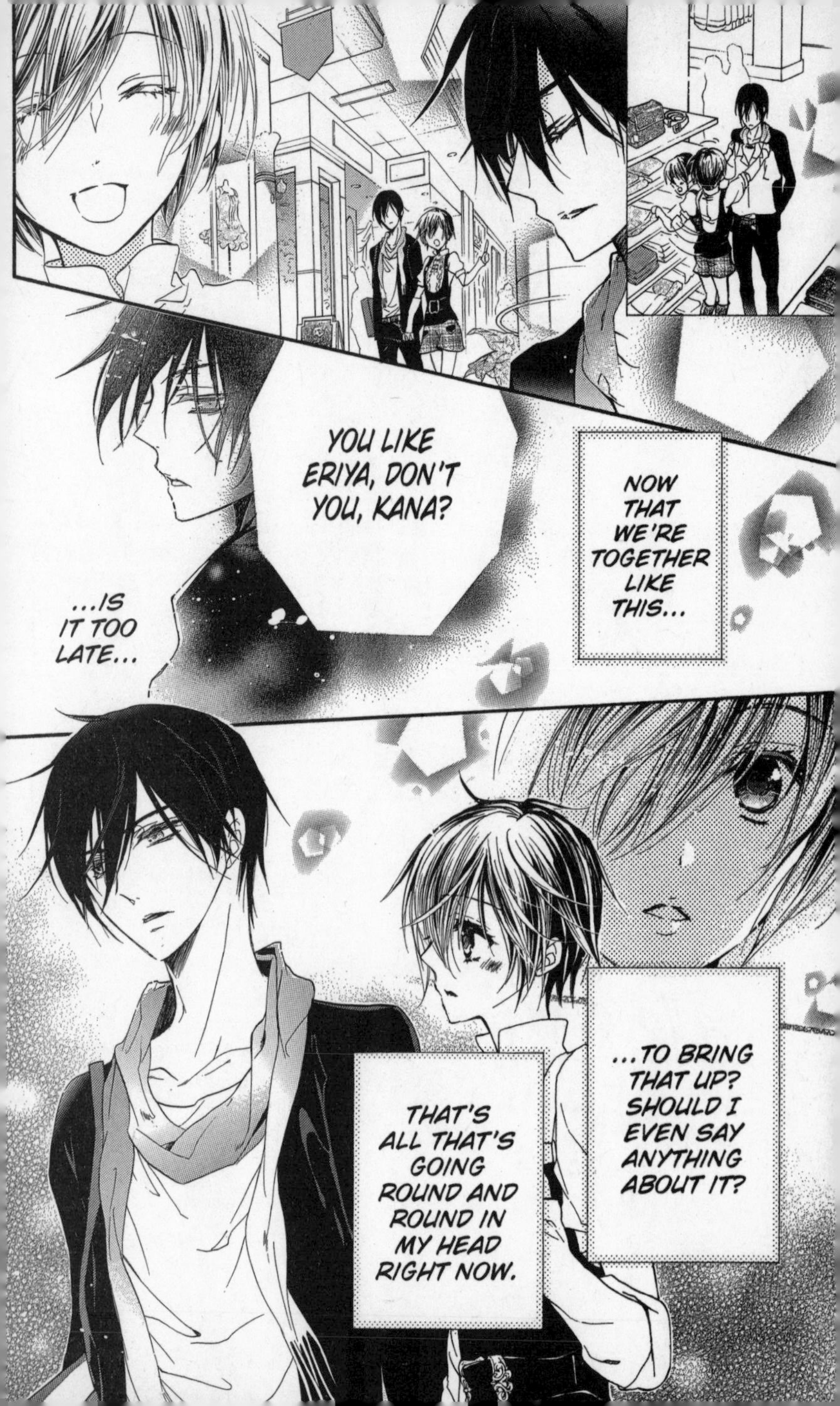
NOW THAT WE'RE TOGETHER LIKE THIS...
YOU LIKE ERIYA, DON'T YOU, KANA?
...IS IT TOO LATE...
...TO BRING THAT UP? SHOULD I EVEN SAY ANYTHING ABOUT IT?
THAT'S ALL THAT'S GOING ROUND AND ROUND IN MY HEAD RIGHT NOW.

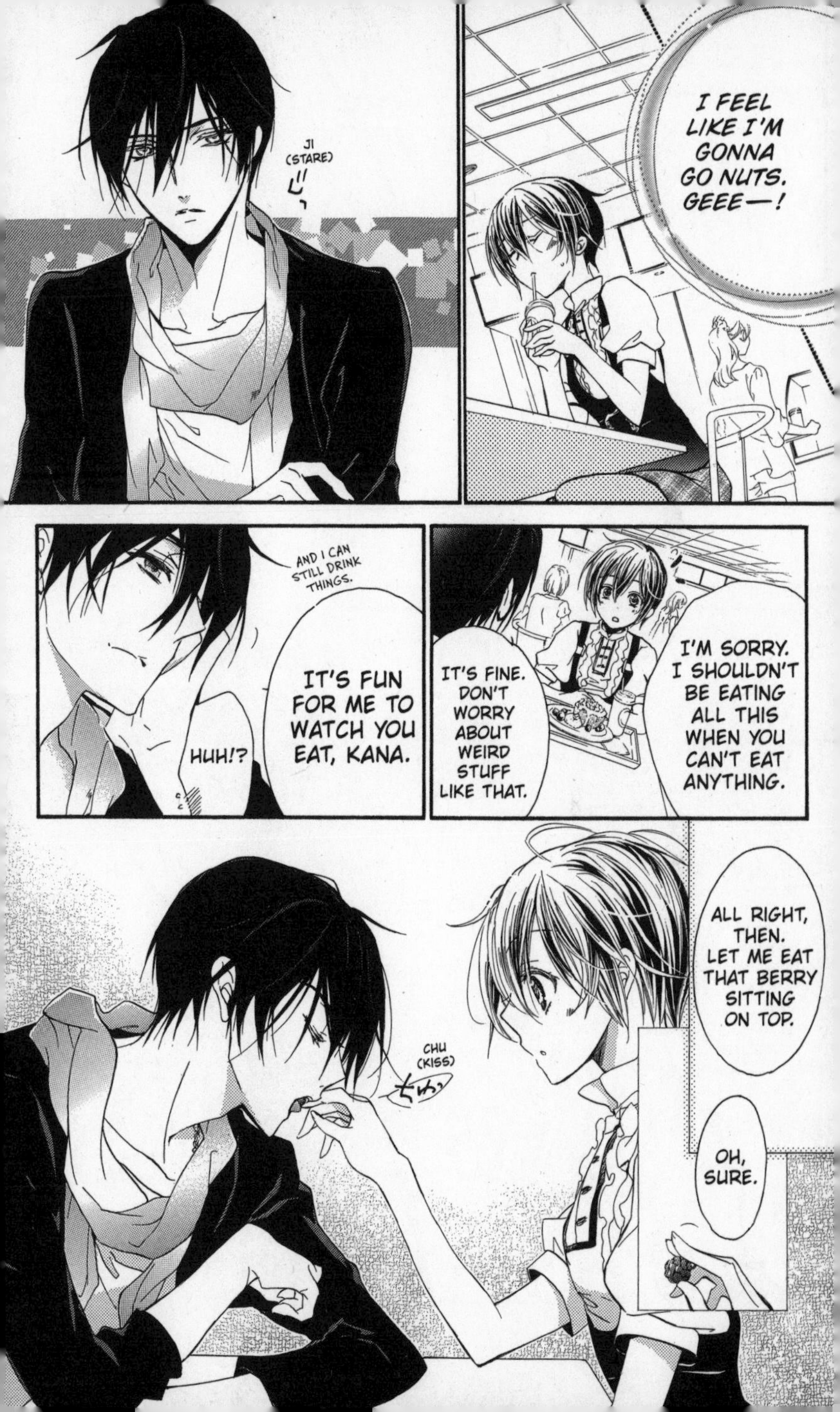

I FEEL LIKE I'M GONNA GO NUTS. GEEE—!
JI (STARE)
I'M SORRY. I SHOULDN'T BE EATING ALL THIS WHEN YOU CAN'T EAT ANYTHING.
IT'S FINE. DON'T WORRY ABOUT WEIRD STUFF LIKE THAT.
IT'S FUN FOR ME TO WATCH YOU EAT, KANA.
AND I CAN STILL DRINK THINGS.
HUH!?
ALL RIGHT, THEN. LET ME EAT THAT BERRY SITTING ON TOP.
OH, SURE.
CHU (KISS)

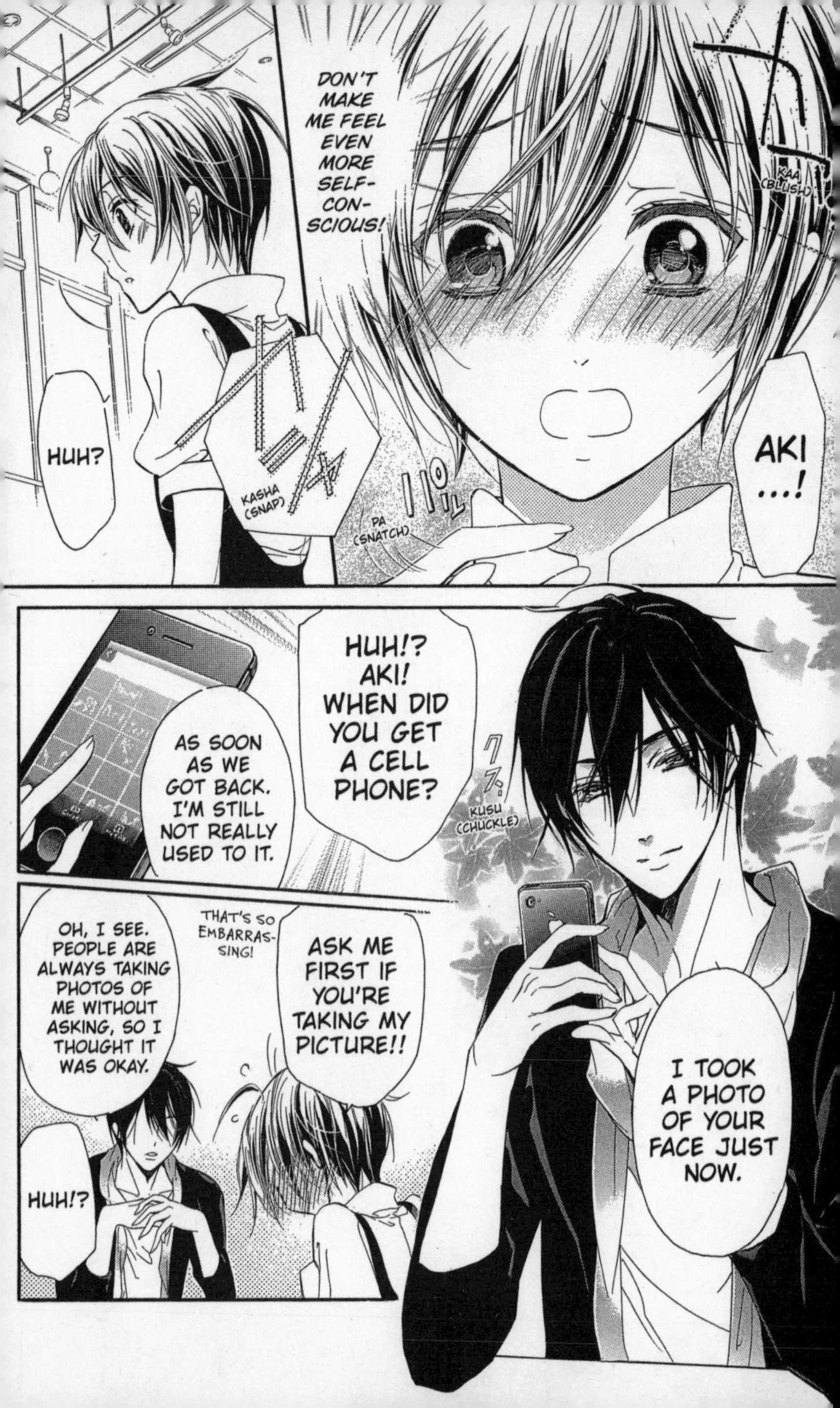

AKI ...!
KAA (BLUSH)
DON'T MAKE ME FEEL EVEN MORE SELF-CONSCIOUS!
PA (SNATCH)
KASHA (SNAP)
HUH?
I TOOK A PHOTO OF YOUR FACE JUST NOW.
KUSU (CHUCKLE)
HUH!? AKI! WHEN DID YOU GET A CELL PHONE?
AS SOON AS WE GOT BACK. I'M STILL NOT REALLY USED TO IT.
ASK ME FIRST IF YOU'RE TAKING MY PICTURE!!
THAT'S SO EMBARRASSING!
OH, I SEE. PEOPLE ARE ALWAYS TAKING PHOTOS OF ME WITHOUT ASKING, SO I THOUGHT IT WAS OKAY.
HUH!?

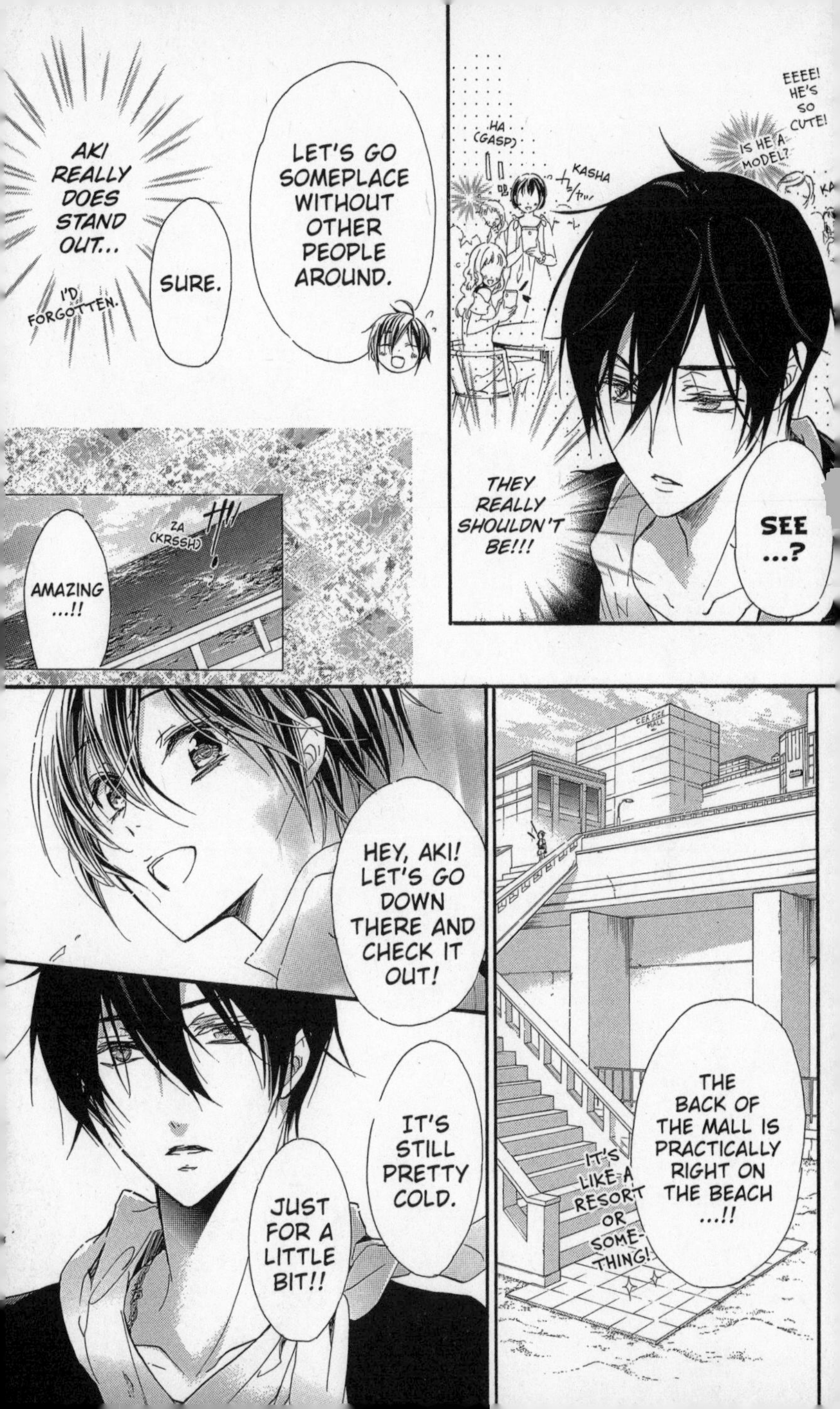
EEEE! HE'S SO CUTE!
IS HE A MODEL?
HA (GASP)
KASHA
SEE ...?
THEY REALLY SHOULDN'T BE!!!
LET'S GO SOMEPLACE WITHOUT OTHER PEOPLE AROUND.
SURE.
AKI REALLY DOES STAND OUT...
I'D FORGOTTEN.
ZA (KRSSH)
AMAZING ...!!
SEA SIDE MALL
THE BACK OF THE MALL IS PRACTICALLY RIGHT ON THE BEACH ...!!
IT'S LIKE A RESORT OR SOME-THING!
HEY, AKI! LET'S GO DOWN THERE AND CHECK IT OUT!
IT'S STILL PRETTY COLD.
JUST FOR A LITTLE BIT!!

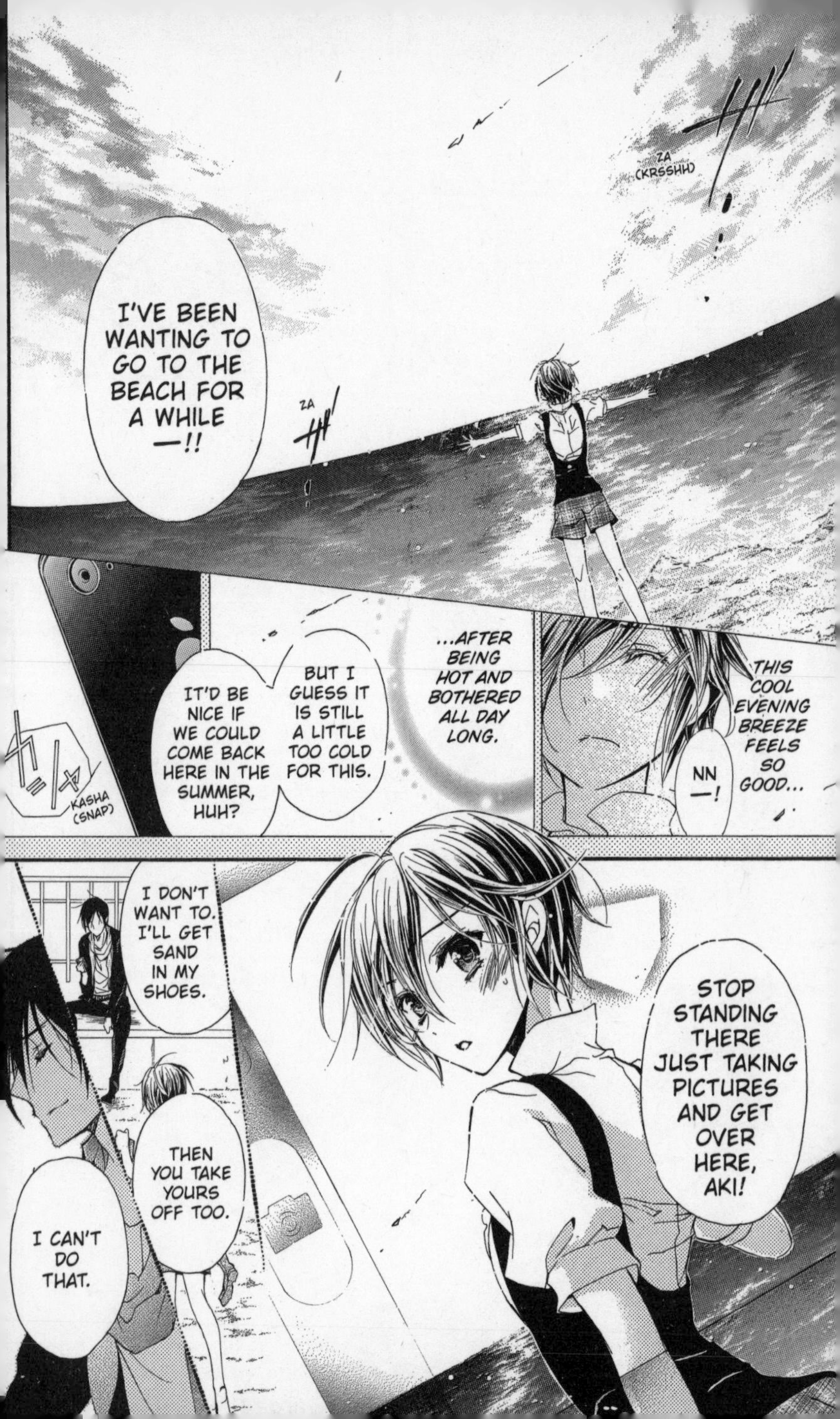
ZA
(KRSSHH)
I'VE BEEN WANTING TO GO TO THE BEACH FOR A WHILE —!!
ZA
THIS COOL EVENING BREEZE FEELS SO GOOD...
NN —!
...AFTER BEING HOT AND BOTHERED ALL DAY LONG.
BUT I GUESS IT IS STILL A LITTLE TOO COLD FOR THIS.
IT'D BE NICE IF WE COULD COME BACK HERE IN THE SUMMER, HUH?
KASHA
(SNAP)
STOP STANDING THERE JUST TAKING PICTURES AND GET OVER HERE, AKI!
I DON'T WANT TO. I'LL GET SAND IN MY SHOES.
THEN YOU TAKE YOURS OFF TOO.
I CAN'T DO THAT.

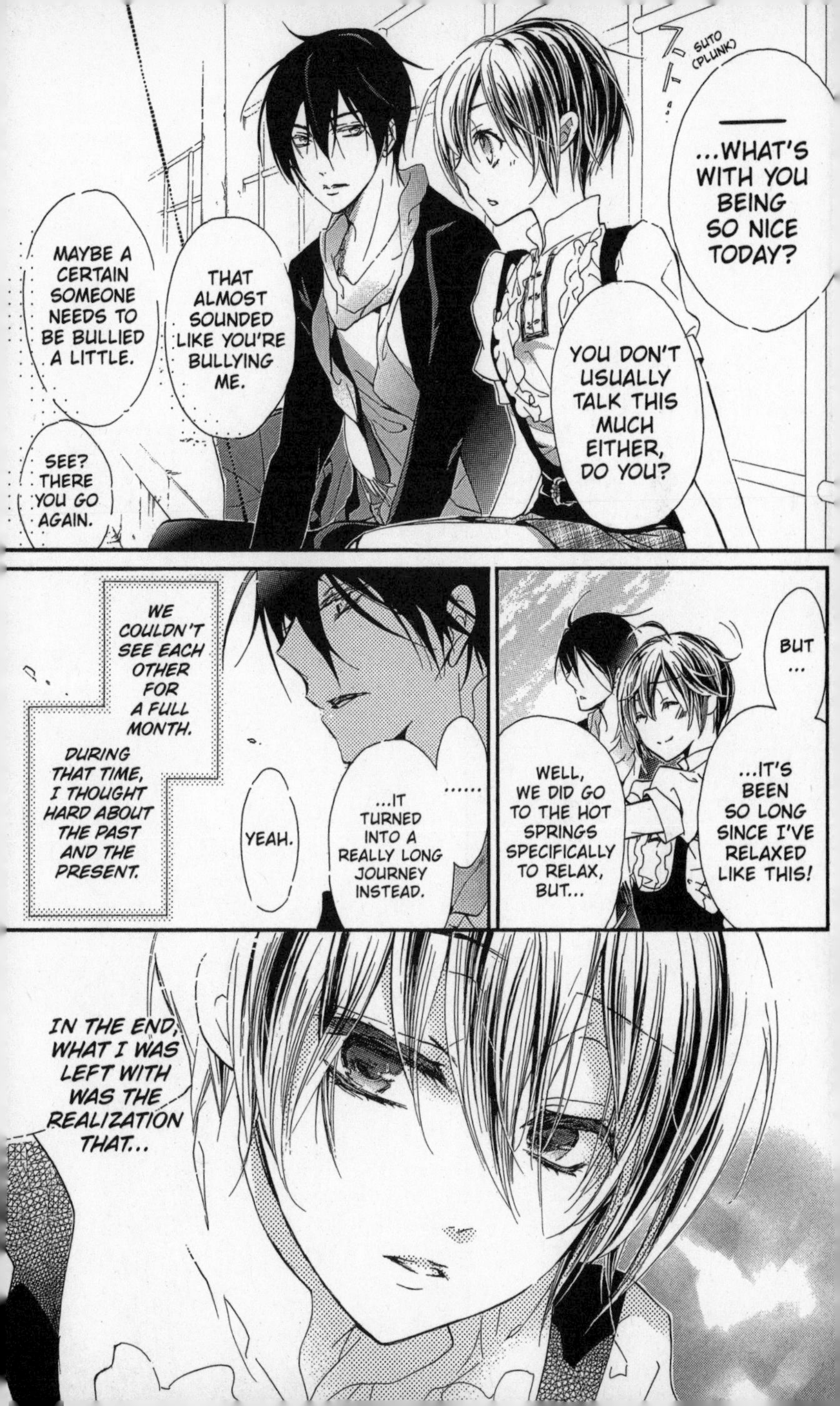
SUTO (PLUNK)
——…WHAT'S WITH YOU BEING SO NICE TODAY?
YOU DON'T USUALLY TALK THIS MUCH EITHER, DO YOU?
THAT ALMOST SOUNDED LIKE YOU'RE BULLYING ME.
MAYBE A CERTAIN SOMEONE NEEDS TO BE BULLIED A LITTLE.
SEE? THERE YOU GO AGAIN.
BUT …
…IT'S BEEN SO LONG SINCE I'VE RELAXED LIKE THIS!
WELL, WE DID GO TO THE HOT SPRINGS SPECIFICALLY TO RELAX, BUT…
……
…IT TURNED INTO A REALLY LONG JOURNEY INSTEAD.
YEAH.
WE COULDN'T SEE EACH OTHER FOR A FULL MONTH.
DURING THAT TIME, I THOUGHT HARD ABOUT THE PAST AND THE PRESENT.
IN THE END, WHAT I WAS LEFT WITH WAS THE REALIZATION THAT…

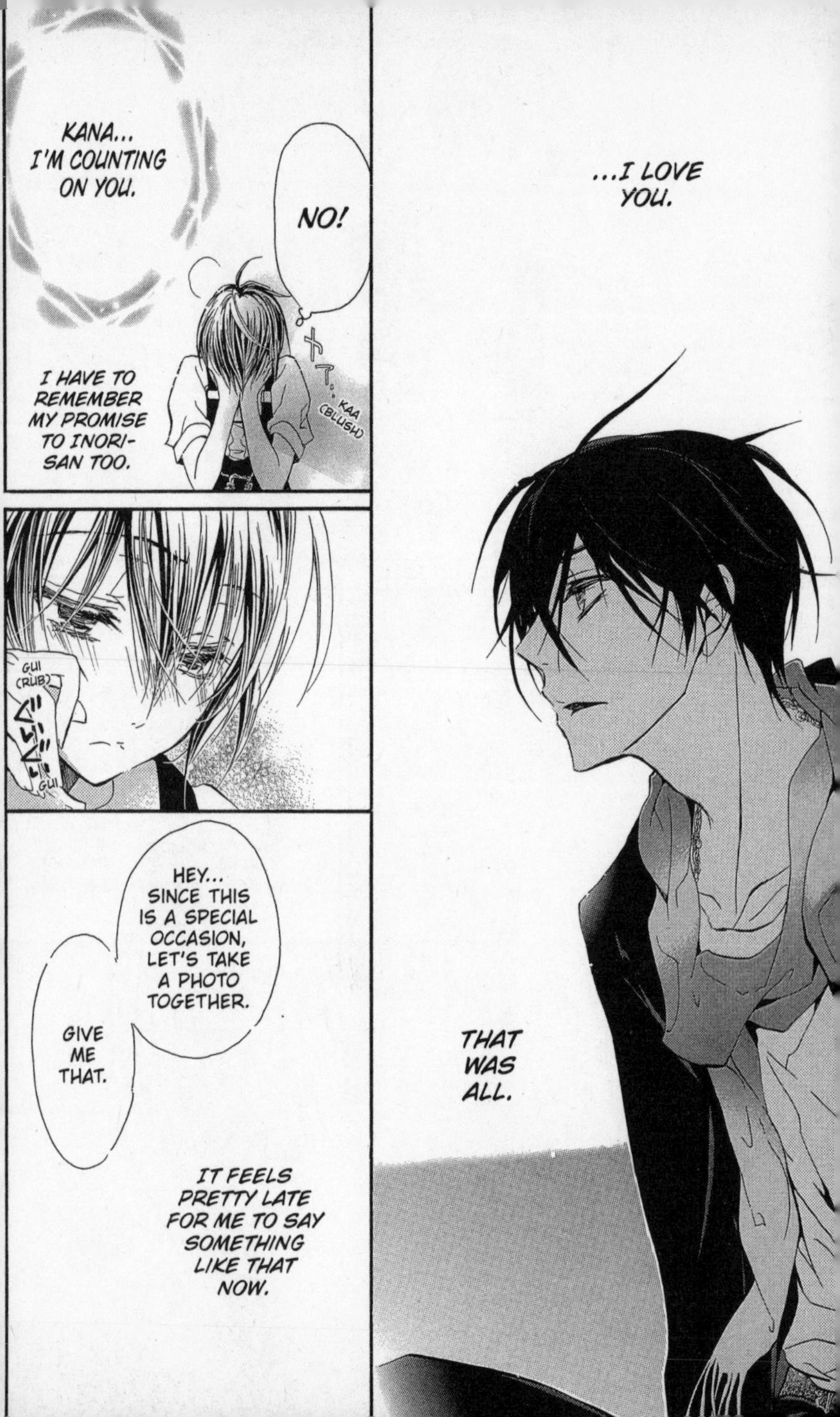
...I LOVE YOU.
THAT WAS ALL.
KANA... I'M COUNTING ON YOU.
NO!
KAA (BLUSH)
I HAVE TO REMEMBER MY PROMISE TO INORI-SAN TOO.
GUI (RUB)
GUI
HEY... SINCE THIS IS A SPECIAL OCCASION, LET'S TAKE A PHOTO TOGETHER.
GIVE ME THAT.
IT FEELS PRETTY LATE FOR ME TO SAY SOMETHING LIKE THAT NOW.

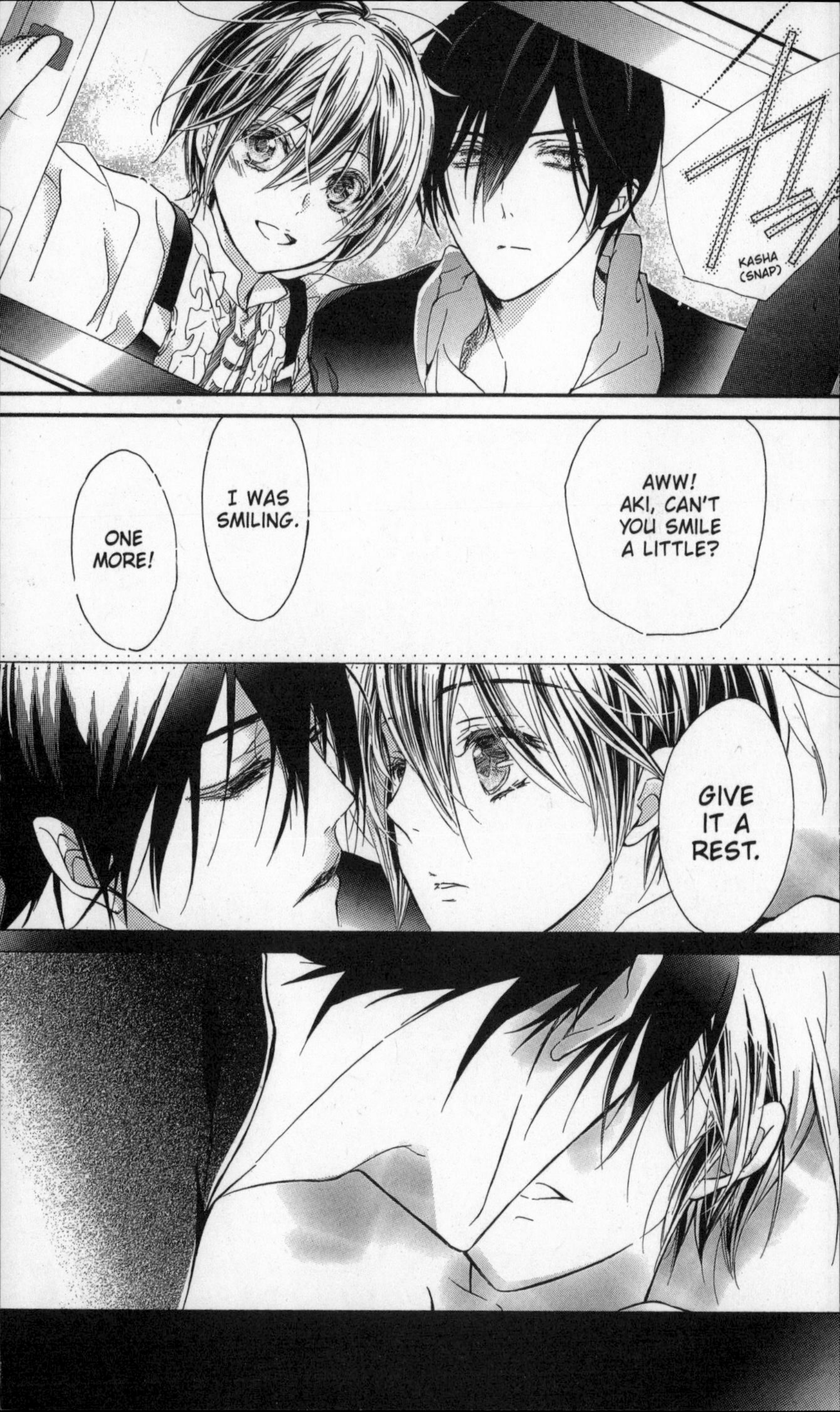
KASHA (SNAP)
AWW! AKI, CAN'T YOU SMILE A LITTLE?
I WAS SMILING.
ONE MORE!
GIVE IT A REST.

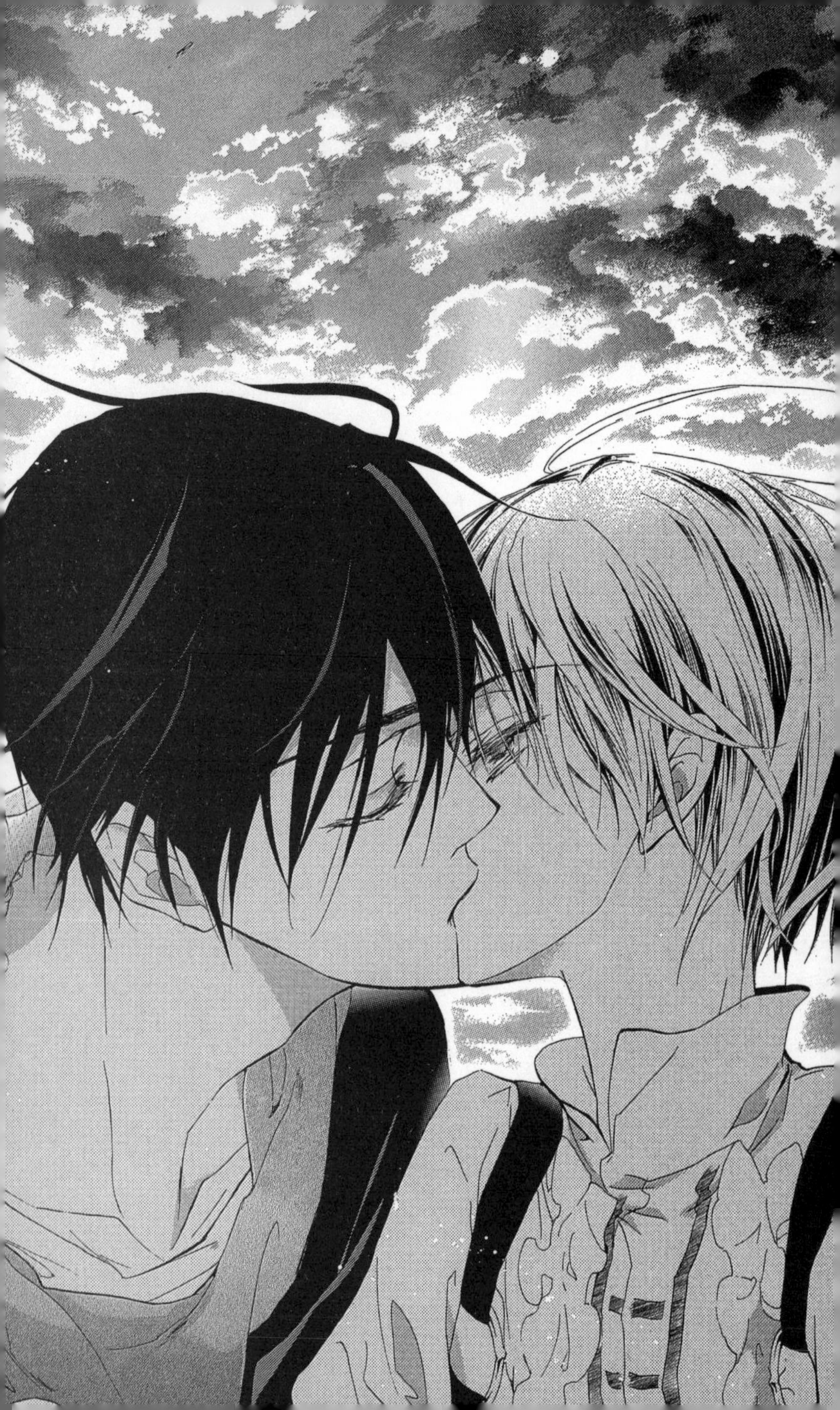

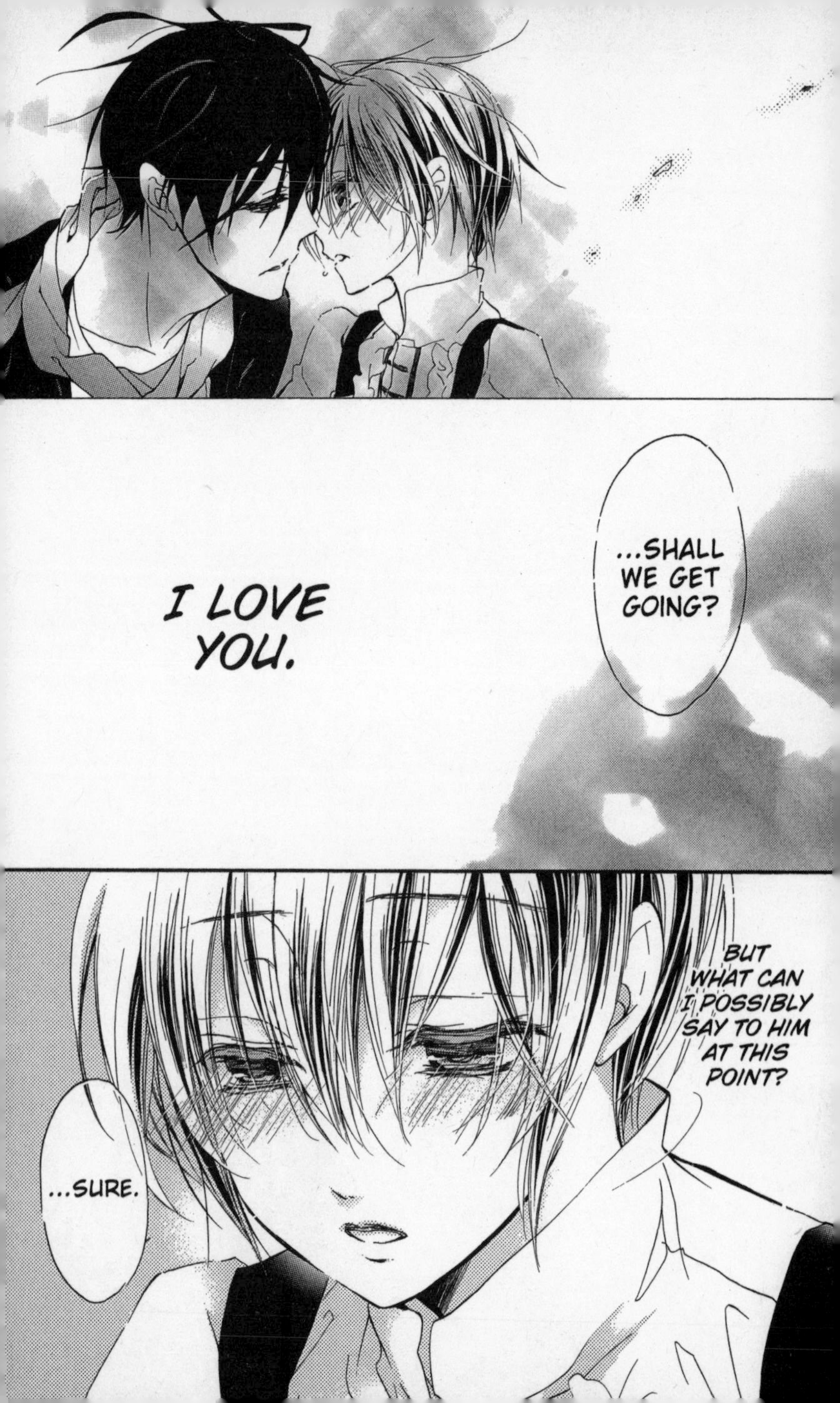
...SHALL WE GET GOING?
I LOVE YOU.
BUT WHAT CAN I POSSIBLY SAY TO HIM AT THIS POINT?
...SURE.

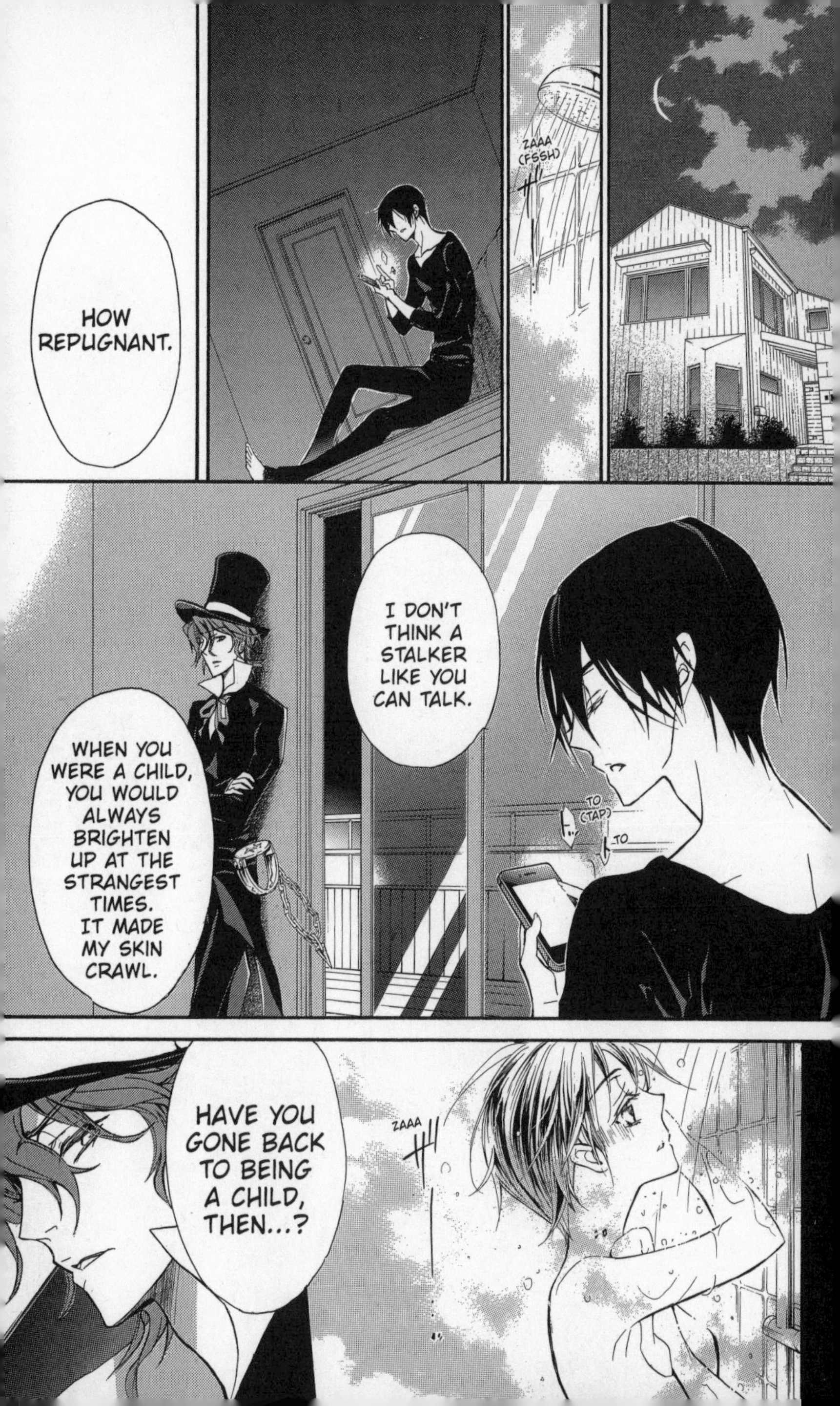

ZAAA (FSSH)
HOW REPUGNANT.
I DON'T THINK A STALKER LIKE YOU CAN TALK.
TO (TAP) TO
WHEN YOU WERE A CHILD, YOU WOULD ALWAYS BRIGHTEN UP AT THE STRANGEST TIMES. IT MADE MY SKIN CRAWL.
ZAAA
HAVE YOU GONE BACK TO BEING A CHILD, THEN...?

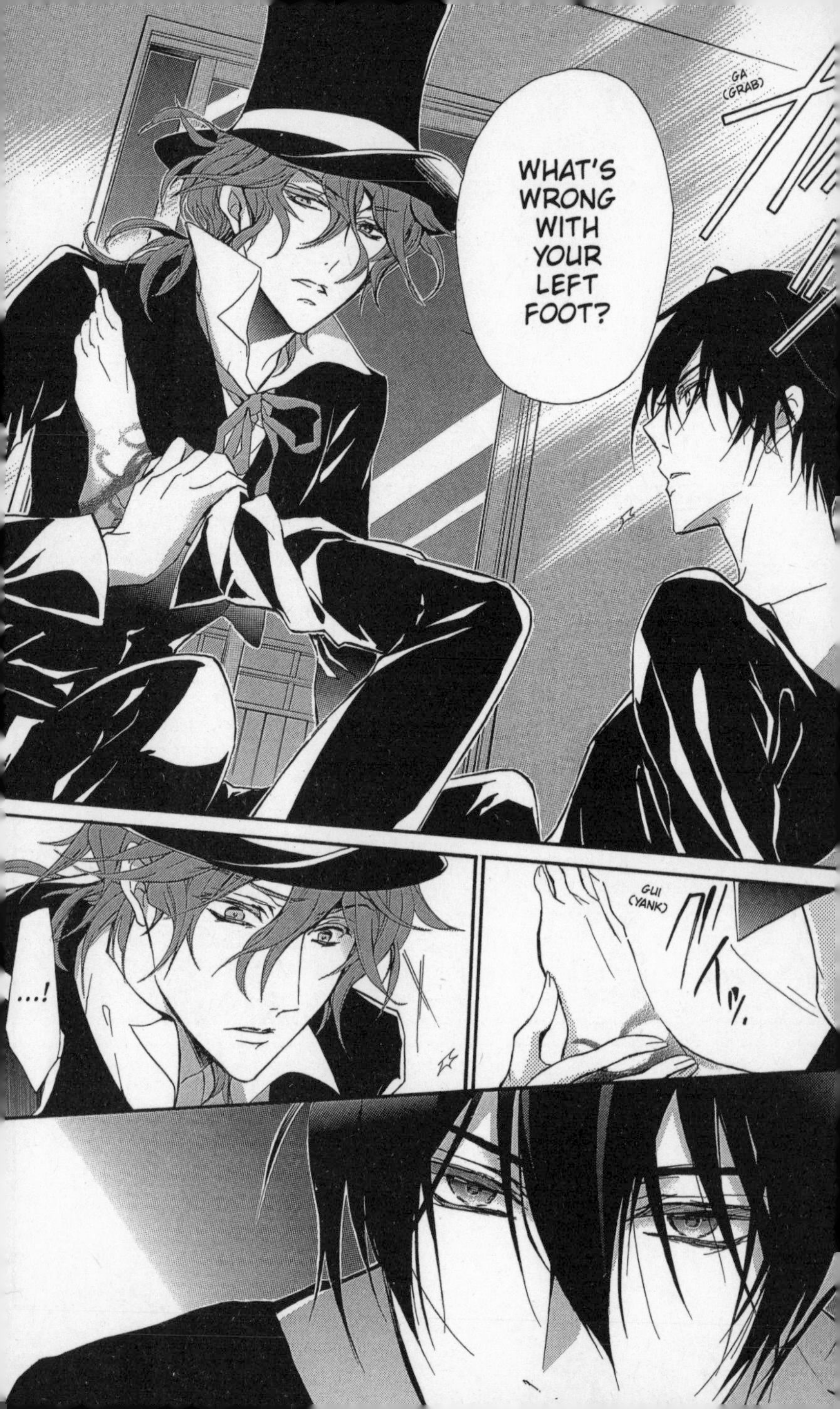
GA
(GRAB)
WHAT'S WRONG WITH YOUR LEFT FOOT?
GUI
(YANK)
...!

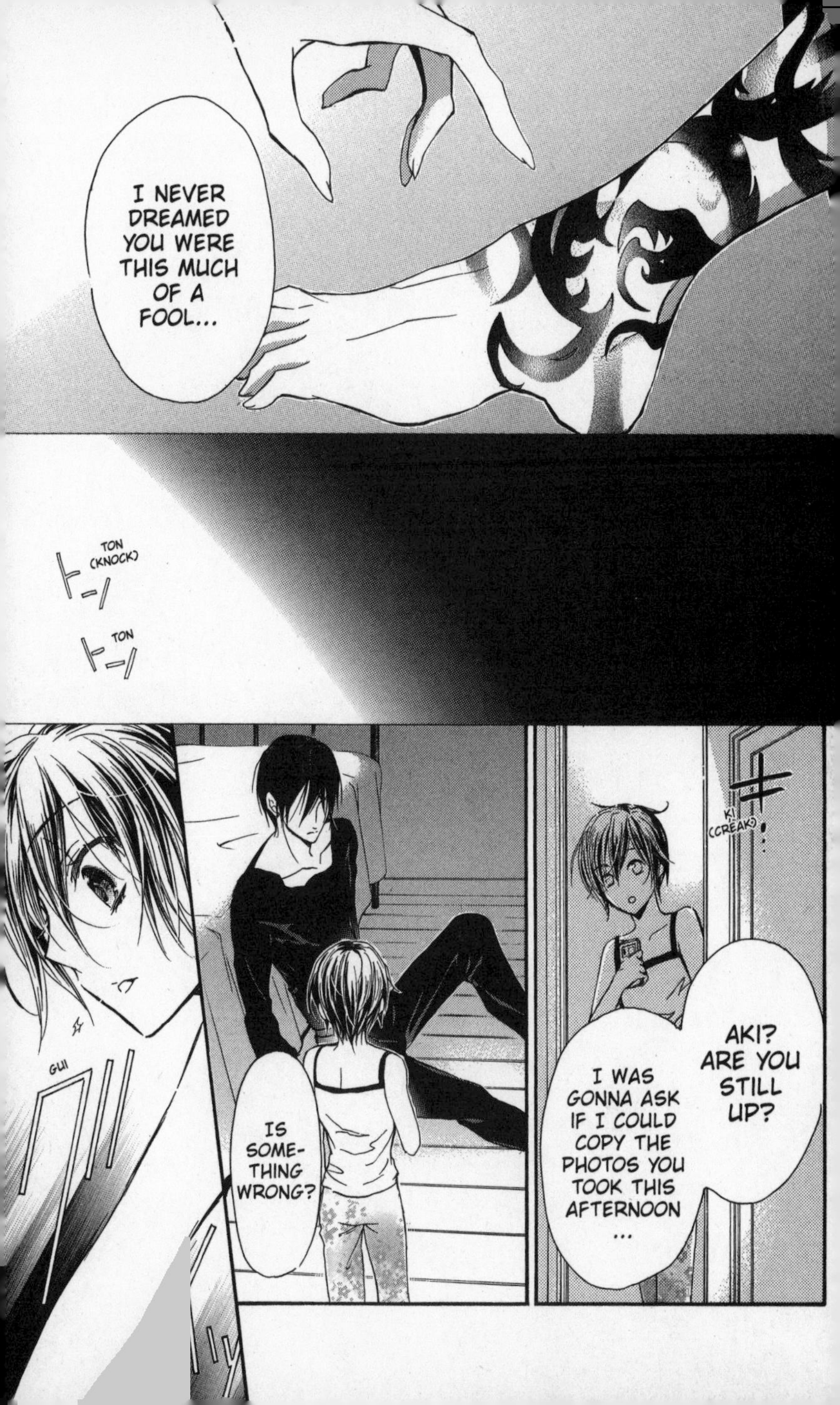
I NEVER DREAMED YOU WERE THIS MUCH OF A FOOL...
TON (KNOCK)
TON
KI (CREAK)
AKI? ARE YOU STILL UP?
I WAS GONNA ASK IF I COULD COPY THE PHOTOS YOU TOOK THIS AFTERNOON ...
IS SOME-THING WRONG?
GUI

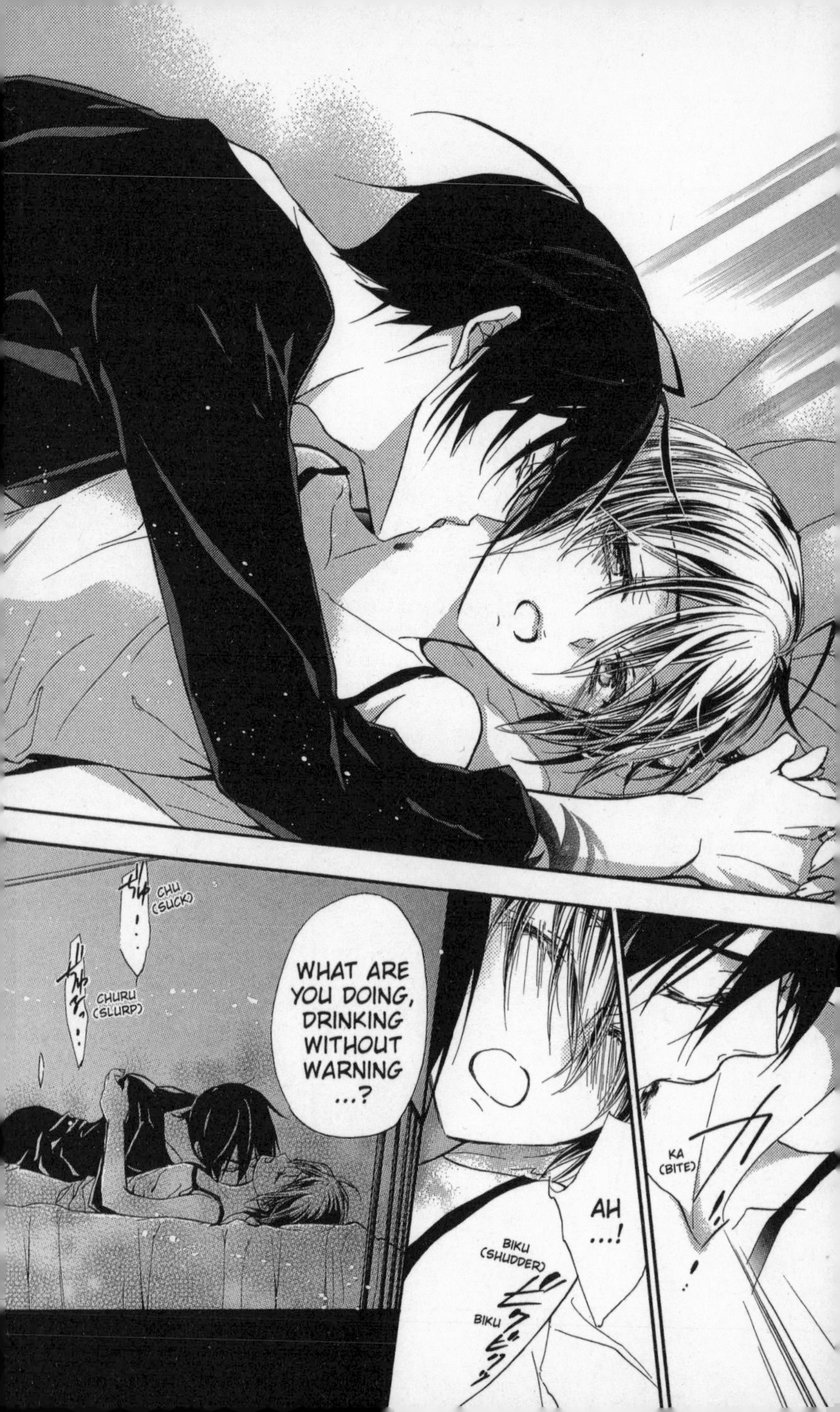
KA
(BITE)
AH
...!
BIKU
(SHUDDER)
BIKU
WHAT ARE YOU DOING, DRINKING WITHOUT WARNING ...?
CHU
(SUCK)
CHURU
(SLURP)

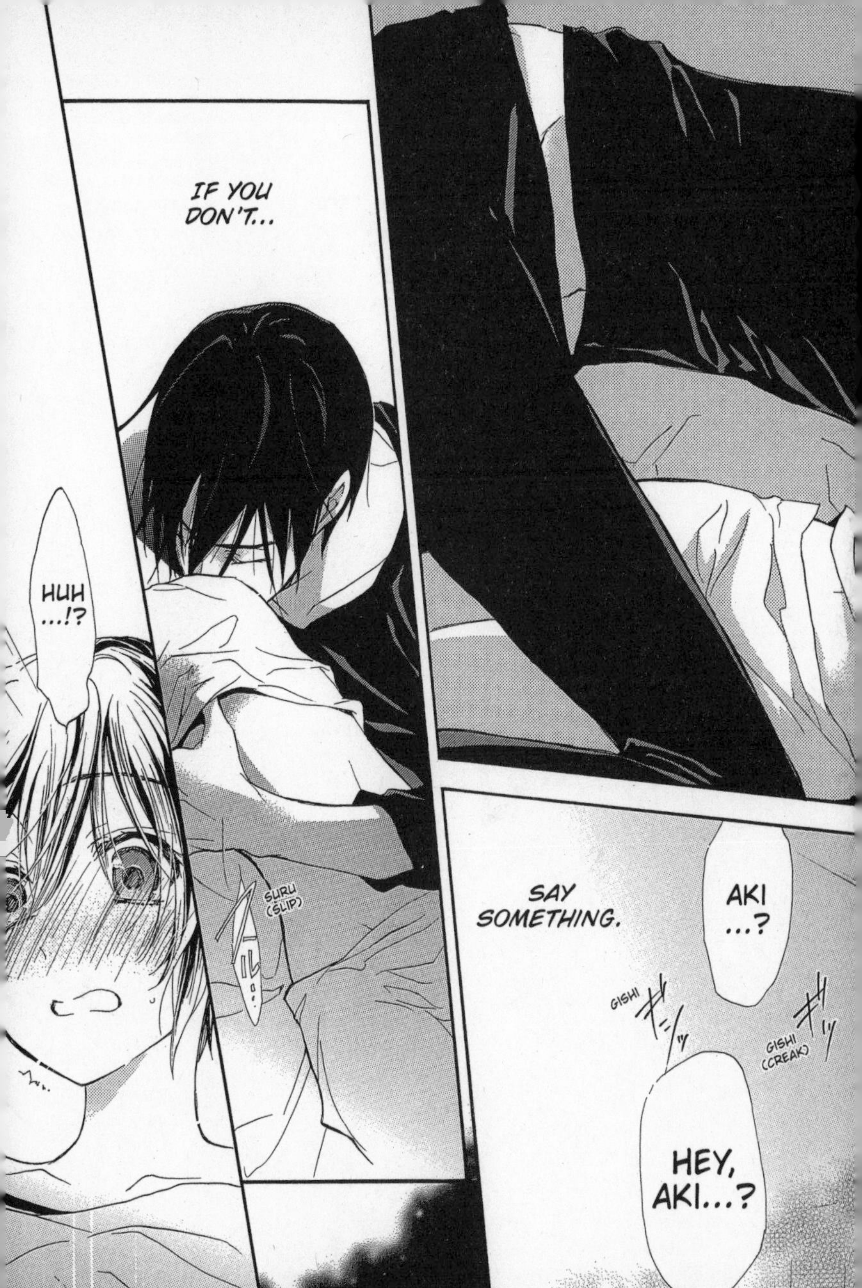
AKI ...?
SAY SOMETHING.
GISHI (CREAK)
GISHI
HEY, AKI...?
IF YOU DON'T...
HUH ...!?
SURU (SLIP)

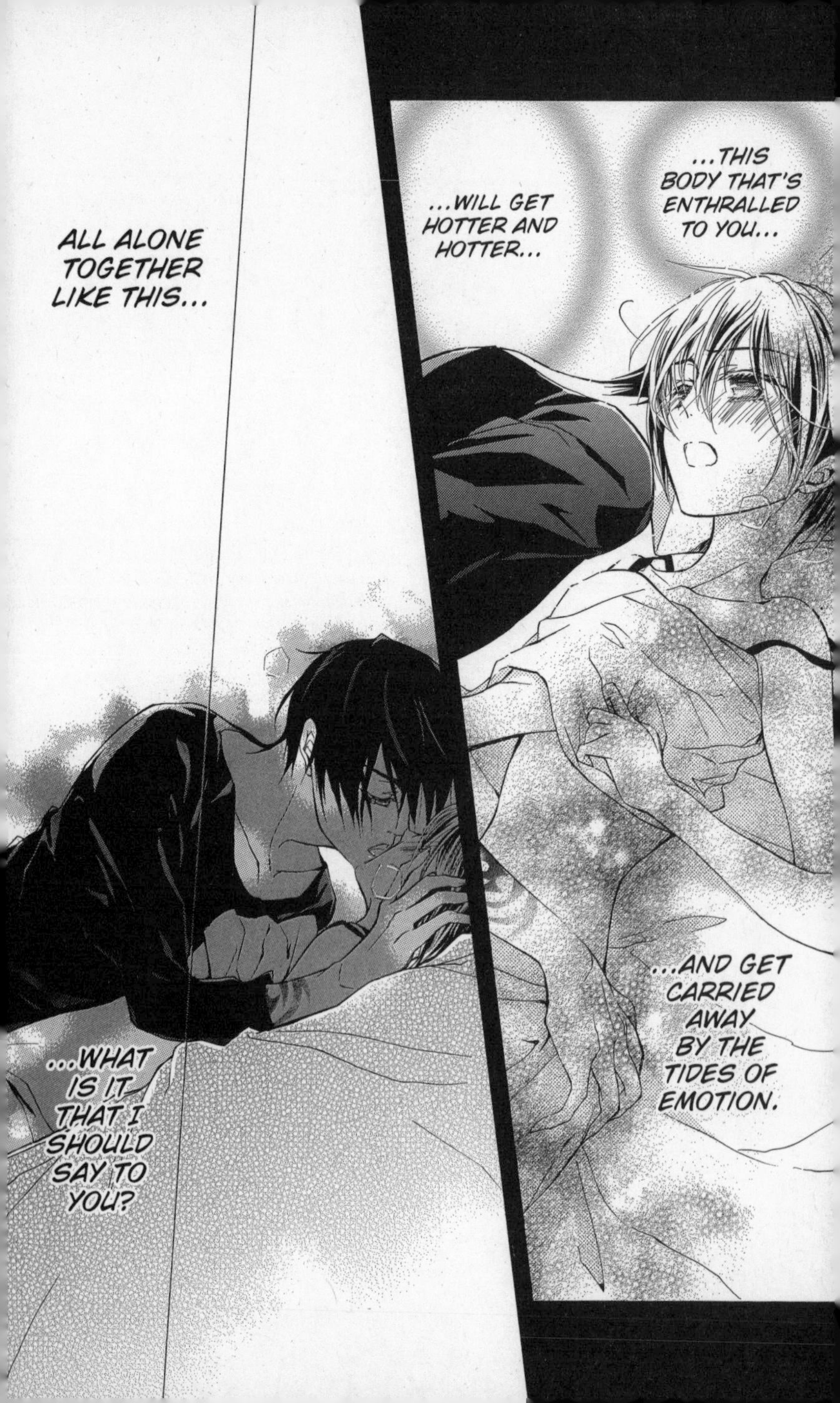
...THIS BODY THAT'S ENTHRALLED TO YOU...
...WILL GET HOTTER AND HOTTER...
...AND GET CARRIED AWAY BY THE TIDES OF EMOTION.
ALL ALONE TOGETHER LIKE THIS...
...WHAT IS IT THAT I SHOULD SAY TO YOU?

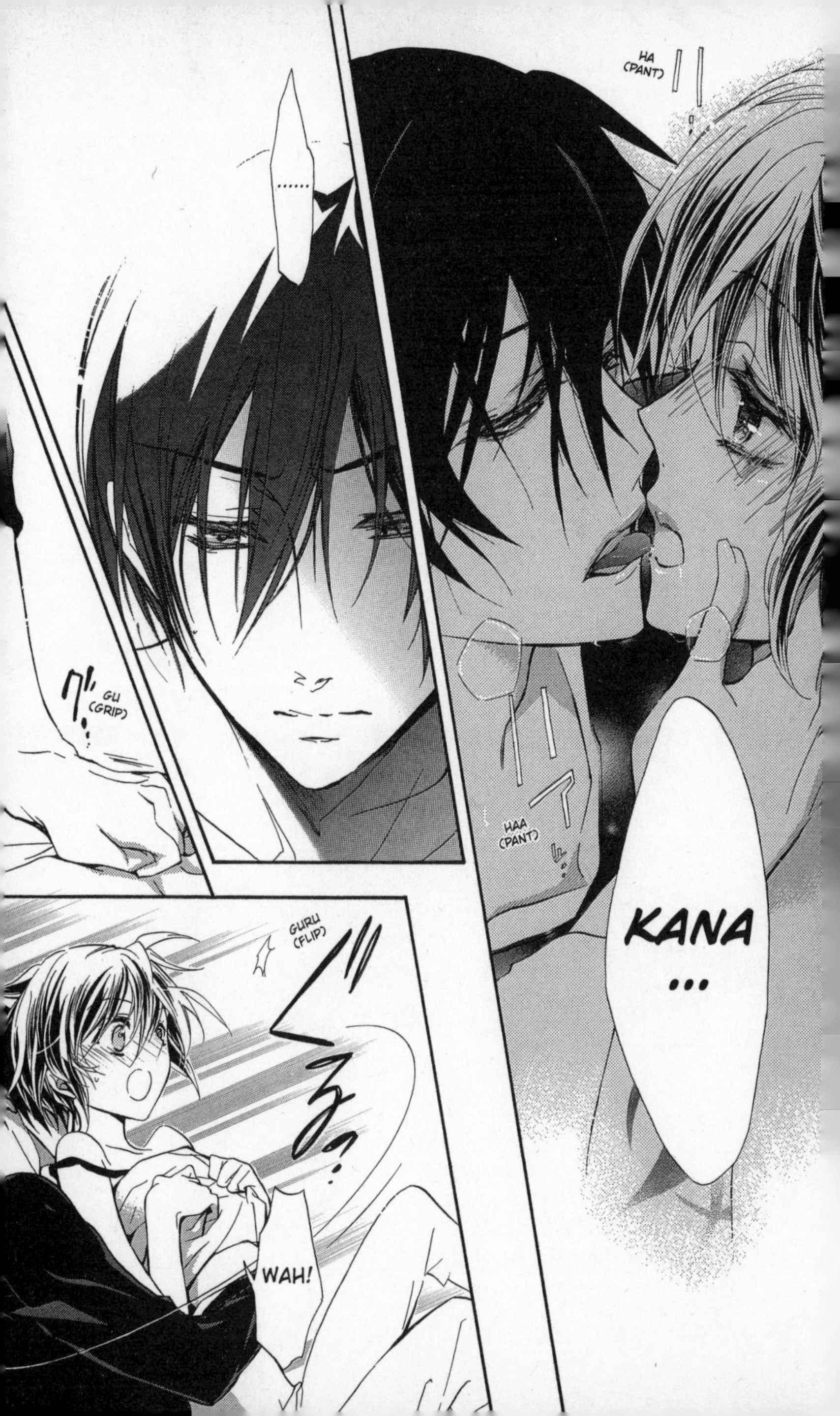
HA (PANT)
HAA (PANT)
KANA ...
......
GU (GRIP)
GURU (FLIP)
WAH!

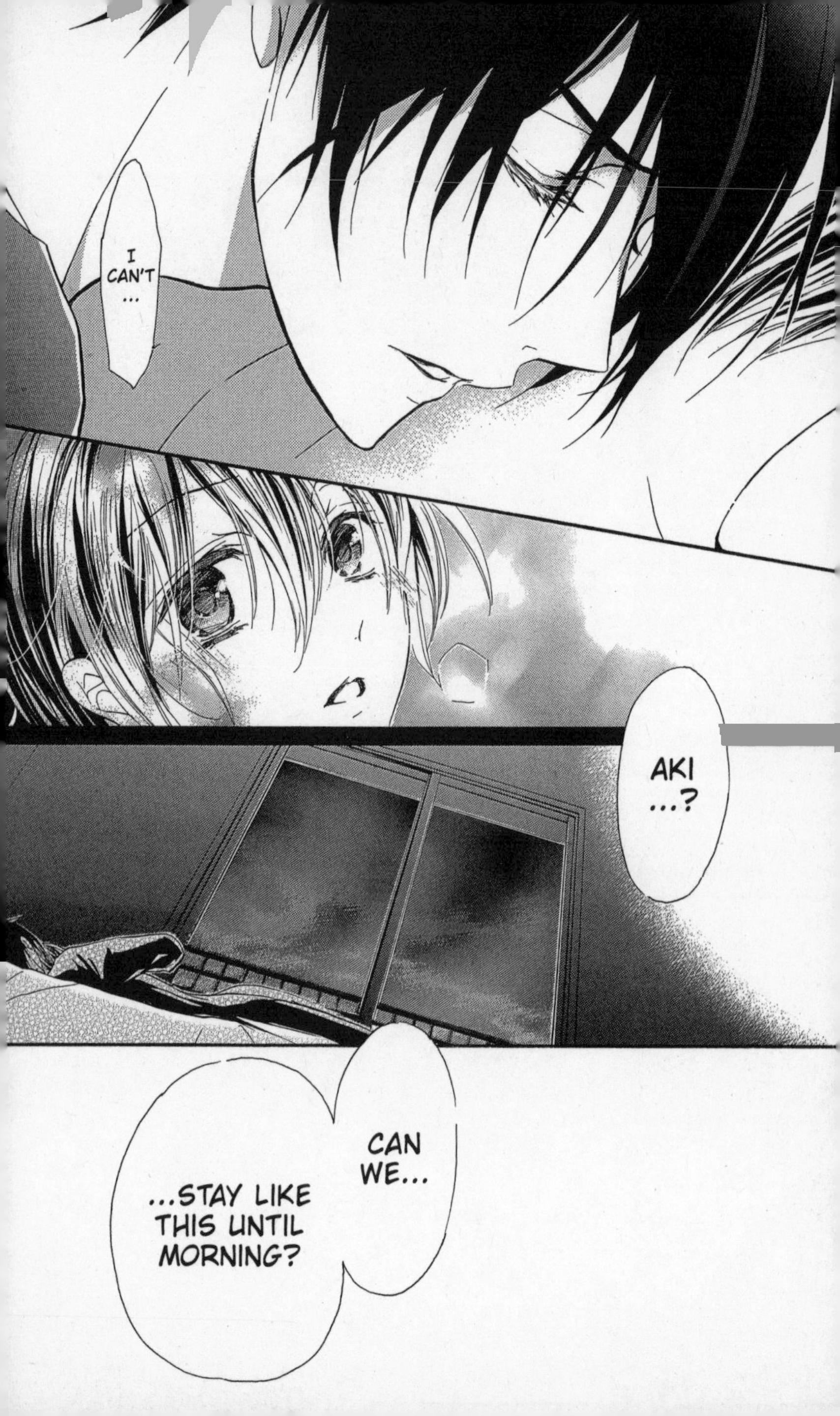
I CAN'T ...
AKI ...?
CAN WE...
...STAY LIKE THIS UNTIL MORNING?

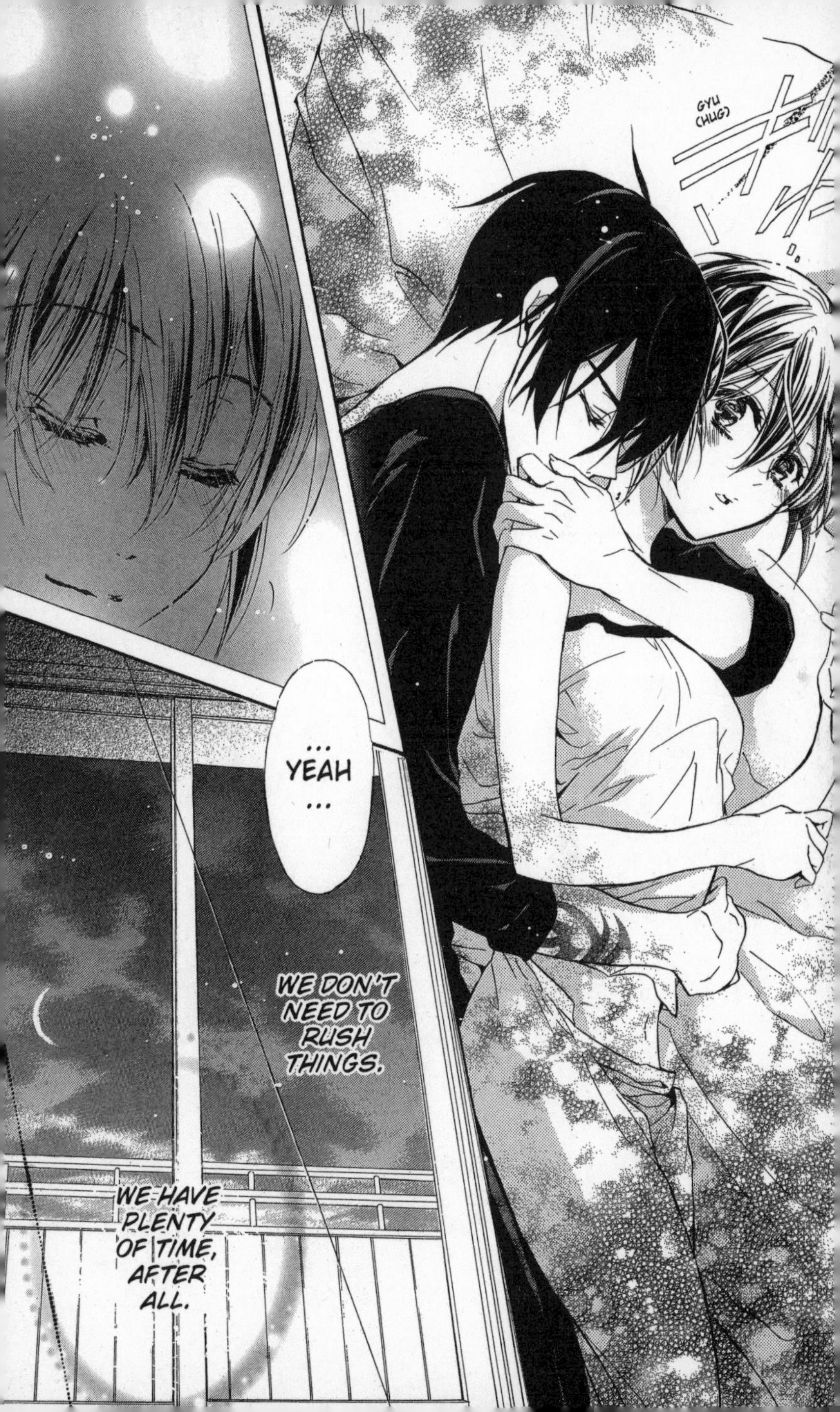
GYU (HUG)
... YEAH ...
WE DON'T NEED TO RUSH THINGS.
WE HAVE PLENTY OF TIME, AFTER ALL.

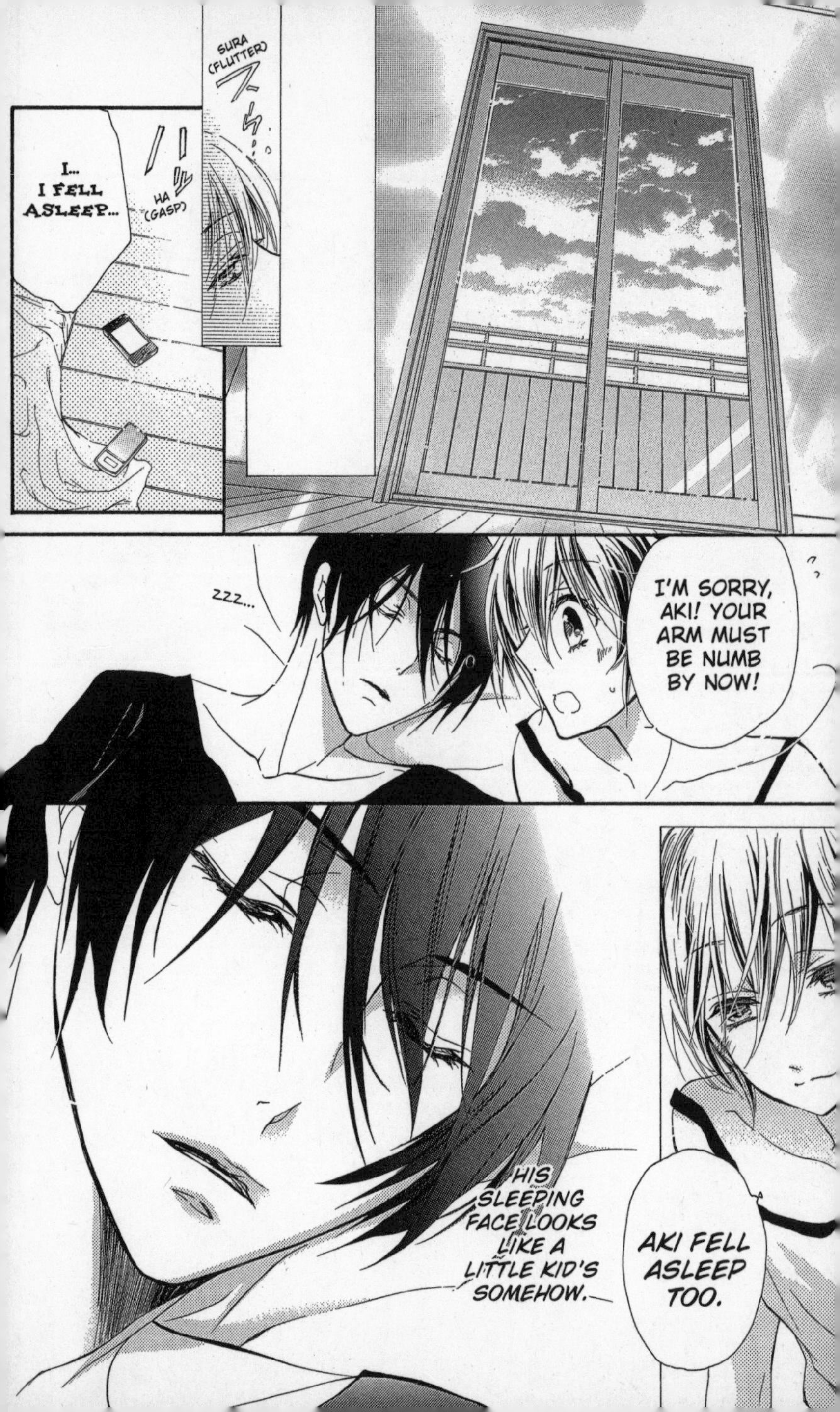
SURA (FLUTTER)
HA (GASP)
I... I FELL ASLEEP...
I'M SORRY, AKI! YOUR ARM MUST BE NUMB BY NOW!
ZZZ...
AKI FELL ASLEEP TOO.
HIS SLEEPING FACE LOOKS LIKE A LITTLE KID'S SOMEHOW.

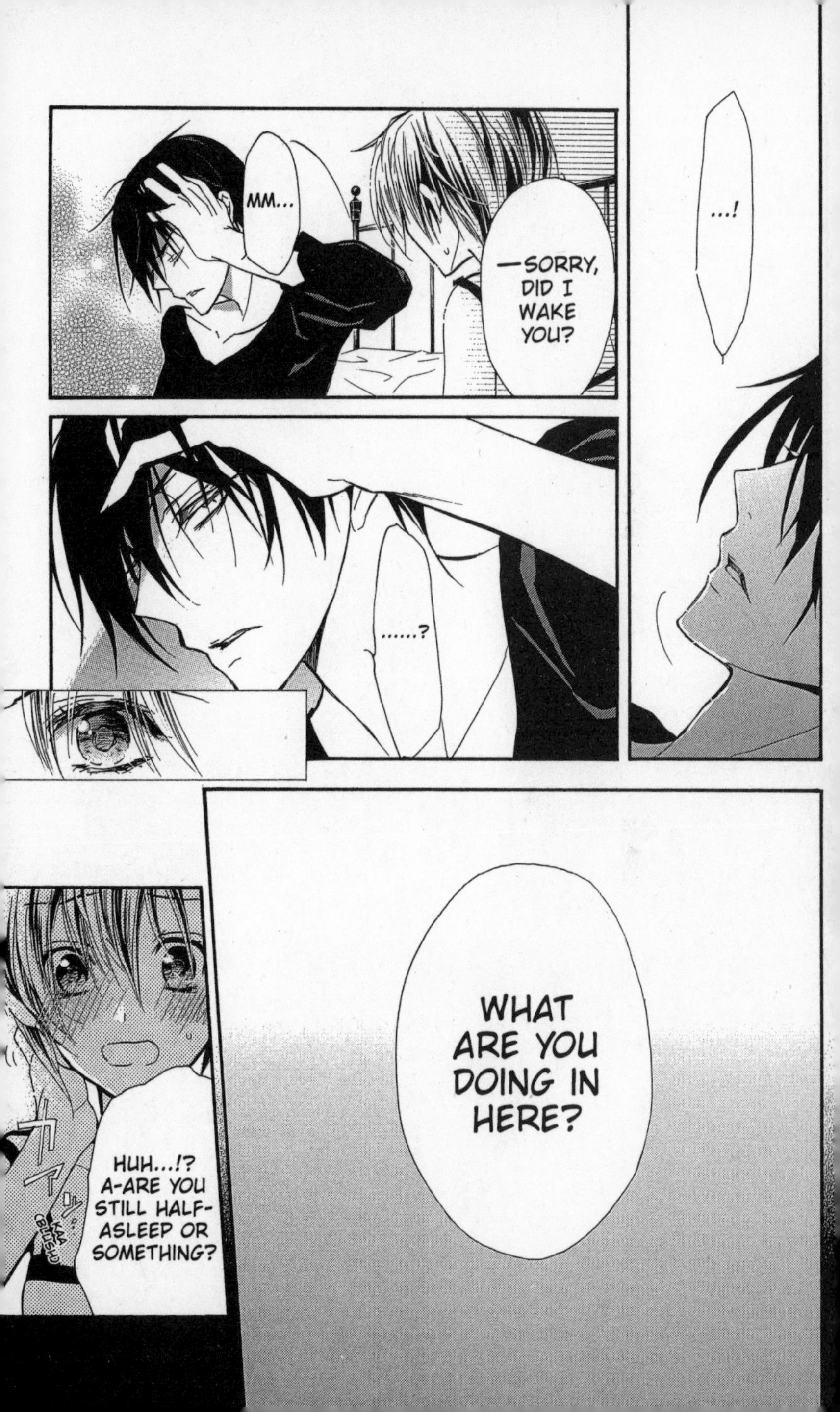
...!
MM...
—SORRY, DID I WAKE YOU?
......?
WHAT ARE YOU DOING IN HERE?
HUH...!? A-ARE YOU STILL HALF-ASLEEP OR SOMETHING?
KAA (BLUSH)

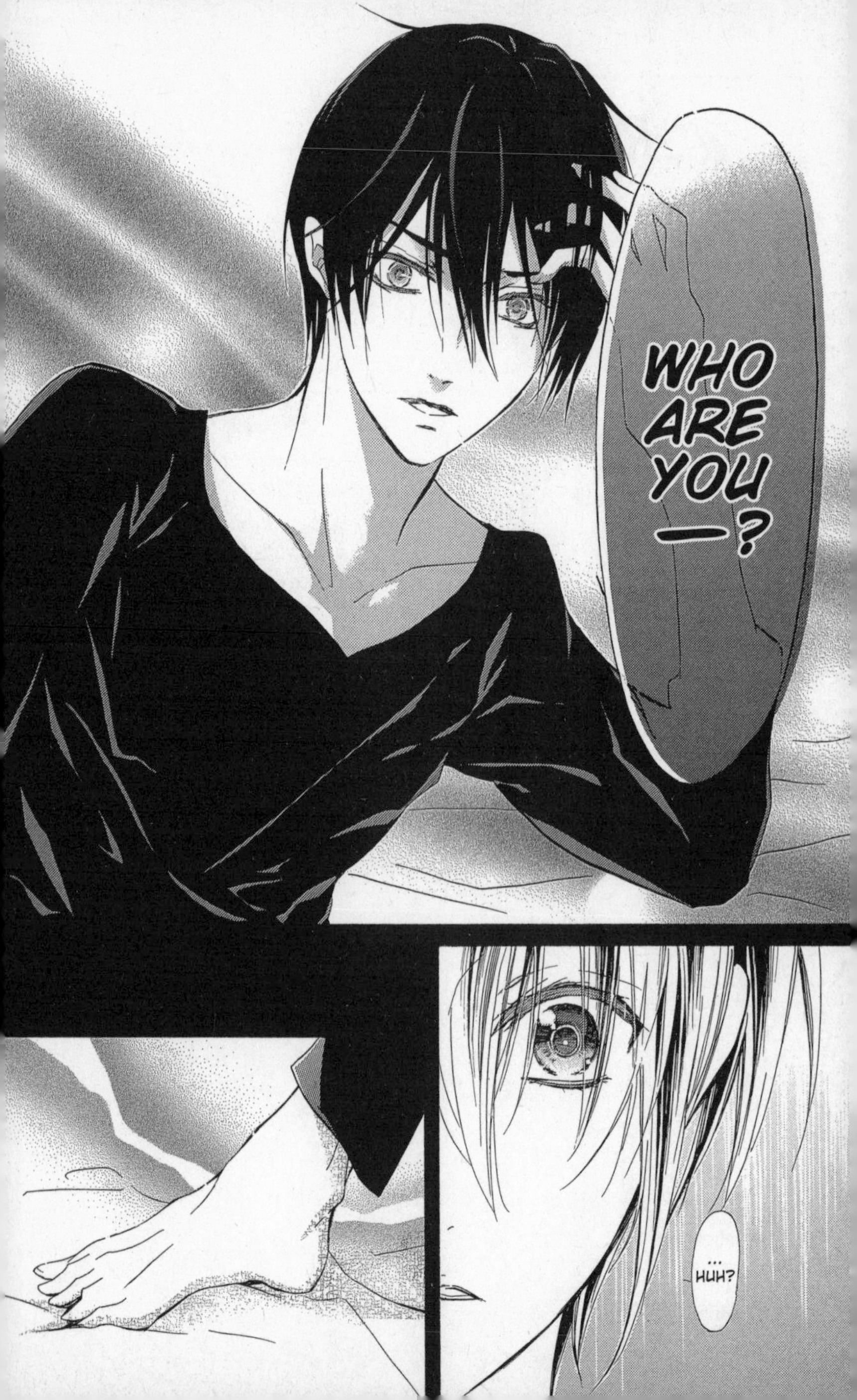
WHO ARE YOU—?
...HUH?

He's my only vampire
Aya Shouoto

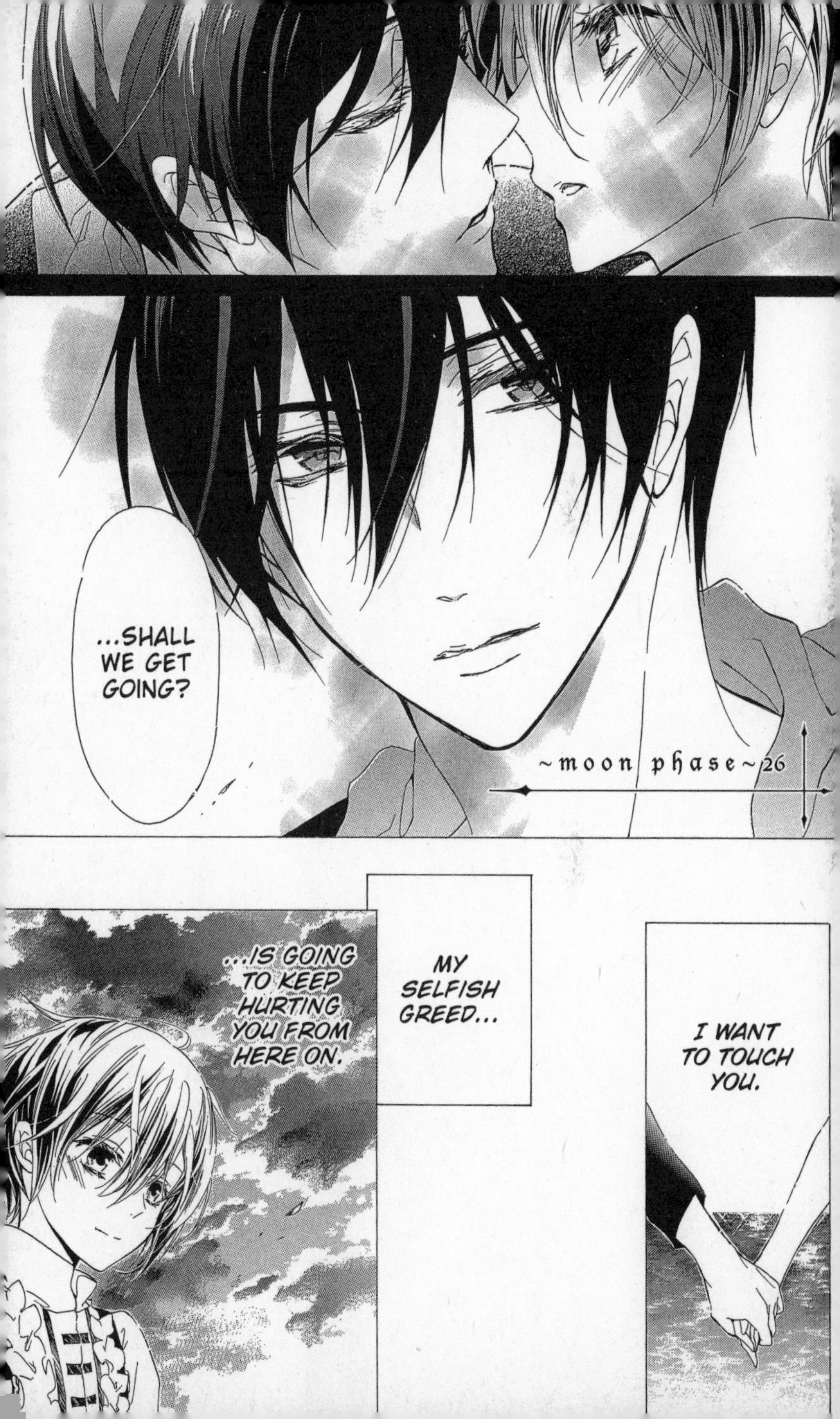
...SHALL WE GET GOING?
~moon phase~26
I WANT TO TOUCH YOU.
MY SELFISH GREED...
...IS GOING TO KEEP HURTING YOU FROM HERE ON.

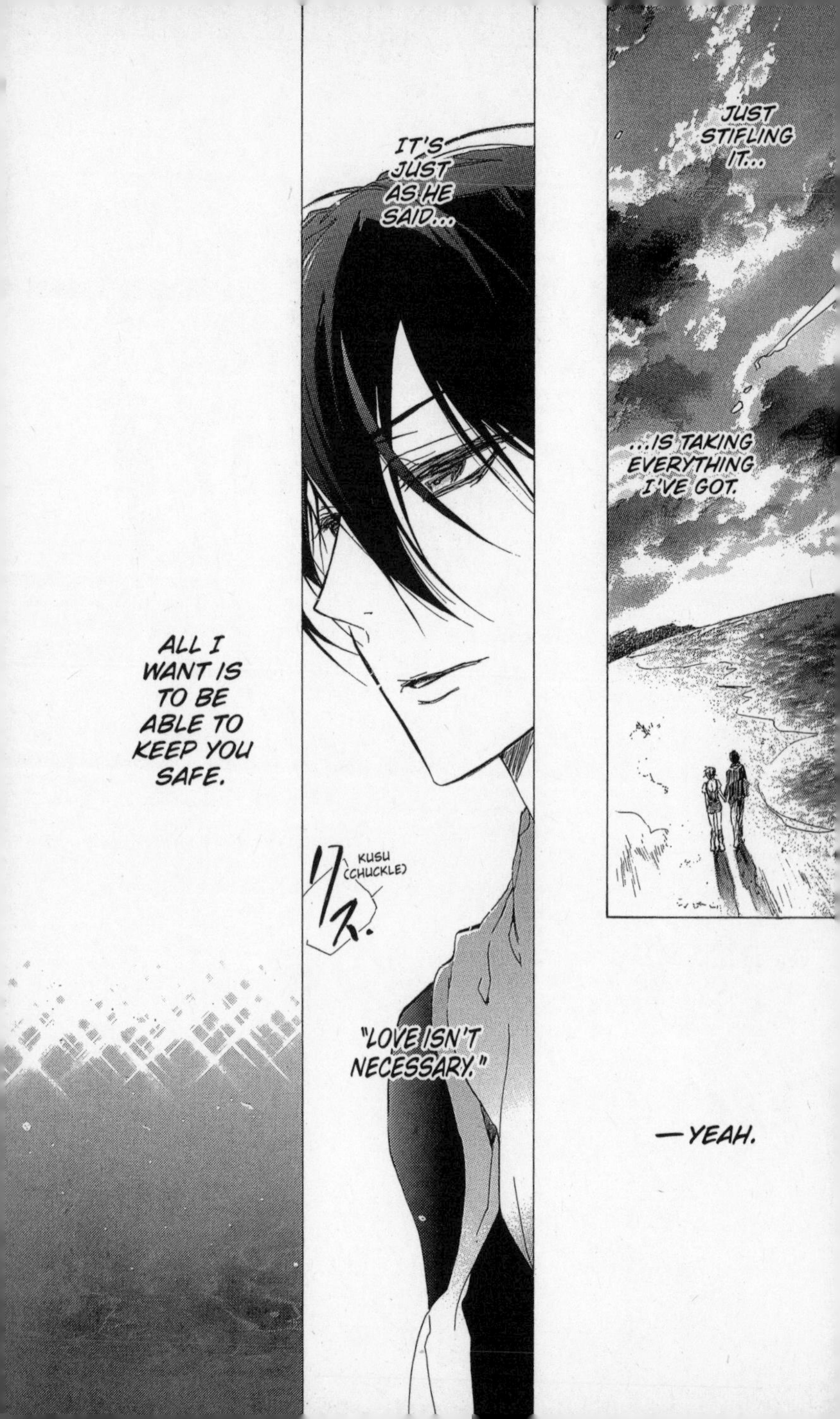
JUST STIFLING IT...
...IS TAKING EVERYTHING I'VE GOT.
—YEAH.
IT'S JUST AS HE SAID...
KUSU (CHUCKLE)
"LOVE ISN'T NECESSARY."
ALL I WANT IS TO BE ABLE TO KEEP YOU SAFE.

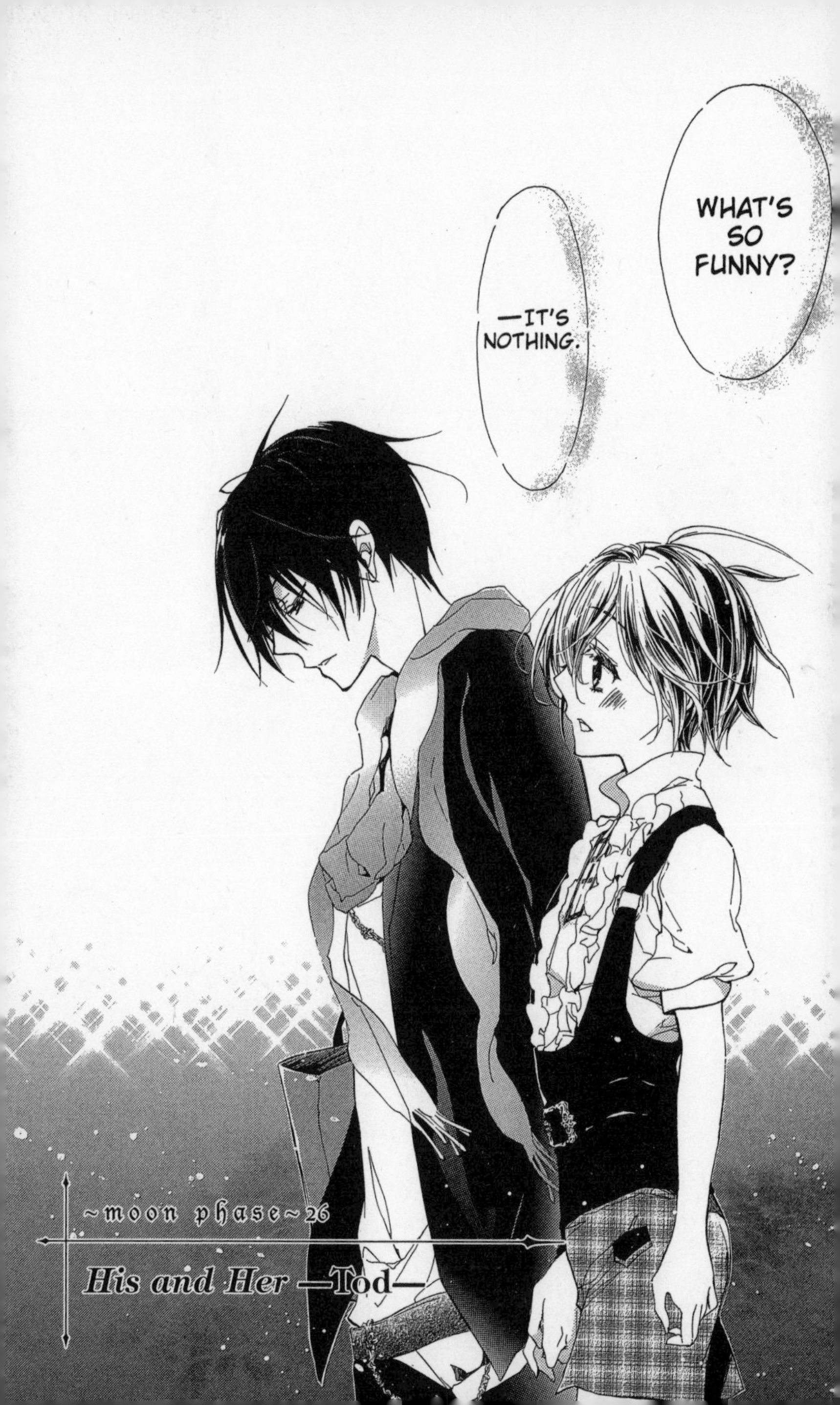
WHAT'S SO FUNNY?
—IT'S NOTHING.
~moon phase~26
His and Her —Tod—

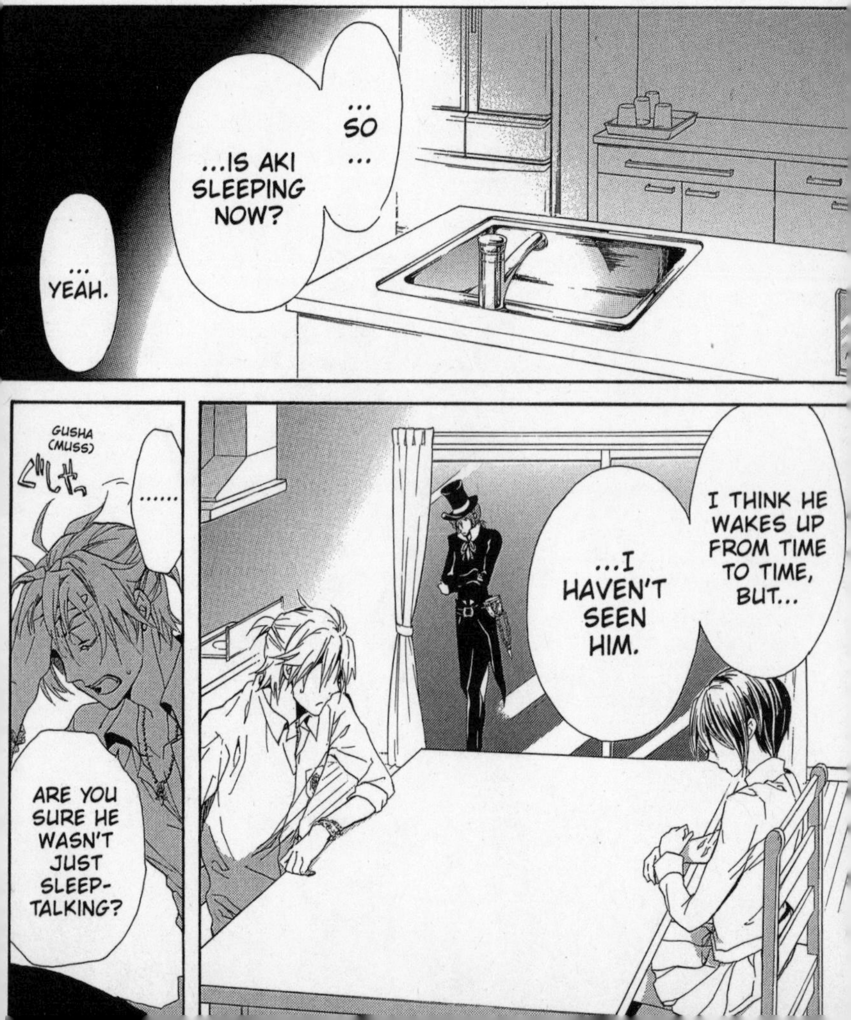
...SO...
...IS AKI SLEEPING NOW?
...YEAH.
I THINK HE WAKES UP FROM TIME TO TIME, BUT...
...I HAVEN'T SEEN HIM.
GUSHA (MUSS)
ぐしゃ
......
ARE YOU SURE HE WASN'T JUST SLEEP-TALKING?

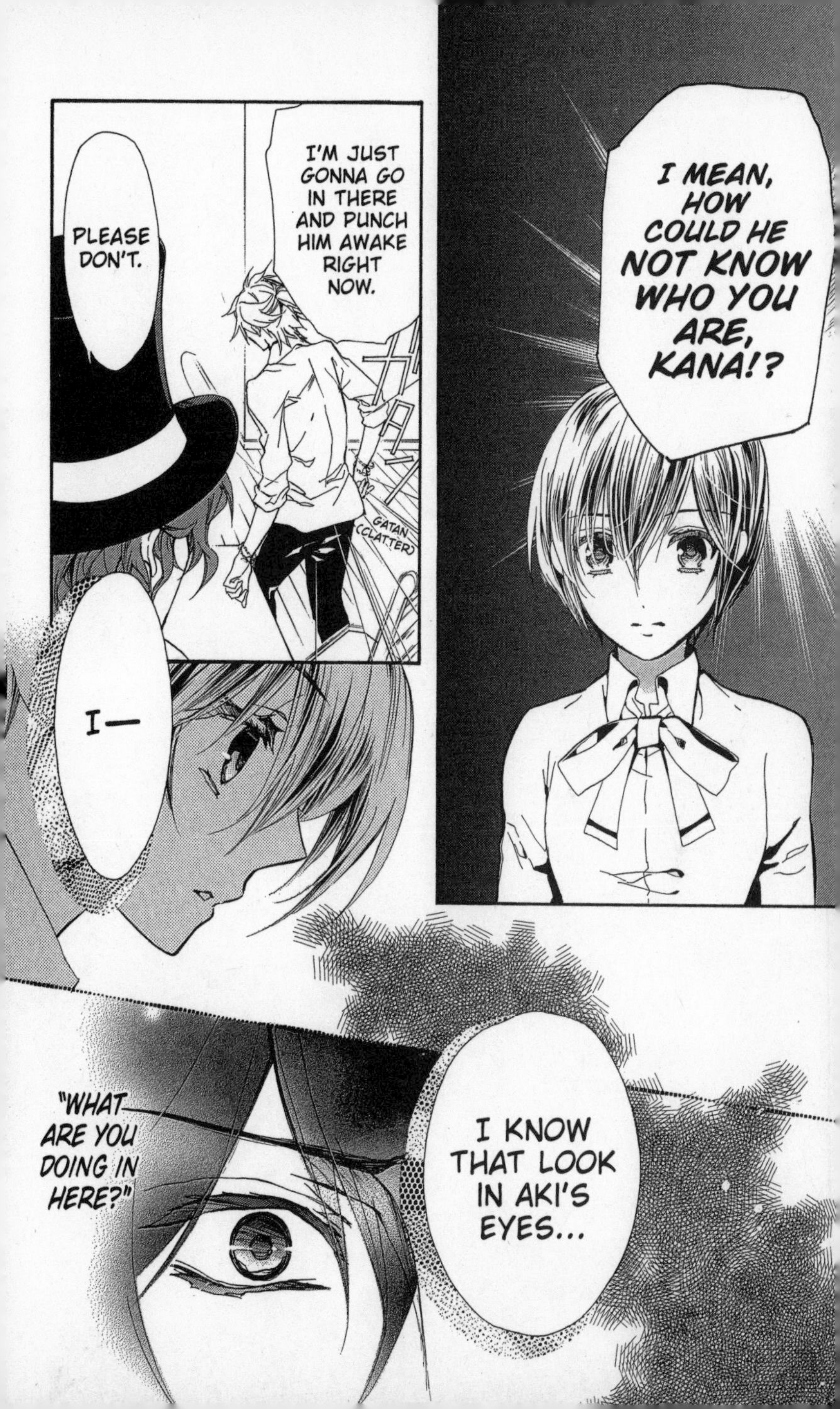
I MEAN, HOW COULD HE NOT KNOW WHO YOU ARE, KANA!?
I'M JUST GONNA GO IN THERE AND PUNCH HIM AWAKE RIGHT NOW.
PLEASE DON'T.
GATAN (CLATTER)
I—
I KNOW THAT LOOK IN AKI'S EYES...
"WHAT ARE YOU DOING IN HERE?"

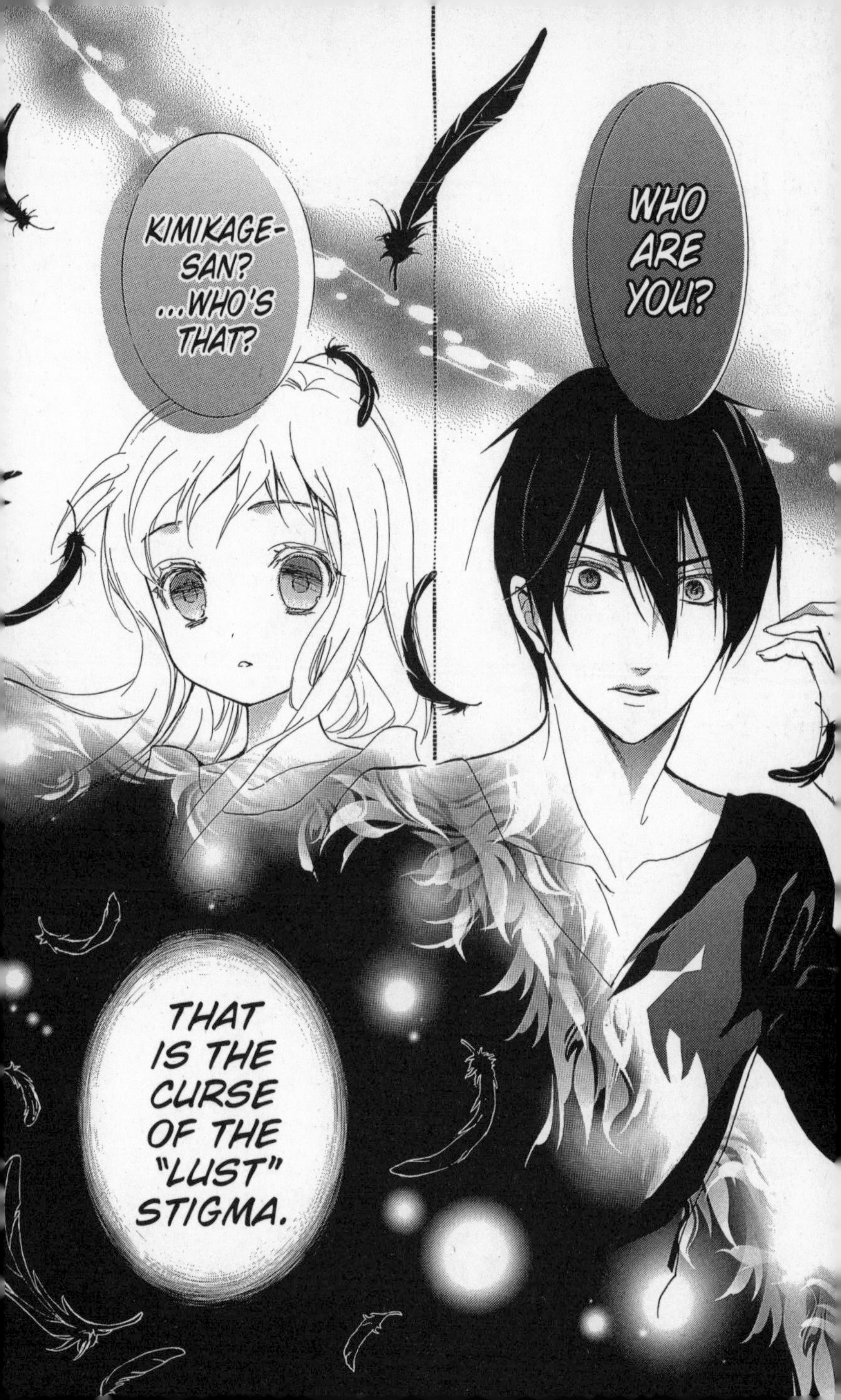
WHO ARE YOU?
KIMIKAGE-SAN? ...WHO'S THAT?
THAT IS THE CURSE OF THE "LUST" STIGMA.

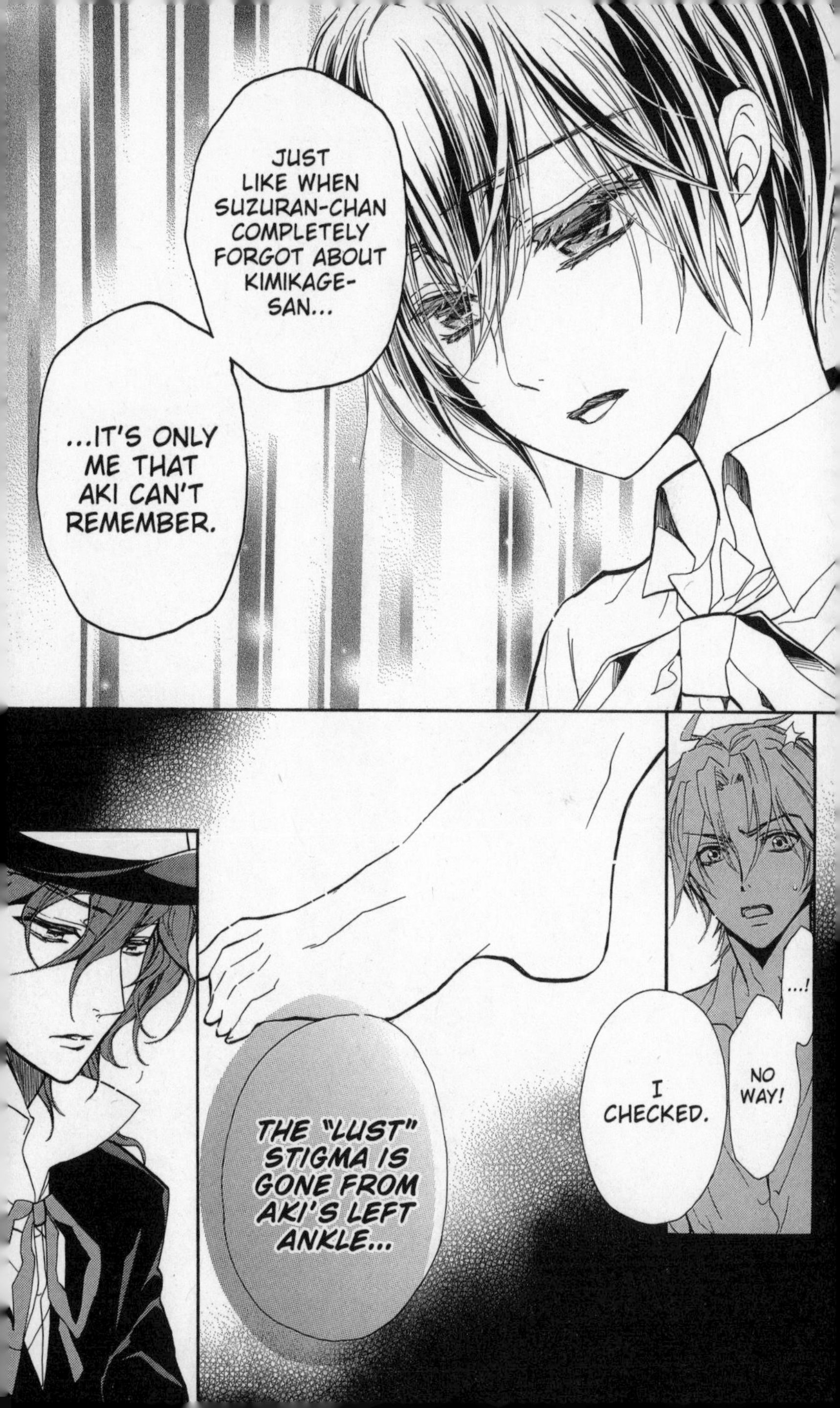

JUST LIKE WHEN SUZURAN-CHAN COMPLETELY FORGOT ABOUT KIMIKAGE-SAN...
...IT'S ONLY ME THAT AKI CAN'T REMEMBER.
...!
NO WAY!
I CHECKED.
THE "LUST" STIGMA IS GONE FROM AKI'S LEFT ANKLE...

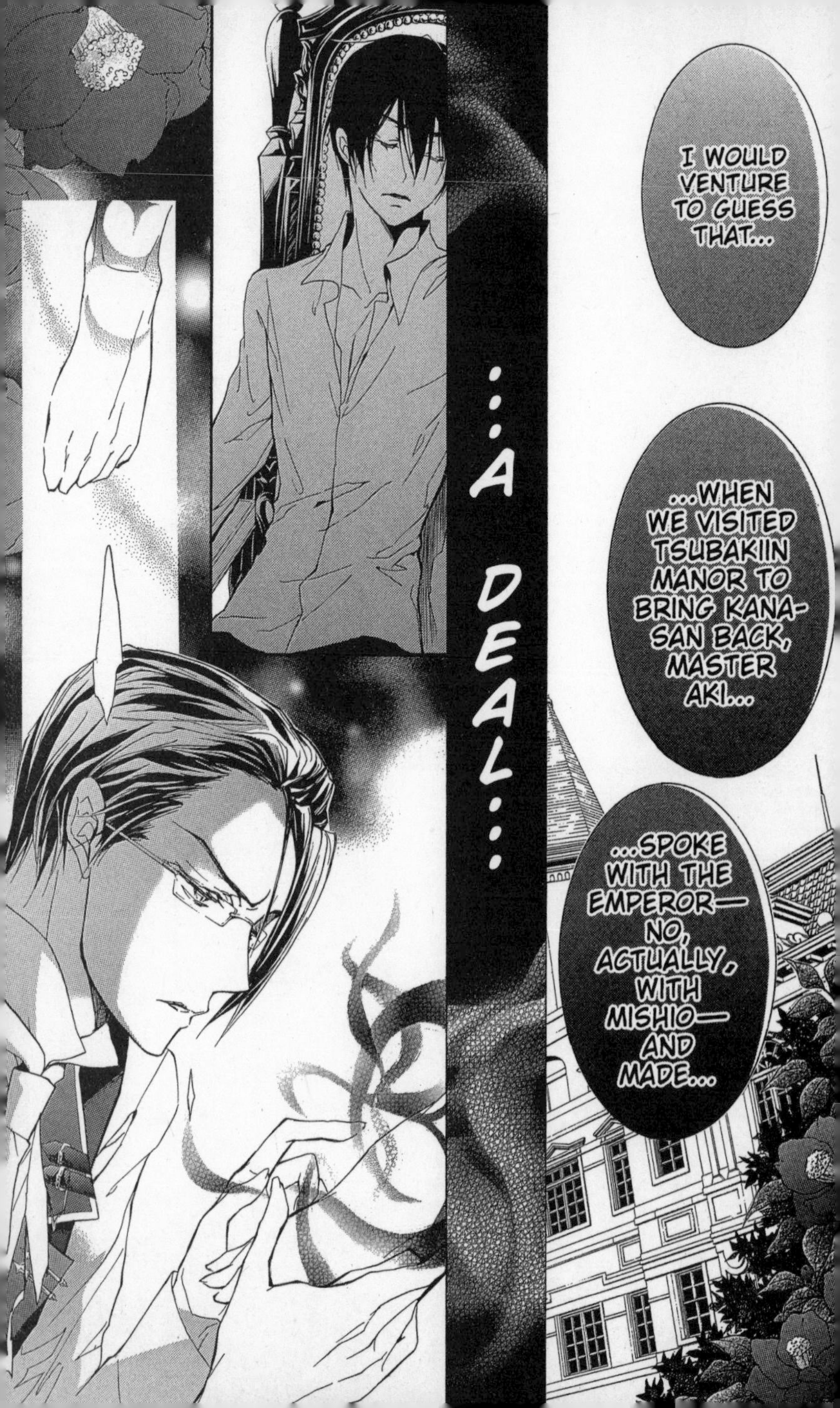
I WOULD VENTURE TO GUESS THAT...
...WHEN WE VISITED TSUBAKIIN MANOR TO BRING KANA-SAN BACK, MASTER AKI...
...SPOKE WITH THE EMPEROR— NO, ACTUALLY, WITH MISHIO— AND MADE...
...A DEAL...

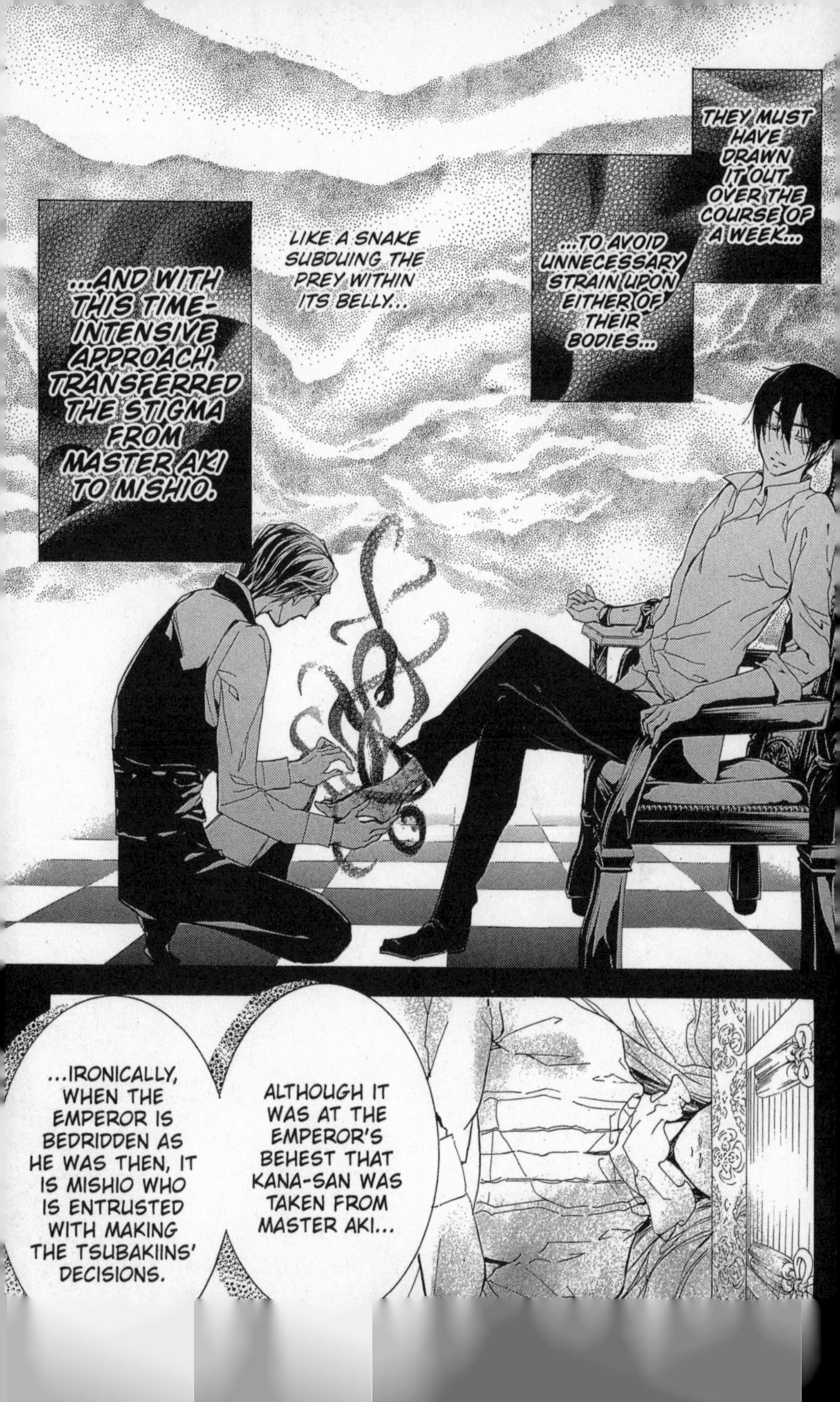
THEY MUST HAVE DRAWN IT OUT OVER THE COURSE OF A WEEK...
...TO AVOID UNNECESSARY STRAIN UPON EITHER OF THEIR BODIES...
LIKE A SNAKE SUBDUING THE PREY WITHIN ITS BELLY...
...AND WITH THIS TIME-INTENSIVE APPROACH, TRANSFERRED THE STIGMA FROM MASTER AKI TO MISHIO.
ALTHOUGH IT WAS AT THE EMPEROR'S BEHEST THAT KANA-SAN WAS TAKEN FROM MASTER AKI...
...IRONICALLY, WHEN THE EMPEROR IS BEDRIDDEN AS HE WAS THEN, IT IS MISHIO WHO IS ENTRUSTED WITH MAKING THE TSUBAKIINS' DECISIONS.

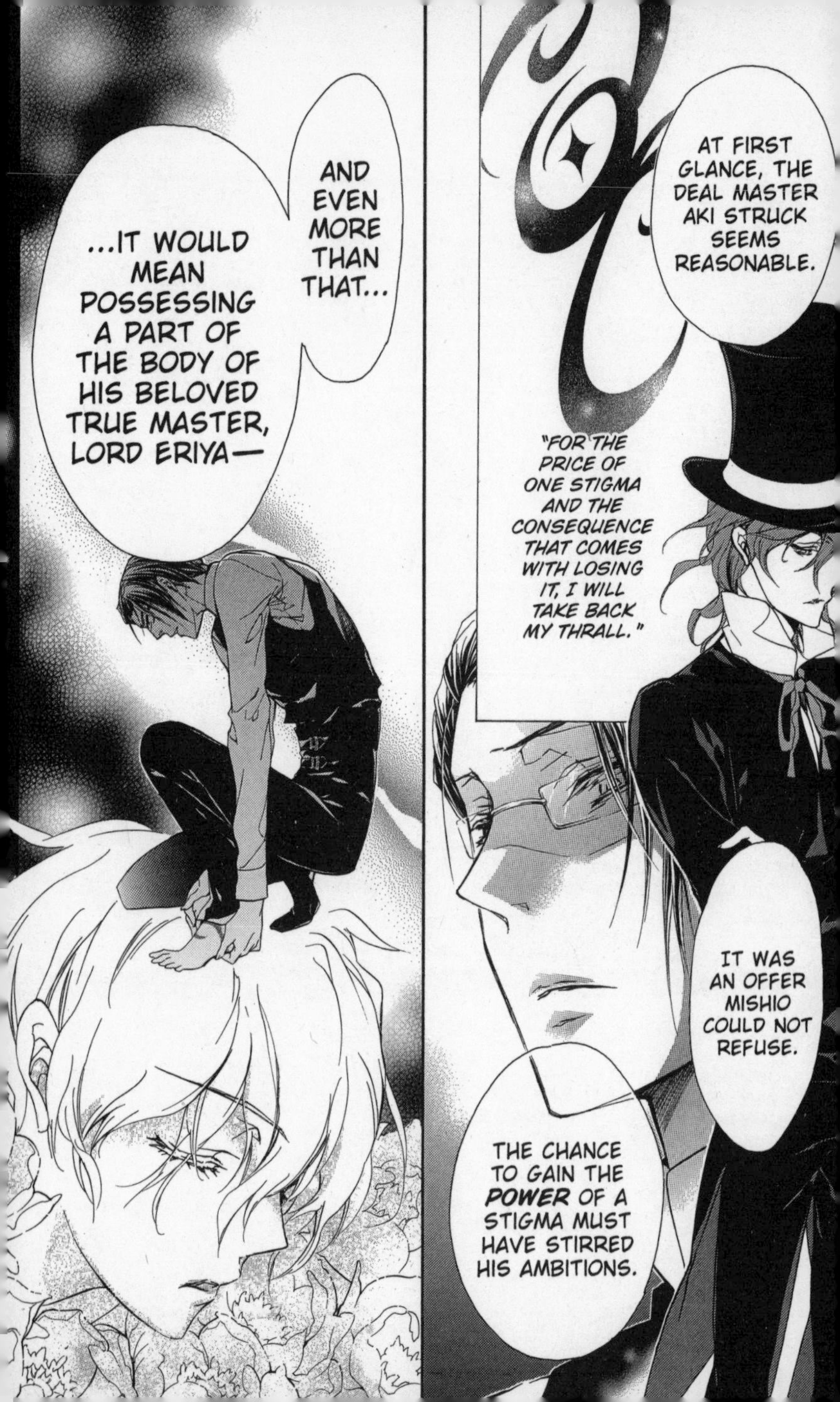
AT FIRST GLANCE, THE DEAL MASTER AKI STRUCK SEEMS REASONABLE.
"FOR THE PRICE OF ONE STIGMA AND THE CONSEQUENCE THAT COMES WITH LOSING IT, I WILL TAKE BACK MY THRALL."
IT WAS AN OFFER MISHIO COULD NOT REFUSE.
THE CHANCE TO GAIN THE POWER OF A STIGMA MUST HAVE STIRRED HIS AMBITIONS.
AND EVEN MORE THAN THAT...
...IT WOULD MEAN POSSESSING A PART OF THE BODY OF HIS BELOVED TRUE MASTER, LORD ERIYA—

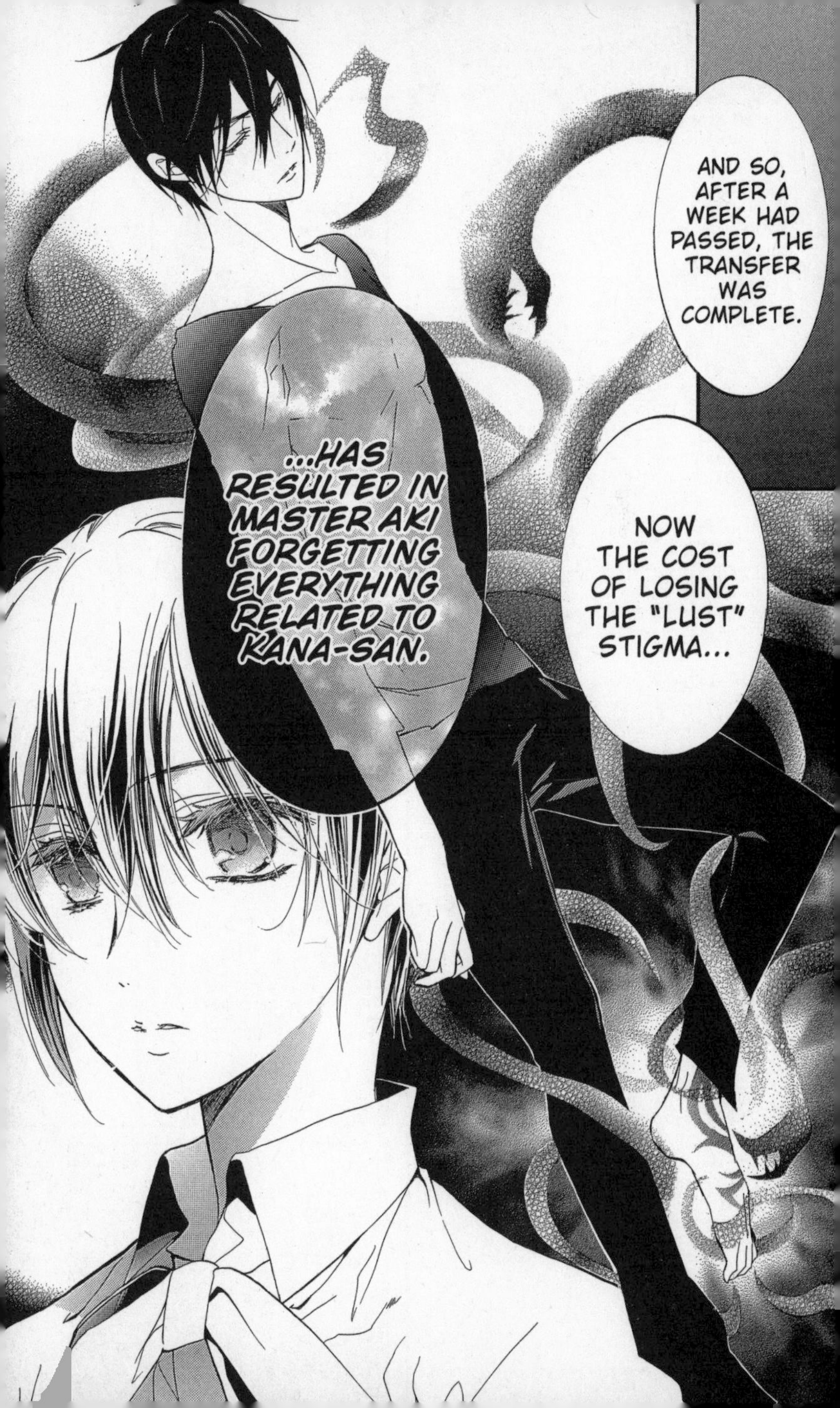
AND SO, AFTER A WEEK HAD PASSED, THE TRANSFER WAS COMPLETE.
NOW THE COST OF LOSING THE "LUST" STIGMA...
...HAS RESULTED IN MASTER AKI FORGETTING EVERYTHING RELATED TO KANA-SAN.

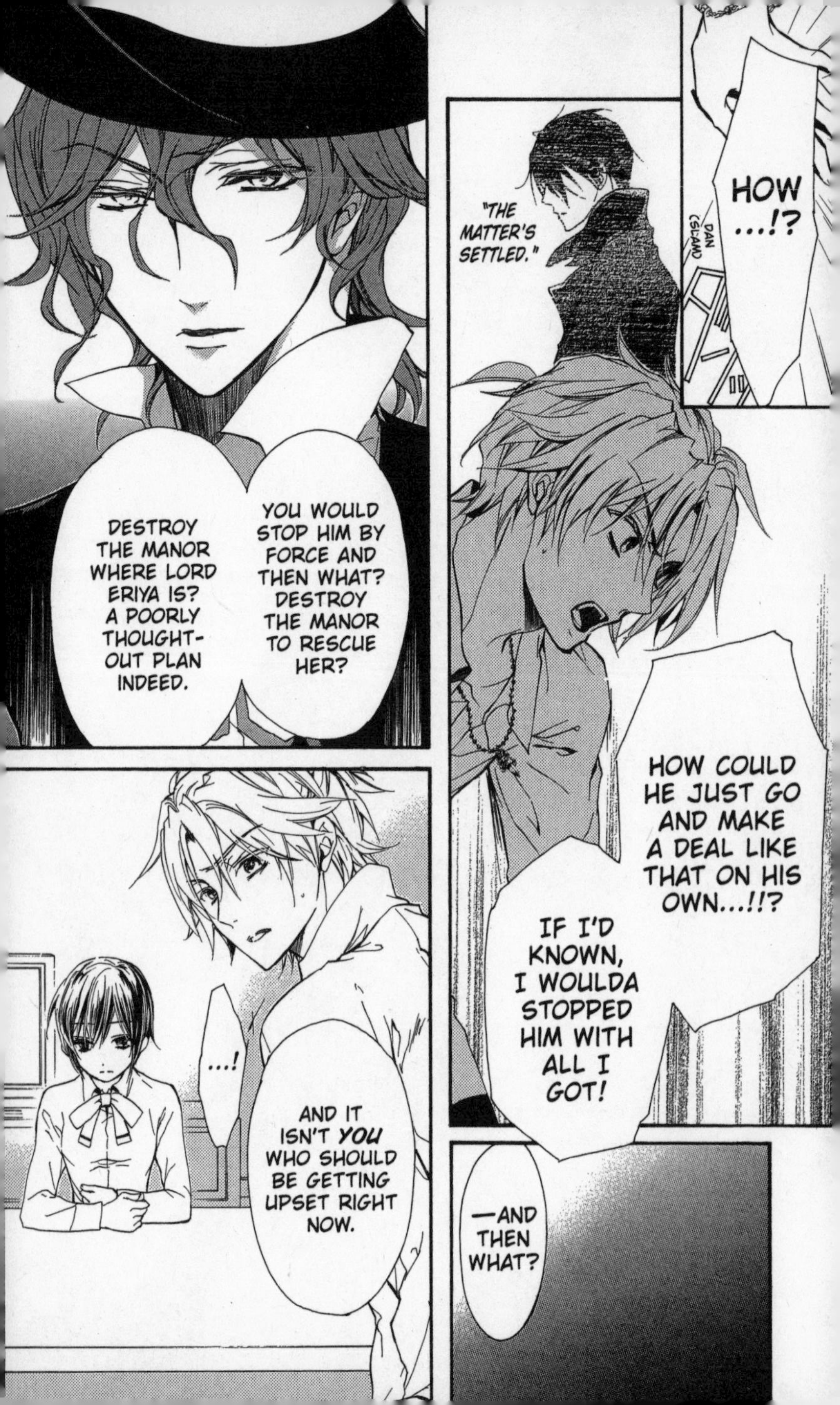
HOW ...!?
DAN (SLAM)
"THE MATTER'S SETTLED."
HOW COULD HE JUST GO AND MAKE A DEAL LIKE THAT ON HIS OWN...!!?
IF I'D KNOWN, I WOULDA STOPPED HIM WITH ALL I GOT!
—AND THEN WHAT?
YOU WOULD STOP HIM BY FORCE AND THEN WHAT? DESTROY THE MANOR TO RESCUE HER?
DESTROY THE MANOR WHERE LORD ERIYA IS? A POORLY THOUGHT-OUT PLAN INDEED.
...!
AND IT ISN'T *YOU* WHO SHOULD BE GETTING UPSET RIGHT NOW.

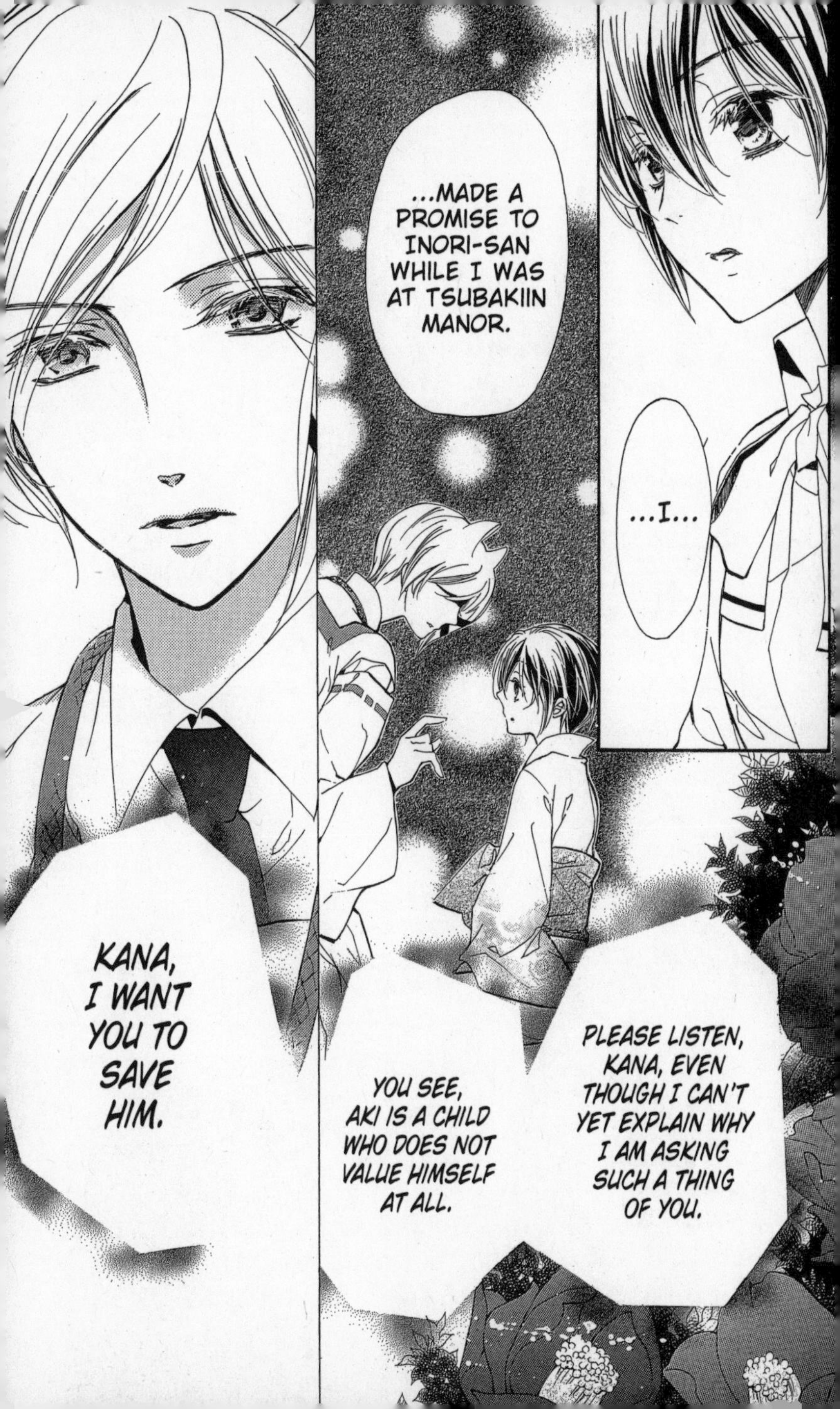
...I...
...MADE A PROMISE TO INORI-SAN WHILE I WAS AT TSUBAKIIN MANOR.
PLEASE LISTEN, KANA, EVEN THOUGH I CAN'T YET EXPLAIN WHY I AM ASKING SUCH A THING OF YOU.
YOU SEE, AKI IS A CHILD WHO DOES NOT VALUE HIMSELF AT ALL.
KANA, I WANT YOU TO SAVE HIM.

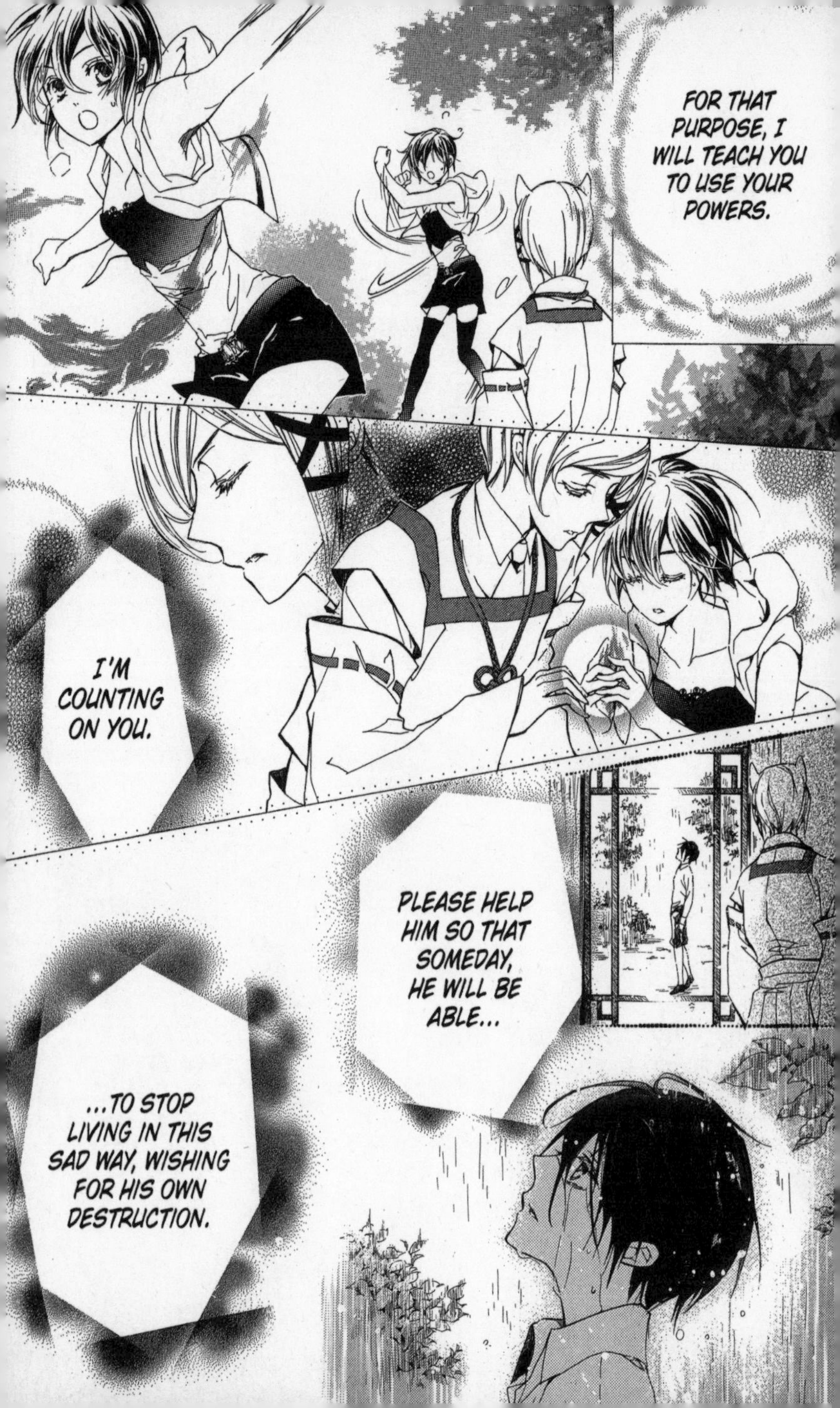
FOR THAT PURPOSE, I WILL TEACH YOU TO USE YOUR POWERS.
I'M COUNTING ON YOU.
PLEASE HELP HIM SO THAT SOMEDAY, HE WILL BE ABLE...
...TO STOP LIVING IN THIS SAD WAY, WISHING FOR HIS OWN DESTRUCTION.

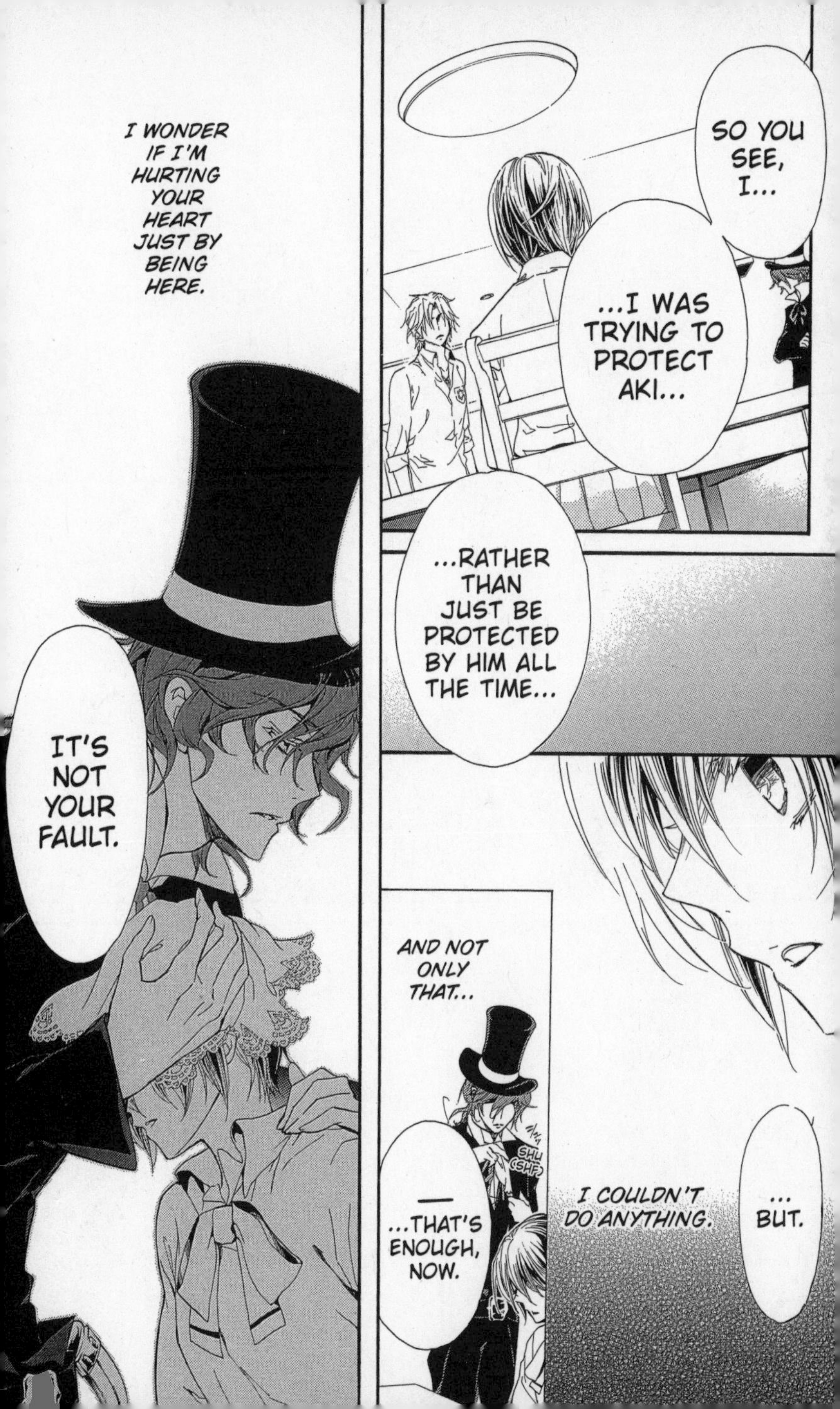
SO YOU SEE, I...
...I WAS TRYING TO PROTECT AKI...
...RATHER THAN JUST BE PROTECTED BY HIM ALL THE TIME...
... BUT.
I COULDN'T DO ANYTHING.
AND NOT ONLY THAT...
SHU (SHF)
—...THAT'S ENOUGH, NOW.
I WONDER IF I'M HURTING YOUR HEART JUST BY BEING HERE.
IT'S NOT YOUR FAULT.

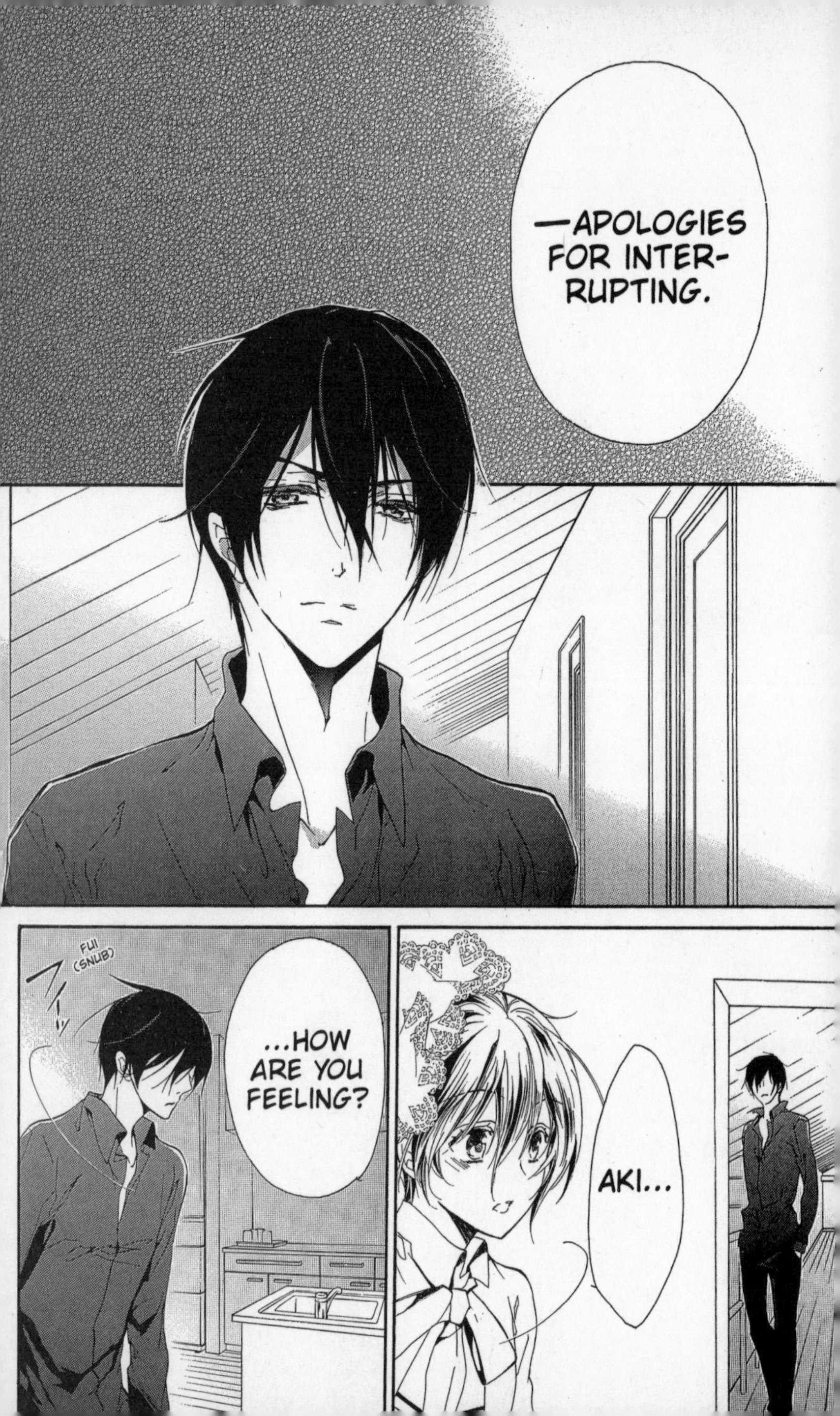
—APOLOGIES FOR INTER-RUPTING.
AKI...
...HOW ARE YOU FEELING?
FUI (SNUB)

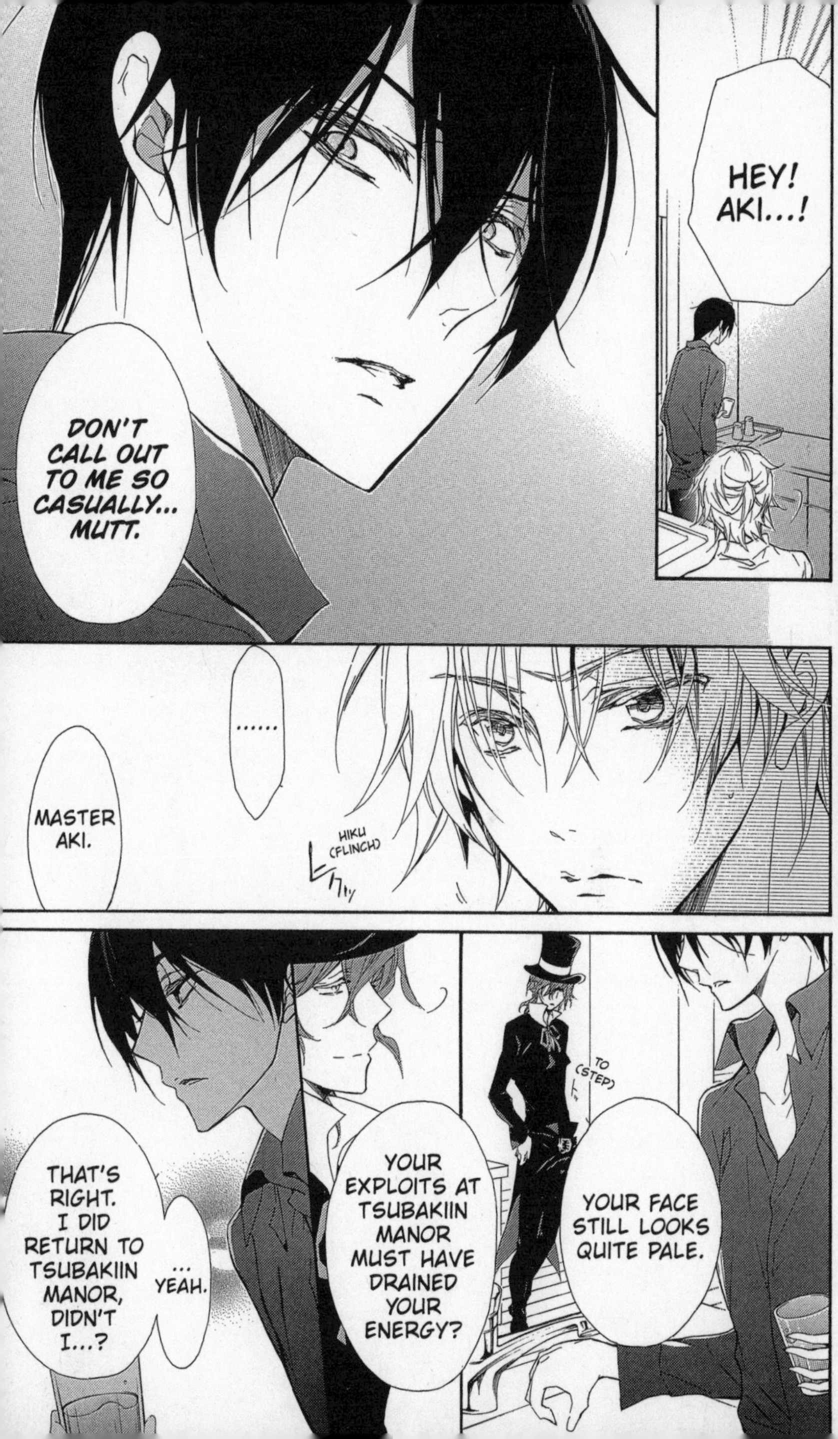

HEY! AKI...!
DON'T CALL OUT TO ME SO CASUALLY... MUTT.
HIKU (FLINCH)
......
MASTER AKI.
TO (STEP)
YOUR FACE STILL LOOKS QUITE PALE.
YOUR EXPLOITS AT TSUBAKIIN MANOR MUST HAVE DRAINED YOUR ENERGY?
...YEAH.
THAT'S RIGHT. I DID RETURN TO TSUBAKIIN MANOR, DIDN'T I...?

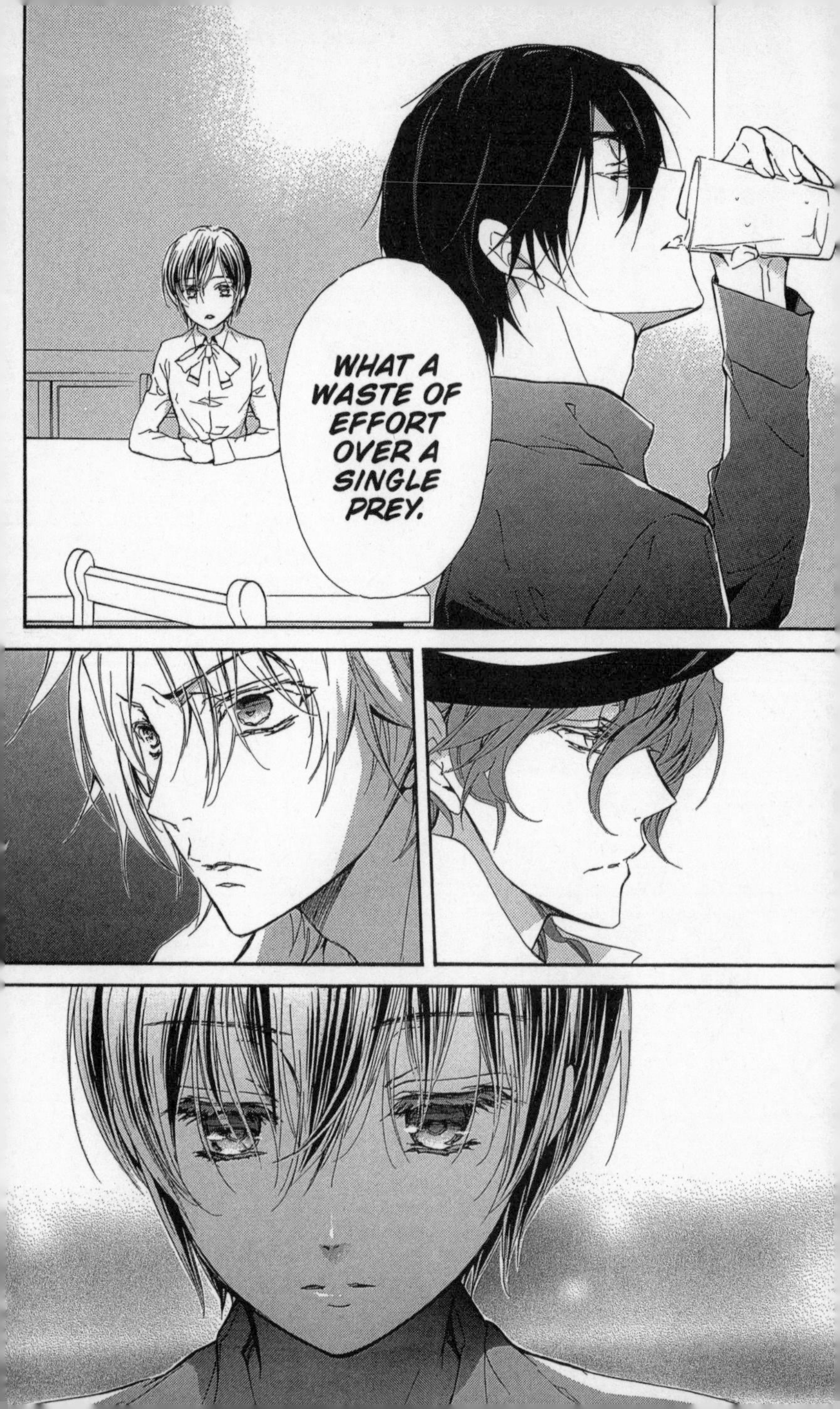
WHAT A WASTE OF EFFORT OVER A SINGLE PREY.

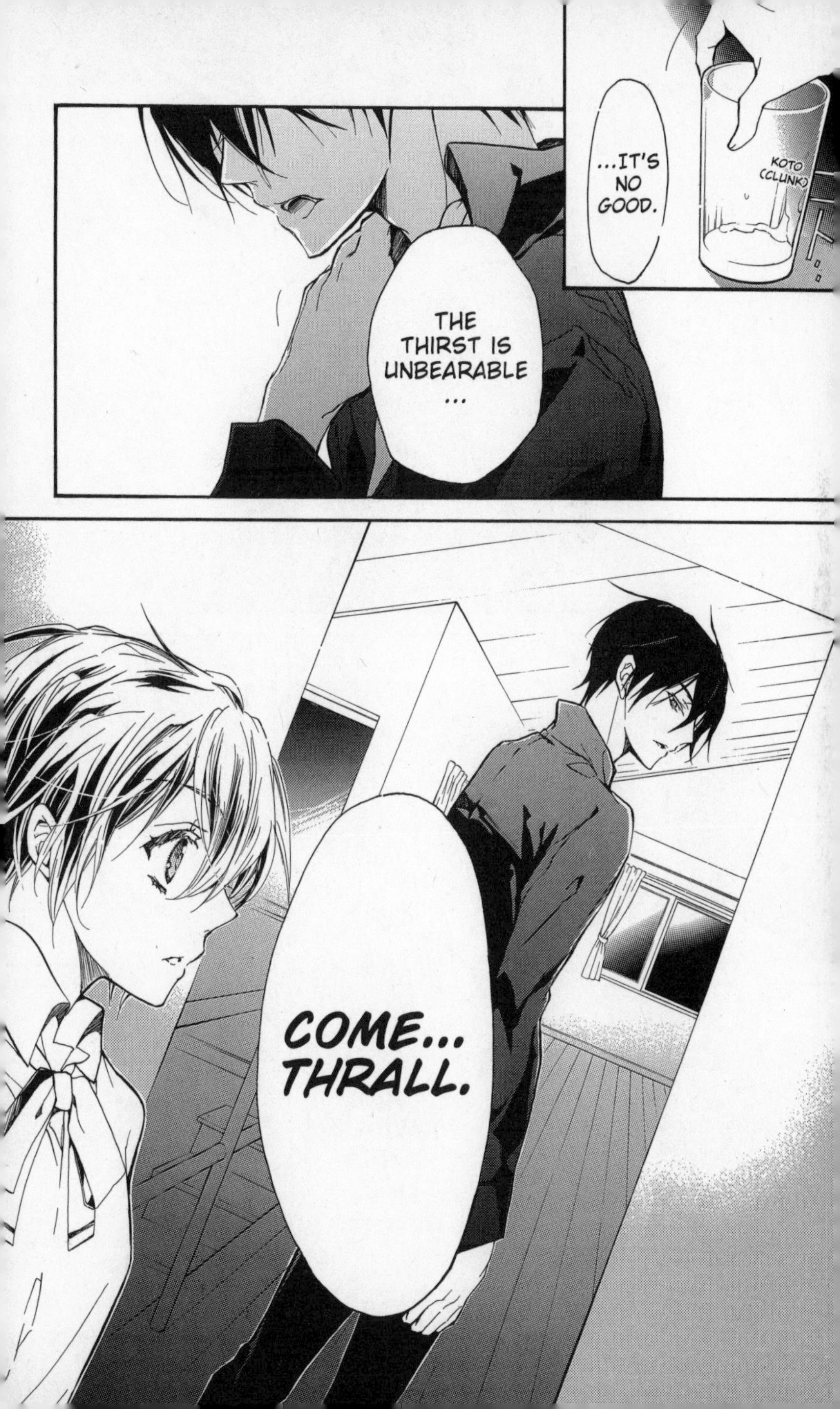
...IT'S NO GOOD.
KOTO (CLUNK)
THE THIRST IS UNBEARABLE ...
COME... THRALL.

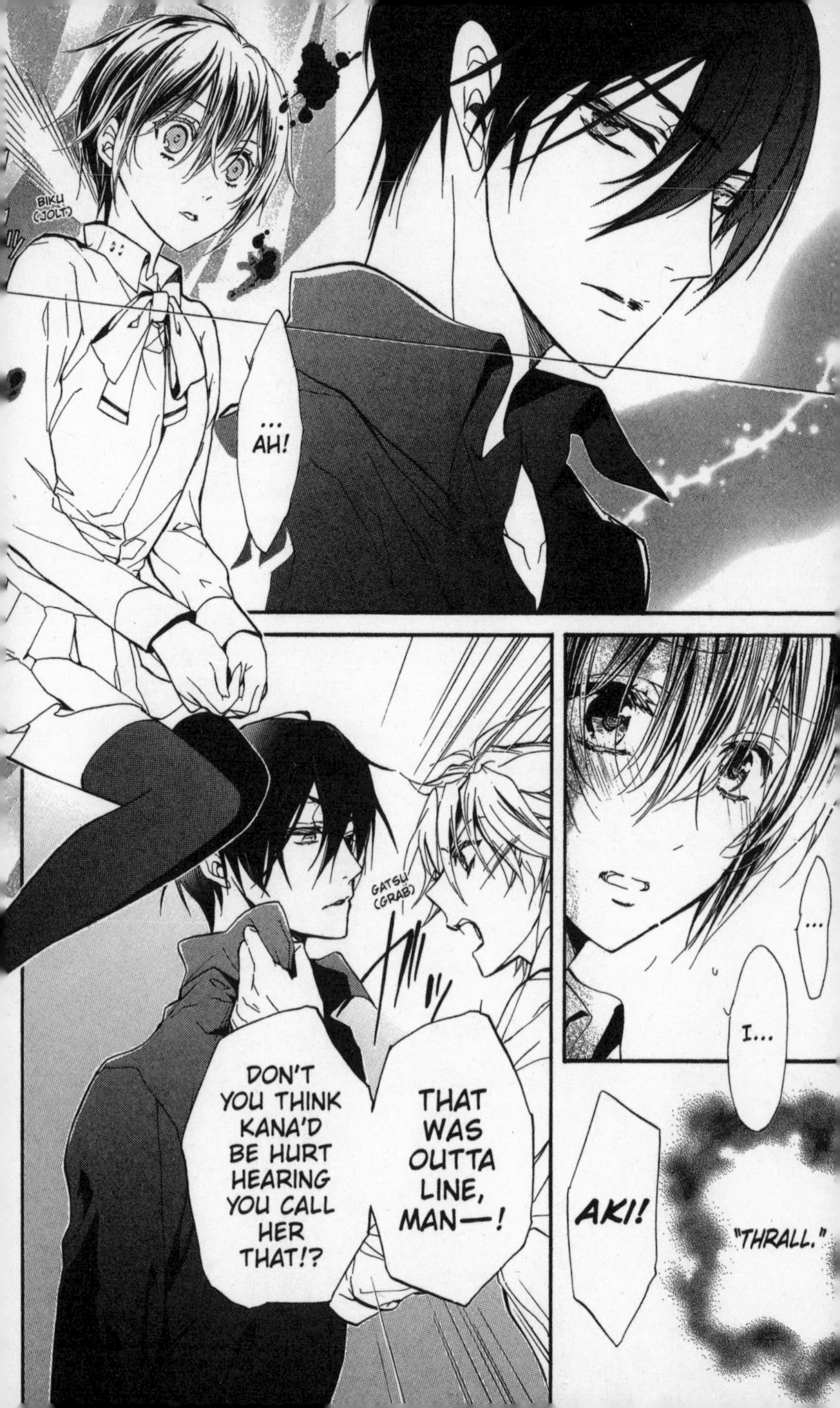
BIKU (JOLT)
... AH!
...
I...
"THRALL."
AKI!
GATSU (GRAB)
THAT WAS OUTTA LINE, MAN—!
DON'T YOU THINK KANA'D BE HURT HEARING YOU CALL HER THAT!?

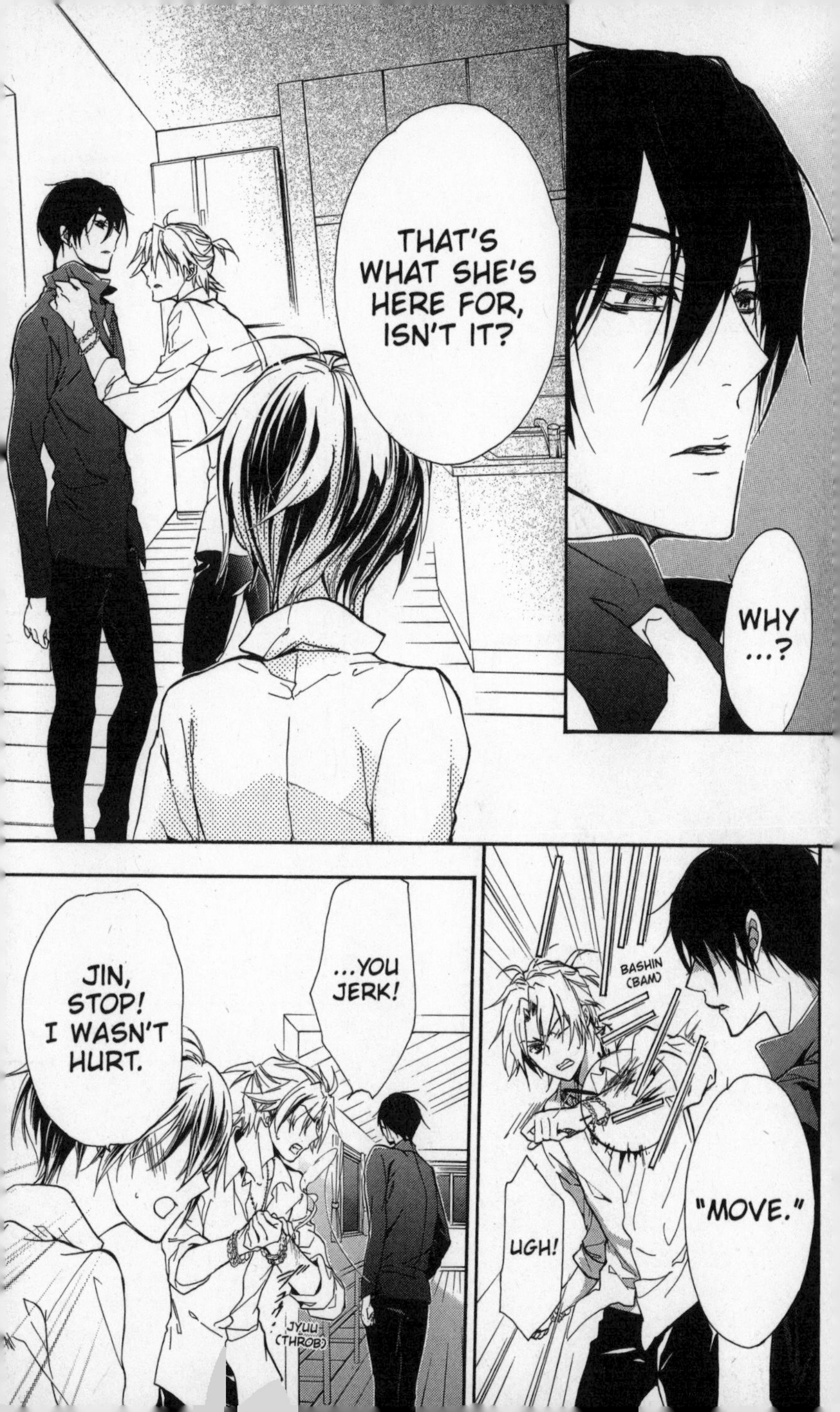
WHY ...?
THAT'S WHAT SHE'S HERE FOR, ISN'T IT?
BASHIN (BAM)
"MOVE."
UGH!
...YOU JERK!
JIN, STOP! I WASN'T HURT.
JYUU (THROB)

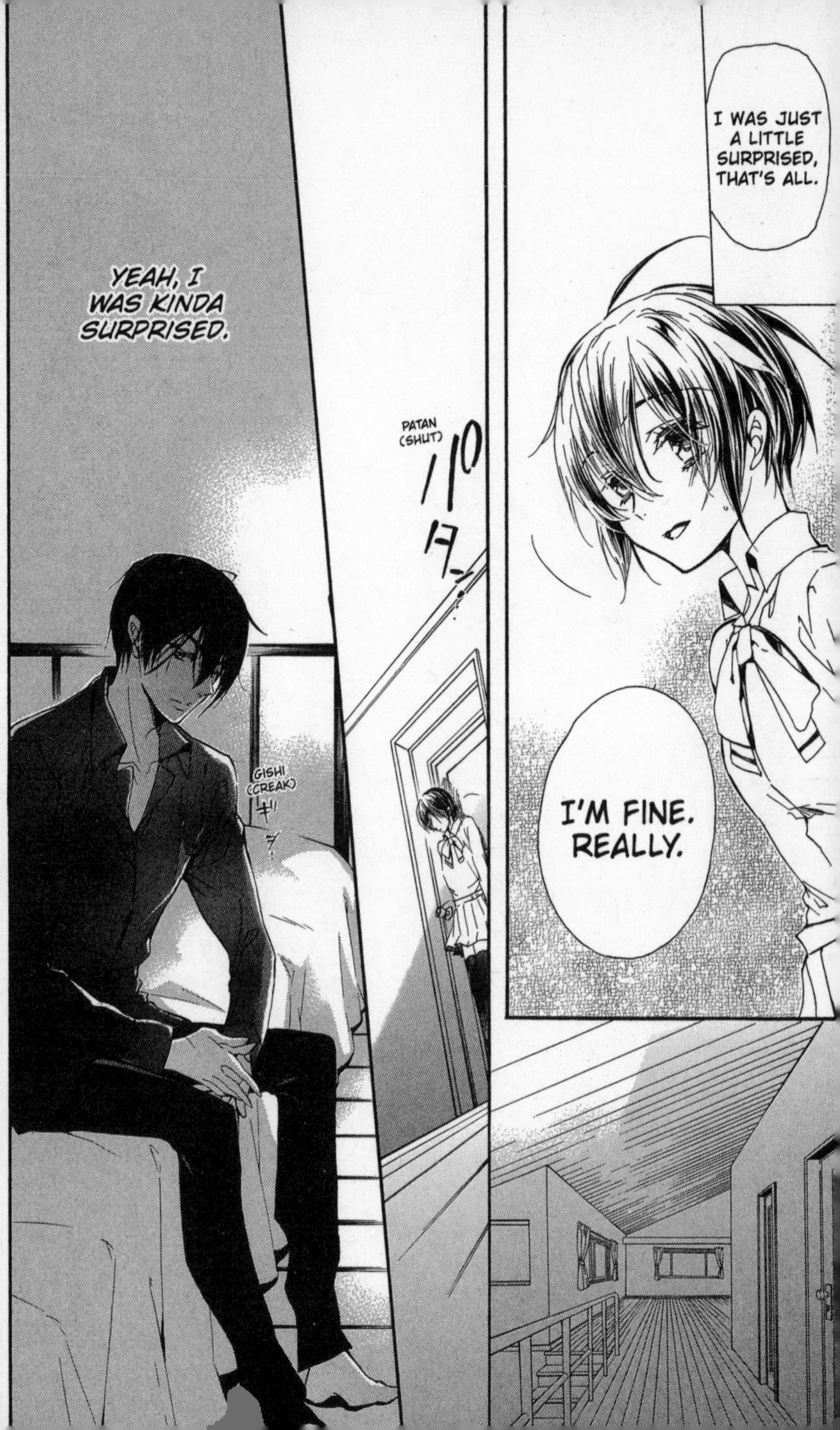
I WAS JUST A LITTLE SURPRISED, THAT'S ALL.
I'M FINE. REALLY.
PATAN (SHUT)
パタン
GISHI (CREAK)
ギシ
YEAH, I WAS KINDA SURPRISED.

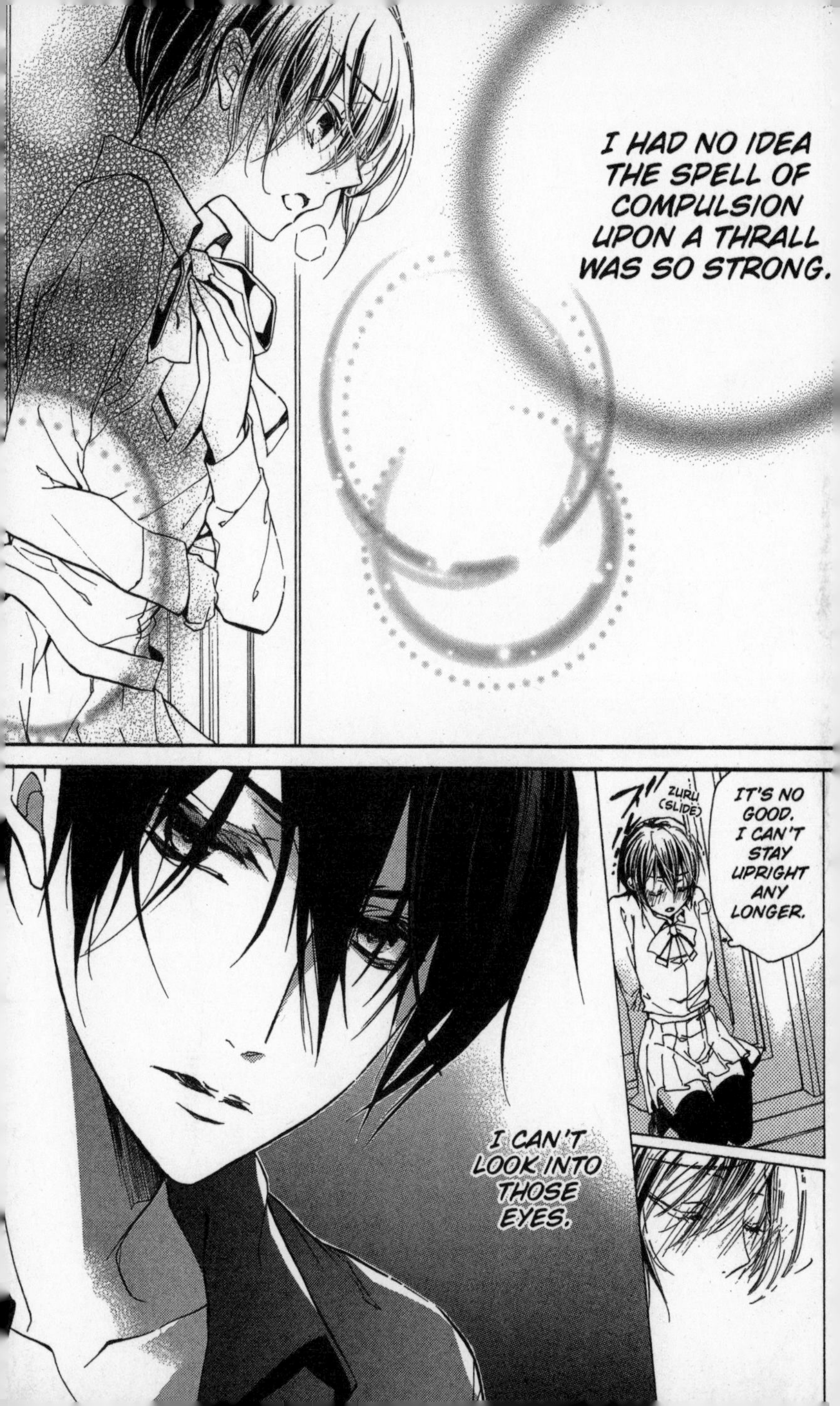
I HAD NO IDEA THE SPELL OF COMPULSION UPON A THRALL WAS SO STRONG.
ZURU (SLIDE)
IT'S NO GOOD. I CAN'T STAY UPRIGHT ANY LONGER.
I CAN'T LOOK INTO THOSE EYES.

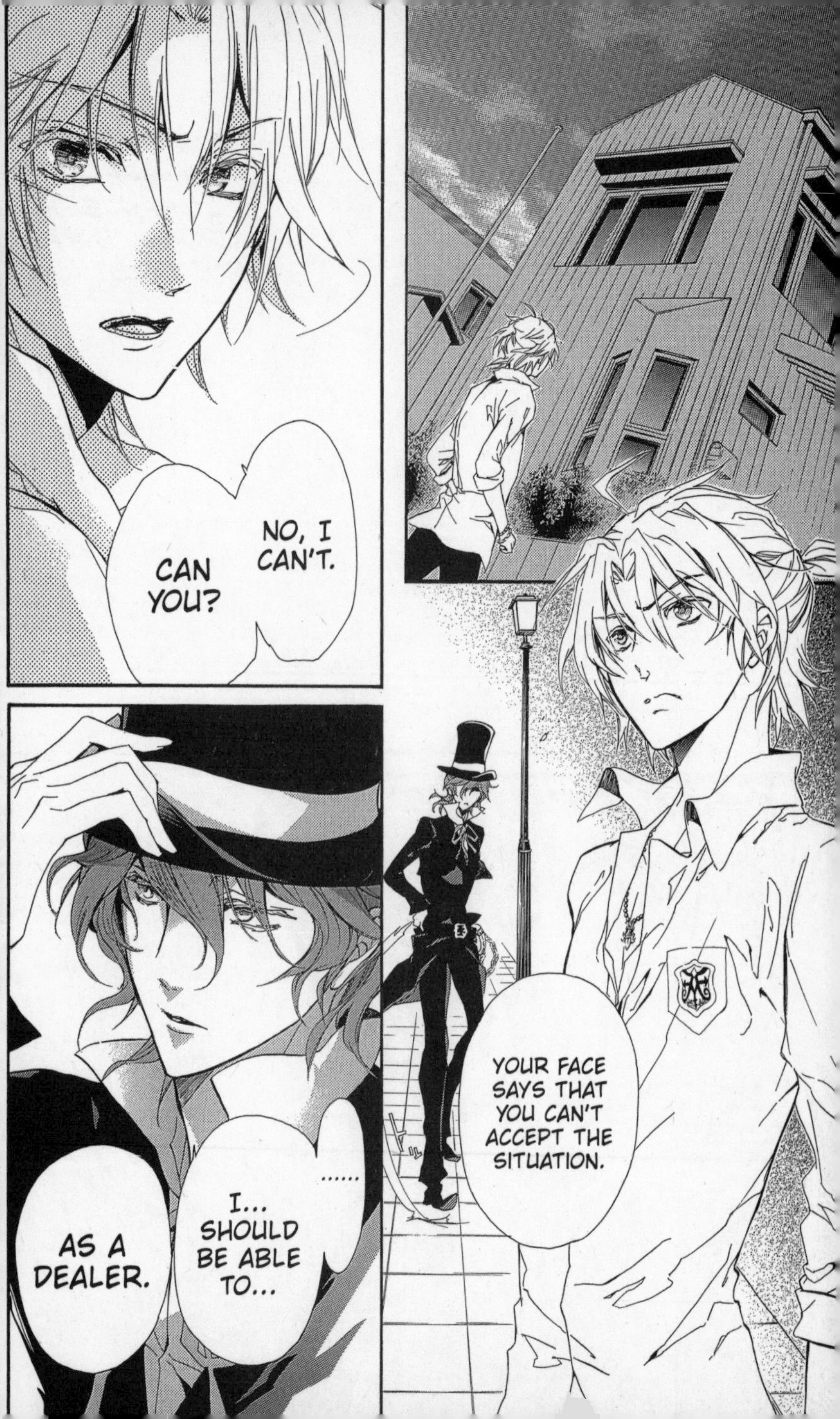
NO, I CAN'T.
CAN YOU?
YOUR FACE SAYS THAT YOU CAN'T ACCEPT THE SITUATION.
......
I... SHOULD BE ABLE TO...
AS A DEALER.

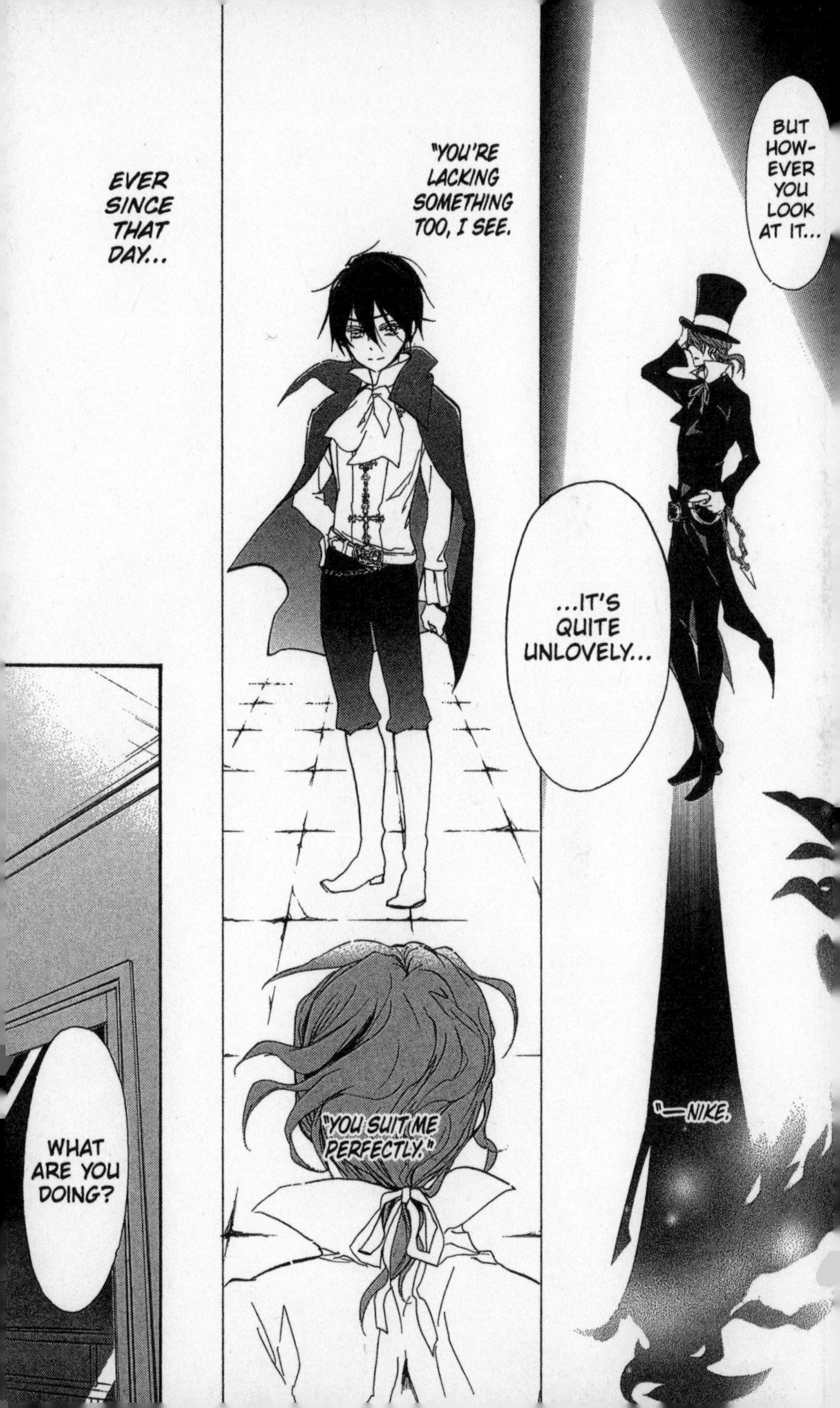
BUT HOW-EVER YOU LOOK AT IT...
...IT'S QUITE UNLOVELY...
"—NIKE.
"YOU'RE LACKING SOMETHING TOO, I SEE.
"YOU SUIT ME PERFECTLY."
EVER SINCE THAT DAY...
WHAT ARE YOU DOING?

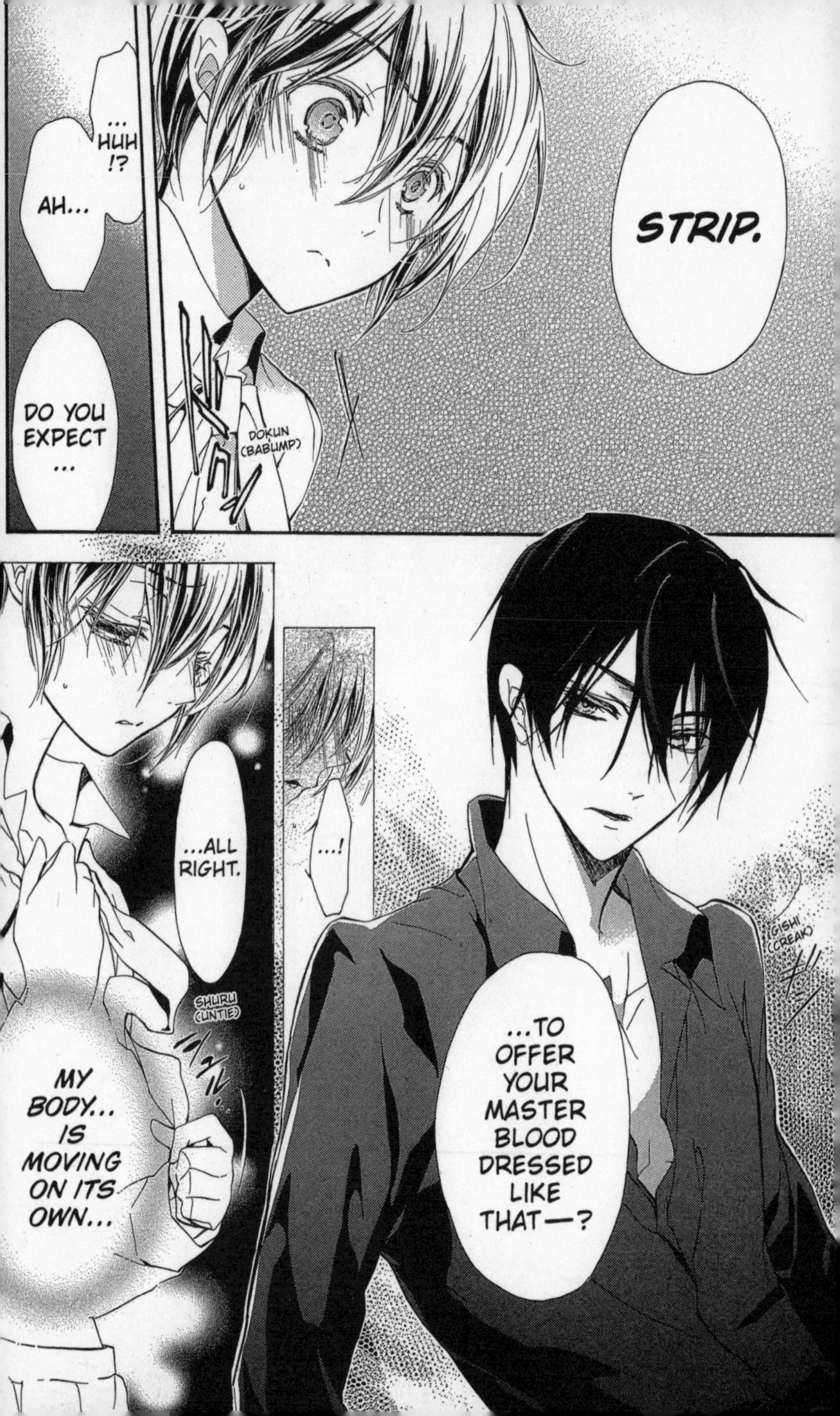
STRIP.
DOKUN (BABUMP)
... HUH !?
AH...
DO YOU EXPECT ...
...TO OFFER YOUR MASTER BLOOD DRESSED LIKE THAT—?
GISHI (CREAK)
...!
...ALL RIGHT.
SHURU (UNTIE)
MY BODY... IS MOVING ON ITS OWN...

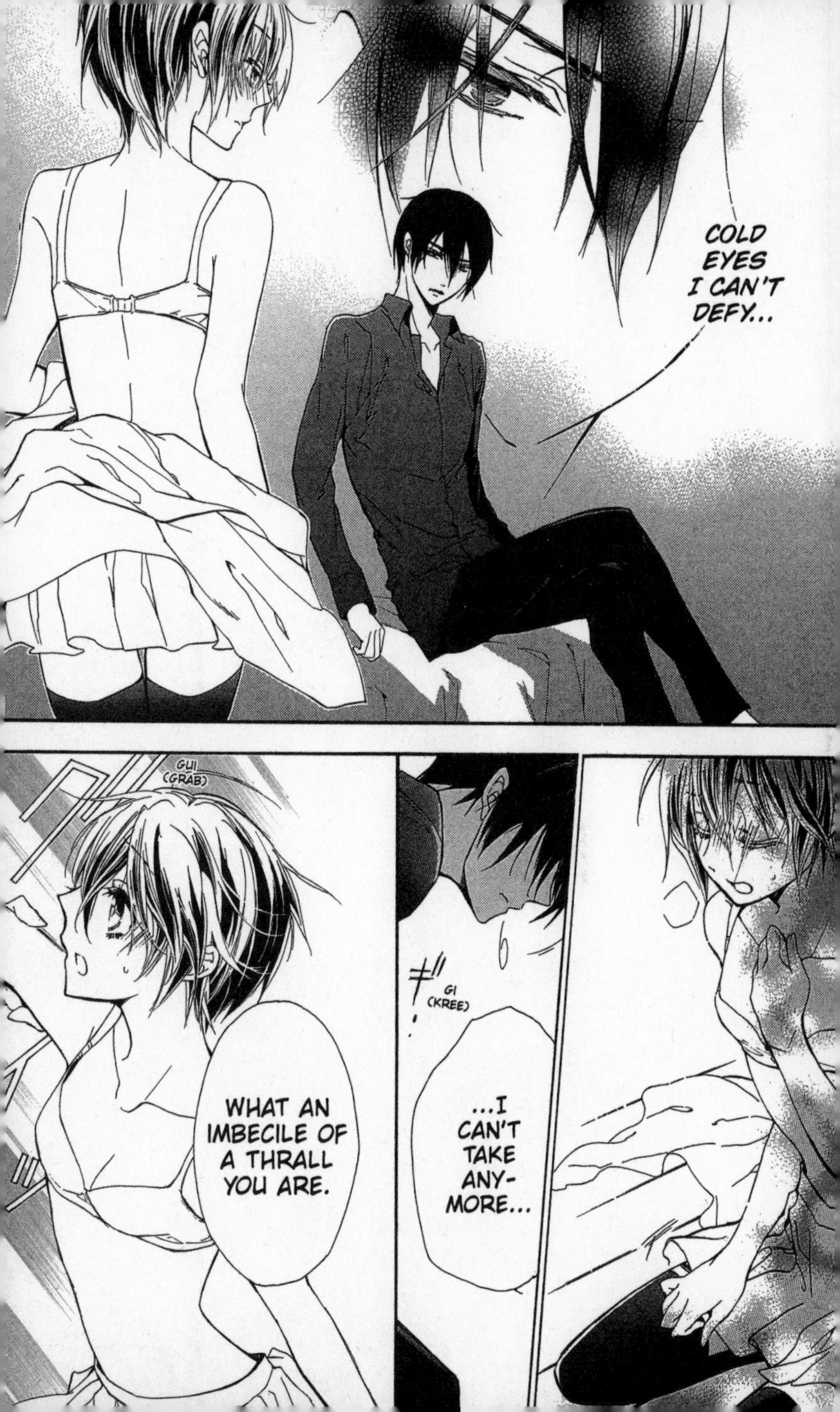
COLD EYES I CAN'T DEFY...
GI (KREE)
...I CAN'T TAKE ANY-MORE...
GUI (GRAB)
WHAT AN IMBECILE OF A THRALL YOU ARE.

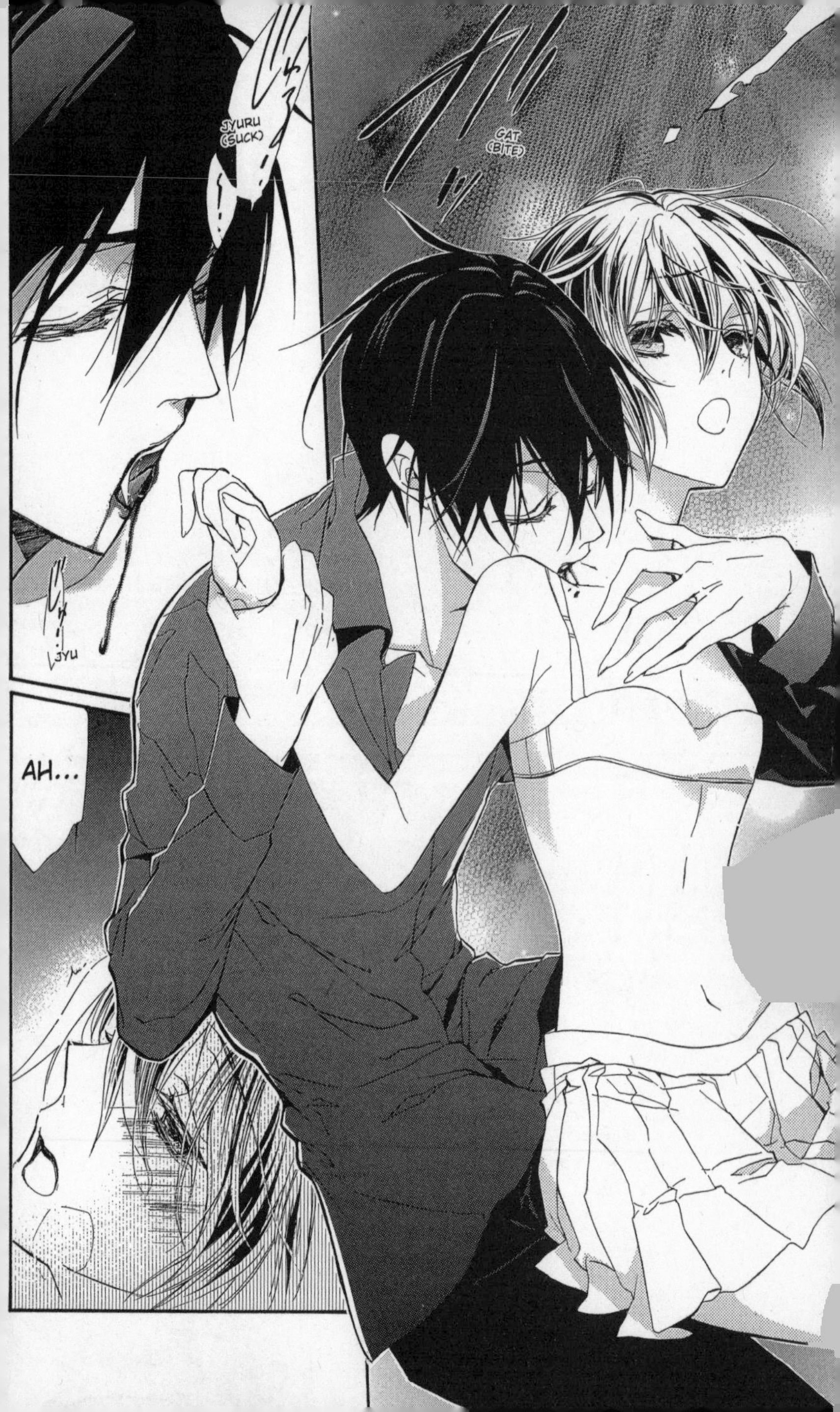
GAT (BITE)
JYURU (SUCK)
JYU
AH...

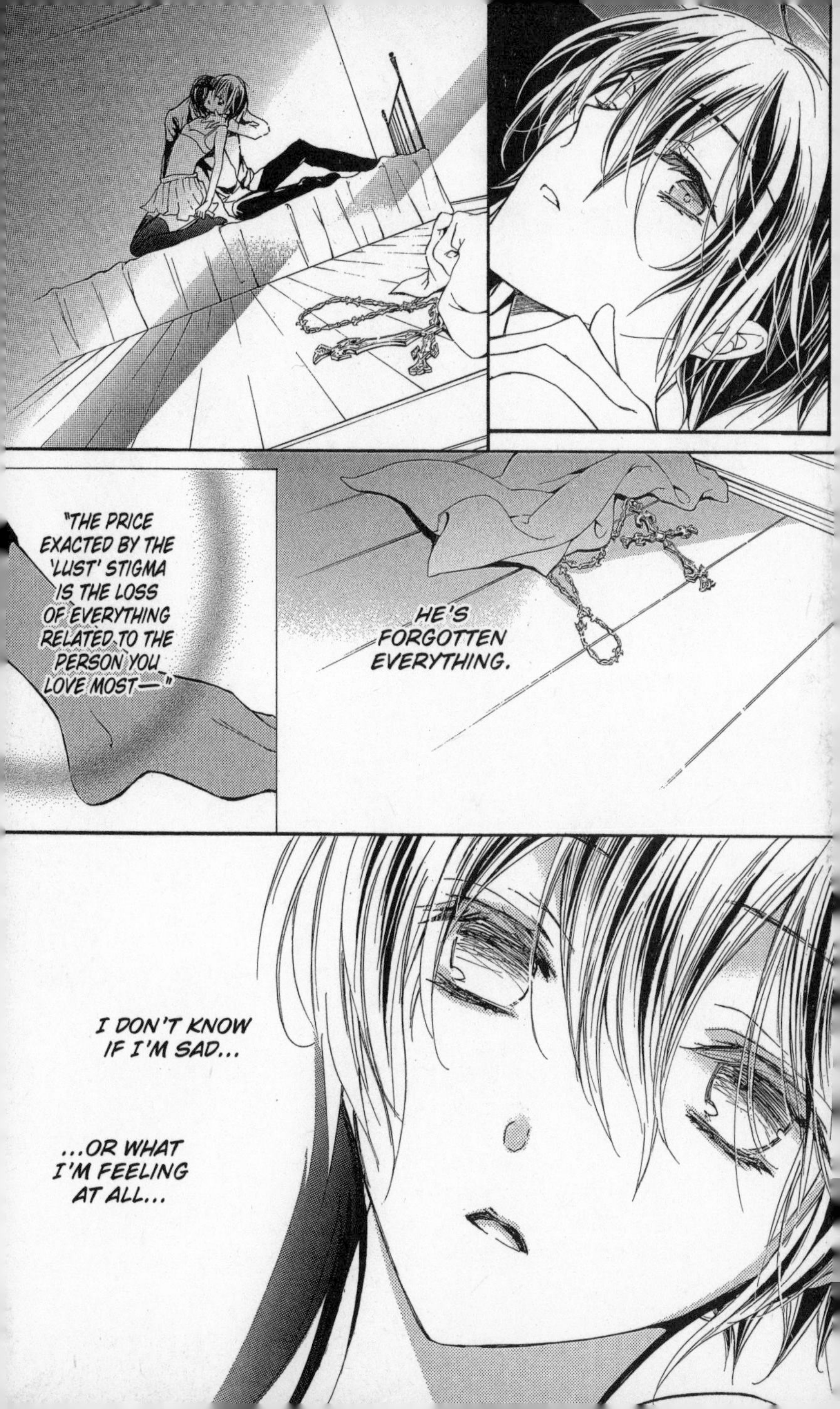
HE'S FORGOTTEN EVERYTHING.
"THE PRICE EXACTED BY THE 'LUST' STIGMA IS THE LOSS OF EVERYTHING RELATED TO THE PERSON YOU LOVE MOST—"
I DON'T KNOW IF I'M SAD...
...OR WHAT I'M FEELING AT ALL...

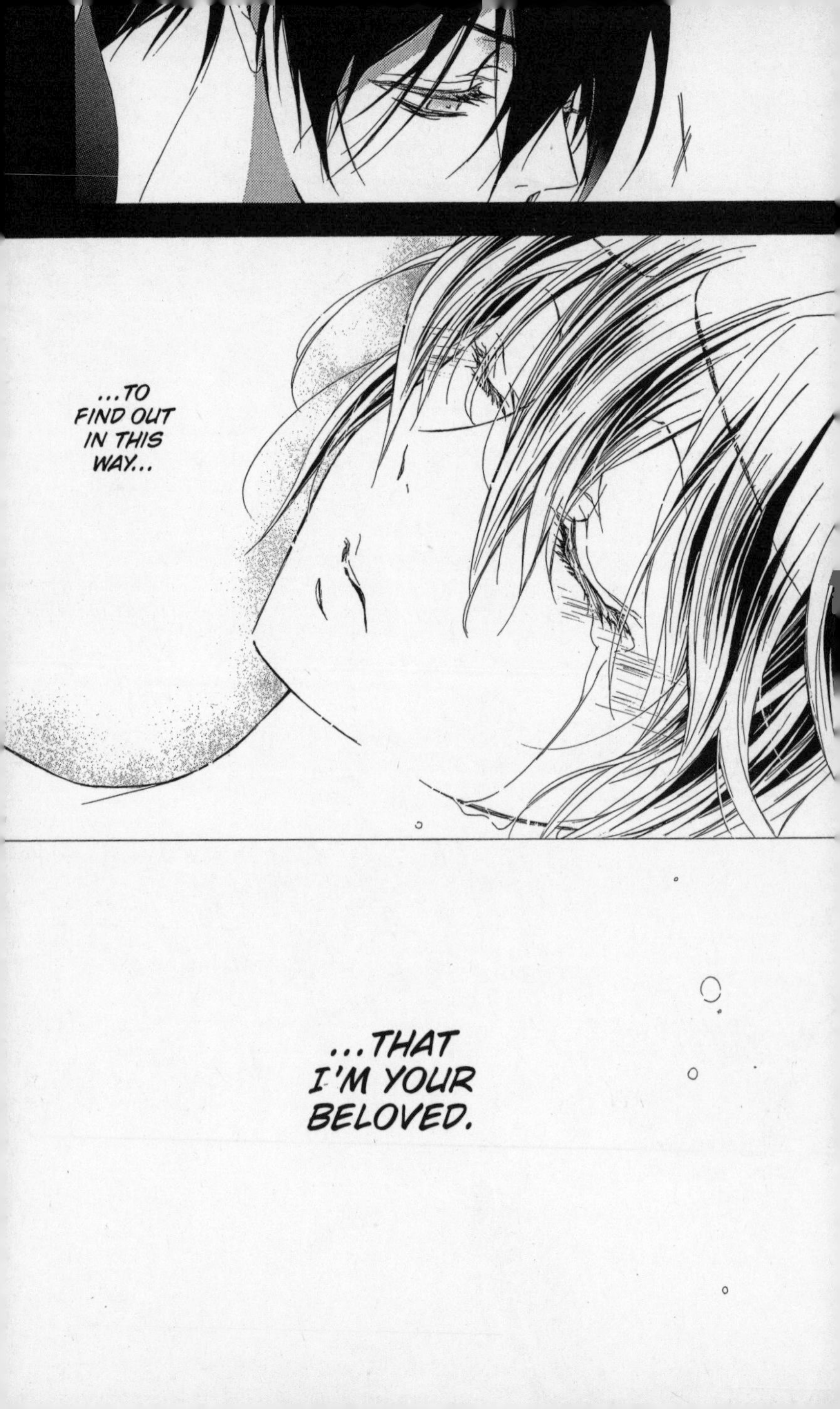
...TO FIND OUT IN THIS WAY...
...THAT I'M YOUR BELOVED.

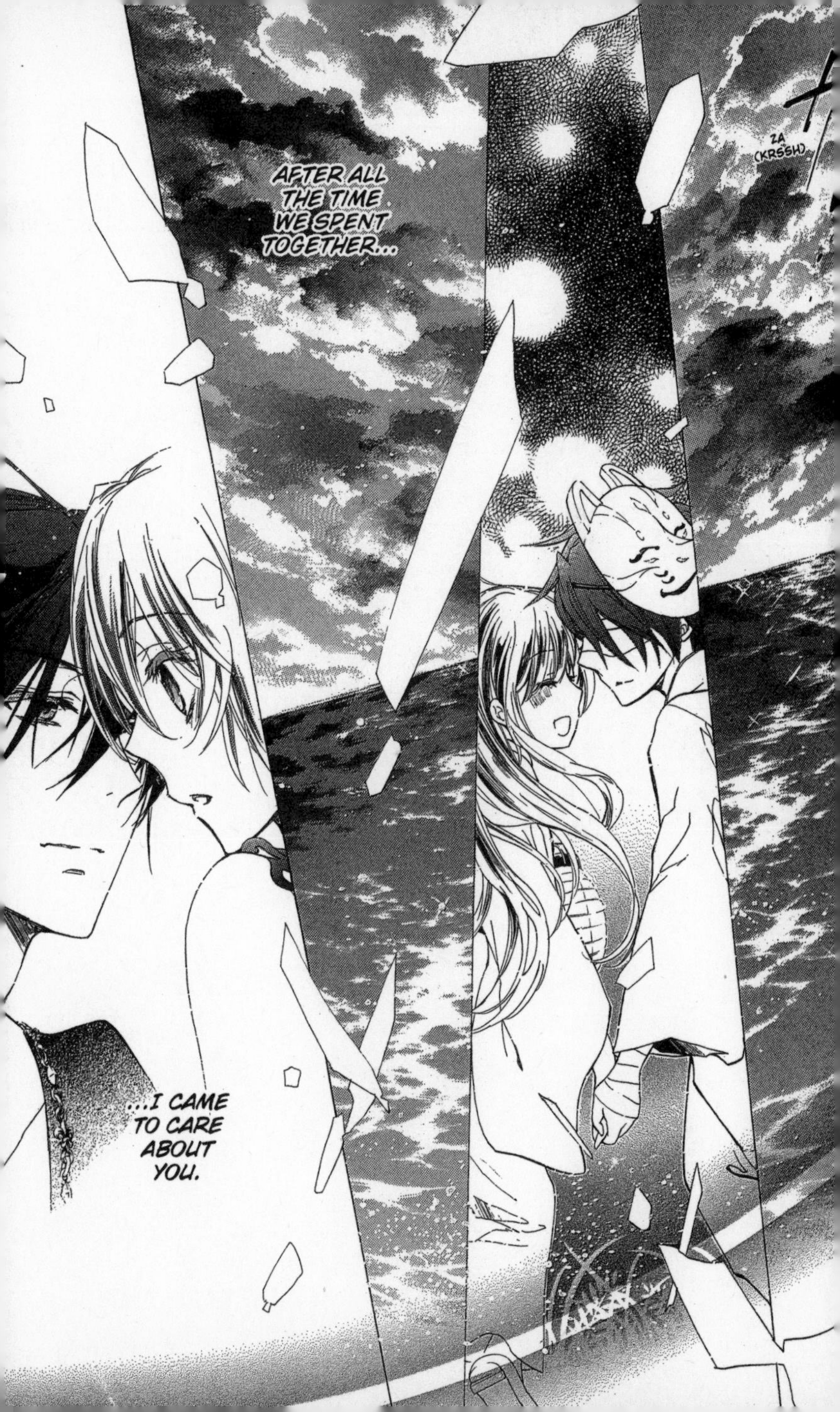
ZA (KRSSH)
AFTER ALL THE TIME WE SPENT TOGETHER...
...I CAME TO CARE ABOUT YOU.

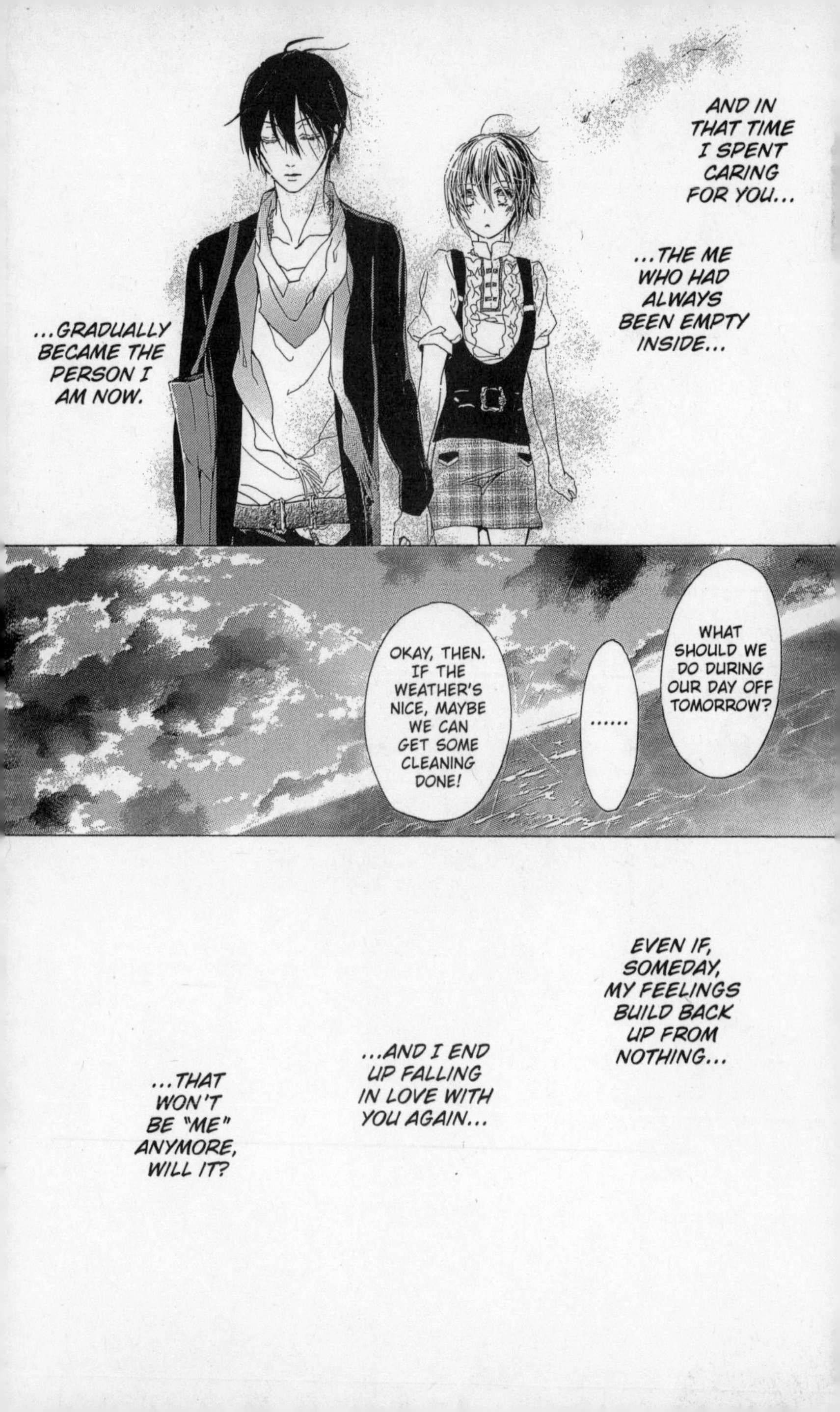
AND IN THAT TIME I SPENT CARING FOR YOU...
...THE ME WHO HAD ALWAYS BEEN EMPTY INSIDE...
...GRADUALLY BECAME THE PERSON I AM NOW.
WHAT SHOULD WE DO DURING OUR DAY OFF TOMORROW?
......
OKAY, THEN. IF THE WEATHER'S NICE, MAYBE WE CAN GET SOME CLEANING DONE!
EVEN IF, SOMEDAY, MY FEELINGS BUILD BACK UP FROM NOTHING...
...AND I END UP FALLING IN LOVE WITH YOU AGAIN...
...THAT WON'T BE "ME" ANYMORE, WILL IT?

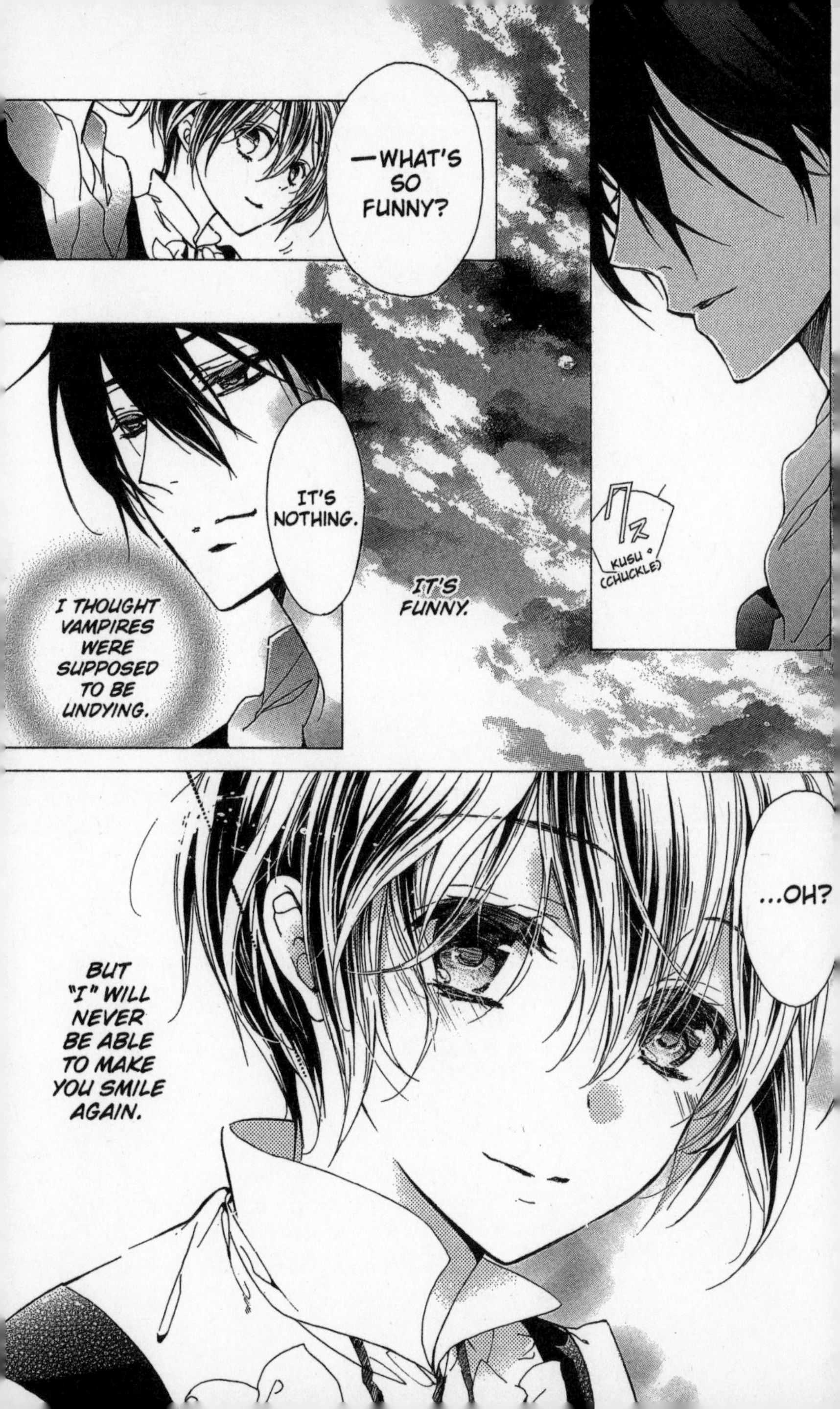
クス
KUSU (CHUCKLE)
—WHAT'S SO FUNNY?
IT'S NOTHING.
IT'S FUNNY.
I THOUGHT VAMPIRES WERE SUPPOSED TO BE UNDYING.
...OH?
BUT "I" WILL NEVER BE ABLE TO MAKE YOU SMILE AGAIN.

IF
THAT
ISN'T
"DEATH,"
WHAT
IS?

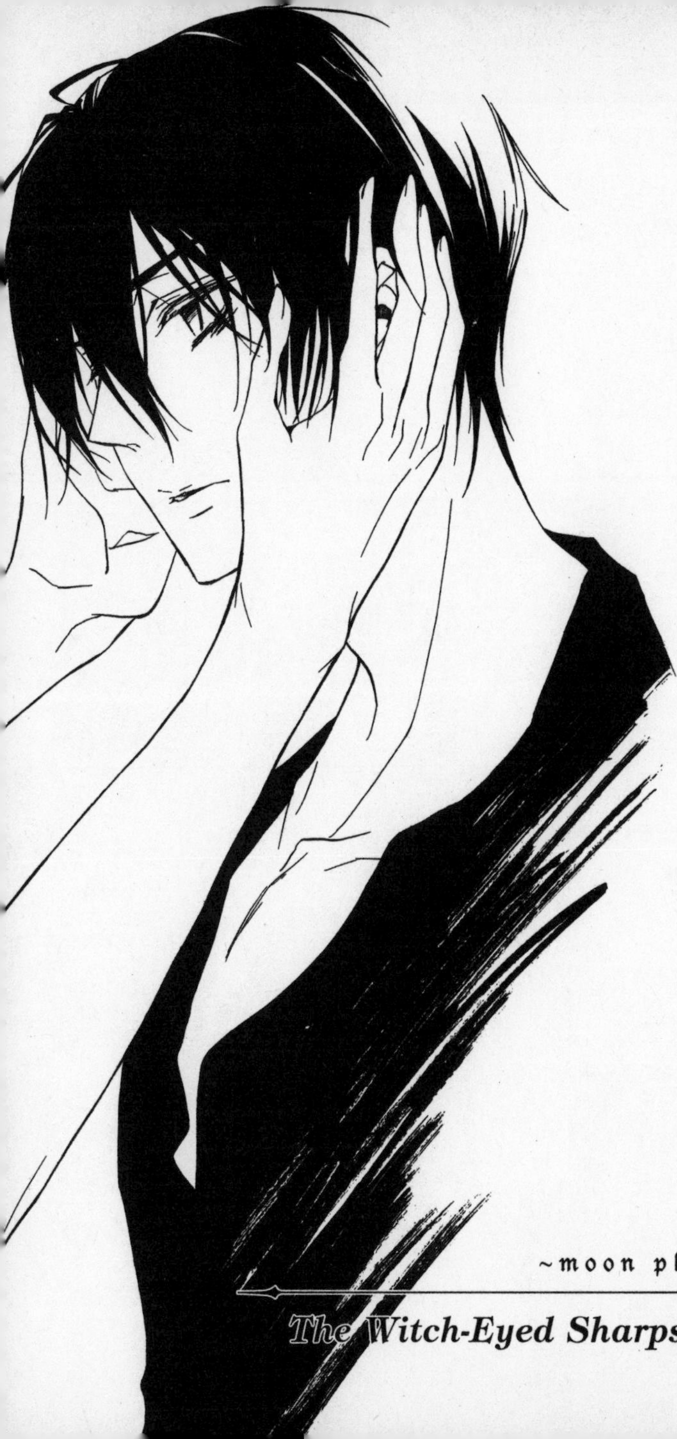

~moon phase~27

The Witch-Eyed Sharpshooter

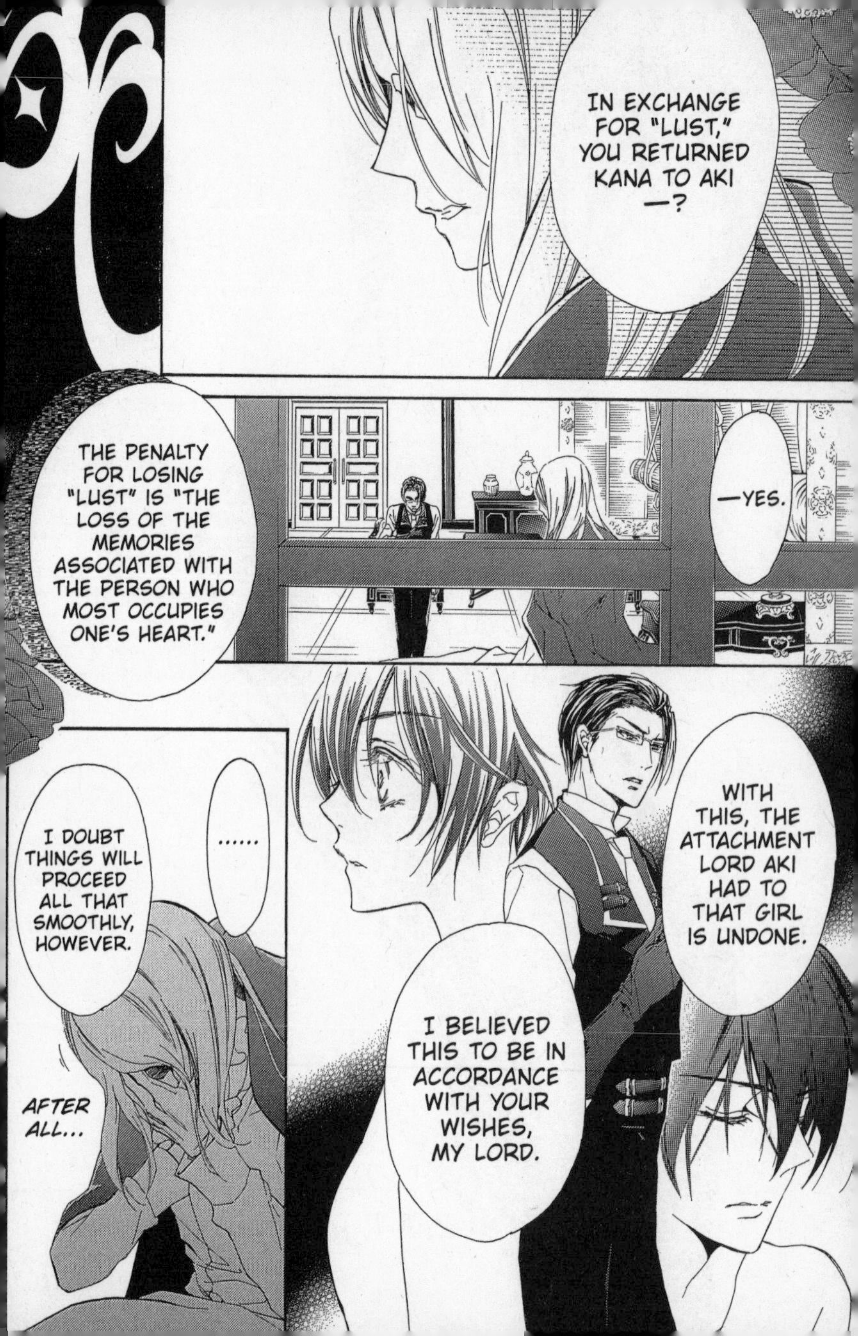

IN EXCHANGE FOR "LUST," YOU RETURNED KANA TO AKI —?
—YES.
THE PENALTY FOR LOSING "LUST" IS "THE LOSS OF THE MEMORIES ASSOCIATED WITH THE PERSON WHO MOST OCCUPIES ONE'S HEART."
WITH THIS, THE ATTACHMENT LORD AKI HAD TO THAT GIRL IS UNDONE.
I BELIEVED THIS TO BE IN ACCORDANCE WITH YOUR WISHES, MY LORD.
......
I DOUBT THINGS WILL PROCEED ALL THAT SMOOTHLY, HOWEVER.
AFTER ALL...

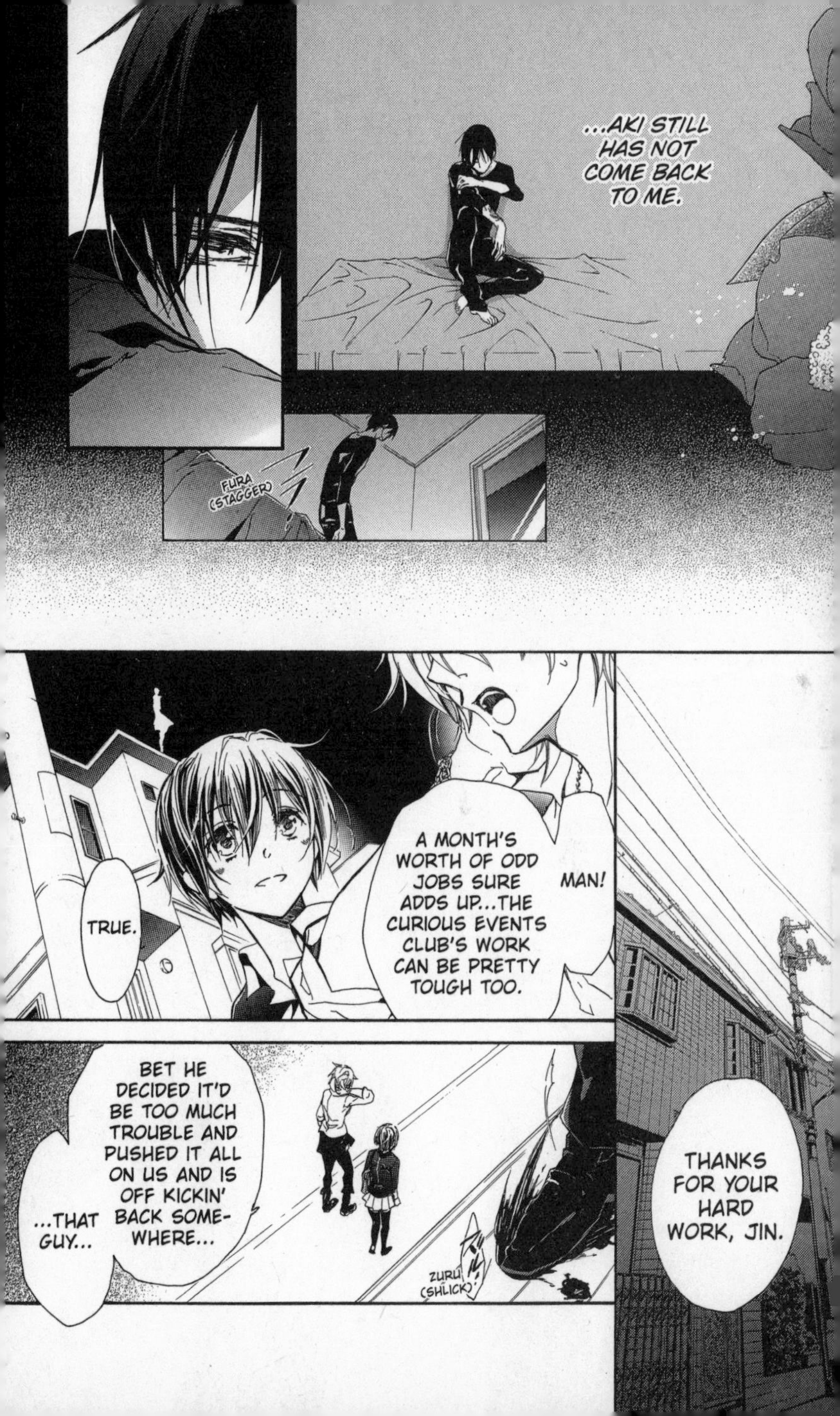
...AKI STILL HAS NOT COME BACK TO ME.
FURA (STAGGER)
THANKS FOR YOUR HARD WORK, JIN.
MAN!
A MONTH'S WORTH OF ODD JOBS SURE ADDS UP...THE CURIOUS EVENTS CLUB'S WORK CAN BE PRETTY TOUGH TOO.
TRUE.
ZURU (SHLICK)
BET HE DECIDED IT'D BE TOO MUCH TROUBLE AND PUSHED IT ALL ON US AND IS OFF KICKIN' BACK SOME-WHERE...
...THAT GUY...

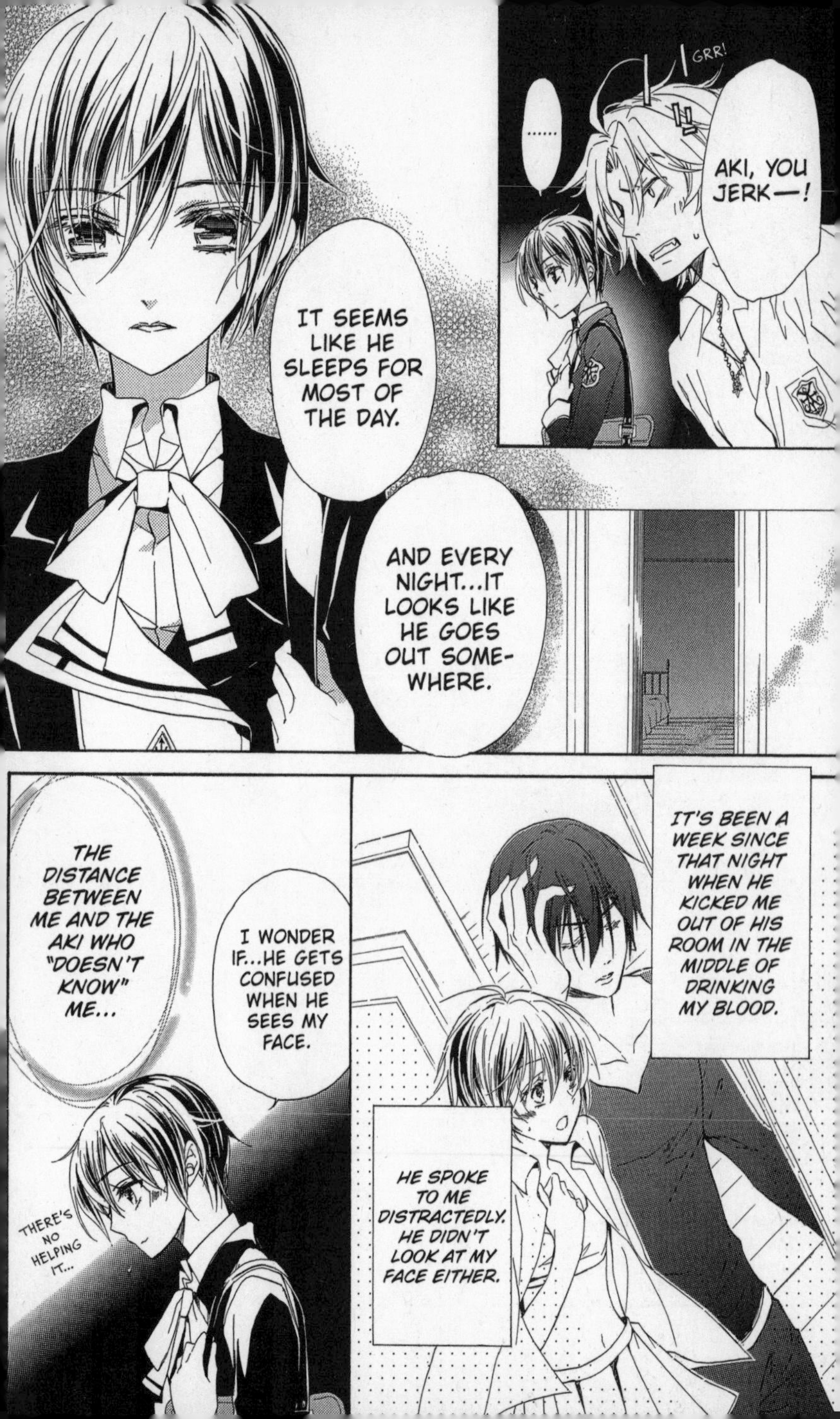
GRR!
AKI, YOU JERK—!
......
IT SEEMS LIKE HE SLEEPS FOR MOST OF THE DAY.
AND EVERY NIGHT...IT LOOKS LIKE HE GOES OUT SOMEWHERE.
IT'S BEEN A WEEK SINCE THAT NIGHT WHEN HE KICKED ME OUT OF HIS ROOM IN THE MIDDLE OF DRINKING MY BLOOD.
HE SPOKE TO ME DISTRACTEDLY. HE DIDN'T LOOK AT MY FACE EITHER.
I WONDER IF...HE GETS CONFUSED WHEN HE SEES MY FACE.
THE DISTANCE BETWEEN ME AND THE AKI WHO "DOESN'T KNOW" ME...
THERE'S NO HELPING IT...

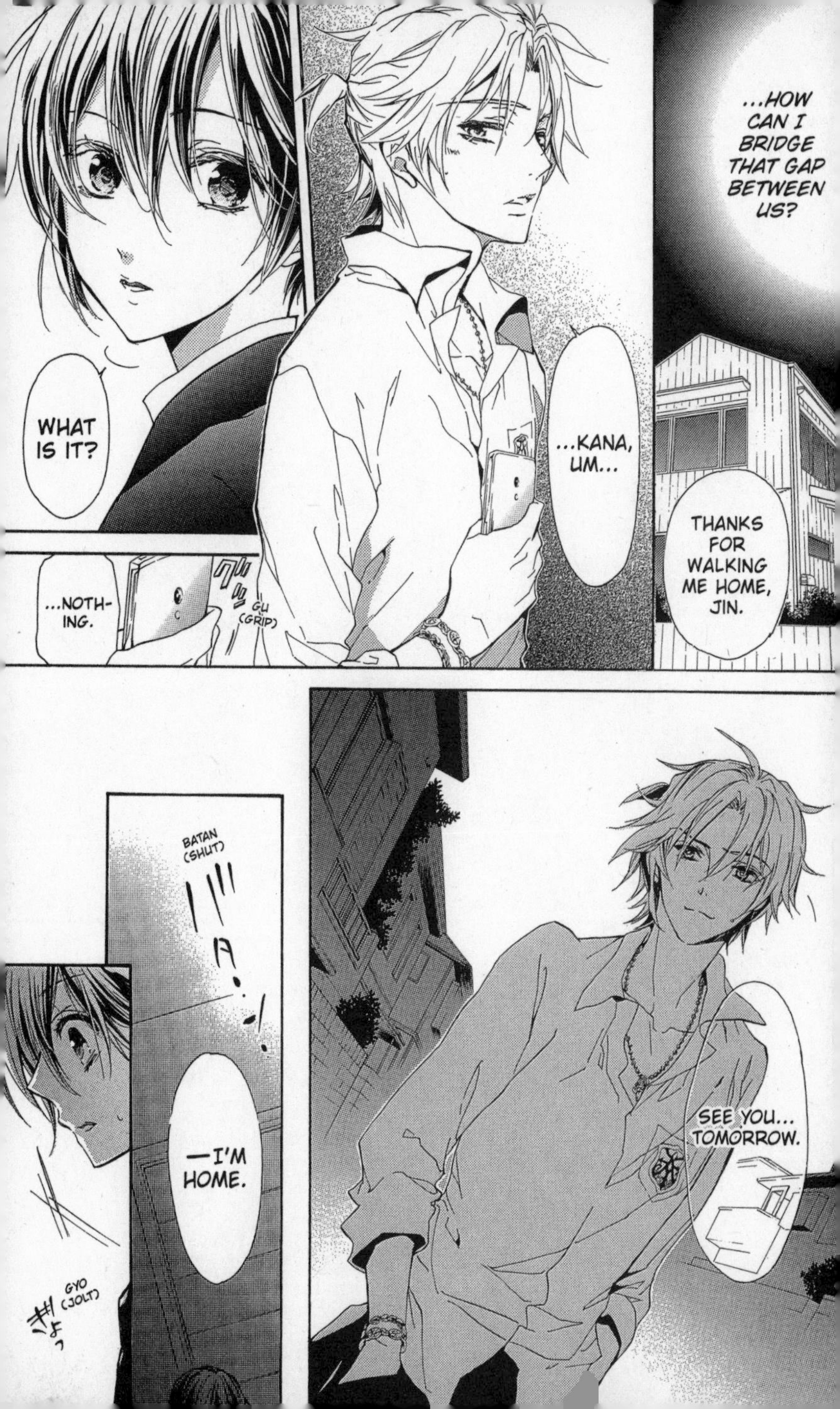
...HOW CAN I BRIDGE THAT GAP BETWEEN US?
THANKS FOR WALKING ME HOME, JIN.
...KANA, UM...
WHAT IS IT?
...NOTH-ING.
GU (GRIP)
SEE YOU... TOMORROW.
BATAN (SHUT)
—I'M HOME.
GYO (JOLT)

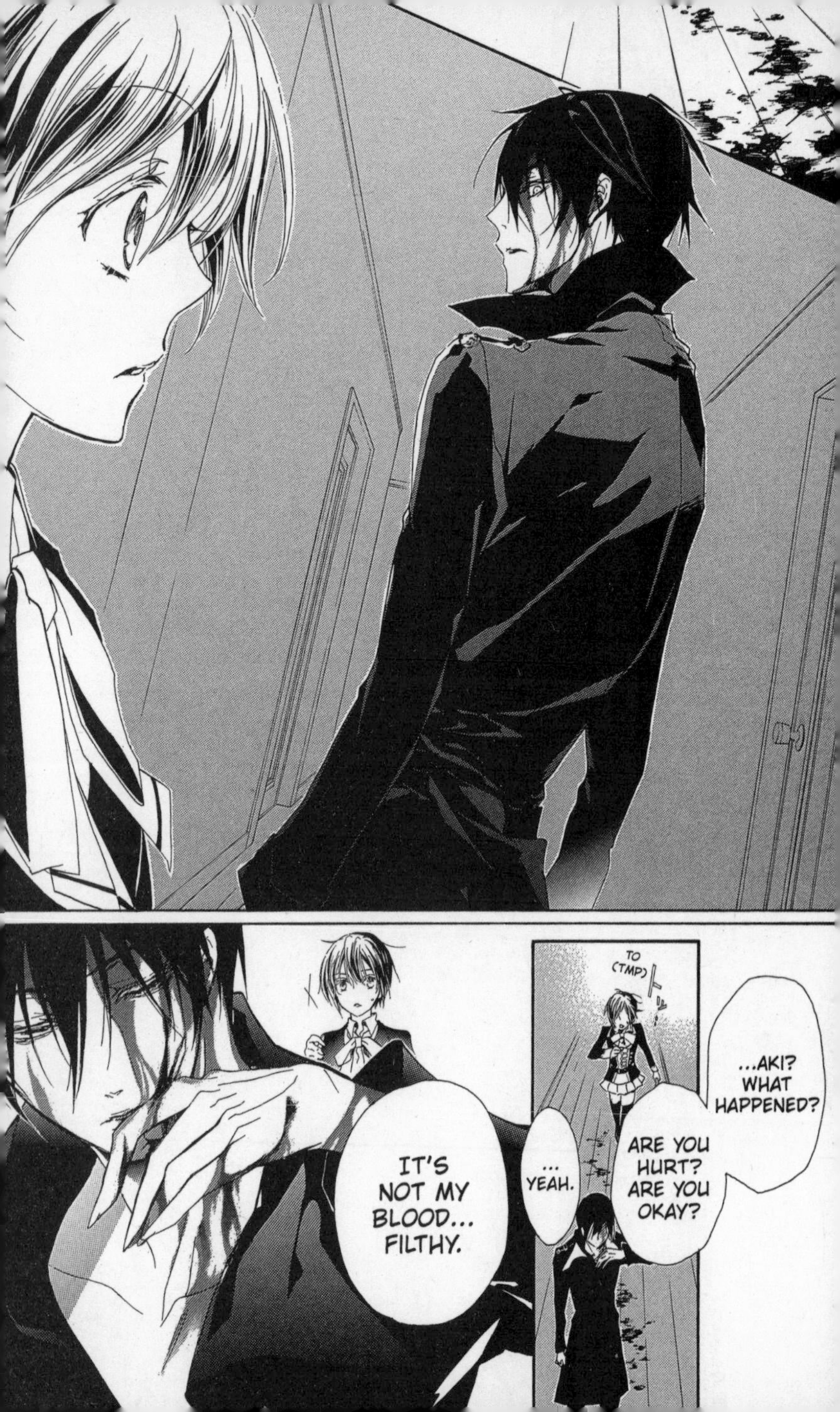
TO (TMP)
...AKI? WHAT HAPPENED?
ARE YOU HURT? ARE YOU OKAY?
... YEAH.
IT'S NOT MY BLOOD... FILTHY.

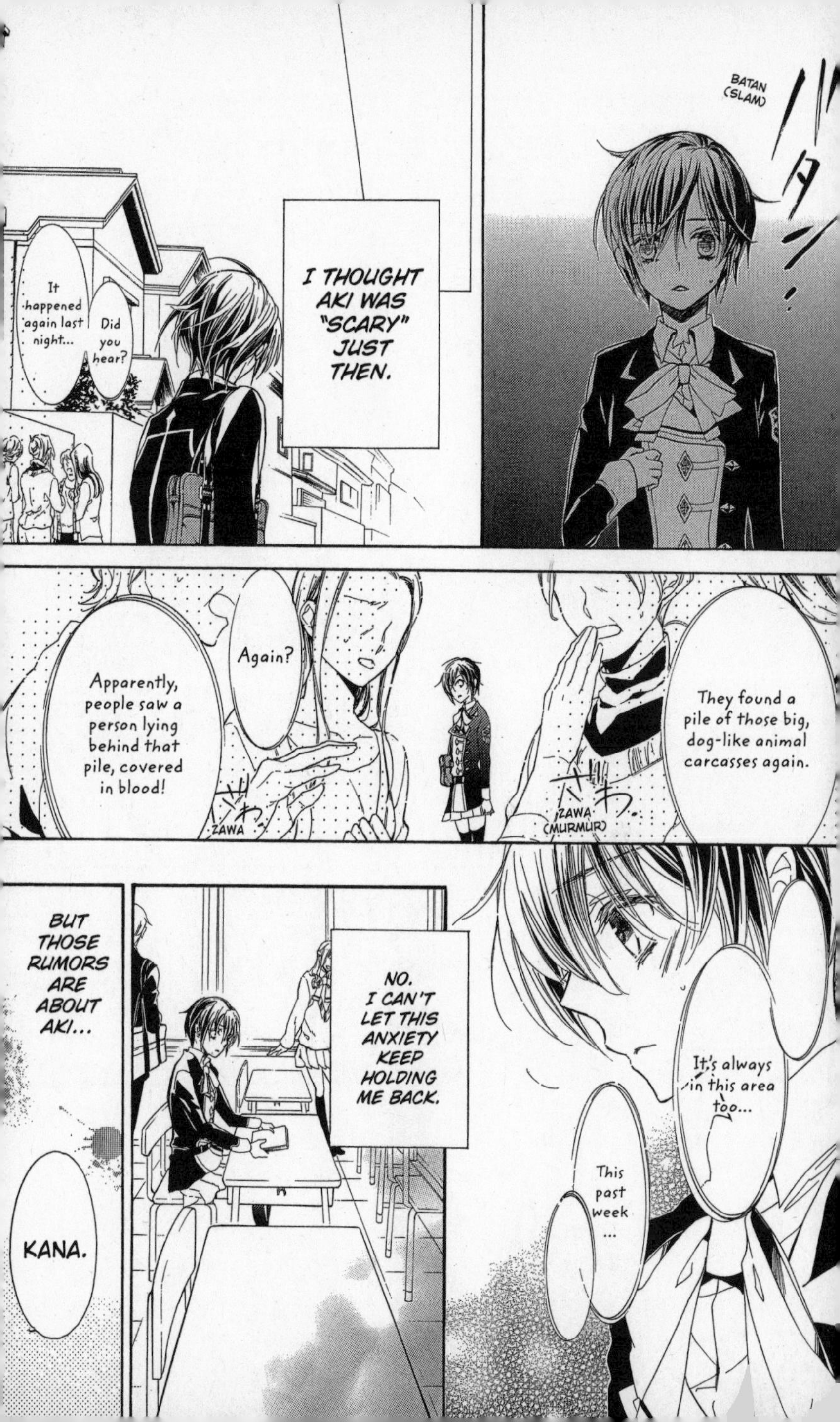
BATAN (SLAM)
I THOUGHT AKI WAS "SCARY" JUST THEN.
Did you hear?
It happened again last night...
They found a pile of those big, dog-like animal carcasses again.
ZAWA (MURMUR)
Again?
Apparently, people saw a person lying behind that pile, covered in blood!
ZAWA
It's always in this area too...
This past week ...
NO. I CAN'T LET THIS ANXIETY KEEP HOLDING ME BACK.
BUT THOSE RUMORS ARE ABOUT AKI...
KANA.

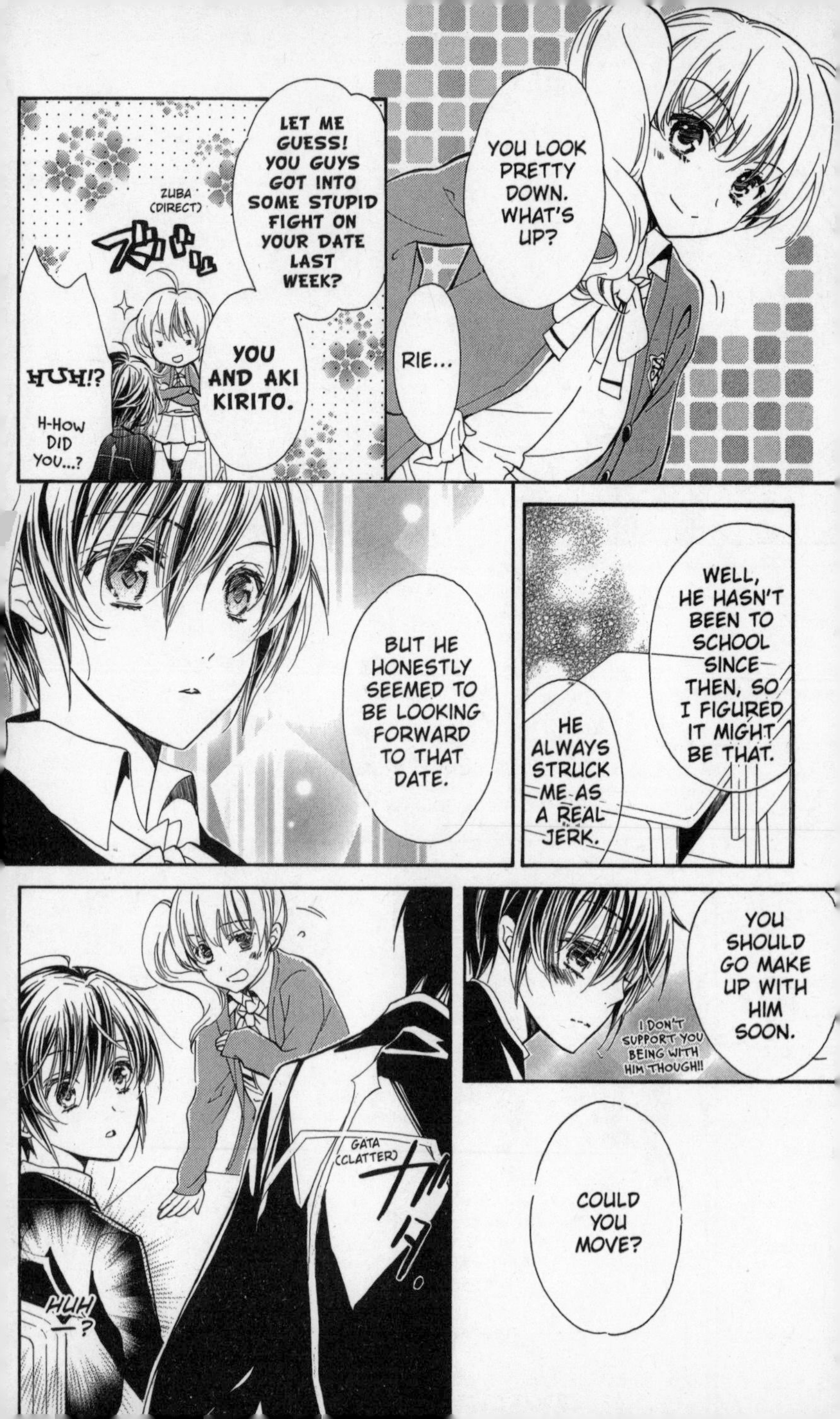
YOU LOOK PRETTY DOWN. WHAT'S UP?
RIE...
LET ME GUESS! YOU GUYS GOT INTO SOME STUPID FIGHT ON YOUR DATE LAST WEEK?
ZUBA (DIRECT)
YOU AND AKI KIRITO.
HUH!?
H-HOW DID YOU...?
WELL, HE HASN'T BEEN TO SCHOOL SINCE THEN, SO I FIGURED IT MIGHT BE THAT.
HE ALWAYS STRUCK ME AS A REAL JERK.
BUT HE HONESTLY SEEMED TO BE LOOKING FORWARD TO THAT DATE.
YOU SHOULD GO MAKE UP WITH HIM SOON.
I DON'T SUPPORT YOU BEING WITH HIM THOUGH!!
COULD YOU MOVE?
GATA (CLATTER)
HUH—?

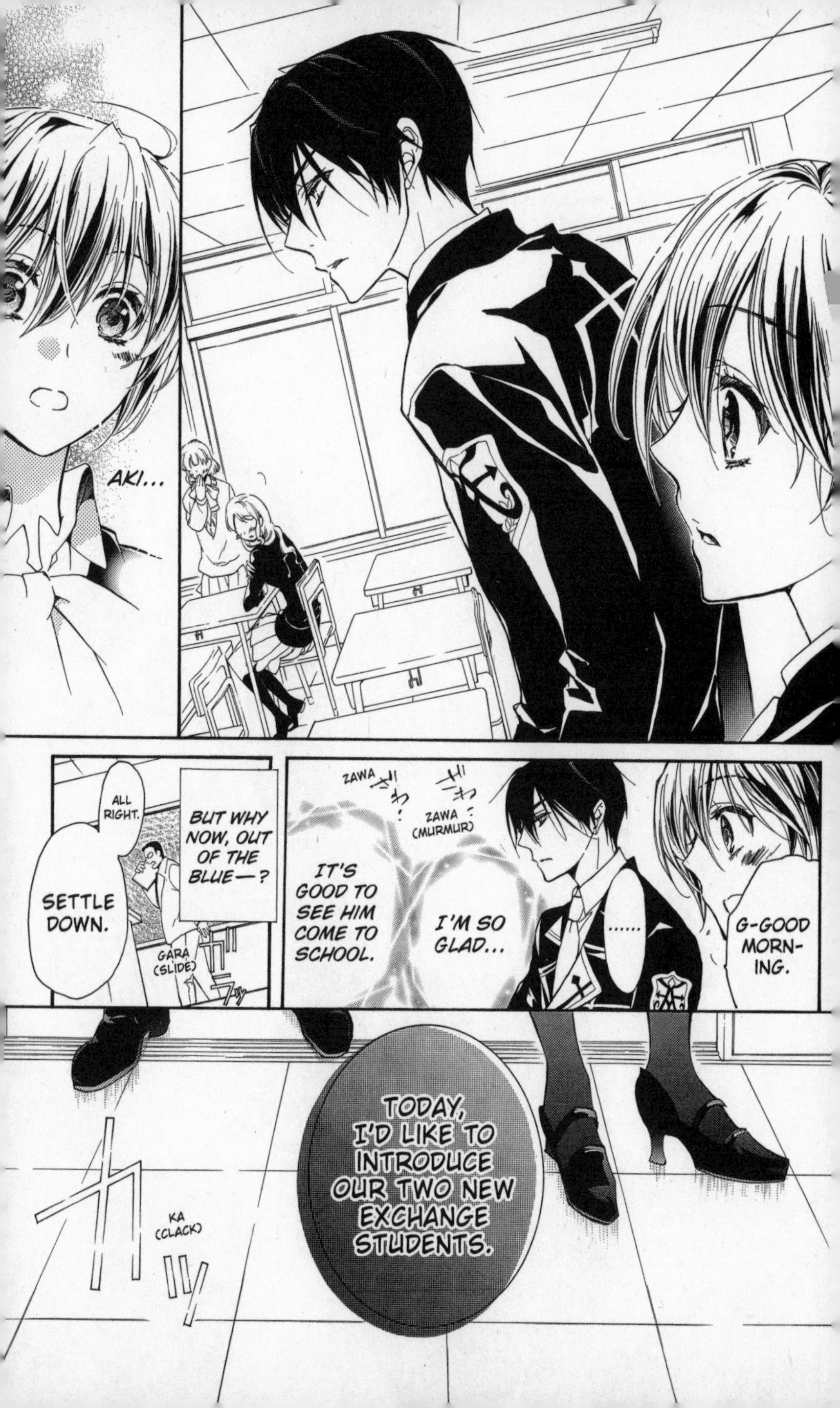
AKI...
ZAWA
ZAWA (MURMUR)
G-GOOD MORNING.
......
I'M SO GLAD...
IT'S GOOD TO SEE HIM COME TO SCHOOL.
BUT WHY NOW, OUT OF THE BLUE—?
ALL RIGHT.
SETTLE DOWN.
GARA (SLIDE)
TODAY, I'D LIKE TO INTRODUCE OUR TWO NEW EXCHANGE STUDENTS.
KA (CLACK)

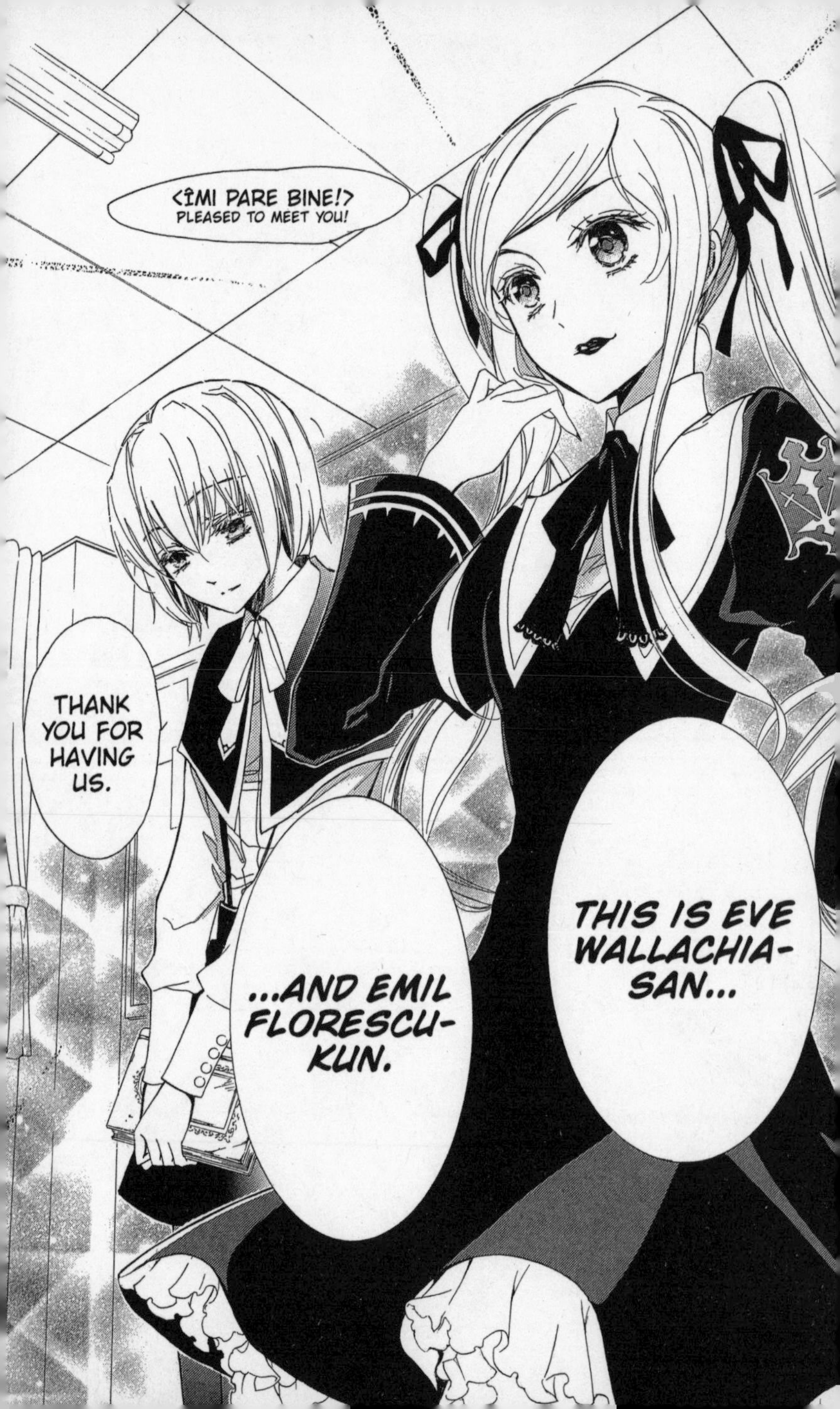
THIS IS EVE WALLACHIA-SAN...
...AND EMIL FLORESCU-KUN.
<ÎMI PARE BINE!> PLEASED TO MEET YOU!
THANK YOU FOR HAVING US.

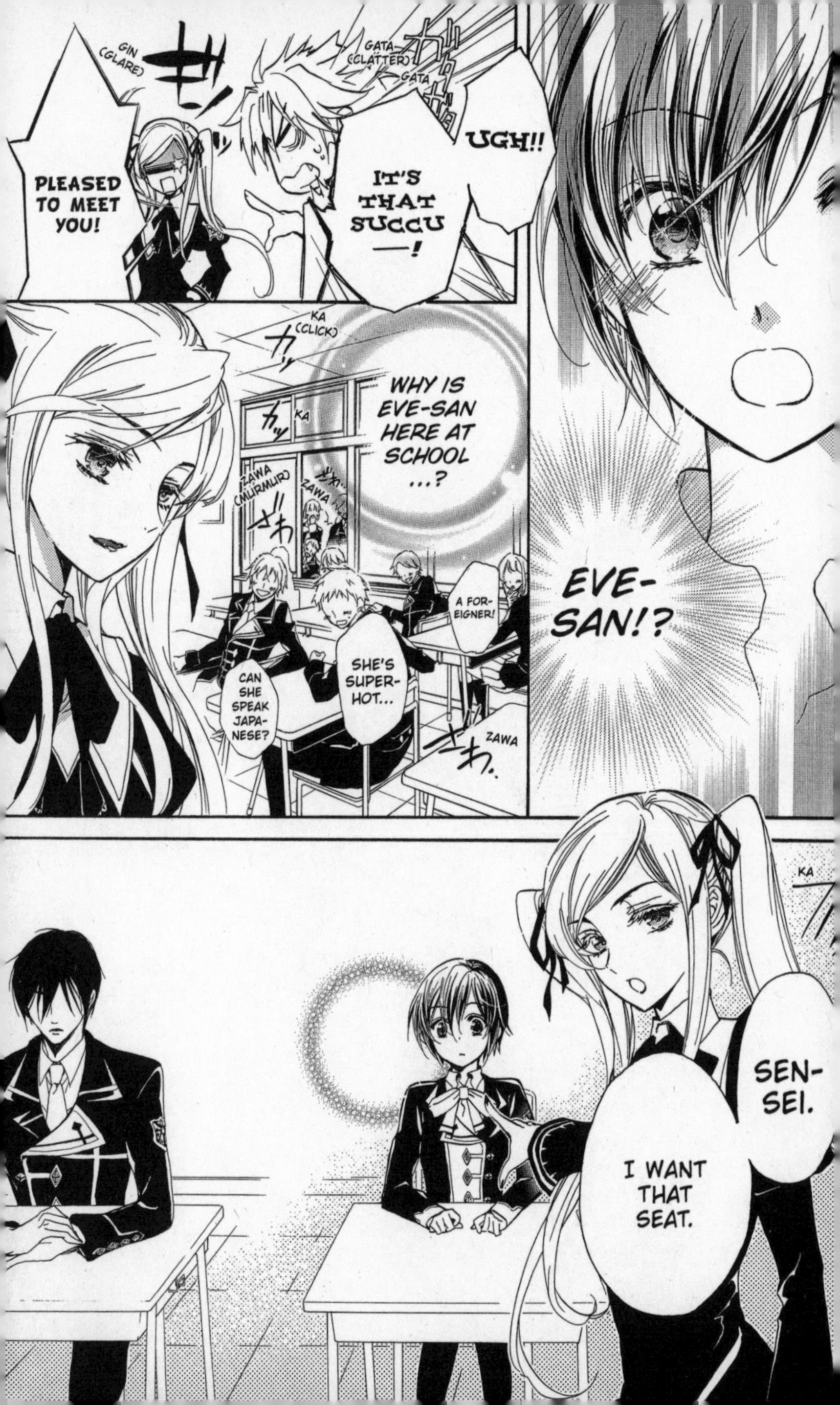
EVE-SAN!?
GATA (CLATTER) GATA
UGH!!
IT'S THAT SUCCU—!
GIN (GLARE)
PLEASED TO MEET YOU!
KA (CLICK)
WHY IS EVE-SAN HERE AT SCHOOL ...?
KA
ZAWA ZAWA (MURMUR)
A FOREIGNER!
SHE'S SUPERHOT...
CAN SHE SPEAK JAPANESE?
ZAWA
KA
SENSEI.
I WANT THAT SEAT.

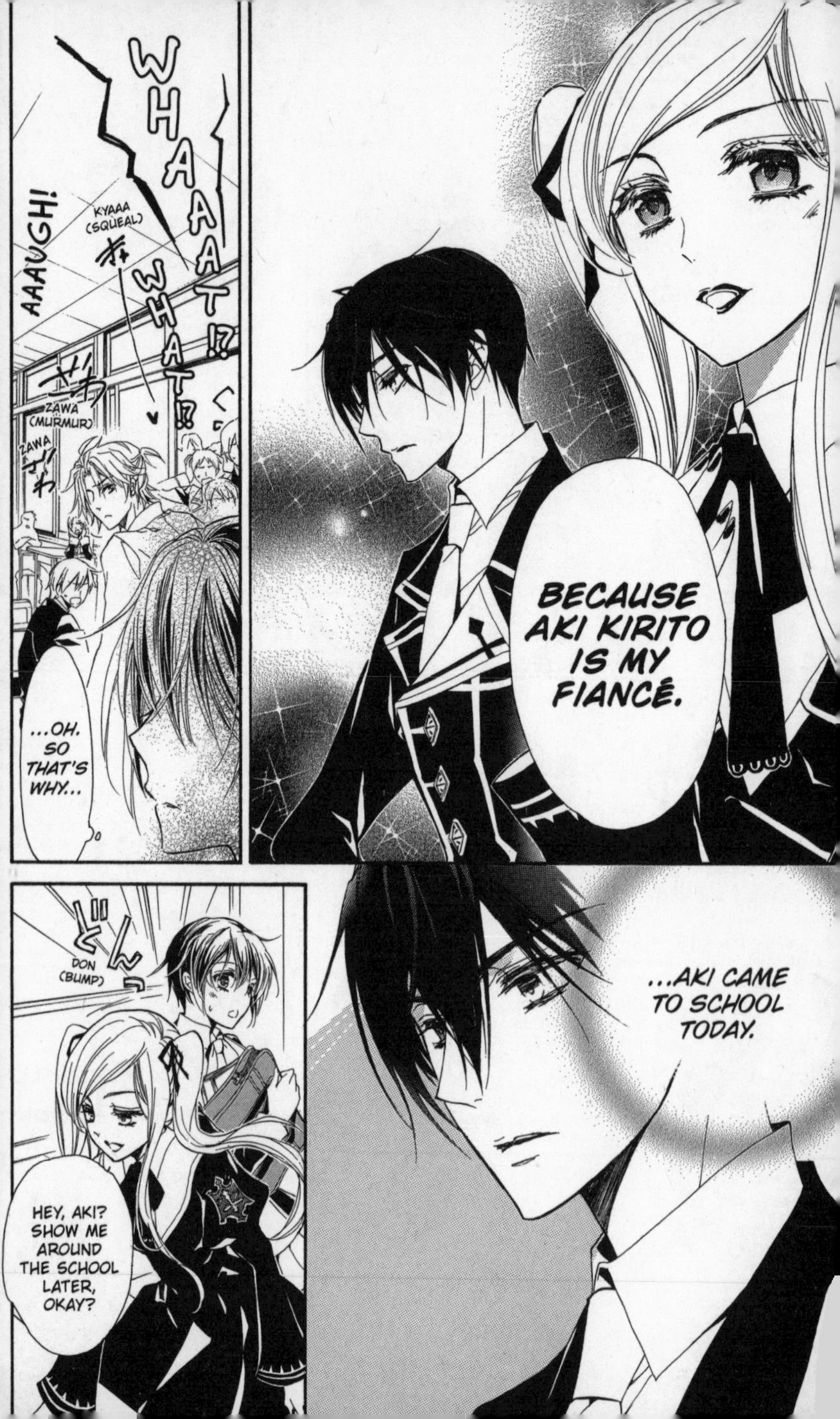
BECAUSE AKI KIRITO IS MY FIANCÉ.
WHAAAT!?
WHAT!?
KYAAA (SQUEAL)
AAAUGH!
ざわ
ZAWA (MURMUR)
ZAWA
ざわ
...OH. SO THAT'S WHY...
...AKI CAME TO SCHOOL TODAY.
どん
DON (BUMP)
HEY, AKI? SHOW ME AROUND THE SCHOOL LATER, OKAY?

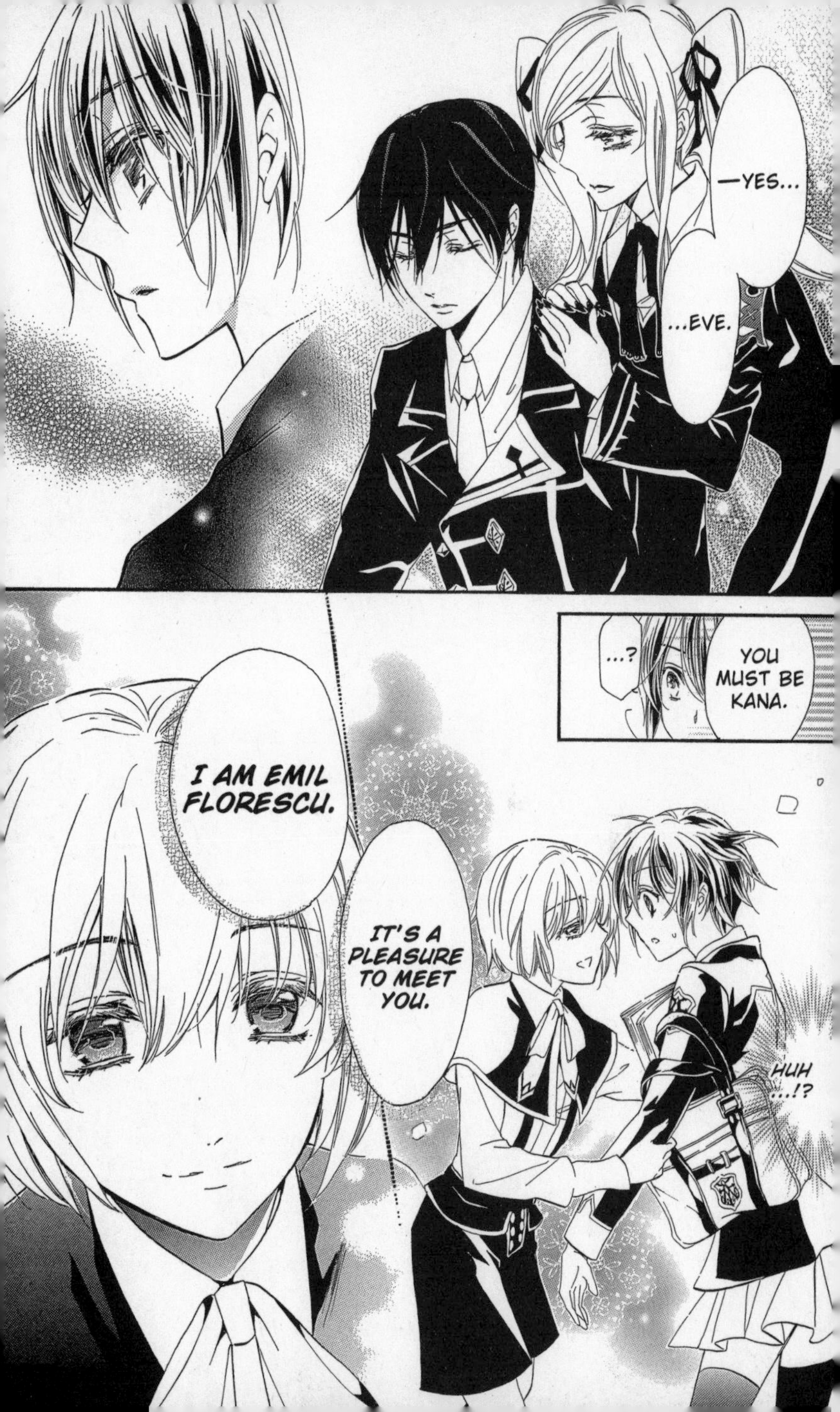
—YES...
...EVE.
YOU MUST BE KANA.
...?
I AM EMIL FLORESCU.
IT'S A PLEASURE TO MEET YOU.
HUH ...!?

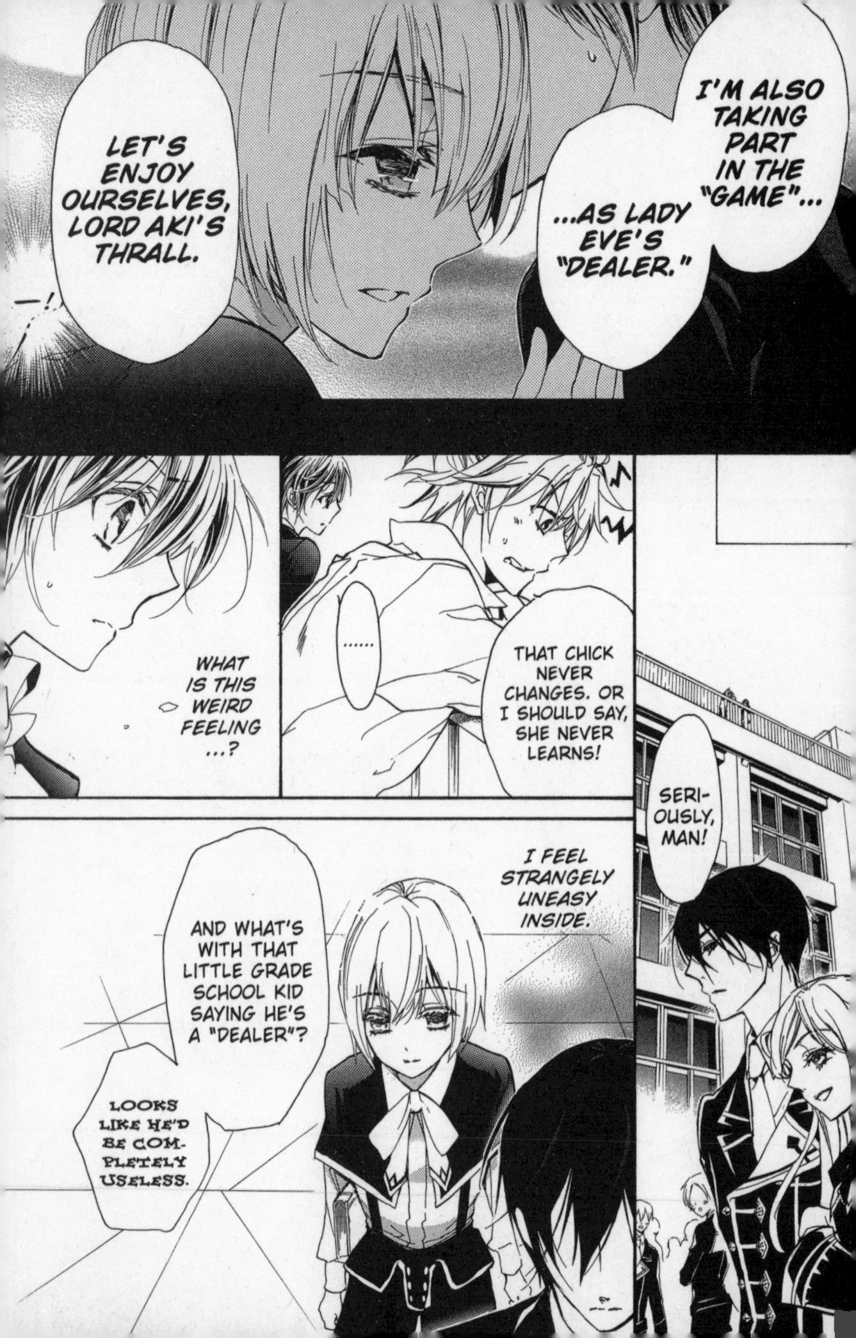
I'M ALSO TAKING PART IN THE "GAME"...
...AS LADY EVE'S "DEALER."
LET'S ENJOY OURSELVES, LORD AKI'S THRALL.
—!
SERI-OUSLY, MAN!
THAT CHICK NEVER CHANGES. OR I SHOULD SAY, SHE NEVER LEARNS!
......
WHAT IS THIS WEIRD FEELING ...?
I FEEL STRANGELY UNEASY INSIDE.
AND WHAT'S WITH THAT LITTLE GRADE SCHOOL KID SAYING HE'S A "DEALER"?
LOOKS LIKE HE'D BE COM-PLETELY USELESS.

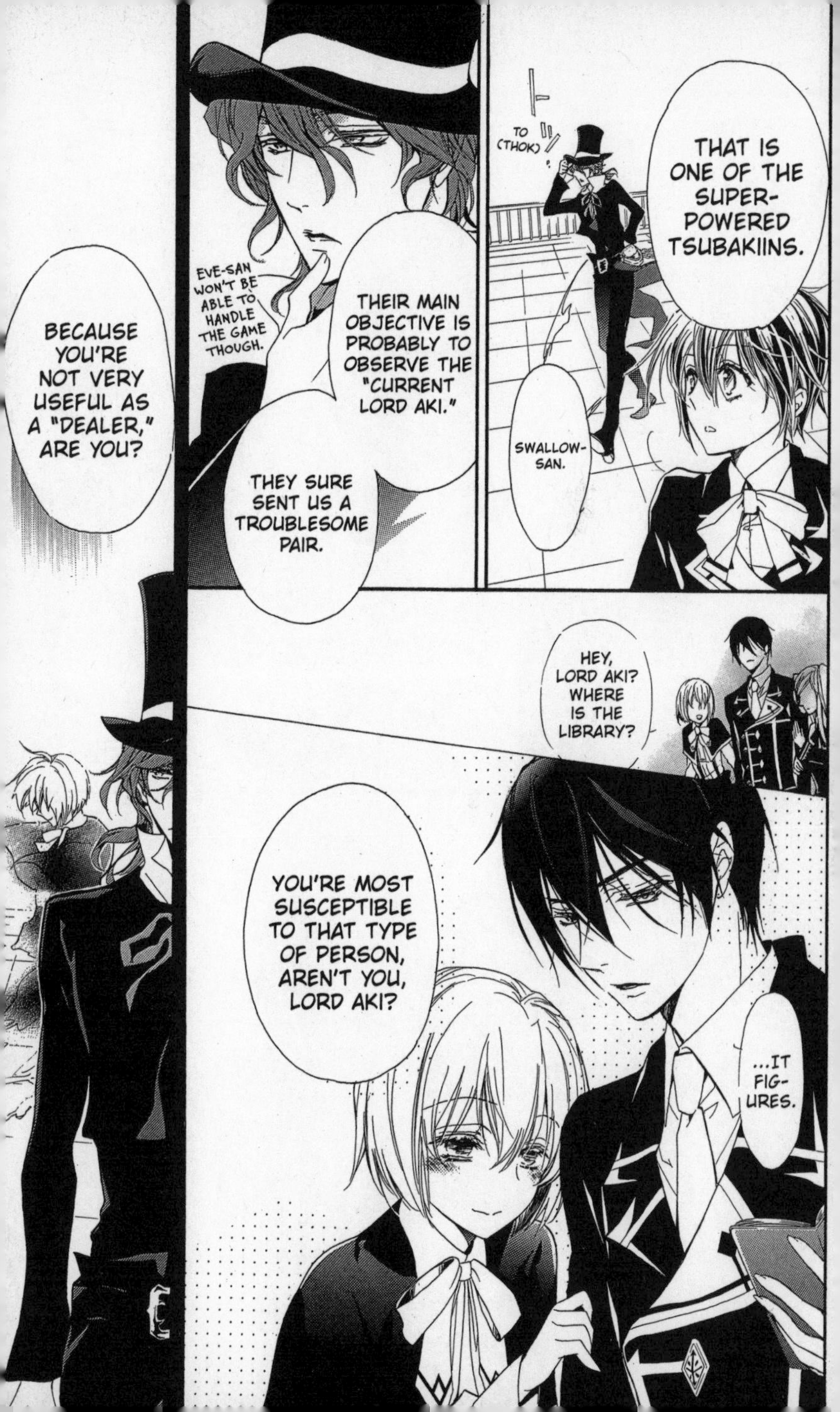
TO (THOK)
THAT IS ONE OF THE SUPER-POWERED TSUBAKIINS.
SWALLOW-SAN.
THEIR MAIN OBJECTIVE IS PROBABLY TO OBSERVE THE "CURRENT LORD AKI."
EVE-SAN WON'T BE ABLE TO HANDLE THE GAME THOUGH.
THEY SURE SENT US A TROUBLESOME PAIR.
HEY, LORD AKI? WHERE IS THE LIBRARY?
YOU'RE MOST SUSCEPTIBLE TO THAT TYPE OF PERSON, AREN'T YOU, LORD AKI?
...IT FIG-URES.
BECAUSE YOU'RE NOT VERY USEFUL AS A "DEALER," ARE YOU?

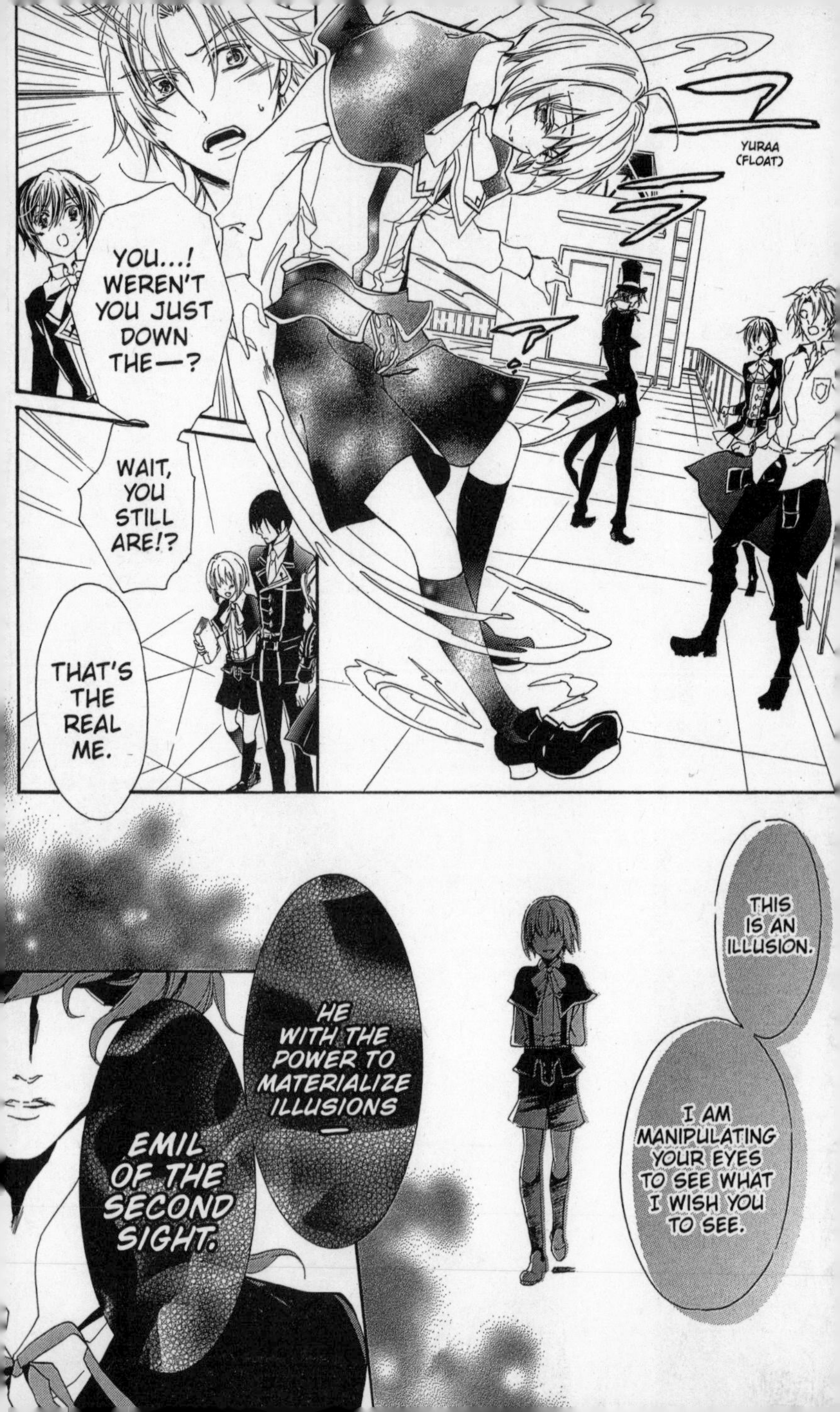
YURAA (FLOAT)
YOU...! WEREN'T YOU JUST DOWN THE—?
WAIT, YOU STILL ARE!?
THAT'S THE REAL ME.
THIS IS AN ILLUSION.
I AM MANIPULATING YOUR EYES TO SEE WHAT I WISH YOU TO SEE.
HE WITH THE POWER TO MATERIALIZE ILLUSIONS—
EMIL OF THE SECOND SIGHT.

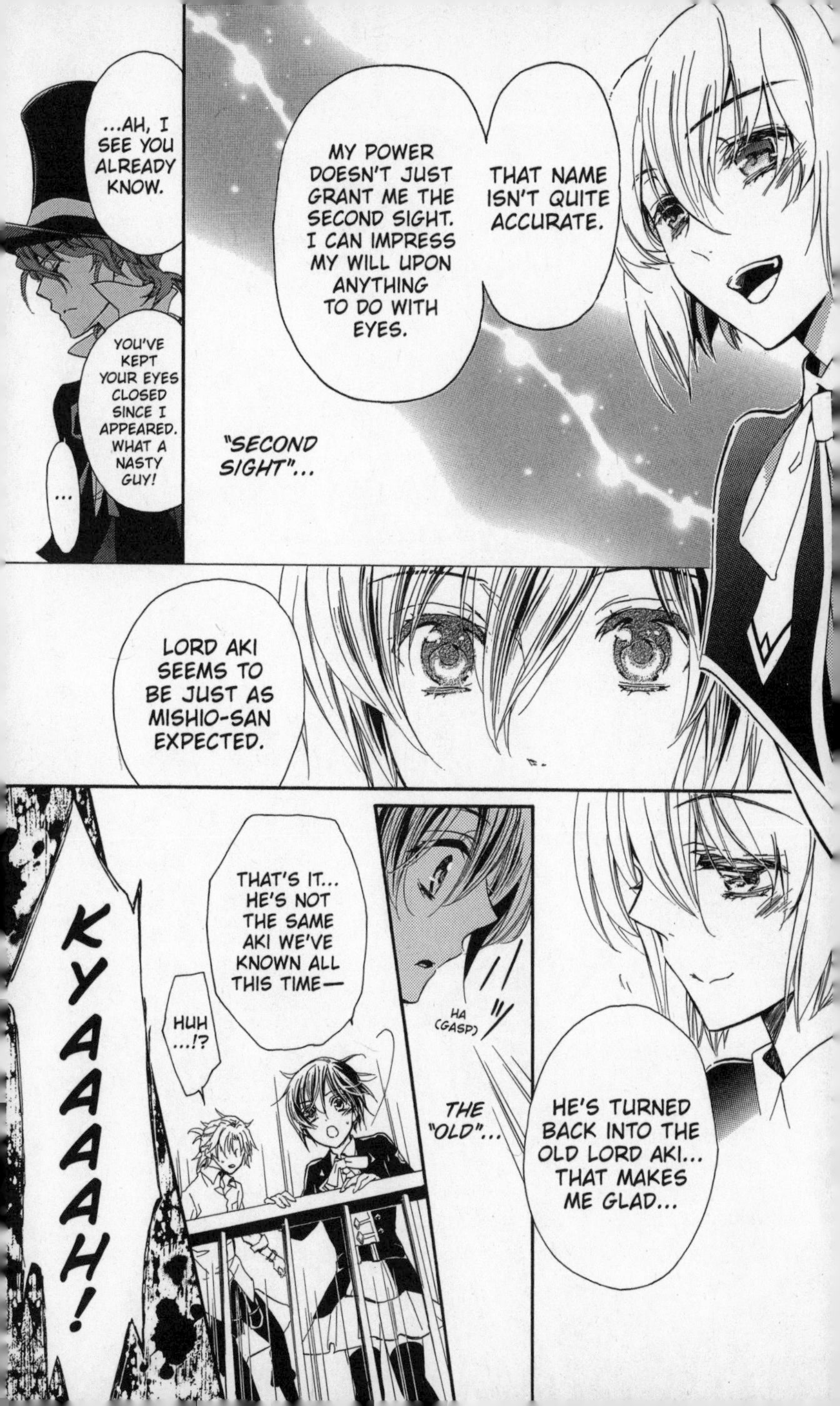

THAT NAME ISN'T QUITE ACCURATE.
MY POWER DOESN'T JUST GRANT ME THE SECOND SIGHT. I CAN IMPRESS MY WILL UPON ANYTHING TO DO WITH EYES.
"SECOND SIGHT"...
...AH, I SEE YOU ALREADY KNOW.
YOU'VE KEPT YOUR EYES CLOSED SINCE I APPEARED. WHAT A NASTY GUY!
...
LORD AKI SEEMS TO BE JUST AS MISHIO-SAN EXPECTED.
HE'S TURNED BACK INTO THE OLD LORD AKI... THAT MAKES ME GLAD...
THE "OLD"...
HA (GASP)
THAT'S IT... HE'S NOT THE SAME AKI WE'VE KNOWN ALL THIS TIME—
HUH ...!?
KYAAAAAH!

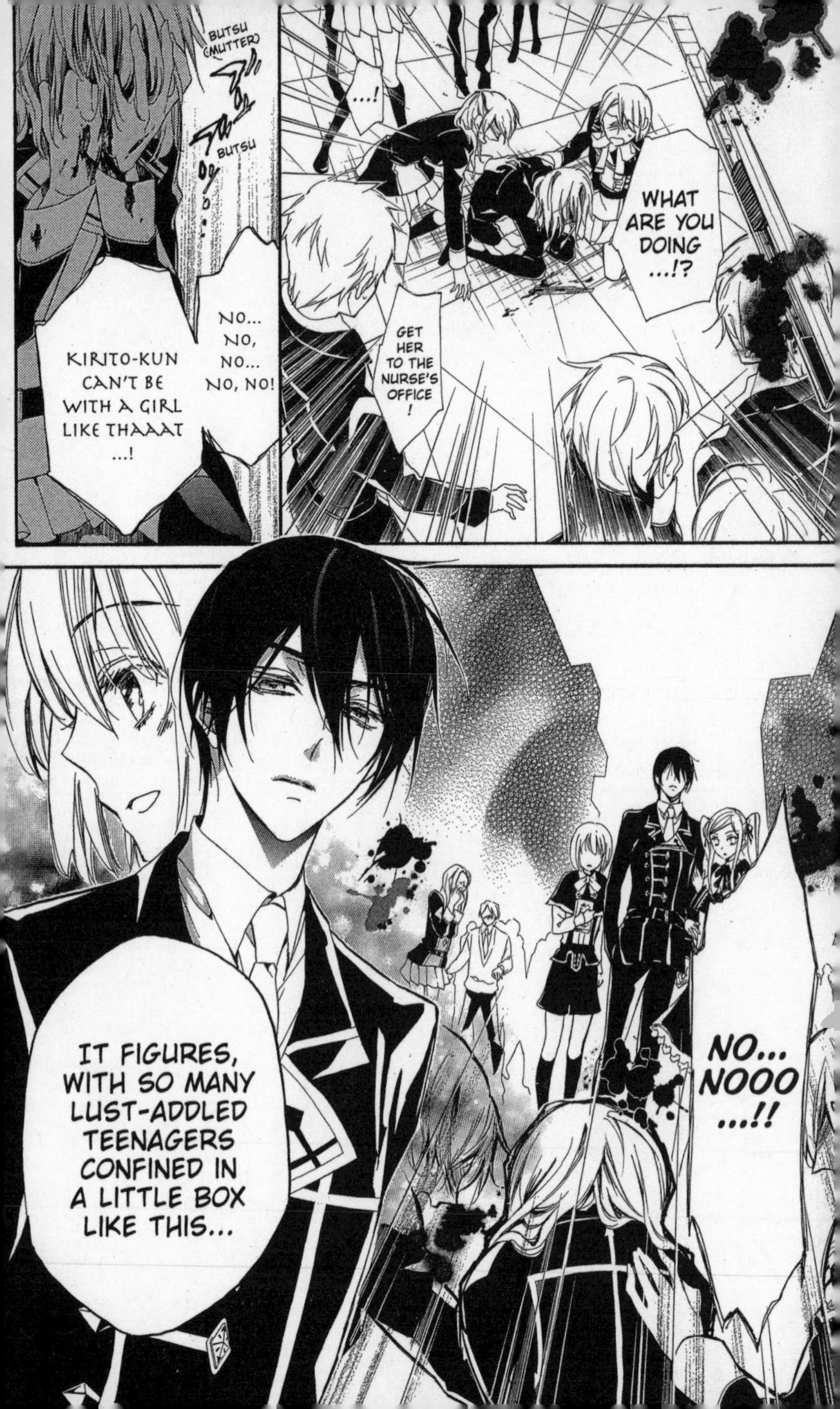
...!
WHAT ARE YOU DOING ...!?
GET HER TO THE NURSE'S OFFICE!
BUTSU (MUTTER)
BUTSU
NO... NO, NO... NO, NO!
KIRITO-KUN CAN'T BE WITH A GIRL LIKE THAAAT ...!
NO... NOOO ...!!
IT FIGURES, WITH SO MANY LUST-ADDLED TEENAGERS CONFINED IN A LITTLE BOX LIKE THIS...

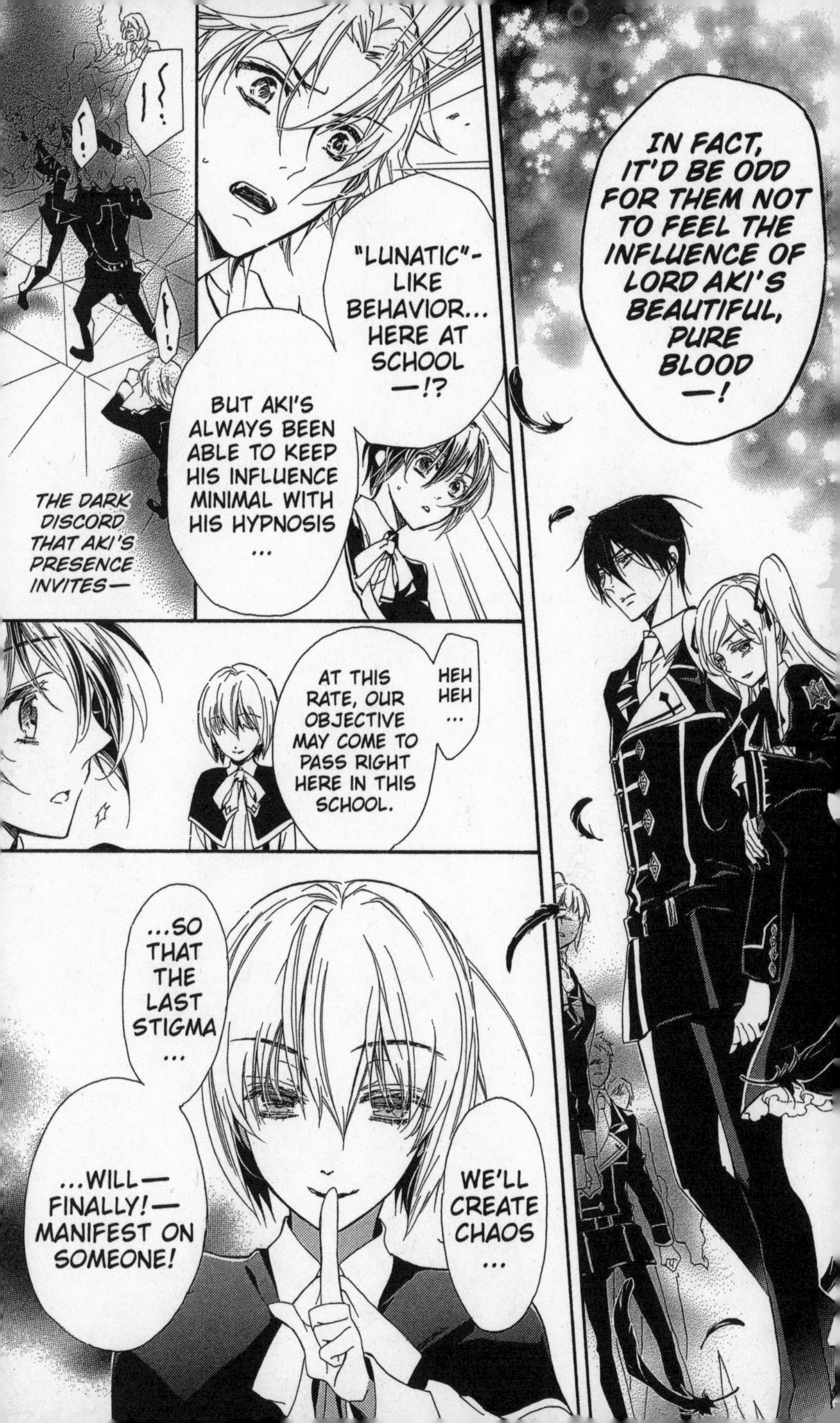
IN FACT, IT'D BE ODD FOR THEM NOT TO FEEL THE INFLUENCE OF LORD AKI'S BEAUTIFUL, PURE BLOOD—!
"LUNATIC"-LIKE BEHAVIOR... HERE AT SCHOOL—!?
BUT AKI'S ALWAYS BEEN ABLE TO KEEP HIS INFLUENCE MINIMAL WITH HIS HYPNOSIS...
!?
!?
!
THE DARK DISCORD THAT AKI'S PRESENCE INVITES—
HEH HEH...
AT THIS RATE, OUR OBJECTIVE MAY COME TO PASS RIGHT HERE IN THIS SCHOOL.
WE'LL CREATE CHAOS...
...SO THAT THE LAST STIGMA...
...WILL—FINALLY!—MANIFEST ON SOMEONE!

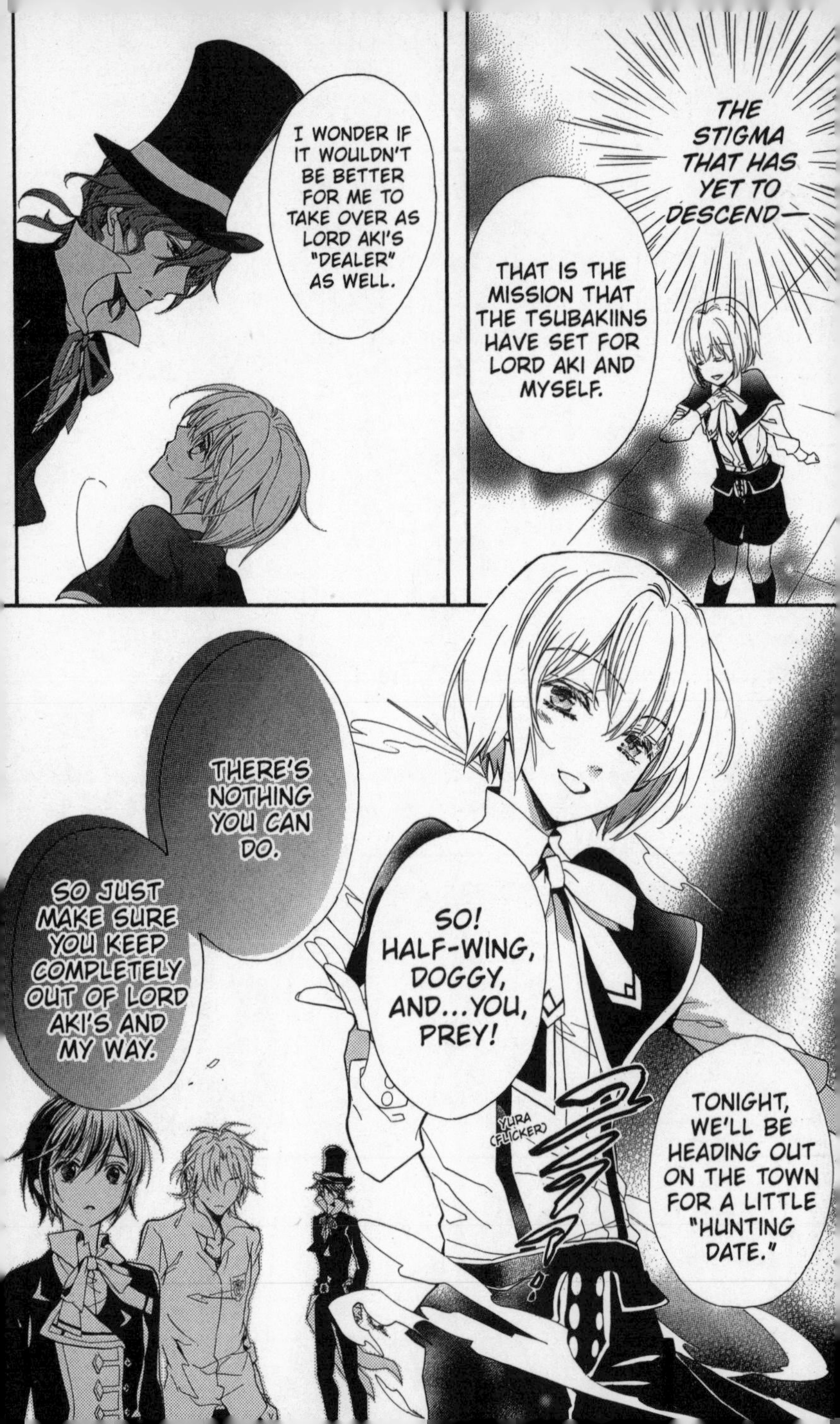
THE STIGMA THAT HAS YET TO DESCEND—
THAT IS THE MISSION THAT THE TSUBAKIINS HAVE SET FOR LORD AKI AND MYSELF.
I WONDER IF IT WOULDN'T BE BETTER FOR ME TO TAKE OVER AS LORD AKI'S "DEALER" AS WELL.
TONIGHT, WE'LL BE HEADING OUT ON THE TOWN FOR A LITTLE "HUNTING DATE."
YURA (FLICKER)
SO! HALF-WING, DOGGY, AND...YOU, PREY!
THERE'S NOTHING YOU CAN DO.
SO JUST MAKE SURE YOU KEEP COMPLETELY OUT OF LORD AKI'S AND MY WAY.

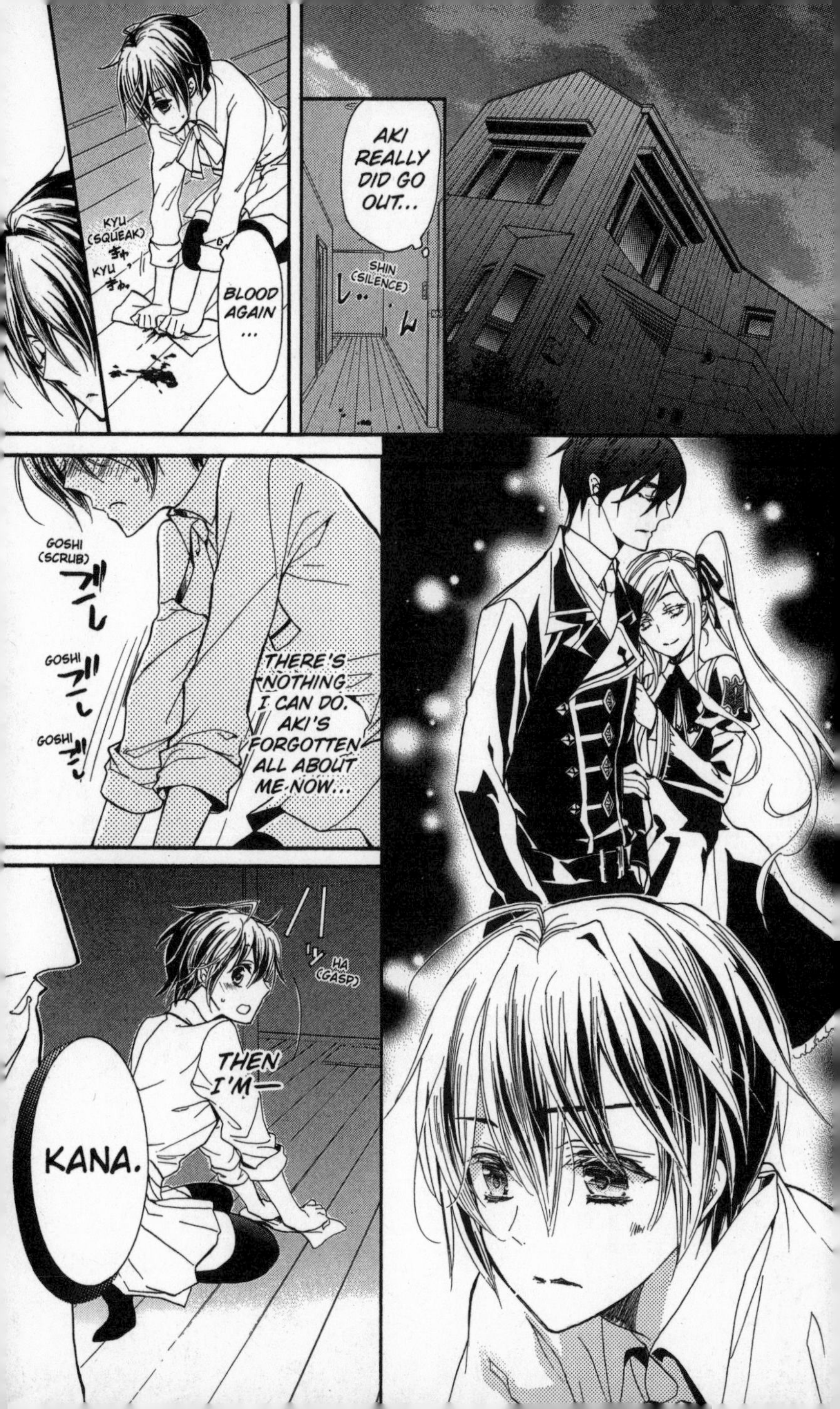

AKI REALLY DID GO OUT...
SHIN (SILENCE)
KYU (SQUEAK)
KYU
BLOOD AGAIN...
GOSHI (SCRUB)
GOSHI
GOSHI
THERE'S NOTHING I CAN DO. AKI'S FORGOTTEN ALL ABOUT ME NOW...
HA (GASP)
THEN I'M—
KANA.

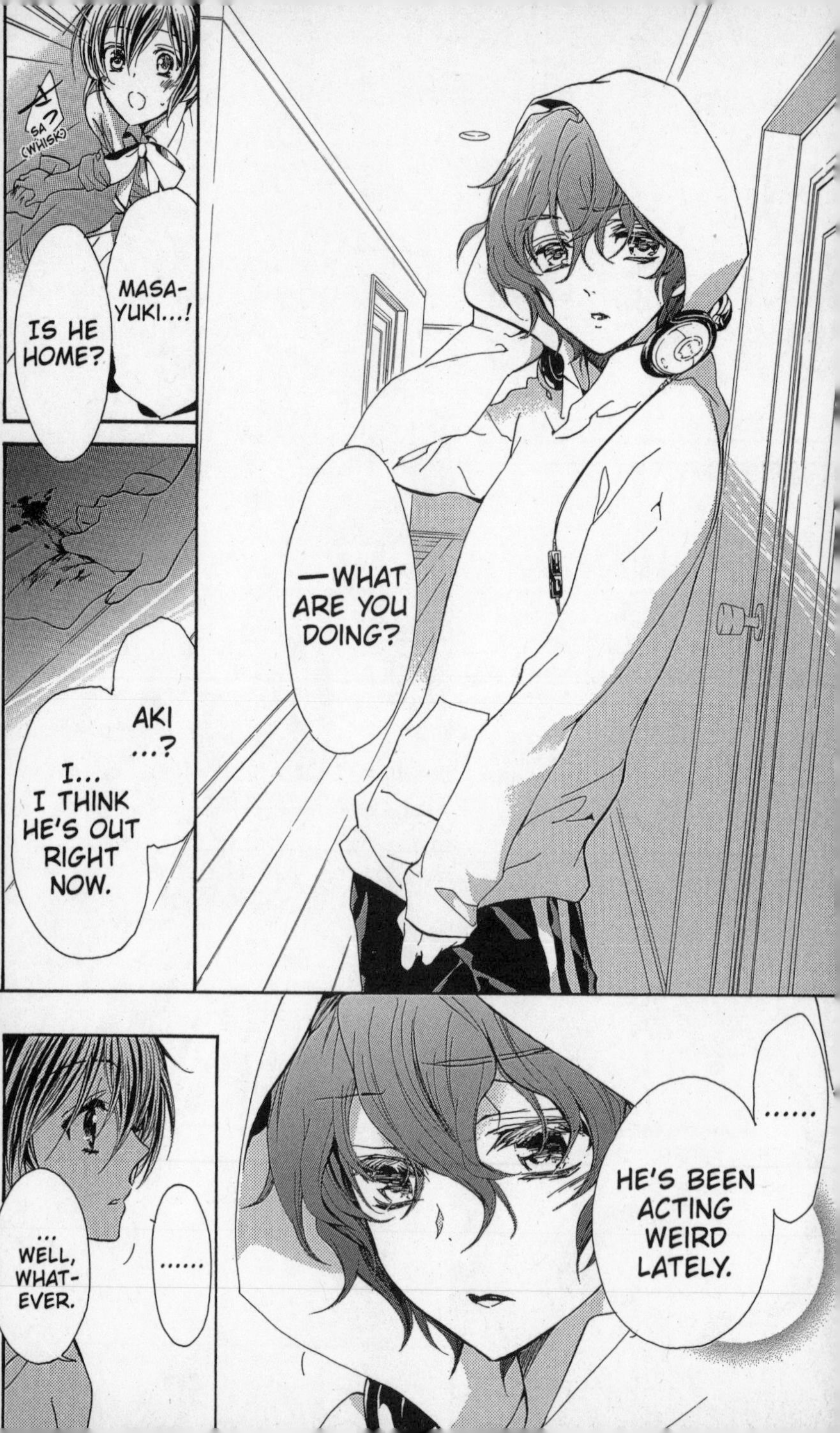
—WHAT ARE YOU DOING?
SA (WHISK)
MASA-YUKI...!
IS HE HOME?
AKI ...?
I... I THINK HE'S OUT RIGHT NOW.
......
HE'S BEEN ACTING WEIRD LATELY.
......
... WELL, WHAT-EVER.

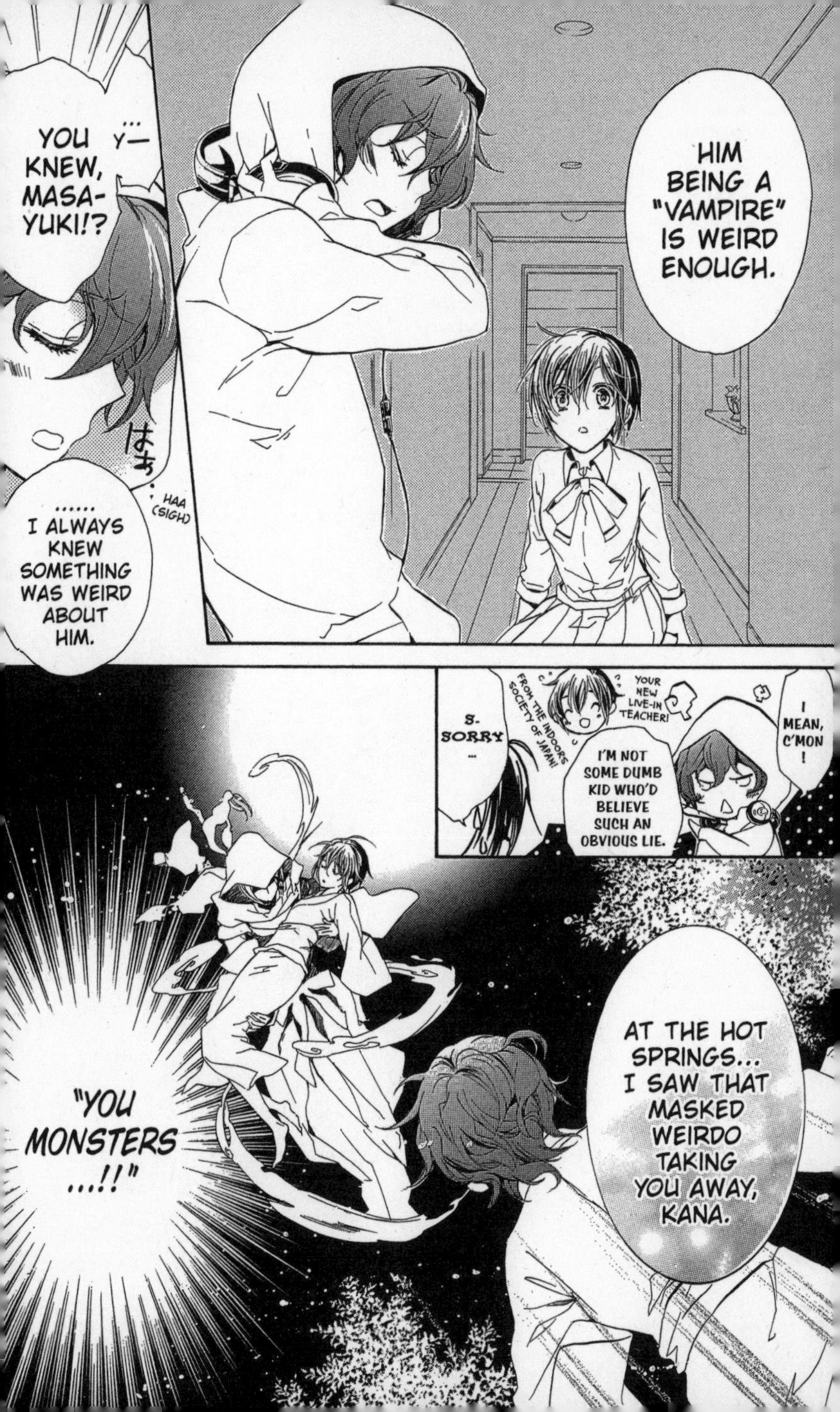
HIM BEING A "VAMPIRE" IS WEIRD ENOUGH.
... Y—
YOU KNEW, MASA-YUKI!?
はぁ
HAA (SIGH)
...... I ALWAYS KNEW SOMETHING WAS WEIRD ABOUT HIM.
I MEAN, C'MON!
YOUR NEW LIVE-IN TEACHER!
FROM THE INDOORS SOCIETY OF JAPAN!
I'M NOT SOME DUMB KID WHO'D BELIEVE SUCH AN OBVIOUS LIE.
S-SORRY...
AT THE HOT SPRINGS... I SAW THAT MASKED WEIRDO TAKING YOU AWAY, KANA.
"YOU MONSTERS...!!"

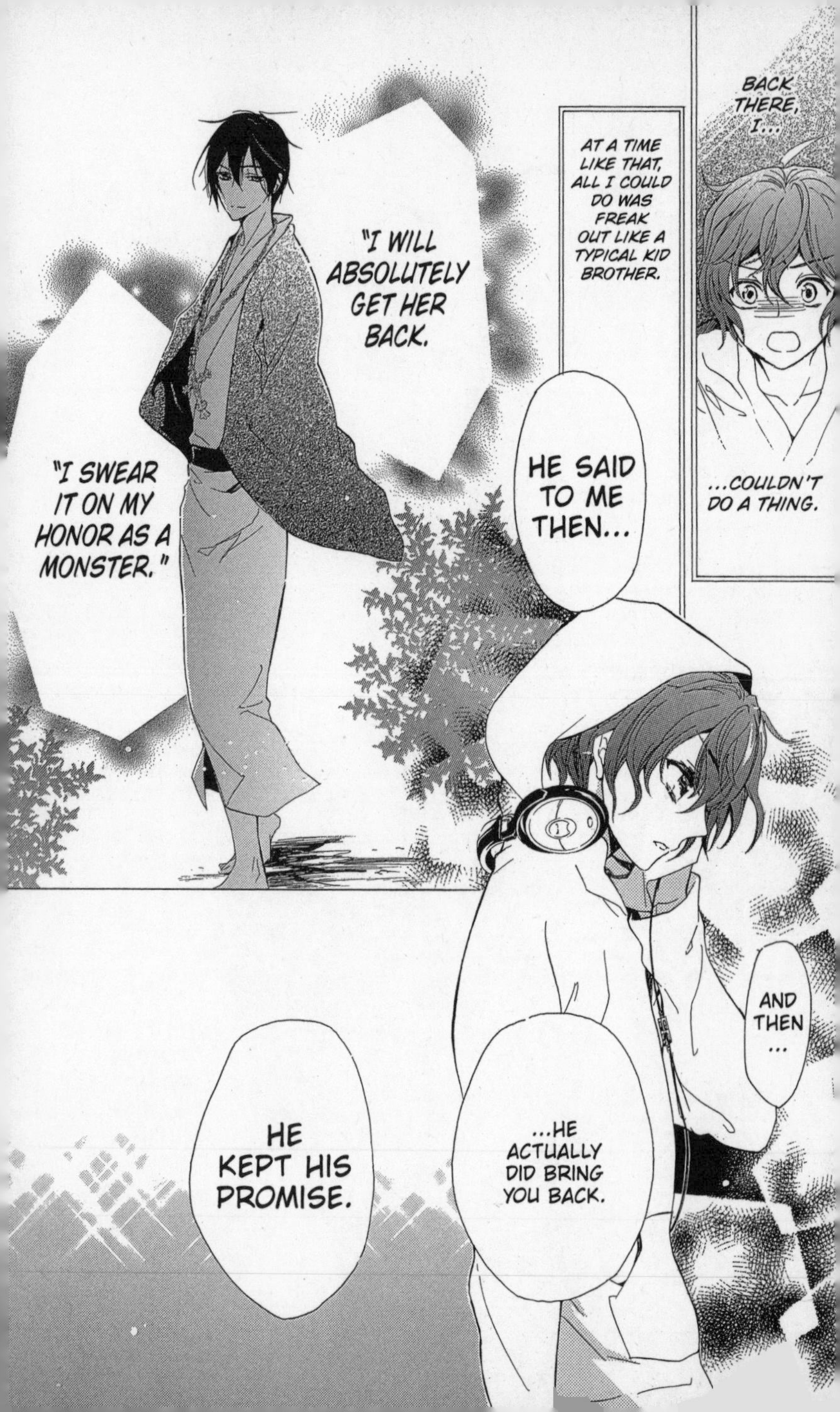

BACK THERE, I...
...COULDN'T DO A THING.
AT A TIME LIKE THAT, ALL I COULD DO WAS FREAK OUT LIKE A TYPICAL KID BROTHER.
HE SAID TO ME THEN...
"I WILL ABSOLUTELY GET HER BACK.
"I SWEAR IT ON MY HONOR AS A MONSTER."
AND THEN...
...HE ACTUALLY DID BRING YOU BACK.
HE KEPT HIS PROMISE.

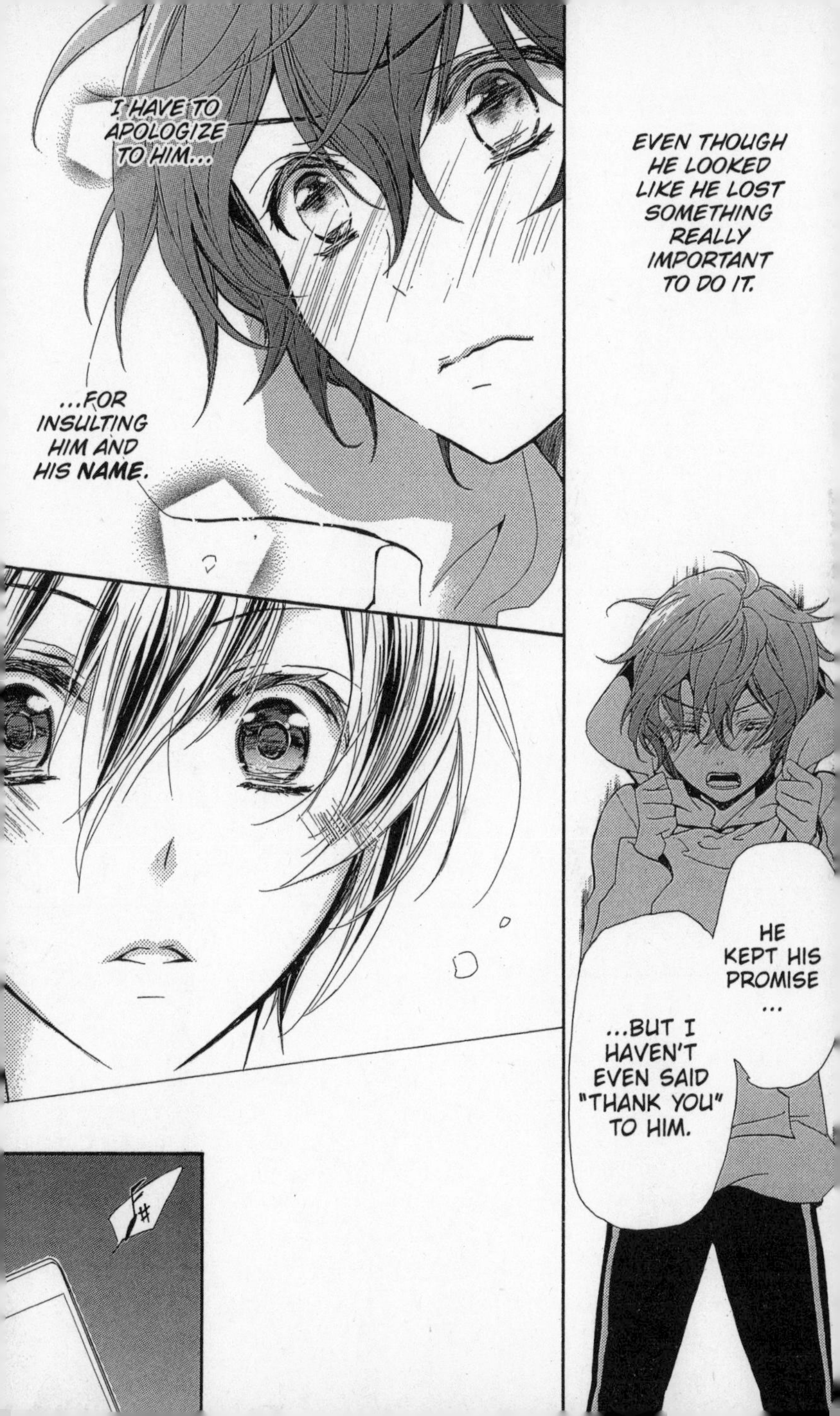
EVEN THOUGH HE LOOKED LIKE HE LOST SOMETHING REALLY IMPORTANT TO DO IT.
HE KEPT HIS PROMISE ...
...BUT I HAVEN'T EVEN SAID "THANK YOU" TO HIM.
I HAVE TO APOLOGIZE TO HIM...
...FOR INSULTING HIM AND HIS **NAME**.

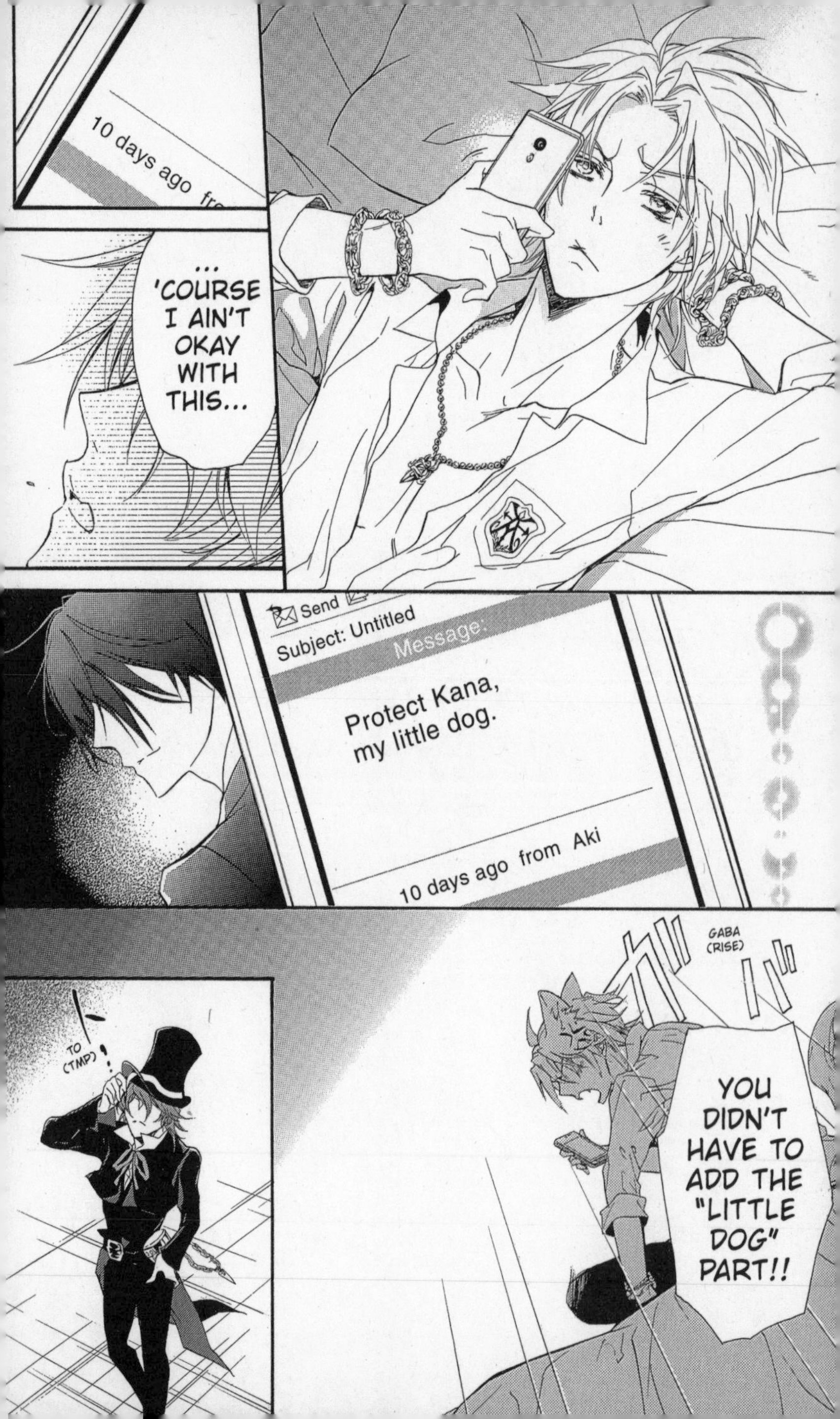
10 days ago
... 'COURSE I AIN'T OKAY WITH THIS...
Send
Subject: Untitled
Message:
Protect Kana, my little dog.
10 days ago from Aki
GABA (RISE)
YOU DIDN'T HAVE TO ADD THE "LITTLE DOG" PART!!
TO (TMP)

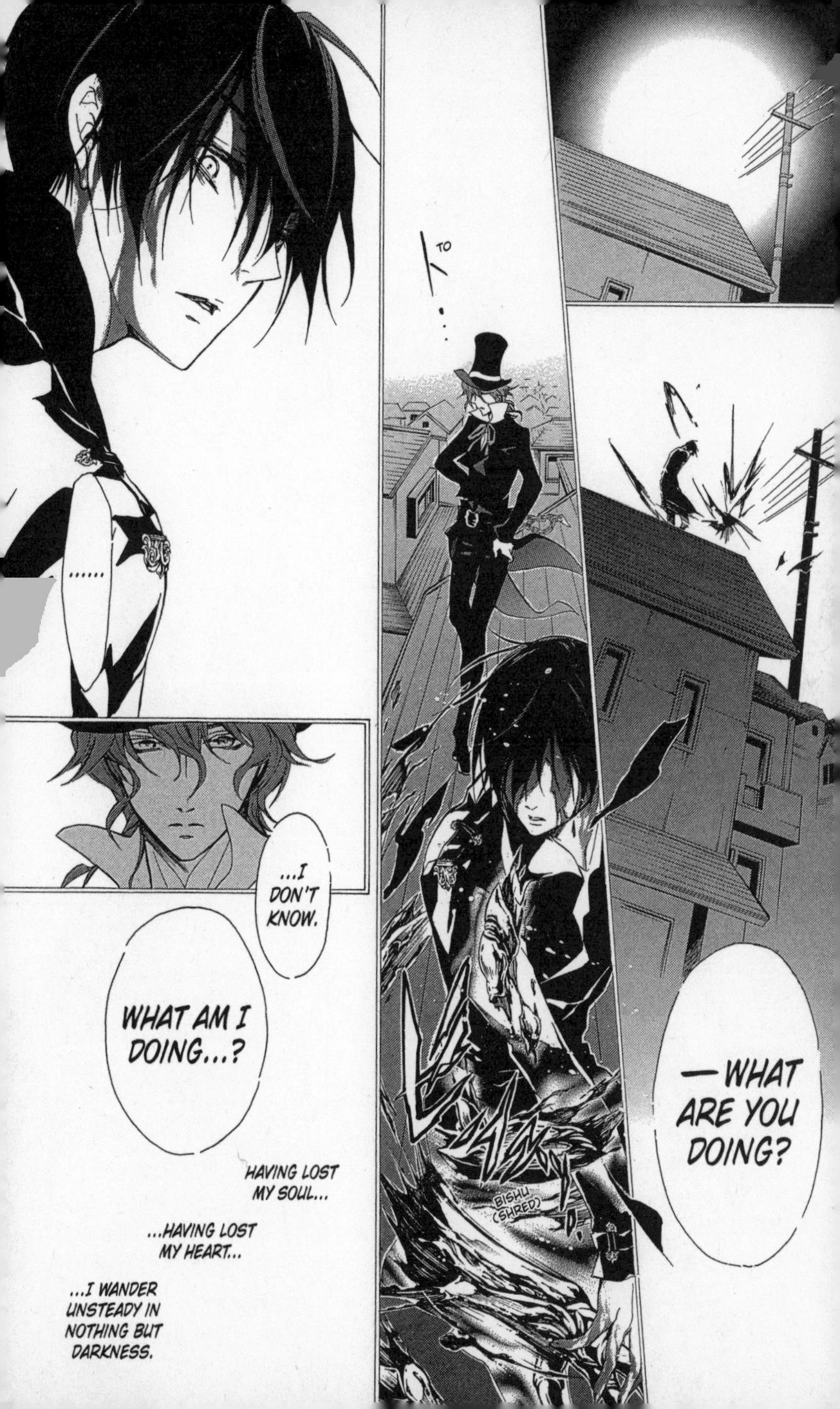

—WHAT ARE YOU DOING?
TO
BISHU (SHRED)
......
...I DON'T KNOW.
WHAT AM I DOING...?
HAVING LOST MY SOUL...
...HAVING LOST MY HEART...
...I WANDER UNSTEADY IN NOTHING BUT DARKNESS.

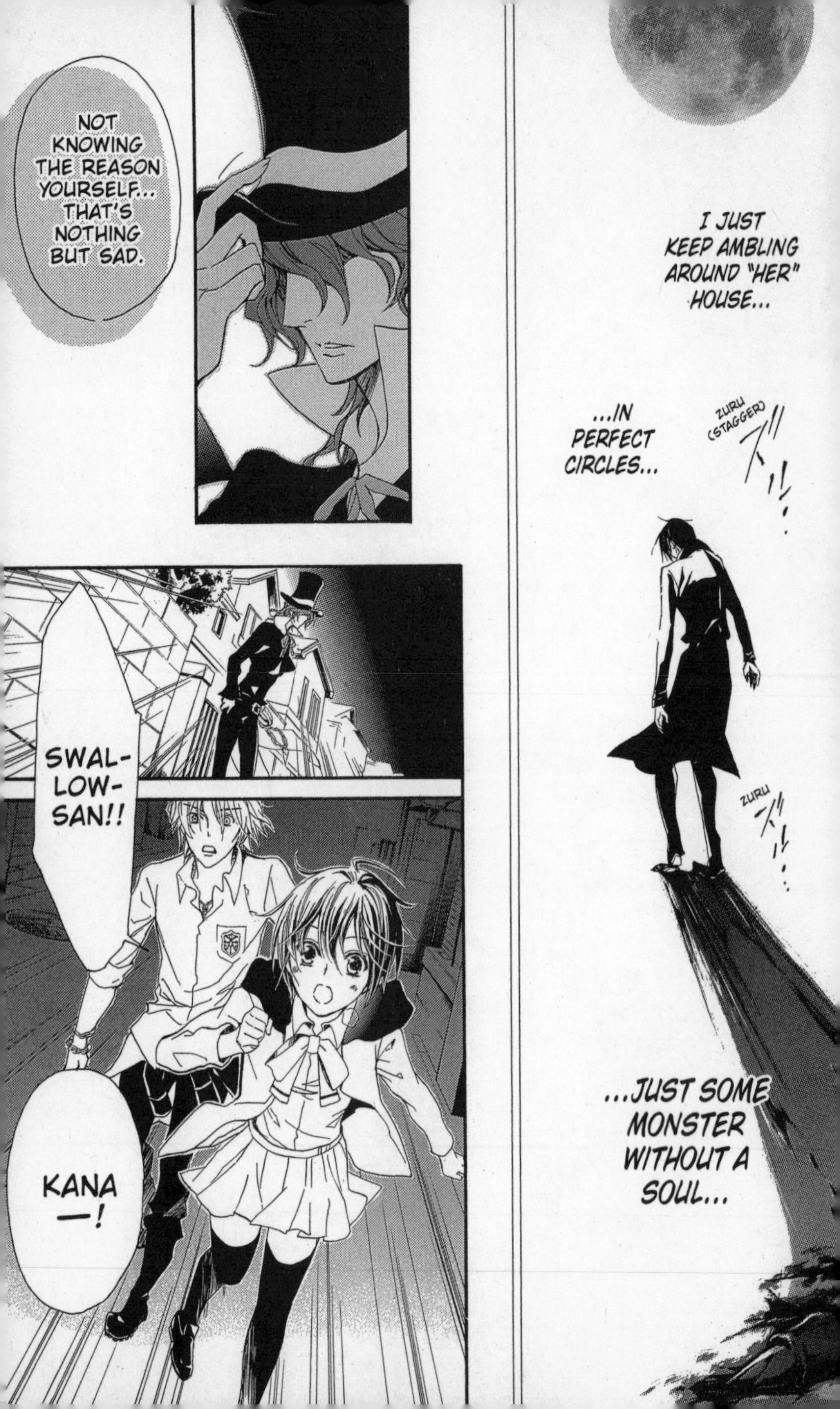
I JUST KEEP AMBLING AROUND "HER" HOUSE...
...IN PERFECT CIRCLES...
ZURU (STAGGER)
ZURU
...JUST SOME MONSTER WITHOUT A SOUL...
NOT KNOWING THE REASON YOURSELF... THAT'S NOTHING BUT SAD.
SWAL-LOW-SAN!!
KANA—!

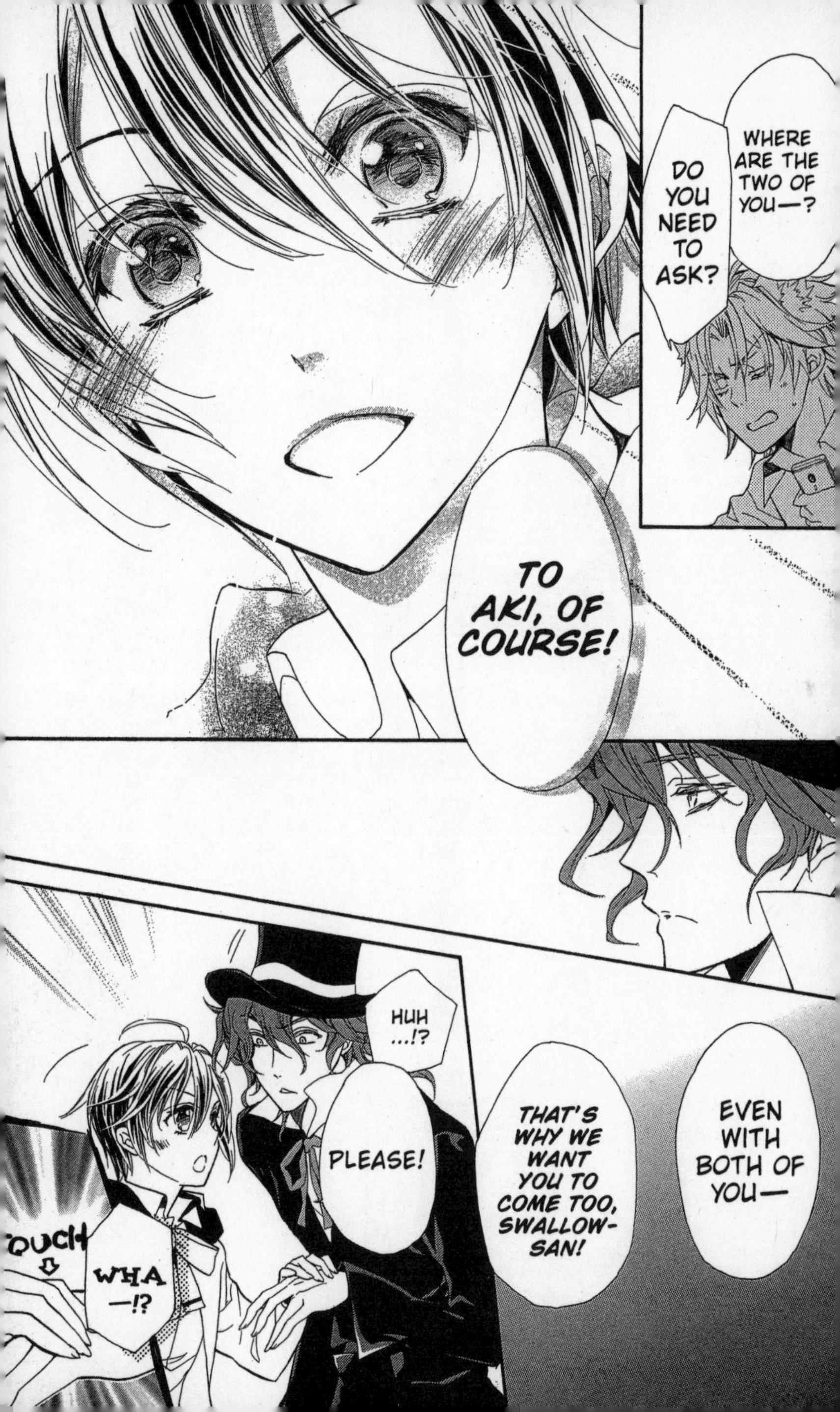
WHERE ARE THE TWO OF YOU—?
DO YOU NEED TO ASK?
TO AKI, OF COURSE!
EVEN WITH BOTH OF YOU—
THAT'S WHY WE WANT YOU TO COME TOO, SWALLOW-SAN!
PLEASE!
HUH ...!?
OUCH
WHA —!?

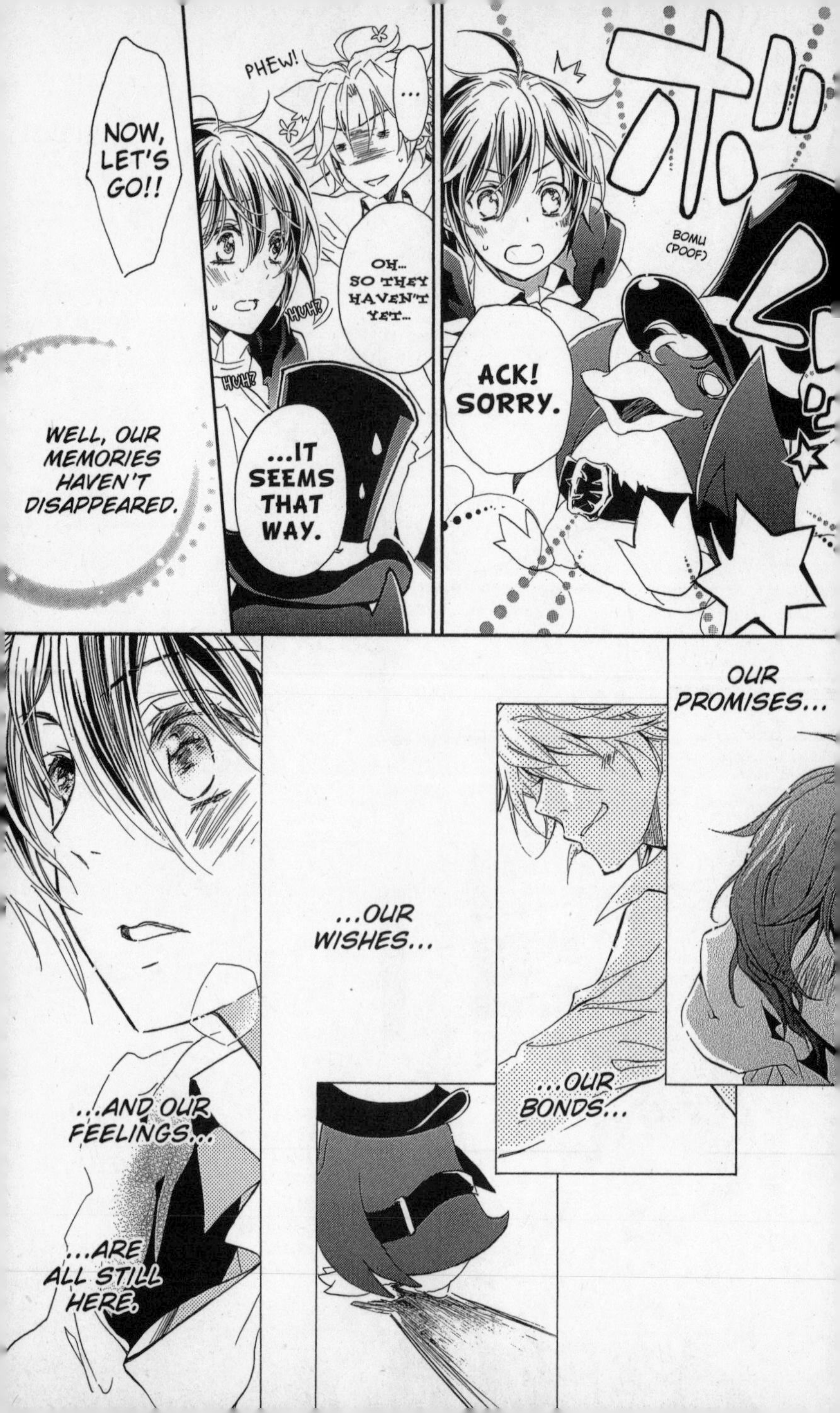
BOMU (POOF)
ACK! SORRY.
PHEW!
...
OH... SO THEY HAVEN'T YET...
HUH?
HUH?
...IT SEEMS THAT WAY.
NOW, LET'S GO!!
WELL, OUR MEMORIES HAVEN'T DISAPPEARED.
OUR PROMISES...
...OUR BONDS...
...OUR WISHES...
...AND OUR FEELINGS...
...ARE ALL STILL HERE.

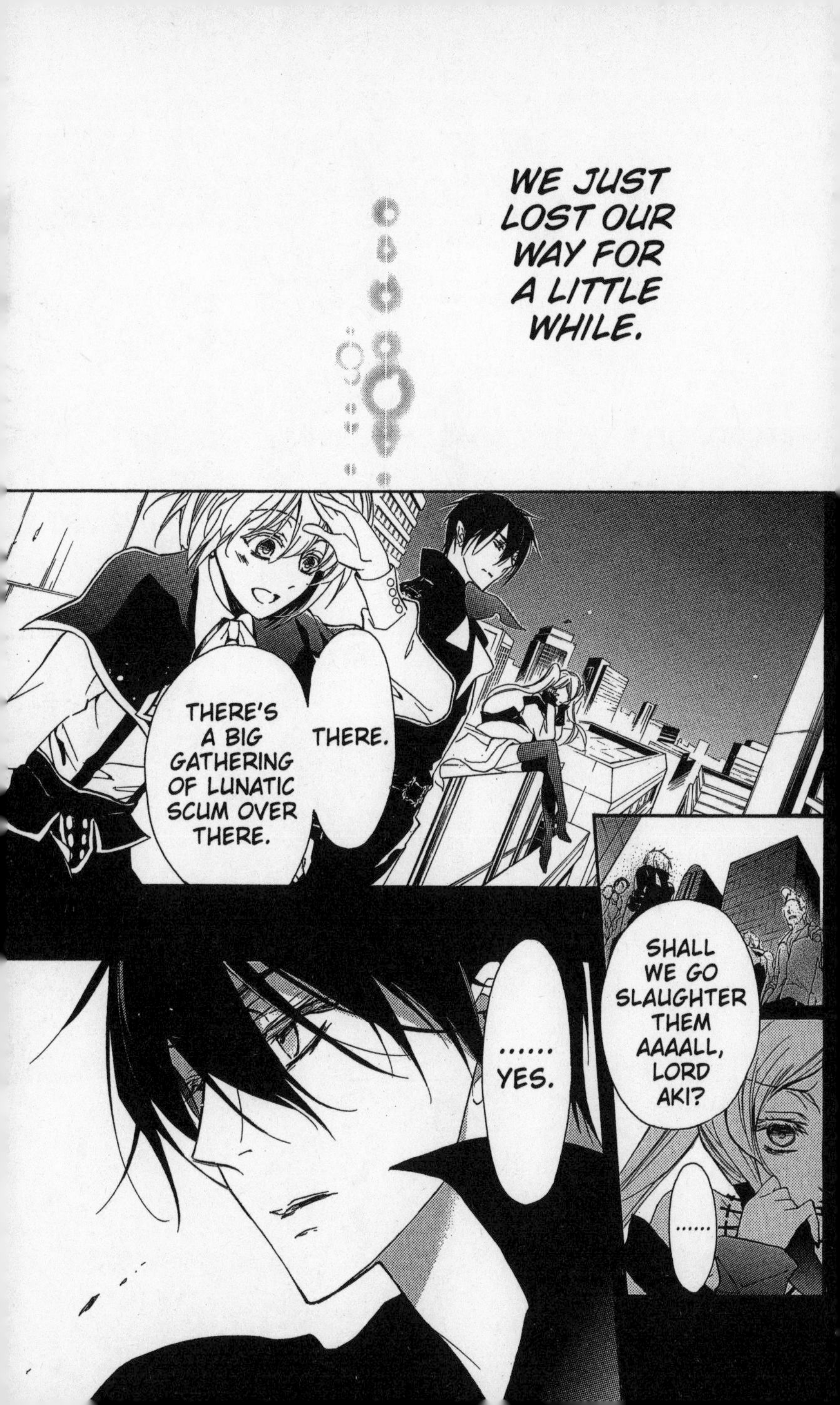
WE JUST LOST OUR WAY FOR A LITTLE WHILE.
THERE.
THERE'S A BIG GATHERING OF LUNATIC SCUM OVER THERE.
SHALL WE GO SLAUGHTER THEM AAAALL, LORD AKI?
......
...... YES.

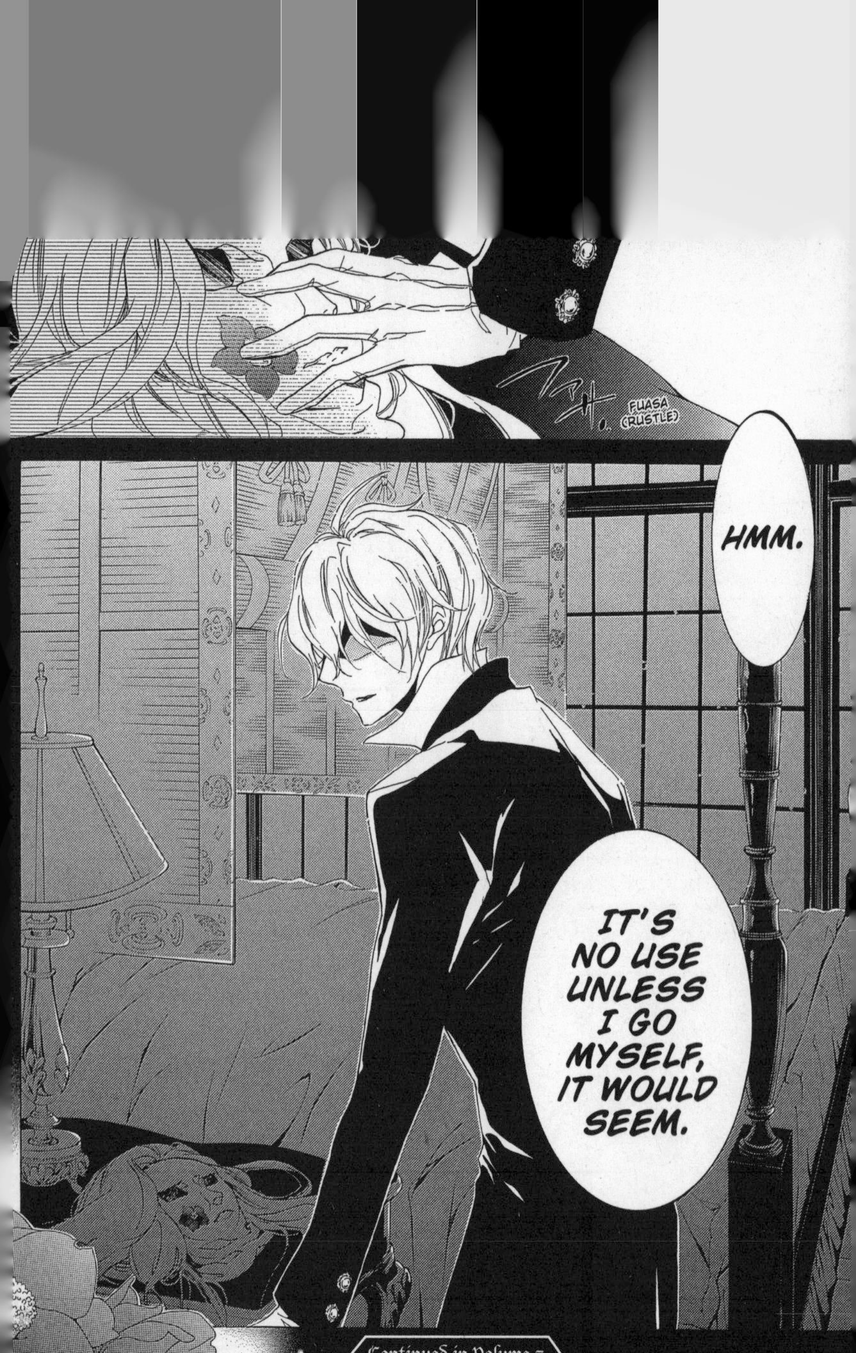
FUASA (RUSTLE)
HMM.
IT'S NO USE UNLESS I GO MYSELF, IT WOULD SEEM.
Continued in Volume 7

He's my only vampire
Aya Shouoto

Next Story

HAVING LOST ALL MEMORY OF KANA, AKI LETS GO OF HIS INHIBITIONS AND THROWS HIMSELF ENTIRELY INTO THE GAME.

UPON WHOM WILL THE FINAL STIGMA DESCEND !?

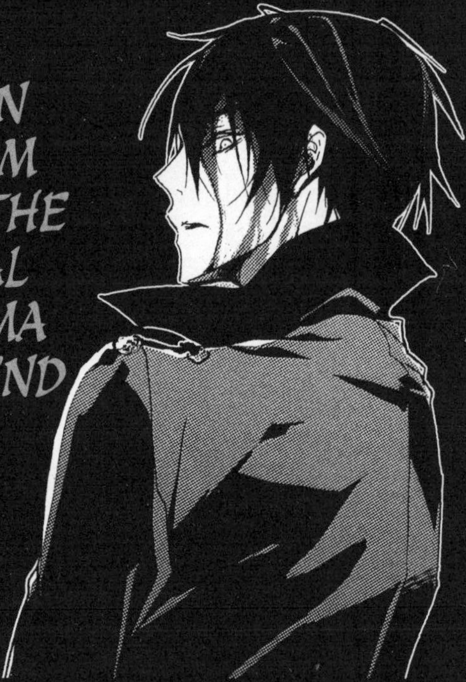

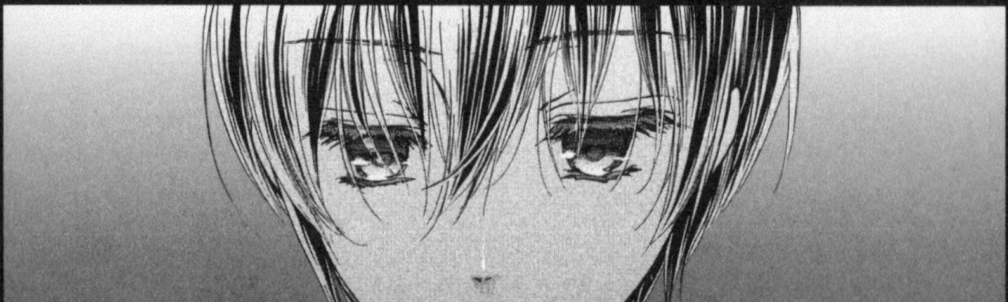

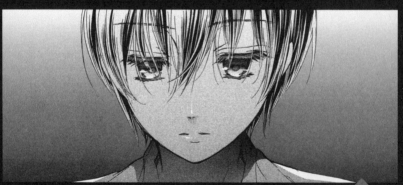

MEANWHILE, THE ACADEMY BRIMS

OVER WITH GREED AND WICKEDNESS—

Coming June 2016

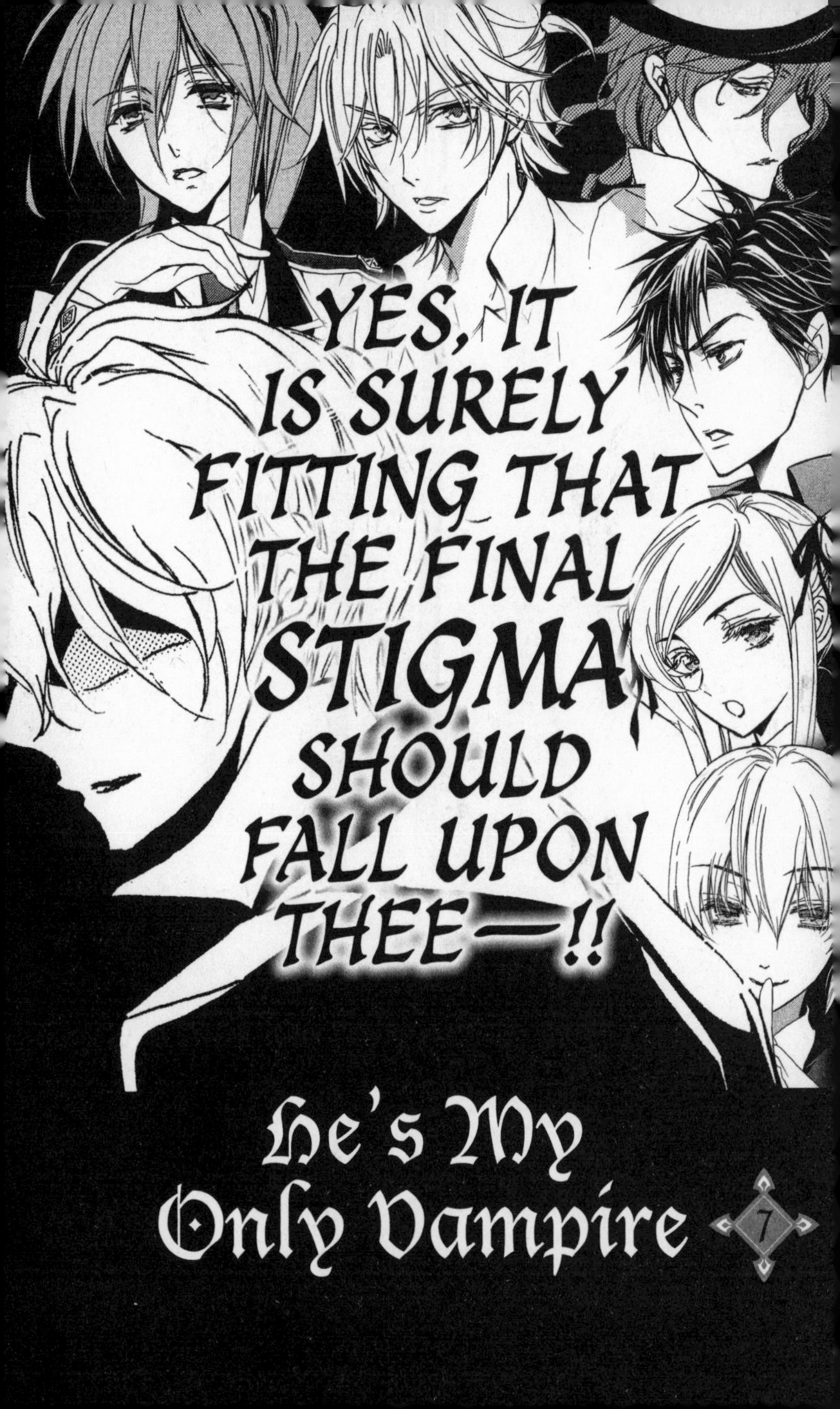
YES, IT IS SURELY FITTING THAT THE FINAL STIGMA SHOULD FALL UPON THEE—!!
He's My Only Vampire
7

He's My Only Vampire ◆ 6
Aya Shouoto

Translation: Su Mon Han † Lettering: Alexis Eckerman

HE'S MY ONLY VAMPIRE Volume 6 © 2013 Aya Shouoto. All rights reserved. First published in Japan in 2013 by Kodansha Ltd., Tokyo. Publication rights for this English edition arranged through Kodansha Ltd., Tokyo.

English translation © 2016 by Yen Press, LLC

Yen Press
1290 Avenue of the Americas
New York, NY 10104

Visit us at yenpress.com
facebook.com/yenpress
twitter.com/yenpress
yenpress.tumblr.com
instagram.com/yenpress

First Yen Press Edition: March 2016

Yen Press is an imprint of Yen Press, LLC.
The Yen Press name and logo are trademarks of Yen Press, LLC.

The publisher is not responsible for websites (or their content) that are not owned by the publisher.

Library of Congress Control Number: 2014504630

ISBN: 978-0-316-34581-1

10 9 8 7 6 5 4 3 2

BVG

Printed in the United States of America